A MUSICIAN DIVIDED:
ANDRÉ TCHAIKOWSKY
IN HIS OWN WORDS

André Tchaikowsky: a portrait photograph by Camilla Jessel Panufnik

A MUSICIAN DIVIDED: ANDRÉ TCHAIKOWSKY IN HIS OWN WORDS

Foreword by
DAVID POUNTNEY

Edited by
ANASTASIA BELINA-JOHNSON

Musicians on Music
No. 10

TOCCATA
PRESS

First published 2013 by Toccata Press, London
© 2013 David Pountney, Anastasia Belina-Johnson
and the estate of André Tchaikowsky

British Library Cataloguing in Publication Data
A catalogue for this book is available from the British Library.

ISBN 978-0-907689-88-1

Set in 11 on 13 point Minion Pro
by Kerrypress, Luton

Printed and bound
by CPI Group (UK) Ltd, Croydon, CR0 4YY

Contents

List of Illustrations

Another portrait photograph by Camilla Jessel Panufnik

Foreword
DAVID POUNTNEY

Where does music go when no-one listens to it? The 'resurrection' of André Tchaikowsky's music, some thirty years after his death, raises this tantalising Platonic issue. One conclusion must be that it slips out of time. Time, and its somewhat more frivolous sister, fashion, is as rigorous a judge of music as it is of anything else, so that music which is heard for the first time in, say, 1984, as André Tchaikowsky's opera *The Merchant of Venice* might have been if the English National Opera had accepted it at that point, is perceived to sound quite different if it is then only heard for the first time, as was the case with this work, in July 2013. At the Bregenz Festival we had already noticed this phenomenon with the re-discovery of another Polish-born composer, Mieczysław Weinberg, whose 1968 opera *Passazhirka* ('The Passenger') was premiered there in 2010: some rather unimaginative critics struggled with the fact that they were hearing new music that had nonetheless been written in the circumstances and aesthetic of an era almost half-a-century earlier.

But when the impact of such a moment of discovery, missed in actual time, is postponed for three decades, as was the case for Tchaikowsky's score, the surrounding world of music theatre and opera can never recapture the changes this operatic version of *The Merchant of Venice* might have brought in the 1980s. Instead, the intervening years were ones of silence, and though silence may be necessary for the composition of music, it is a terrible fate to befall it afterwards, especially an opera, with its colossal investment of work in writing down those many thousands of dots on the page.

There are, of course, many neglected and unrecognised composers, but this fate is perhaps above all the fate of the émigré. Music likes to advertise itself as the language without borders, but once you cross a real border, an unbridgeable gulf of indifference and neglect opens up beneath your feet. You will suddenly find that your music is not played, or heard, any longer. In that vulnerable stage between recognition and oblivion, the obligation of a national radio station and the network of support from fellow students, composers and impresarios are decisive. These factors have played a hugely important role in deciding the fate of many Polish artists, driven abroad in the nineteenth and early twentieth century by the Tsarist occupation, briefly flowering in independent Poland between the two World Wars, and then brutally affected by the Nazi invasion, followed by Soviet occupation. From Chopin onwards, the experience of the Polish composer has been all too typically the experience of exile.

Tchaikowsky, after his experiences as a child escaping from the Ghetto and then being in hiding for the remaining three years of the war, survived but was left with a deeply traumatised psyche. Being a depressive and a homosexual was no recipe for a positive experience in Soviet-occupied Poland. He escaped to Britain, where he was a foreigner by birth, and an outsider by nature but also, in a cultural sense, an Anglophile. He knew more about Shakespeare than most of his contemporary British citizens, and wrote better English than most of them, too! His foreign but intensely well-informed operatic view of Shakespeare was something to be treasured, but in the end it too met with silence.

I was part of that silence. Now I am part of the noise. It was with enormous excitement that I prepared the performance of Tchaikowsky's opera – the most important operatic interpretation of Shakespeare since the nineteenth century – and the rediscovery of his extraordinary personality, biography and view of the world which this book presents in such a lively form.

Preface
ANASTASIA BELINA-JOHNSON

The purpose of this book is to introduce the life and work of the Polish-born composer and pianist André Tchaikowsky (1935–82) through his own writings – his diaries, a testimony he gave after the Second World War and excerpts from his letters – and the memories of his friends and colleagues.[1] The intention of the many extensive quotations from original sources is to enable the reader to 'hear' the composer's own thoughts and views on life and his work. Tchaikowsky was a protégé of Arthur Rubinstein, a student of Stefan Askenase and Nadia Boulanger, and a prize-winner of the Chopin International Piano Competition in 1955 and Queen Elisabeth International Piano Competition in 1956. He performed with important orchestras and conductors around the world and recorded for such major record labels as RCA Victor and Columbia Marconi. Among his compositions are two piano concertos, two string quartets, works for voice and the opera *The Merchant of Venice*. The volume in hand is a part of a larger project, which will result in a comprehensive biography; the current volume will, I hope, serve as an introduction to André Tchaikowsky and his fascinating world.

The complexity of his personality, his wonderful sense of humour, his astonishing literary talent, his erudition, memory, dedication to his work, his love for his friends and his outstanding support for friends in times of trouble may make him difficult to capture in words, and yet he is an ideal subject for a biographer: he was a part of the history of the Holocaust and his story of survival is touching and sobering; he was volatile; he had a professional conflict, one that many have faced, of composer *v.* pianist; his sexual orientation – he was homosexual – caused him much self-doubt at various stages of his life; and the list of people he worked with and knew is almost as long as the list of those he offended with his scathing remarks. I hope that this book succeeds at showing the many sides of his character.

---

[1] Tchaikowsky began to work on a document he entitled 'Autobiography' in 1974 (*cf.* p. 134, below). It is not included in this collection because he did not wish to see it in print, having confessed in his diaries (*cf.* p. 274, below) that he invented many events described there. In view of the fact that research into Tchaikowsky's life and career is in its infancy, it was felt that his views should be respected until a researcher can make a convincing case for publishing the text and steer the reader between fact and fantasy.

On 18 July 2013 *The Merchant of Venice* was given its world premiere, 31 years after its completion, at the Bregenz Festspiele. It was a true discovery for the artists and audiences alike: the work is a serious, complex and profound interpretation of Shakespeare's play, with music that reflects and supports its complexity and intricate plot. The discovery of Tchaikowsky did not end with the opera: a week-end symposium, organised by the Festspiele, introduced his life and other works to the Bregenz public: people who knew Tchaikowsky, heard him perform or had researched his life and works came from all over the world to take part. What became clear in the course of the symposium was that, although Tchaikowsky was unquestionably a trying personality, he was also someone one could not help liking, admiring, even loving. The memories of the people who knew him are mostly funny, happy, exciting and touching. One could not keep being upset at this man, even after being shut out – 'given the treatment'.[2]

When Martin Anderson, the publisher of this book, read the first draft of the edited diaries, he immediately asked me if I had considered whether Tchaikowsky might have suffered from Asperger's syndrome. Suddenly, everything seemed to make sense: Tchaikowsky's difficulties in maintaining healthy relationships and friendships, his love of solitude, his erratic and unexplainable 'treatments', and his often pathological fear of large gatherings and after-show parties.[3] Although everyone who knew him remembers him as the soul of any party, his apparent love of being the centre of attention had a dark undercurrent: he believed that people had expected him to be funny, entertaining, ready to tell a joke or an interesting story. He suffered enormously from this imagined burden, which was most probably the reason behind his frequent escapes from company and numerous parties he was expected to attend as a concert pianist. This outlook is well documented in his diaries, which show the extent of his often self-imposed suffering.

Part One is an introductory biographical essay, based on diaries, letters, interviews and other such materials. Its aim is to give the outline of Tchaikowsky's life, focusing on the most important events and on his

---

[2] Judy Arnold described (in an interview with Anastasia Belina-Johnson, 10 September 2012, London) being 'given the treatment' as a sudden and complete break, which could be face to face or via a letter, often for no other reason than Tchaikowsky's impulsive decision to cut all the ties. No one was safe from it, and many of his friends either experienced it or came dangerously close to it themselves, or witnessed others in their circle receiving it.

[3] Martin Anderson put this 'diagnosis' in context in a contribution to the Bregenz symposium, arguing that Asperger's syndrome, or at least some degree of autism, is probably a unifying characteristic among major composers and offering in evidence Alkan, Bach, Beethoven, Brahms, Brian, Bruckner, Janáček, Langgaard, Magnard, Martinů, Mozart, Prokofiev, Shostakovich, Weinberg and many others as company for Tchaikowsky.

major compositions and introducing people who were significant to him. Part Two is the testimony he gave to the Jewish Historical Institute in 1947. Part Three contains excerpts from his diaries, covering the period between 1974 and 1982. The entries were chosen in order to present as widely as possible the breadth of Tchaikowsky's interests, his thought-processes, ideas, relationships and friendships, and his reactions to music, theatre and literature. Finally, all his known compositions and his recordings are documented.

Tchaikowsky research is still in its initial stages, and there is still much to be discovered and understood about the composer. It is my hope that this book will make a modest contribution to existing knowledge, and consolidate David Ferré's research with mine.[4] This publication had to be put together in less than twelve months, and while every effort has been made to check that all information here is correct, if there are any inaccuracies or mistakes, I take full responsibility for them.

I use the westernised spelling of André Tchaikowsky throughout the book as that was the name he used when living in the west. In Poland he is still known as Andrzej Czajkowski.

---

[4] David A. Ferré, *The Other Tchaikowsky: A Biographical Sketch of André Tchaikowsky*, self-published, Chwelah, WA, 1991, available online at http://andretchaikowsky.com.

Acknowledgements

This book would not exist without two people: Lewis Owens, who first alerted me to André Tchaikowsky's opera *The Merchant of Venice* in 2011, and David Pountney, who in 2012 asked me to write the text. I must confess that I was familiar with neither the opera nor its composer, but discovering neglected operas has always been my passion, and one written on a famous play by Shakespeare was something I could not ignore.

The process of discovering André Tchaikowsky as a person, pianist, composer, friend, lover and son would have been much more difficult without the help and advice of many people who knew him personally, knew his music, or were passionate about getting his name and his music known to wider audiences. Eve Harrison, his close friend and devoted supporter, enabled me to look at the composer's diaries and other documents, and I am grateful for her unreserved help. She also read through the draft of the book, helping to eliminate a number of inaccuracies, and contributed generously towards my research costs. Michael Menaugh answered any questions with speed and insight, holding nothing back, and quickly becoming a dear friend. John O'Brien, whom I met in Bregenz in July 2013, shed light onto various aspects of Tchaikowsky's personality, and gave a detailed account of the process of the work on *The Merchant of Venice*. I would like to thank those of André Tchaikowsky's colleagues and friends who agreed to be interviewed or answered my questions by e-mail: Wanda Wiłkomirska, Halina Janowska, Judy and Michael Arnold, Stephen Kovacevich and Jody Fitzhardinge. Liz Smith and her team at entertaining:tv were enthusiastic about the composer, producing a beautiful documentary that will help further promote his work. The director of the documentary, Mark Charles, spent hours discussing ideas with me, which always led to new discoveries and insights.

My heartfelt thanks go to my outstanding research assistant, David Ferré. His generosity and humble spirit, his support and encouragement were more than welcome and received with gratitude. In a vital service to Tchaikowsky's future biographers and scholars, David interviewed many of Tchaikowsky's friends, relatives and colleagues from 1985 onwards, compiling an impressive archive of interviews (both on tape and in transcription), at the time when memories of the man were still fresh and vivid. David was very helpful in preparing material for the discussion of Tchaikowsky's music in Part IV and also contributed financially to the production of this book. David helped, moreover, with the organisation of the illustrations and with details for the captions, and he designed and drew the family tree on p. 22.

For permission to use the illustrations I am indebted to the following: Judy Arnold (pp. 59, 64, 70, 360 and 374), Milein Cosman (pp. 71, 105 and 147), Camilla Jessel Panufnik (frontispiece and p. 8) and the Jewish Historical Institute, Warsaw (p. 87), with the remainder either in the public domain or courtesy of the André Tchaikowsky estate. I also acknowledge permission from the Jewish Historical Institute for use of the André Tchaikowsky Testimony of 1947 (pp. 85–98). I have endeavoured to acknowledge, and obtain permission from, all owners of copyright material; if I have unwittingly infringed anyone's copyright, I ask for notification so that any subsequent edition can be corrected.

My thanks go to the inspirational David Pountney, without whom *The Merchant of Venice* would still be waiting its turn on the operatic stage: in 2011 he agreed to meet me and listened to my suggestion that the opera be staged at Bregenz. Without his acute sense of the stage and recognition of outstanding music, this project would undoubtedly have taken many more years to complete. I must also thank him for putting his trust in me when commissioning this book, and for always being there and making sure the process was never impeded by any problems or worries.

A distinguished historian and dear friend, Dr Nir Arielli, helped with contextual research about the Warsaw ghetto and understanding Holocaust-related issues, and was always there to help with any questions or to lend support. Vania Čelebičić-Arielli is a special being who was there for me from the inception of my research and writing, and through to its completion. I thank her for being ready to talk about my work any time I needed it. Professor Derek Scott always found time whenever I had to talk to him about my research and provided necessary encouragement and advice.

Lyndsay Weir, a close family member and a retired New Zealand-based psychiatrist, helped me to understand Tchaikowsky's childhood traumas and put them in context. His encouragement and advice throughout the entire process are warmly acknowledged.

Séan Gray, the director of Tchaikowsky's publisher, Josef Weinberger, lent every ounce of support and encouragement, as did his colleagues Lewis Mitchell, Alex Dangerfield and Christopher Moss. The company contributed substantially towards the costs of my research and the production of this book. Séan and his colleagues provided help with scores and any information, always replying with incredible speed and efficiency. Without them, the production of this book might not have happened at all, or would have been much delayed.

Martin Anderson of Toccata Press has proven once again to be the best editor and advisor I have ever worked with (with his usual blunt modesty, he even challenged me on the veracity of that statement). His phenomenal musical and historical knowledge were, and remain, hugely inspiring, and I can safely say that to this day I have not met anyone else whose erudition equals his.

The Adam Mickiewicz Institute in Warsaw generously offered grants for three visits to Warsaw, to research and write the book, and I am grateful for their support. It has been a pleasure to work with a cultural organisation such as this one without having to deal with extensive paperwork. All my questions and requests were answered and complied with without any delay. I thank Paweł Potoroczyn, Aleksander Laskowski, Ewa Bogusz-Moore, and Bogusława Marszalik for all their help.

Piotr Maculewicz and Magdalena Borowiec at the Biblioteka Uniwersytecka w Warszawie-Archiwum Kompozytorów Polskich (University of Warsaw Library-Archives of Polish Composers) made available any materials I wanted to look at, so that my research there was pleasant and obstacle-free. Izabela Zymer gave her time freely during my research in the archives of the Polish Music Information Centre and Polish Composers' Union in Warsaw, and helped with translations of some documents. Marek Bykowski, spokesman for the Fryderyk Chopin University of Music in Warsaw, helped find a file of documents related to Tchaikowsky's student years there, and was very encouraging of my work.

Boutique B&B in Warsaw was where I produced the early draft of the book. Its inspiring atmosphere made the work flow, and I met many people who supported and promoted book not yet in existence. Jarosław Chołodecki, the owner of the hotel and a passionate supporter of Polish music and arts, patiently complied with my requests for writing-desks and meeting-spaces and helped with contacts. And Mrs Atha's café in Leeds, where I live and work, were happy to put up with me spending entire days there, setting up an office and writing.

Warsaw is the most inspiring place I have ever worked in. The energy of the city and its people hugely contributed to my efforts. I felt immediately accepted by everyone I met there, and I thank especially two people who have become close friends, Irena Makarewicz and Krzysiek Bielecki, for letting me become a part of their lives.

Most of all, I must thank my wonderful husband Daniel, whose support during research and writing of this book meant that I could keep focused while he patiently took care of all daily tasks. He also helped with proof-reading the drafts and set the two music examples presented in the book.

Finally, I dedicate this book to the memory of my father Alexander Belin (1952–98), a wonderful man and talented musician and composer, who died of stomach cancer in New Zealand at the age of 46. He once told me that there is nothing to be afraid of in this life, and it is because of these words I have often found the bravery to do things that did not always seem possible.

Anastasia Belina-Johnson
September 2013

I
BIOGRAPHICAL
OUTLINE

Anastasia Belina-Johnson

From Birth to Ghetto

In the Warsaw Ghetto

It took only 27 days – from the onset of the attack on Warsaw on 1 September 1939 – for the invading Germans to claim the city as an occupied territory. The Jews living there were ordered to relocate into one neighbourhood in the centre, which was sealed by a wall in November 1940. At its peak, approximately 445,000 people lived within its walls.[1]

A spacious apartment on 1 Przejazd Street in the ghetto area was home to two generations of a Jewish Polish family: Celina and Nicolas Sandler, Ignacy and Irena Rappaport, and Felicja and Karl Krauthammer. Celina Sandler (1888–1955), the grandmother of André Tchaikowsky, was an enterprising woman with a strong spirit, whose fearless determination would save her grandson's life during the German occupation. She had many useful connections, and knew practically everybody who could be of any help to her and her business, a beauty school and cosmetics factory in the fashionable area of Plac Trzech Krzyży ('Three Crosses') in the centre of Warsaw. The business made Celina very rich, but she spent more money than she made, through careless spending and gambling. Eventually, facing bankruptcy, she was forced to sell her factory in 1933.

She was married twice, first to Ivor Rappaport, a doctor in the Russian army, in 1910. With him she had two children: a son, Ignacy, in 1911, and a daughter, Felicja, in 1913. In 1918 she divorced Rappaport and married a Warsaw lawyer, Nicolas Sandler. Felicja Rappaport was well educated, a talented pianist and singer, spoke five languages, and was remembered for her fashion sense and for frequent changes to the colour of her hair. Tchaikowsky's uncle Ignacy studied chemistry at Liège University, and, like his sister, was talented in languages and piano. He belonged to an underground liberation movement during the occupation, and was executed by the Germans during the Warsaw Uprising in 1944.

In 1933, Celina moved to Paris, where Felicja studied cosmetology without much success but enjoyed spending time with friends and visiting the nightclubs. In one such club in the summer of 1934 she met Karl Krauthammer, a disillusioned young lawyer with no obvious prospects. A

---

[1] Nir Arielli, 'Emanuel Ringelblum and the Warsaw Ghetto *Oneg Shabbat* Archives – A Story of Historical Awareness', *Hayo Haya*, Vol. 2, 2003, p. 2.

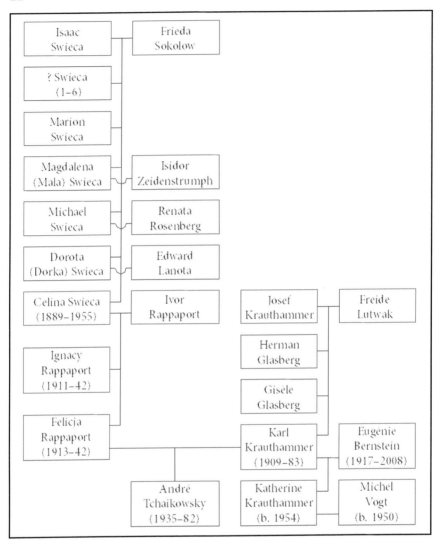

Tchaikowsky's family tree

relative remembers that Felicja attracted Karl's attention by dancing on a table.[2] The courtship was short, and Karl and Felicja were married in Paris on 11 December 1934, both in a civil ceremony and a Jewish Orthodox service. In March 1935 Felicja found out that she was pregnant, and her mother decided that it would be wiser for all of them to move to Warsaw,

[2] Halina Malewiak (Tchaikowsky's cousin), in a telephone interview with David Ferré on 29 November 1985, Israel. Transcript and tapes of this and all other interviews taken by David Ferré are held in the Warsaw University Library, in the Andrzej Czajkowski archive.

Family group, c. 1932, left to right: unknown; Felicja Aleksandra Rappaport (Tchaikowsky's mother); Marian Swieca (Tchaikowsky's great-uncle), Kazimierz Zeidenstrumph (later Charles Fortier, Tchaikowsky's cousin); unknown; unknown; Ignacy Rappaport (Tchaikowsky's uncle); the violinist Roman Totenberg

where Karl would have better employment opportunities, and she intended to re-establish her cosmetics business. Tensions arose immediately after the marriage, and by the time Felicja was five months pregnant, Karl returned to Paris. It is difficult to establish why their relationship failed; some accounts show that Karl was fooled by Celina's pretence of being rich at the same time as he misled Celina into believing that he himself was so wealthy that he did not need to work.[3]

André Tchaikowsky was born on 1 November 1935 in Warsaw and named Robert Andrzej Krauthammer. It is unclear if Karl was in Warsaw when his son was born. Both Halina Malewiak and Irena Paszkowska stated that Karl went back to Warsaw to bring Felicja and Andrzej to Paris; Karl's second wife, Eugenie Krauthammer, believed that he was in Paris in November 1935.[4] Karl's sister later recounted that her brother was very upset at being shut out, and made efforts to reunite the family in 1939.[5]

---

[3] Eugénie Krauthammer, interviewed by David Ferré on 23 July 1985, Paris.
[4] Halina Malewiak, *loc. cit.*; Irena Paszkowska (the wife of Tchaikowsky's uncle Ignacy), interviewed by David Ferré, 4 April 1987, Warsaw; Eugénie Krauthammer, *loc. cit.*
[5] Eugénie Krauthammer, *loc. cit.*

Three photographs of Robert Andrzej Krauthammer as toddler (left)
and three-year-old

As a child, the young Krauthammer was energetic and talkative; he absorbed languages, behaviours and ideas at lightning speed, and enjoyed the attention of adults. By the age of three-and-a-half, he could read in Polish, German and Russian, and at the age of four his mother began to teach him piano. He was fascinated by the idea that one could read music in the same way as one reads the written word, and his mother showed him the relationship between printed notes and piano keys. His grandmother immediately began to plan for his future, announcing that he would become the best and most famous pianist in the world.

When Celina's apartment was enclosed into the ghetto area, she defiantly moved out to the 'Aryan' side of Warsaw, claiming to be a Christian, while Felicja decided to remain with her son. Although Celina's family had never observed the Jewish faith, it was still a huge risk for her to live openly as a non-Jew, especially with her daughter and grandson staying in the ghetto. When Tchaikowsky later told the story to Gervase and Katia de Peyer[6] and they asked why his grandmother was not in hiding, he answered: 'There was no reason – she thought nothing would happen to her'.[7] This boldness was typical of Celina – she went about accomplishing her heroic tasks every day without fear. For the next two years, Celina singlehandedly supported her family by bringing food and necessary provisions. She made money

---

[6] Gervase de Peyer (b. 1926), English clarinettist and conductor, and his wife Katia.
[7] Katia de Peyer, interviewed by David Ferré, 3 November 1986, New York.

*Tchaikowsky's grandmother Celina Janina Sandler-Czajkowska (c. 1935)
and (right) his mother, Felicja Aleksandria Rappaport-Krauthammer (c. 1934)*

by trading in various goods, buying them cheaply in the ghetto and selling them on the other side.

Andrzej's mother sent him to the ghetto kindergarten, where he was looked after by his 23-year-old cousin Halina Malewiak. She remembered that he was a difficult child, causing problems even when he was transferred into different groups in order to avoid trouble. Some time in spring or early summer of 1942, Halina remembered, he threw a stone at the head of one of the teachers and, after being told that they would inform his mother about it, started crying and begging them not to tell her. He very dramatically explained that she would beat him if she found out. Halina thought it was not true, but he was such an impressive actor that everyone believed him.[8]

He did play the piano, but seldom, as the family piano was still in the apartment, and Felicja was still allowed to play it from time to time.[9] In later years Tchaikowsky himself did not like to talk about his life in the ghetto, and his friends could glean only a few details here and there. It is possible that he witnessed a death of a child, shot by a German soldier, and also had a gun pointed at him. Nevertheless, his family concealed the reality from him so much that not until decades later did he realise he did not really know what was going on in the ghetto.

---

[8] Halina Malewiak, *loc. cit.*
[9] *Ibid.*

In the early summer of 1942 it became apparent that Felicja and Andrzej must try to escape. By that time Felicja was married to Albert Rozenbaum, a dentist with a good position in the hospital and a member of the Jewish police.[10] Celina arranged false documents for herself, Felicja and Andrzej, but Felicja decided to stay. It is possible that she did not want to leave Albert, or thought that Celina would have a better chance of saving the seven-year-old Andrzej without herself in tow. In July 1942 the Germans began expelling the residents of the Warsaw ghetto, most of them to the death camp at Treblinka. By that stage it was almost impossible to get anyone out of the ghetto, but Celina brazenly led her grandson out dressed in girl's clothing, dyeing his hair, eyebrows and even eyelashes blond. It was thought that she either bribed one of the German soldiers at a check point, or escaped through the cellar of her house to the outside, as the house was just by the ghetto wall.[11]

A month later, in August 1942, Felicja was transported to and murdered in Treblinka. Tchaikowsky idolised his mother and felt her loss acutely for the rest of his life. This tragedy caused the development of a complex set of emotional problems based on issues of abandonment, for Tchaikowsky believed that his mother had chosen her new husband over her son and thus had not followed him and Celina to safety. In a letter to Halina Janowska he explained:

> Twenty years later, under psychoanalysis, I came to realise that I resented my mother's death greatly because she *could* have saved herself: granny had prepared false papers, a hiding place etc., but she didn't do it because of my stepfather Albert: she didn't have the heart to leave him in the ghetto.[12]

Only when Tchaikowsky went to Israel in 1980, where he for the first time visited Yad Vashem[13] and read, among other things, documents in the Emanuel Ringelblum Oneg Shabatt Archive,[14] did he understand and

---

[10] The marriage took place in the ghetto, but no corroborative documents have survived.

[11] In her interview with David Ferré, Halina Malewiak thought the escape took place in July 1942; Tchaikowsky stated in his testimony (*cf.* p. 88, below) that it was 7 August.

[12] Tchaikowsky's letter to Halina Janowska, dated 13 February 1977, quoted from *...my guardian demon*, Jacek Laskowski's unpublished English translation of *...mój diabeł stróż*, 1996, p. 124 (*cf.* note 79, p. 72, below).

[13] Established in 1953, Yad Vashem in Jerusalem is the world centre for research into, documentation of and education about the Holocaust.

[14] From 1939 to early 1943 a group of historians, writers, rabbis and others, under the leadership of the Jewish historian Dr Emanuel Ringelblum (1900–44) set about the systematic documentation of life in the Warsaw Ghetto; their archive was buried in milk cans and metal boxes in three separate locations, two of which yielded up their secrets after the War (the third site has yet to be located). It

Karl Krauthammer,
Tchaikowsky's father,
photographed in 1932

forgive his mother. He also realised a significant fact: his own traumatic history was not unprecedented, and in many ways less harrowing than the histories of many Jewish people and families whose accounts were preserved in the Archive.

A Child without a Childhood

In 1942, to help ensure his survival, Robert Andrzej Krauthammer became Andrzej Robert Jan Czajkowski,[15] and Celina Janina Sandler became Celina Czajkowska. The name was chosen for a practical reason: Celina had a worker in her factory by the name of Czajkowska, a lady of similar age and looks and, if ever either lady's documents were checked, they looked so similar that it would be difficult to detect that the face did not match the photograph. Later Tchaikowsky grew to abhor his surname, believing that it was a terrible handicap; he wanted to make his mark as a composer, but he felt overshadowed by his Russian near-namesake.

Between July 1942 and January 1945 Celina embarked on a dangerous and difficult journey of hidden existence. She arranged at least ten hiding-places for her grandson and herself; only a few of these places did they share. Tchaikowsky's testimony lists a number of addresses,[16] although it is

is in the Emanuel Ringelblum Jewish Historical Institute that Tchaikowsky's 1947 deposition is held (*cf.* pp. 85–98).

[15] This name is given in some of Tchaikowsky's official documents, such as his application for studying at the Fryderyk Chopin University of Music in Warsaw, held in the University's archives.

[16] *Cf.* pp. 86–97, below.

not easy to know if the information he gave there was entirely correct. He was difficult to conceal: he liked to talk, he drew attention to himself, and he even told a group of children he was playing with in one of his hiding-places in the Polish countryside that his name was actually Krauthammer, and that he was Jewish. The next day saw him living in a different location.

One of the hiding-places was outside the ghetto area, with a Catholic mother and daughter, a Mrs Balińska and Monica, who concealed Tchaikowsky in a wardrobe. The following excerpt from Tchaikowsky's unpublished autobiography describes his impressions of that particular chapter of his life:

> How long had I been in this wardrobe? Seven weeks, two years? I had meant to count the days, but I'd forgotten. Anyway, there weren't any days in the wardrobe, or any hours: the dark was always equally complete, and the chamber-pot in one of its corners had to be located by touch. I had now learnt to do that, as I had learnt to use it silently. This had been very difficult at first. Once I upset the pot and some of the mess seeped out into the room. This made St. Monica[17] very angry. Never mind the filth, she said, though that's bad enough, she had to clean up after me with her own hands, but what if a neighbour or some stranger had been in the room? Do I want the Gestapo to make an end of them all at one go? That's what they get for saving my shitty life at the risk of theirs. Would I rather be moved down to the cellar, where the rats will eat me? No? Then I'd better watch out and keep quiet. For God's sake it's not as if a lot had been asked of me: just don't move and make no noise, that's all. And shit where you've been told to. Why, any animal could have been trained to do that in much less time, but it's beyond our dear wonder-boy!
>
> I was very contrite after that, and I did keep quiet. At least my body did; and hopefully, after a time, my mind would grow numb as well, the pot apart, there was nothing in the wardrobe but darkness and me. Kola had told me that Eskimos saw no daylight at all for half the year. Had I been here half a year? And would it turn me into an Eskimo? Did Eskimos also bite their fingernails? No, they had other occupations: building igloos, training seals for circuses… Sometimes they saw the Northern Lights high in the sky. But that only happened once or twice a year, when the Eskimos had been particularly good and God saw fit to grant them a reward; the lights went off again at the first sin. This, of course, was also the reason why I could not see the halo round St. Monica's head: it was visible only to the worthy.
>
> Even without the halo, the evidence of Monica's holiness was quite strong enough! A positive miracle had taken place in that humble abode. In a few months' time Monica was going to be blessed with a baby – and she wasn't

---

[17] Because Monica was expecting a child but was not married, the young André thought she was the new Holy Virgin.

married. The mystery of the Immaculate Conception had only recently been explained to me, and it took me some time to realise that the hitherto unique privilege had been bestowed again, and on my hostess's daughter! Awed by the revelation, I knelt down inside the wardrobe and prayed, silently of course, to the New Holy Virgin. I also thanked the Lord for making me a witness of his Second Coming. For this was indisputably at hand: all the signs were there. The Word was to become Flesh again – Monica's flesh.

By the time she unlocked the wardrobe door that evening, my greeting had been thoroughly rehearsed. 'Blessed be the fruit of Thy womb!' I chanted, adding whatever other bits of Scripture seemed relevant to the special majesty of the occasion. My eyes were lifted heavenwards, so the sudden blow on my cheek took me by surprise, but I managed to keep up the litany through the slaps and kicks that now followed. Monica's own litany, louder than mine and, if anything, even more fervent, was addressed directly to myself.

'You shit! You filthy stinker! You crass Jewish louse! They should have cut your big tongue off, not your foreskin. I'll teach you to stick your hooked nose into matters that do not concern you! I'll teach you to spy and eavesdrop on people whose one toenail is worth more than your stupid head. Though no, your head *is* worth something in ready cash, and in fact it might come in handy'; she added with a sudden smile. At the same time, to my confusion, she began to cry. 'Oh, what have I done, what have I done to deserve all this? Even this little rat now laughs at me. Rat! RAT!'

At last I understood: Monica was feeling unworthy. Full of Christian humility as only a saint could be, she found herself overwhelmed at being not just the object, but the actual vessel of Grace. It was vital that she be reassured.

'Dry your tears, Star of the Sea', I intoned. 'If you had not deserved it, it wouldn't have happened. You know this as well as I…Ow!'

I had to yell, for Monica had grabbed my hair and was now spitting in my face, again and again, with what I realised must be righteous wrath. She then let go of me, rushed into the next room and came back carrying a soda-water syphon. The jet went straight into my face and I fell sideways into a corner of the wardrobe, happily missing the full chamber-pot. St. Monica then slammed and locked the door.

By that time, of course, I was thoroughly used to spending my nights in the wardrobe. At first, Monica usually took me out about eleven at night, when no neighbour was likely to drop in, and put me into bed right in the front room on a sofa that might not have been quite adequate for an adult, but was ample for me. Monica and her invalid mother always said it was asking for trouble, and one night a lady from the next flat did drop in on them; there was just enough time to throw a bedcover and a couple of cushions over me. Covered by these I could not judge whether Monica had succeeded in making the sofa look unoccupied. But the lady must have been taken in for she refused the proffered arm-chair and sat heavily down on the sofa an inch or two from my foot. Unable to move or breathe I concentrated on the conversation in which the two terrified women did their best to sound casual. 'Are you sure you wouldn't be more comfortable in the rocking chair?' 'Oh no, thanks, you know I love your sofa.' At some point I must have passed out.

After that, my keepers decided it was too risky to let me out into the room, except on Grams' [Celina's] weekly visits, during which Monica would stand guard at the window while her mother listened for footsteps outside the front door. At a whisper from her, I would be rushed back into the wardrobe and all traces of my presence obliterated. While drying their shoes on the outside doormat, the visitors could hear Monica's strident voice reciting French irregular verbs, which Grams corrected whenever it seemed plausible. The neighbours came to be quite impressed by the calm fluency of Monica's French teacher.

Grams was due to visit me the day after the revelation. It never occurred to me to ask where she lived, how often she was forced to change her hiding place or set about finding me a new one, or where she found the money to pay for my keep and for herself. I took it for granted she would appear on the appointed day, and she always did. My hosts looked forward to her visits far more than myself. She brought them money, and me love.

She also invariably brought some cotton wool and a vial of oxygenated water. This was used to dye my hair blond in order to make me look less Semitic, just in case I was found (the implausibility of a Gentile child living in a wardrobe never seemed to occur to her). It also enabled Grams to keep in practice for the new beauty parlour she would undoubtedly open as soon as the war was over. At present, she was clearly off form: sometimes she used too much dye and made me an albino, and once she burned right through the hair and left me with a round bald patch on the top of my head, making me look, as Monica observed, just like the saint I thought myself to be. But what I hated most was the dyeing of my eyebrows and eyelashes. I kept my eyes tightly shut lest the stinging acid found its way through my lids and burn my sight out: then the world would become a wardrobe.

While this took place, Grams would submit me to an examination. She asked me to recite the Lord's Prayer and Ave Maria, and posed random questions on the tenets of the Roman Catholic religion. This was easier for me than for her, as she obviously didn't know them herself and could seldom have spotted a mistake. Then she would make me recite all the details of my latest identity: name, birthplace, my parents' names and where I had been brought up. This was a far harder test, as Grams thought it safer to obtain fresh identity papers every week or two, and I constantly had to memorise, digest and identify myself with a new set of data. Usually I managed all right, but I still knew far more about Jesus' life than about my own; above all, he felt to me more *real*. Sometimes both catechisms were combined in an attempt to catch me off my guard, somewhat like this:

– Where was Jesus Christ born?
– In Bethlehem.

– And you?

– In Pinsk.

– Idiot! That was last time. Can't you read anymore?

– Bialystok.

– That's better. What's your father's name?

– Adam Yanowski.

– And the Holy Virgin's husband's

– Saint Joseph.

– Who massacred the innocents?

– Herod.

– And who does it today?

– The Jews. They crucify Christian children and then drink their blood. This last answer always made my hosts smile.

The night before this particular visit, I found it harder than usual to run over the required answers in my mind. The imminence of the next incarceration made all my knowledge of the first seem dull and old-hat, and my own identity too contemptibly small an affair to deserve attention. Besides, I was hungry: Monica had forgotten my dinner. Or perhaps, in preparation for the second Advent, I was meant to fast? Saints had lived on locusts in the desert. There were no locusts in the wardrobe, only numerous lice; Grams' bleach kept them out of my hair, but not out of my clothes. Still I wasn't tempted to eat lice, not yet.

In the morning a silent, stern Monica opened the door and pointed out into the room. The smell of food was far more important to me than Grams' presence. While I ate, Monica's mother gave the usual exhaustive account of the risks and emotions my presence in the house continually exposed them to. Grams heard it with composure and a show of contrite sympathy, waiting for the other woman to come to the point. She knew that, among other vicissitudes, the cost of living would inevitably come to be mentioned, and this was her cue for offering to raise the terms on which I was kept. This time the transition from lament to negotiation seemed particularly long in coming, and Grams finally found it necessary to take the initiative. Would they, she asked, find a twenty per cent rise adequate? The mother was about to answer, but Monica silenced her with an abrupt gesture.

'Look here!', she said impulsively, 'we have just about *had* your brat. Take him away, will you? He stinks.'

This was true. I did.

'Why, what has he done?' exclaimed Grams. She turned to me with a frown and asked me the same question in her most disciplinarian voice. I was opening my mouth to explain, when Monica hastily cut in.

'Oh, never mind what he's done! He's been true to his own filthy self. There's no point in going into it, just take him and go. Hear me? Go!'

'Now? In broad daylight? Where can I take him to?'

'What do *I* care? We've had our share of him. Take him to the Gestapo and claim a reward!'

'Now, Miss Monica…'

'To the Gestapo! That's where he belongs! We should have done it long ago, and we may yet, if you don't hurry up…'

'Monica!' said the mother. 'Are you crazy? The whole house can hear you!'

'Let them!' yelled Monica. 'Let them all come! Let them see the little vermin for themselves. I'll call them!' She took a step towards the door.

But Grams was already standing there, her arms crossed, feet apart, and a set look on her face that made it very hard to believe she had no teeth of her own. I saw Monica's mother reach out for the soda-water syphon and realised where the trick came from. She directed it at Monica, who did not see it. There was a very short silence.

'Very well, Miss Monica', said Grams quietly. 'The Gestapo are two streets away. Won't they ask us a few questions, though? Won't they be curious to know where the boy has been, who had hidden him, fed him and looked after him? It's only fair, after all, that so much kindness should not go unrecognised.'

'Are you blackmailing *us*?'

Monica now sounded amazed rather than angry, and her mother softly put down the syphon on the table. They both stared at Grams.

'That *would* be a change, wouldn't it? Think for yourselves. You may yet come to prefer the little vermin, as you call him, not to be discovered. The penalty for hiding a Jew is the same as for being one, and you know what that is, don't you? Even Gentiles are mortal, you know: you can see them hanging from the lampposts all over town. Sometimes they are hanged upside down, which takes much longer… You wouldn't look your best that way.'

Grams' voice was calm and patient, just as if this was another French conjugation. She stared straight at Monica, who by now was quite silent, and allowed herself more and more time between the phrases.

'Whatever happens to the boy shall happen to you, Miss Monica: I will see to it that it does. Don't worry, he won't abuse your generous and disinterested hospitality for a minute longer than necessary; I also want him out of here, for *his* sake. It is only a question of finding him another place. This may take an hour or a month – I cannot tell which. Till then, I am afraid you will have to go on putting up with him, especially as you seem to be making a speciality of unwanted children.'

Strangely enough, this last puzzling remark upset Monica more than anything else. She hurled herself at Grams, who seized her arms.

'You Jewish scum! How dare you?'

'Shhh!' from the mother.

'If I didn't dare, Miss Monica,' said Grams, still gripping her opponent's arms, 'neither my boy nor myself would be here. All I do is dare – every minute of every day. It takes far more than you to frighten me. Remember, the boy knows your name, your address, he's been here for two months, and he even knows that you've repeatedly accepted payment for defying the authorities. If he doesn't tell the Gestapo when he's caught, I will. See to it that he's safe.'

She let go of Monica and went over to the mother's wheel-chair. There was no haggling this time: Grams simply took some money out of her bag and put it into the woman's hands. I don't know if the amount had been increased.

'And that's the gratitude we get!' said the mother. 'We should have known.'

I couldn't help thinking that she was taking a leaf out of Grams' own book. 'You get all the gratitude you deserve', replied Grams. 'And anyway, you don't want gratitude: you want cash. Stop giving yourselves airs you can't afford.'

She kissed me on the forehead and went out, without even dyeing my hair. The silence seemed to go on forever. I was afraid of making the least movement which might attract the two women's attention. Somehow I felt that I could only be punished, atrociously and irredeemably, for Grams' sins and for all my forefathers'.

Monica had sat down and was now crying. I was longing to comfort her, but I didn't dare. What apology could possibly have made up for Grams' blasphemies? What atonement for the inexplicable fact that despite Monica's holiness Grams had managed to cut more of a figure? It was a wonder God had allowed that.

After a while they began to talk, of small things, without any reference to Grams or myself. They sounded tired. The mother presently took up a book, Monica got up and moved a few things about the room. There was nothing to tidy up, but Monica acted as if there was, and this was how she came across me.

She pulled me to my feet and gave me a long, silent look, which terrified me. I wholeheartedly endorsed her evaluation of myself as vermin. Do lice *know* they are vermin? If they do, they must be miserable. There was nothing in me but shame, dirt and fear, and Monica took her time reading these from my cringing face. Still silent, she pointed out the wardrobe with her chin. I went in and sat down in my usual corner. The lock clicked. I slept.

It was a great relief when the next day she reprimanded me in the usual vehement way. I'd been afraid that she would never speak to me again. Why should someone who had conversed with the archangel Gabriel talk to the likes of me?

During the war not only did Tchaikowsky endure the loss of his mother and years of secrecy: at the age of seven he also underwent three traumatic operations to reverse his circumcision.[18] A family friend, a doctor, performed the first operation in a private flat; Tchaikowsky stated

---

[18] This fact is confirmed by Halina Malewiak and Irena Paszkowska in their interviews, and by Tchaikowsky himself in his diaries. The only person he told about the operations was his close friend Michael Menaugh.

in his testament that he did not have any pain relief and had to keep silent. The psychological trauma of this event was further increased by the fact that Celina had a habit of making hurtful remarks about this operation.[19] During these difficult years, Tchaikowsky began to develop a number of character traits present in his adult persona, one of which was the desire to cause sensation by saying controversial and often shocking things which on many occasions, particularly at the start of his concert career, alienated his agents and promoters. He also had a pathological need for acceptance and love, and punished those he thought did not show it to the expected degree.

Emerging Pianist

Łódź, 1945–48

Before the war, the city of Łódź was an important place of music and culture; after the conflict, with Warsaw in ruins, it was one of the first Polish cities to re-instate its music school, and on 1 March 1945 the Łódź Academy of Music, founded at the beginning of the twentieth century, was re-opened as the State Music Conservatoire, at 32 Gdańska St. The conservatoire was famous for a number of prominent musicians, including Kazimierz Wiłkomirski,[20] Maria Wiłkomirska[21] and Emma Altberg[22] who taught piano, and Kazimierz Sikorski,[23] who taught composition. Under the auspices of the Conservatoire, in the Music High School, André Tchaikowsky began his piano studies with Emma Altberg.

His talent was immediately obvious. He had a tremendous facility for sight-reading and learned his lessons quickly. He also began composing. Altberg did her best to foster in her student a sense of discipline and methodical practice, but the task was not difficult, since he simply did not have to work hard: he could play anything he was asked without any obvious effort. Tchaikowsky liked his teacher, and maintained a correspondence with her after he finished his studies.

---

[19] Halina Malewiak, *loc. cit.*
[20] Kazimierz Wiłkomirski (1900–95) was a Polish cellist, composer, conductor and teacher, brother of Wanda, Maria and Michael Wiłkomirski. In 1945–47 he was the president of the Academy of Music in Łódź.
[21] Maria Wiłkomirska (1904–95) was a Polish pianist, soloist and chamber musician, a professor of the State Higher School of Music in Warsaw and Łódź in 1945–81.
[22] Emma Altberg (1889–1983) was a Polish pianist, pedagogue and journalist. She studied piano in Paris, St Petersburg and Łódź, and taught in Łódź Academy of Music in 1945–61.
[23] Kazimierz Sikorski (1895–1986) was a Polish music-theorist, composer and pedagogue. He taught composition, harmony, counterpoint, musical forms and instrumentation in Łódź in 1945–51, and in 1951–66 music theory and composition at the State High Music School in Warsaw.

In Łódź Tchaikowsky lived in a small apartment with his grandmother and her recently widowed sister Dorota Swieca (Dorka). Celina once again had to earn money to support her now much smaller family, and it is thought that she was making hats and took any jobs in the beauty industry. In 1947 Celina had a heart attack (her second; the first had occurred in 1938), and it is most likely that she thought it would be easier to move to Paris where her sister Magdalena Swieca (Mala) would help her. There Tchaikowsky would also be able to continue his piano studies at the Paris Conservatoire with the famous professor of piano, Lazare Lévy,[24] suggested by Emma Altberg.

Paris, 1948–50

The move to Paris in January 1948 was made possible because Tchaikowsky's father provided all the necessary travel documents and passports. Father and son met for the first time, but there was no bond between them and, as time went on, they drifted further apart. Although Tchaikowsky recorded their final break in his unpublished autobiography, it is almost certain that he invented the details of this break. What is certain is that they had some kind of an argument that ended with Tchaikowsky calling his father a 'cunt'. Because Karl slapped André in public, he took an immediate decision to cut off all relations with his father and, in his own mind, 'left' him, just as his mother had done thirteen years previously.

Some of Tchaikowsky's relatives believed that Karl supported his son financially, although Tchaikowsky himself later wrote[25] that his grandmother would not accept a penny from him:

> 'My mistake was in providing for you alone, instead of offering to support her as well,' said Father. 'I had too strong a grudge against her to volunteer that.'
>
> This was ridiculous: Grams would never have accepted a centime from a man she loathed and despised, and they would have torn me apart between them. But I did not contradict Father: there was no point.

It is likely that, if Karl indeed gave money for his son's piano lessons, he did it through a family member. Tchaikowsky's cousin Charles Fortier was most probably that person.[26] Whatever the case, Celina struggled for money. Once again, faced with a difficult financial situation, she found a solution: she enquired at the Polish Embassy in Paris about some kind of financial assistance. Tchaikowsky was asked to give a recital at the Embassy,

---

[24] Lazare Lévy (1882–1964) was an influential French pianist, organist, composer and pedagogue. He taught at the Paris Conservatoire in 1914–16, 1920–23, 1923–40 and 1944–53.

[25] In a diary entry dated 14 April 1980; *cf.* p. 284, below.

[26] Charles Fortier, interviewed by David Ferré, 28 December 1985, Paris.

The twelve-year-old André giving a concert in Paris,
with his grandmother (front, centre) looking on

which became his first public performance, on 1 May 1948, when he played Chopin's Scherzo in B minor, *Nocturne* in F minor, and some of his own compositions that included a *Nocturne*, which he called Op. 1, No. 1. He was twelve. The recital proved successful: the Embassy offered him a monthly stipend that enabled him to study at the Paris Conservatoire until 1950.

In July 1948 Tchaikowsky auditioned for the class of Lazare Lévy, who was immediately impressed with the young pianist and gave him two trial lessons. The first took place on 5 July 1948; after the second, Tchaikowsky was accepted to the Conservatoire, starting piano lessons with Lévy's assistant, Marcelle Fossier-Brillot. He wrote to Emma Altberg:

> Professor Lévy's assistant is giving me very difficult pieces to make me work because she has already learned what an idler I can be. And she changes the programme every second week, so that I won't be bored and discouraged from work. After the *Pathetique* there was Chopin's *Fantasie Impromptu* in C sharp minor, and later the *Moonlight*. Encouraged, I asked for Chopin's Etude in F minor, Opus 25, Number 2, and I received two: this one and F major Opus 25, Number 3. Then, my greatest effort so far, *Scherzo* in B minor by Chopin, which I played on 1 May at the Polish Embassy. I'm enclosing a bit of a review, where they exaggerated my age. The other piece I played at the Embassy was a *Nocturne* in F minor, the one you instructed me

Lazare Lévy with some of his students – Tchaikowsky on the left – in 1950

in. At a school recital, I played the *Moonlight*, one of my own compositions, the *Nocturne* (the same), and two pieces of Professor Lazare Lévy. Now I'm playing Beethoven's *Variations* in C minor, Chopin's *Polonaise* in E flat minor, Chopin's *Etude* in A flat major, Opus 25, Number 1, Bach's *Prelude and Fugue* in C minor from volume I, and two *Etudes* of Clementi, the C major (3rd), and the B major (25th). From Saturday, my new program is Bach's *Italian Concerto*, a theme with variations by Fauré, and also Clementi's *Etude* in A flat major (29th). I'll be playing on Mother's Day, *Le Coucou* of Daquin, Chopin's *Fantasie Impromptu*, and my own composition.

For my examinations (20 Oct. 1948), I'll be playing one piece, the same as everyone else, for comparison, and then three individual pieces (probably Beethoven's C minor *Variations*, Fauré's *Variations*, and Chopin's B minor *Scherzo*, which I haven't started yet). Maybe some changes will happen. Clementi's etudes, written for the right hand, I also play with the left hand.

Oh, I have almost forgotten the most important thing – I have broken relations with my father because he didn't want me to learn music and wanted to take me away from my grandma. He should be grateful, but he hates her. As for our finances, it's harder now, but my brave and loving grandma got a job and somehow, without father and quarrels, we manage. I work a lot to be able to help grandma as soon as possible.[27]

In October 1948 Tchaikowsky took part in the competition for the higher course at the Conservatoire, which meant that he would be able to start lessons with Lévy himself. In early November four candidates were chosen from 340, Tchaikowsky being one of them. He describes the competition and his musical activities in his letter to Altberg:

As 'morceau imposé' we were given *Grande Polonaise Brillante* by Chopin, Opus 22 for piano and orchestra. As 'morceau choisi' I selected the great Fantasia in C minor by Mozart. As for the 'morceau de déchiffrage', I composed it especially for this event, lest anyone should know it. The 'jury' consisted of twelve professors, each time different, and they were awfully strict. I was just lucky! Here in the conservatory, it's different than in Poland: after playing, a student can't walk out of the class; you have to be there from 9 to 12 and listen to the others play.

I'm now repeating the *Moonlight*, and working on the Prelude and Fugue in A flat major from Bach's volume I, exercises by Czerny and Philipp, and one *Mephisto valse* by Liszt, which for the time being I've put aside until after Christmas, so one has to wait until January.

I've been writing a lot of compositions for the piano, and even for orchestra (symphony in B major). Professor Lazare Lévy and his assistant, Mme Fossier-Brillot, are working on two piano sonatas I wrote and dedicated to them. Here's the plan for the sonatas:

Piano Sonata in F minor (for Mme Fossier-Brillot)
I – *Allegro*. Very widely developed with the dynamics of constant crescendo and polyphonic transformation. It's great.
II – *Theme and Variations*. 35 variations based on a theme of a friend of mine from Łódź.

[27] Letter to Emma Altberg dated 12 July 1948, quoted in *The Other Tchaikowsky, op. cit.*, p. 57.

Piano Sonata in C sharp minor (for Professor Lazare Lévy)
I – Introduction and Allegro
II – Aria and 27 Variations. It's in the form of a Fugue, Waltz, Nocturne, Recitative, March, Funeral March, etc.
III – Grande Fugue. For four voices, Cadenza, Recitative, Finale and Coda.

The sonatas are treated symphonically, which is hard to achieve for an average pianist, but for my professor, it's nothing. Unfortunately, I myself can't play these sonatas yet.

It quickly became obvious that for Tchaikowsky composition was more interesting and challenging than playing. It would remain so for the rest of his life.

At the Conservatoire National de Musique he studied piano performance, solfège, instrumentation, history of style, sight-reading and the history of music. In June 1950, at the end of his final year, he entered the competitions in piano performance and solfège and received gold medals in both disciplines. At fourteen years of age Tchaikowsky was the youngest competitor, and one of the youngest graduates of the Paris Conservatoire with its highest honours.

Poland, 1950–56

Polish Composers' Union

Because Tchaikowsky had received funding from the Polish Ministry of Culture, he was invited back to Poland, with promise of further financial assistance. He decided to accept the invitation and on 17 July 1950 he returned to his home country. As was to be the case for the rest of his life, his activity there was divided into composition and performance. It is clear that he wanted to focus on composing, and a file kept in the archives of the Polish Music Information Centre, Polish Composers' Union, Warsaw, contains documents relating to his membership. On 13 June 1950 Tchaikowsky made an application to the Youth Circle (Koło Młodych) of the Polish Composers' Union, in which he informed the committee:

I was born in Warsaw on 1 November 1935. My father, Karol Ignacy, was a doctor of law. My mother, Felicja Alexandria, was without occupation. They were both murdered during the German occupation and I was left under the care of my grandmother, Celina Czajkowska. Shortly after the war, I began my musical studies. In 1948, because of the bad state of health of my grandmother, I went with her to Paris, where I continued my studies up to the year 1950 and graduated with high accord, with first medals in piano and sight-reading. On the invitation of the ministers' council, I came back to Poland for the course at Łagów. Accepting the proposition of the Minister of Culture, I decided to settle permanently in Poland to continue my studies. Beginning with the school year 1948, I've had a scholarship from the Polish Government.[28]

This letter shows Tchaikowsky's desire to distance himself from his father even further, by 'killing' him in print. All his official biographies, and entries in dictionaries, incorrectly refer to the death of both his father and mother.

The Composers' Union requested a list of Tchaikowsky's compositions, which he sent on 6 November 1950, and which listed only two extant works among others that were lost or 'in preparation':

(10) Dances (manuscript is lost)
(10) Etudes (manuscript in preparation)
Sonatina in G major
Suite for piano
Piano Sonata in F minor (lost)
Piano Sonata in A major (lost)
Variations on a theme of Handel (lost)
Variations on a theme of Cohen (in preparation)
Variations on an original theme (lost)
Concerto for piano and orchestra (lost)
Concerto for violin and orchestra (in preparation)
Sonata for violin and piano (lost)
Concerto for flute and orchestra (in preparation)[29]

The influential Polish composer Zygmunt Mycielski[30] evaluated Tchaikowsky's Suite for Piano, reviewing it in a letter to the committee of the Union on 8 November 1950:

I wish to draw the attention of the Polish Composers' Union to the fact that Andrzej Czajkowski shows considerable composing talent through his musical inventiveness, which is remarkable for such a young boy. On the basis of his piano *Suite* that I have read, I can state that Czajkowski undoubtedly possesses a great talent, musicality, and originality. The Suite consists of four pieces:

[28] The letter, held in the archives of the Polish Music Information Centre, Polish Composers' Union, Warsaw, is quoted in *The Other Tchaikowsky*, op. cit., pp. 62–63.
[29] The archives of the Polish Music Information Centre, Polish Composers' Union, Warsaw.
[30] Mycielski (1907–87) studied first in Kraków before moving to Paris to study composition with Paul Dukas and Nadia Boulanger. His own compositions include six symphonies and other orchestral pieces, two piano concertos and much chamber, instrumental and vocal music.

Early Tchaikowsky: three piano pieces – a Nocturne *he styled
his Op. 1, No. 1 (1948), a study marked* Prestissimo possible *(1949)
and another merely* Presto *(1955) – and a clean copy of a 1955 setting
for soprano and piano of Christ's words on the cross
(from Matthew 27:46)*

1. *Preludium* – It is Scriabin-like, but I prefer it to many compositions that are built on the piano arpeggiare. It is still a youthful search, but it is not a copy of any style.
2. *Variations* – He couldn't introduce a great variety, he struggles, but still his inventiveness shows through the descending chromaticism.
3. *Waltz* – Not enough variety in the right hand, but it has an inborn sense of style and form.
4. *Lullaby* – Shows an outstanding musicality, although it contains a lot of wrong notes. It is not precisely put down, but I prefer these childish mistakes to school routine and correctness.

> In my opinion, Andrzej Czajkowski should be trained by the best teachers, who will be able to develop his talent and at the same time respect his musical individuality, which is shown by his first piano pieces.[31]

Based on Mycielski's appraisal, the committee granted Tchaikowsky membership of the Youth Circle – and, as a member, he used the resources available to him to the full. He requested a piano, which was lent to him and delivered to his new address in Warsaw, he asked for manuscript paper, and he took part in performances of his own and other composers' works. He also actively sought commissions, and made an application to the committee to grant him a commission for the following three proposed works:

> A cycle of 12 piano studies, aimed at students of Music Schools that would address a variety of technical problems, with modern rhythms, and meant for performance, not just practice.

> A Piano Concerto F minor for full symphony orchestra, or possibly an augmented one. The concerto will be in three movements, *Allegro, Andante, Rondo-Allegro.*

> A Flute Concerto H moll in three movements: *Allegro moderato, Andante* or *Lento* (the first movement was not yet decided), *Scherzo – Allegro vivace* or *Prestissimo,* and *Rondo – Allegro.*

At the end of the letter, he asked the Union for financial support that would enable him to finish the compositions. An official stamp on the document shows that his application was approved on the same day, 5 January 1951.[32]

[31] *Ibid.*
[32] *Ibid.*

From the documents kept in his file it is evident that he was treated as a promising composer, and all his requests were complied with almost immediately. He was granted financial support, and invited to take part in various events. For example, for a performance of his own Prelude and Fugue in 1951 he was promised the considerable amount of 200 zlotys, paid on the day of the concert.[33] His membership started in 1950, and expired in 1958, after which he was expected to apply for the full, adult, membership of the Composers' Union. But he did not apply because in 1957 he left Poland again, this time permanently.

Warsaw

When Tchaikowsky returned from Paris, he had spent the summer of 1950 in a music camp in Łagów in central Poland, and then a year in Sopot, a seaside town in northern Poland, where he studied at the Music High School, but he found the piano course undemanding and concentrated on composition. When he came back to Warsaw, he received, as promised by the Ministry of Culture and the Composers' Union, his own apartment, and a grand piano in September 1951.

Tchaikowsky enrolled at the State Academy of Music in Warsaw (today The Fryderyk Chopin University of Music), to study piano with Stanisław Szpinalski and composition with Kazimierz Sikorski.[34] Szpinalski, at the time the Director of the School, immediately realised the extent of Tchaikowsky's talent and all his written appraisals comment on his student's extraordinary musical ability, both as pianist and composer. Appraisals of students' progress as members of the Communist generation were also required, and Szpinalski duly noted Tchaikowsky's dedication to self-development, and sound knowledge of Marxist-Leninist ideologies.[35]

The Tchaikowsky file in the University archive contains documents relating to his study-period between 1951 and 1956.[36] They include a letter of application, with details of his French education, regular appraisals and examination results. In 1953, parallel to his studies at the Warsaw University, Tchaikowsky finished his course at the secondary school Korespondencyjne Liceum Ogolnoksztalcace No. 3, graduating with A+ grades in Polish and French, A in history, astronomy, physics, biology, chemistry and study of

---

[33] *Ibid.*

[34] Stanisław Szpinalski (1901–57) was a Polish pianist and teacher of piano at the State High Music School in Warsaw in 1951–57.

[35] Personal Characteristic, undated, by Prof. S. Szpinalski, Andrzej Czajkowski file, the Frederyk Chopin University of Music.

[36] The file was discovered in February 2013 when enquiries were made about any documentation relating to Tchaikowsky's student years.

With a lifeguard at Sopot, on the Baltic coast near Gdansk, in 1950

the constitution, and B in mathematics, geology and geography.[37] His essays on various topics already show a considerable talent for writing.

Tchaikowsky then applied for and was granted the year 1954–55 off, so as to prepare for the Chopin competition without the additional workload of other subjects. But he did not concentrate solely on the piano, as his report to the Composers' Union shows: he composed a sonata for viola and piano, two preludes and two études for piano and a song for soprano and piano set to words by the Polish poet Julian Tuwim.[38] During the preparation for the competition he spent the summer months in Sopot, where he met the young Chinese pianist Fou Ts'ong, who recalled Tchaikowsky's reputation as the most incredibly talented, 'extraordinarily brilliant'[39] pianist. Tchaikowsky was extravert, demonstrative in a physical way, always hugging and kissing

---

[37] Secondary School Certificate, Andrzej Czajkowski file, the Fryderyk Chopin University of Music.

[38] The archives of the Polish Music Information Centre, Polish Composers' Union, Warsaw. Tuwim (1894–1953) was one of the leaders of the group of Polish poets called Skamander. Mieczysław Weinberg was another composer who responded strongly to Tuwim's poetry, using it in a number of song-settings and as the basis for his Eighth and Ninth Symphonies (1964 and 1940–67) and the cantata *Piotr Plaksin* (1965).

[39] Fou Ts'ong, interviewed by David Ferré, 31 August 1986, London.

his friends, and in particular a very beautiful girl of about fourteen or fifteen, who often accompanied him.[40] He already exhibited the kind of intensity that made his company exhausting for many of his friends later in life. 'He was always full-on, almost hysterical in his sarcasm and enthusiasm', said Fou Ts'ong. But he was also 'if not the most, then one of the most intelligent people I met in my life'.[41]

The sharp-tongued Tchaikowsky was never lost for words. A typical story from this period of preparation for the competition is about his practice of Chopin's F minor Piano Concerto. He was working on a difficult section of the finale, very fast and technically challenging. Fou Ts'ong's teacher, the most senior professor there, heard Tchaikowsky practise and criticised his playing. Tchaikowsky's response was: 'It's only because you can't [play it], you are jealous'.[42]

The jury awarded Tchaikowsky eighth place (out of 77 competitors from 25 countries), which delighted him since he did not consider himself a particularly good interpreter of Chopin's music. He was also given special awards as the youngest Polish pianist (he was nineteen at the time) in the competition: a piano, 10,000 zlotys, and a concert tour in Poland and Bulgaria. In today's money, 10,000 zlotys would be about 6,000 euros, 5,000 pounds sterling or 8,000 US dollars, a generous prize by all standards.

One of the jury members was the Polish-Belgian pianist Stefan Askenase (1896–1985) who, impressed by Tchaikowsky's talent, invited him to study in Brussels. He later remembered: 'André had a wonderful gift. When I heard him the first time, I wanted to stop playing'.[43] Askenase said that the lessons he gave Tchaikowsky were more conversations and consultations, because he was already an artist in his own right.[44] Their relationship lasted until Tchaikowsky's death.

Tchaikowsky also met the famous Polish pianist Arthur Rubinstein (1887–1982), who took considerable interest in the young musician and recommended that he take part in the Queen Elisabeth Competition in Brussels in 1956. This time Tchaikowsky achieved more success, being awarded third prize, coming behind Vladimir Ashkenazy and John Browning. Asked why he did not win the first prize, Fou Ts'ong reflected:

---

[40] *Ibid.*
[41] *Ibid.*
[42] *Ibid.*
[43] Stefan Askenase, interviewed by David Ferré, 16 July 1985, Bad Godesberg, Germany.
[44] *Ibid.*

Tchaikowsky's enrolment card at the Music School in Sopot (above), and (right) the leaving certificate awarded in Sopot on 17 September 1951, with highest marks ('very good') for Analysis and Counterpoint, Musical Style and Piano Performance but only 'satisfactory' for the study of Marxist-Leninist theories.

He was very, very individual. Such individuality is never going to get the first prize. [...] André never won any first prize, and he was one of the most talented, incredibly talented pianists, or musicians altogether, I have ever known.[45]

Tchaikowsky's cousin Halina Malewiak believed that the prize of 1,000,000 French francs (about €1,500, £1,200 or $2,000 today) clouded his mind, and showed to full extent his recklessness with money: just like his grandmother Celina, he spent without restraint. Fame, success, money and Rubinstein's attention and support, she thought, went to his head and unbalanced him, and created the foundation for his future professional problems.[46] Halina Janowska also recounted that Tchaikowsky brought with him from Brussels an expensive Grundig radio, and at least thirty gold Swiss watches, in addition to other expensive purchases.[47]

---

[45] *Loc. cit.*
[46] Halina Malewiak, interviewed by David Ferré, 28 March 1987, Paris.
[47] Letter to David Ferré dated 10 April 1992.

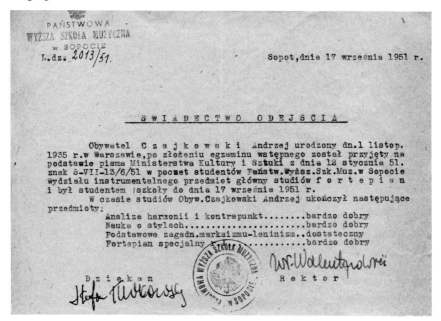

The Queen Elisabeth Competition brought international engagements, Rubinstein's support and further lessons with Stefan Askenase – a dream come true for anyone interested in the career of concert pianist. But Tchaikowsky was not dreaming of a concert career, and found the demands placed on him by this early success very difficult. He never went back to the State Academy of Music after his year off, and the Director issued an order to expel him in 1957 for failing to return, as promised, to continue his studies of 1955–56.[48]

On 5 November 1955 Tchaikowsky's grandmother died, and with her died the last link to his past. By all accounts, their relationship was not a straightforward one; for him, it was deeply ambivalent: as a child, he was very much attached to her and, as a youth, he both loved and hated her. John O'Brien summed it up in 1987:

> He hated her. And yet he owed her so much he couldn't get over the guilt of it. He tried very hard to love her, but he couldn't. I think it tore him apart. For years and years he battled, but he could not. She was so powerful, so overbearing. And obviously so determined that he had a mission of some sort. Clearly a musical mission.[49]

---

[48] Andrzej Czajkowski file, the Fryderyk Chopin University of Music.

[49] John O'Brien, interviewed by David Ferré, 2 January 1987, Syracuse, New York.

All the official statements Tchaikowsky made in Poland show his respect for the only surviving member of his immediate family. Celina was the star of his own story, not only the powerful force that saved him but the person who set him on his professional path, although also bestowing on him severe handicaps that resulted from her high expectations and pressure.

Enfant Terrible

The stories about Tchaikowsky's outbursts, shocking behaviour and disregard for any social norms during the early years of his concert tours are legendary and could fill an entire book. Perhaps one of the most famous stories was told by fellow pianist John Browning, who remembered that at a reception after the Queen Elisabeth Competition Tchaikowsky said to the ex-Queen of Italy and member of the Belgian royal family, Valérie José, that he wanted 'to have sex with her, then push her off a fast-moving train'.[50] Browning said that Tchaikowsky just wanted

> to be amusing, just to be a little monkey. She looked straight ahead, typical royal reaction, as somebody whisked him off and told him never to do that again. He was a prankster. He loved doing shocking things. He tried very hard to be shocking and unconventional. It was very difficult to tell how much of the eccentricities were real and how much were fake. But he was a very sweet boy. He was really very kind and very decent.[51]

Tchaikowsky's first American tour started on 13 October 1957, when he played Prokofiev's Third Piano Concerto with the New York Philharmonic and Dimitri Mitropoulos. He was represented by the world's most famous impresario, Sol Hurok, who was also Arthur Rubinstein's agent and who took on Tchaikowsky purely on Rubinstein's recommendation. Rubinstein significantly cut the number of his own appearances there in order to give his protégé a better chance. But Tchaikowsky instantly created conflicts. Hurok promoted him with a biography that drew heavily on emotionally charged accounts of Tchaikowsky's parents' deaths in Treblinka, and Tchaikowsky felt he was being showcased in America as a 'sort of Anne Frank of the keyboard'.[52] Hurok was also uncomfortable with promoting Tchaikowsky, who had essentially escaped from Poland, at the same time as promoting other Polish and Russian musicians who did not leave their

[50] John Browning, interviewed by David Ferré, 12 December 1986, Syracuse, New York.
[51] *Ibid.*
[52] Halina Janowska, interviewed by Anastasia Belina-Johnson, 20 February 2013, Warsaw.

Tchaikowsky (centre) with a group of friends in Warsaw c. 1954

countries; indeed, he wanted Tchaikowsky to go back to Poland, and that created another conflict.[53]

The pianist Peter Frankl remembered a story from Tchaikowsky's concert in Dallas during his 1957–58 tour that illustrates his frustration and intense dislike of after-concert parties:

> André ruined his American career. He used to say: 'I showed those Americans that you can't get away with this!' André was against the kind of 'rich ladies' who were sort of leading the musical life in the US, especially in Texas. Well, in Dallas there was a lady called Mildred Foster who all the time made her appearance, contacted the artists, and made them kind of obey whatever she said. [...] But André made up his mind that he wasn't going to go to see her. She insisted that she is Rubinstein's friend, and so on. He finally went to her party. When André was asked to speak, he said: 'I'm not a polite speaker at dinner parties. In fact, I'm not very good at dinner parties; in fact, I hate dinner parties. I didn't want to come to this party and I'm not suitable to this party because when I get excited, I get nose bleeds in public and I feel one coming on and will have to leave soon. You really don't want me at your party. I am a communist, I eat with my fingers, I never take a bath, I'm Jewish, I pick my nose, I believe in equal rights of whites and blacks, and, finally, I'm a homosexual.'[54]

---

[53] Terry Harrison, interviewed by David Ferré, 25 June 1985, London.
[54] Peter Frankl, interviewed by David Ferré, 3 July 1985, London.

Conversing with Queen Elisabeth of Belgium at the 1955 Chopin competition

Needless to say, this kind of behaviour did little to endear him to his patrons and promoters, and he never did have the kind of American career that he could have had if he had been interested in developing his profile there.

Nonetheless, he did receive invitations to the USA after his first season, and Hurok organised a follow-up tour for the 1958–59 season. Tchaikowsky was supposed to make recordings with RCA and Fritz Reiner, but his late arrivals for rehearsals, missed concerts and insulting and erratic behaviour, combined with his refusal to play any of the concertos by Tchaikovsky, Rachmaninov, Grieg, Saint-Saëns or the Beethoven 'Emperor' Concertos, did not help Hurok's endeavours to develop his career. He made no secret that he developed a severe dislike of America, and when Hurok confronted him about his destructive behaviour, Tchaikowsky rebelled completely, and continued in the same fashion. He did not want to be back, and burned bridges as he went along.

When the season was over, Hurok refused to work with Tchaikowsky who, in turn, refused to accept any other invitations to the USA. Although the reviews from his concerts proclaimed him to be an excellent musician, his fame as an artist impossible to work with was even more widespread. Tchaikowsky had only two other performances in America: in Houston with Lawrence Foster in 1975, and in Rochester with David Zinman in 1978.

David Zinman remembered another story, this time associated with Tchaikowsky's concert performance on 3 March 1960 in Bergen, Norway. Because of his phenomenal ability to learn new works very fast, his repertoire list included concertos that he had not played before. For the Bergen concert he had to perform the Ravel G major Concerto, for which Tchaikowsky did not even have the music.

> André said: 'This was one of the concertos in my repertoire that I haven't got around to learning, but I've got two weeks. I'll learn it'. He had heard it and liked it. So he went to town and bought the score. The next morning, he came down after having his breakfast, went to the piano, and opened the score. Just then, the telephone rang. It was some friend of his coming to town, so immediately they went out and had lunch together and partied for a couple of days. Somehow, without his knowing it, about a week had gone by, but he still had a week left, naturally. So he opened the score again, and the telephone rang again. It was his manager, or somebody, and André had to go and replace somebody up in the provinces, so he went and did a concert there. He came back and now he had about two days left. Then some other friend of his arrived. So it was now the day before the concert and he still hasn't learned it at all. So he had a problem. André figured that instead of flying, he'd leave that day by train, and since he's fantastic at learning by study, and has a fantastic mind, he would learn the score just by looking at it, and then play it from memory. Of course, when he got to Bergen, he would practise it, but he would learn it on the train just by looking at it.
>
> So he took the train and they went across the English Channel and got on another train. André opened his brief case to get the score out and realised he left it at home on the piano. So there he was, arriving in Bergen, Norway, to play music he didn't have, and for which, in fact, he had never even seen the score.
>
> André was met at the train station by the conductor and secretary of the Bergen orchestra. They're going to drive him to the hotel. So he gets in the car, absolutely not knowing what to do. The conductor of the orchestra says to him: 'Mr Tchaikowsky, there's a small problem. You are playing the Ravel Concerto, and as you know there's a very important harp part. Our harp player is sick from food poisoning. Would you consent to doing the concerto without the harp player?'
>
> André says: 'Under no circumstances would I permit myself to do such a thing'. So the conductor says, 'What are we going to do? André replies: 'We'll have to play another concerto, that's all'. 'It's the last second. Which concerto can we do?' says the conductor. André says, and this is clever of André: 'I think we should play a Mozart concerto'.

This was at the beginning of André's career. He didn't have that many Mozart concertos in his repertoire. The conductor asked which one he would like to play? André answers: 'I don't know, because I play all of them.' The conductor said that they would go to their library and get out all the Mozart piano concertos they had there. So they go immediately to the library and get out all the scores.

André goes to the piano in the artists' room and plays each one a bit: 'No, this is too early.' 'This is a lovely one, but I don't think it's right.' Finally he comes to No. 25, к503, the only concerto he knows, and says: 'Let's play this one.' Then, of course, he plays it completely from memory the next day, no problem, without practising. The orchestra is in ecstasy and the critics, who found out about this, just think it's the greatest thing.

After the concert, they decided to throw a wonderful party for André with wine and beer. André was a very bad drinker, couldn't hold his liquor at all, and would get topsy-turvy. Everyone was making toasts to the great André Tchaikowsky and this fantastic feat that he had done. So, finally, André stood up and said: 'I have a toast, and a confession. The toast is to all of you for being such wonderful hosts and hostesses, and to this marvellous orchestra, and your talented conductor. The confession: I don't know and have never played a note of the Ravel G major Concerto; the only Mozart concerto I know is No. 25; and I was the one who poisoned the harpist.' Then he sat down, and there was this unbelievable silence.[55]

Tchaikowsky was not invited back to Bergen after this event. Stories like this one are peppered throughout his career, and many of those who knew Tchaikowsky would have at least one such tale to tell.

Arthur Rubinstein

After meeting Tchaikowsky in 1955, Rubinstein wanted to support and promote him as a pianist, giving him glowing references and even providing him with a room in his house in Paris. But Tchaikowsky found the responsibility of being a protégé of the famous pianist unwelcome and, combined with his nonchalant attitude, spiky personality and reluctance to do anything against his own will, problems followed almost immediately. The Canadian pianist Janina Fialkowska (b. 1951), a pupil of Rubinstein, recounted her conversations with Rubinstein about Tchaikowsky. She thought that Rubinstein did not understand Tchaikowksy because

he had a hard time understanding any sort of nervous, impulsive behaviour. Rubinstein was a man of the last century. Things like behavioural aberrations, you didn't discuss those things, and you certainly didn't flaunt them. In

---

[55] David Zinman, interviewed by David Ferré , 14 December 1986, Rochester.

TUNE-UP TIME FOR A NEW SEASON—The New York Philharmonic, above, is scheduled to open its 116th season on Thursday evening at Carnegie Hall. In inset, conductor Dimitri Mitroupolos and André Tchaikowsky, Polish pianist, who will make his New York debut on the opening program, playing Prokofieff's Piano Concerto No. 3.

Tchaikowsky with the conductor Dimitri Mitropoulos pictured in The New York Times *in a 1957 feature article announcing the highlights of the new season*

his day it was kept sort of hush hush. He didn't understand depression or anything like that.[56]

She remembered that the break between Tchaikowsky and Rubinstein happened because of an insult similar to that he made to the member of Belgian royalty, delivered by Tchaikowsky to Rubinstein's mother-in-law:

> Arthur is very, very loyal. Demanding, but loyal. To have had to break off he must have done something pretty horrible. Arthur would have put up with a lot for the sake of that kind of talent. But then in a funny way Rubinstein was a family man. He had this idea of how families should be. And he couldn't have someone insult this idea.[57]

Rubinstein was hurt by the break. Had Tchaikowsky wanted to promote himself as a pianist, he could not have found a better, more influential supporter, but he did not care for such promotion, and left Rubinstein's protection without, it seems, any regrets.

During a tour of the USA in 1957–58, Tchaikowsky already displayed the characteristics of his later years: extreme nervousness before performances, dislike of practising, frequent disregard for social etiquette, and abhorrence of social functions and receptions after concerts. He shocked the patrons of

---

[56] Janina Fialkowska, interviewed by David Ferré, 28 February 1987, Syracuse, New York.
[57] *Ibid.*

*An autographed Hurok promotional
picture from 1957*

American concerts by saying rude things to the very people who subsidised
his tours, he did not forge good relationships with conductors and
orchestras, and seemingly enjoyed the reactions he created. Tchaikowsky
often told the story of being invited to play for Horowitz at his home after
a concert on 13 October 1957. He was looking forward to going, but he
was kept waiting for over an hour and so, when he was finally admitted
and asked to play, he dropped a thunderous C major chord, saying that it
was the only thing he could play by memory. Horowitz's reaction can be
easily imagined.[58] But the letter he then wrote to Halina Janowska provides
a much blander account, not mentioning his hair-raising behaviour at all.[59]
As with many of Tchaikowsky's stories, it is not possible to tell fiction from
truth; with every repeat, he would embellish the stories so much that the
true version of events would be completely forgotten, and lost.

England

Tchaikowsky left Poland in October 1956 and, although he returned to
Warsaw briefly in 1957, he decided later that year to leave permanently –
although it is thought that he never renounced his Polish citizenship. The
New Zealand music-critic Ian Dando remembers:

[58] Quoted in *The Other Tchaikowsky*, p. 146.
[59] Letter dated 8 November 1957.

On tour in South America in 1958

He had a strange relationship with Poland. He was always suspicious of Poland, never wanted to go back. In fact, when I was at the Warsaw festival, and staying with Halinka, a number of the Warsaw festival people said 'If you know André, please persuade him to come back and give some recitals in Warsaw. We'd love to have him back'. I passed this onto André, and André said 'No, no. If I went back to Warsaw they might cancel my visa, I might be imprisoned there, I mightn't be able to get out again. No, I don't trust any countries east of the Iron Curtain.' André would never go back to Poland for that reason.[60]

Tchaikowsky's friend Stanisław Kolodziejczyk commented that he 'didn't want to go back to Poland because it

was the country of very unpleasant and frightening war experiences. This was his association. The second such element, I think, was the death of his grandmother which he took very hard.[61]

---

[60] Recollections of Ian Dando, recorded on tape on 22 December 1987 and sent to David Ferré.
[61] Stanisław Kolodziejczyk, interviewed by David Ferré, 16 September 1986, Warsaw.

He remembered that Tchaikowsky was with him when his grandmother died, and he never forgave himself that he was not with her.

> With her death, the last link with Poland disappeared, and he left never to return. He was worried about visas and passports, and not being able to travel freely. Did not like this control. But he did not officially deny his Polish citizenship, and he carried [a] double citizenship card with him.[62]

After leaving Warsaw in 1957, Tchaikowsky lived in Brussels, Paris and London, moving from one friend's place to another's, and spending a few weeks in Fontainebleau in 1957, where he took composition lessons with Nadia Boulanger. He was introduced to her by Zygmunt Mycielski, who thought Tchaikowsky would benefit from lessons with her, as Mycielski himself had over three decades earlier. As with Rubinstein, he left Boulanger on bad terms. During his brief study period he lived in Boulanger's house but was asked to vacate his room when she expected another student (presumably still being able to continue with lessons). Now the feeling of not being wanted took over, and he punished Boulanger in the only way he knew – by severing all relations.

The legend goes that Tchaikowsky decided to settle in England after reading *The Diary of a Nobody* (1888–89) by the brothers George and Weedon Grossmith. He was delighted with the book, and believed that people really did live and think in the way the protagonist – the celebrated Charles Pooter – described. England provided a longed-for stability, even if it took him some years to settle there properly.

Tchaikowsky lived for three years (1963–66) in the home of Michael and Judy Arnold, whom he met in Hong Kong in 1961 during a tour of the Far East. The Arnolds, who lived in Hong Kong for several years, returned to England in 1962, and when Tchaikowsky was looking for somewhere to live in 1963, they offered him a room in their house. From then on, until 1969, Judy looked after all his paperwork and some concert affairs. In 1966 Tchaikowsky finally moved into his first flat, at Waterlow Court, Heath Close, London NW11, a quadrangle of flats in Hampstead Garden Suburb, not far from Hampstead Heath. The purchase of the property had been made possible with the help of Charles Napper, a wealthy patron of the arts who supported young musicians and who had arranged a 100% mortgage for Tchaikowsky. The flat was very small, Tchaikowsky was nervous about practising for fear of upsetting his neighbours and he felt he was too readily accessible while living in London. He eventually decided to sell it and buy

---

[62] *Ibid.*

somewhere better suited to his professional activities. His final move took place in 1976, when he bought a small house (built in the 1960s) in Cumnor, a village to the south-west of Oxford. It was his close friend Eve Harrison who had made it clear he could sell Waterlow Court and buy something more appropriate. Tchaikowsky had met Eve since she was married to his agent Terry Harrison, and the two quickly became friends. Eve was a special presence in Tchaikowsky's life, the only person around whom he could truly relax and be himself. His diaries show how much he treasured her friendship, and how he valued her opinions on life, music and relationships. It was Eve who organised the sale of the Waterlow Court flat, the purchase of the house Tchaikowsky eventually chose and the move to Cumnor. There he prepared for his concerts, and composed in between tours. His next-door neighbour, Pat Allison, helped him with the daily running of the house and looked after his paperwork.

A Reluctant Pianist

Between 1957 and 1960 Tchaikowsky gave close to 500 concerts around the world. His international career began with the Chopin Competition, but after the Queen Elisabeth Competition in Belgium it entered a new phase when he was represented by Hurok. While Hurok promoted Tchaikowsky in the United States, his European manager was Wilfrid van Wyck, who organised his English debut. It took place in London on 29 January 1958 (in the middle of his American tour) in the Royal Festival Hall, when he played Prokofiev's Second Piano Concerto with the Pro Arte Orchestra conducted by Anthony English. Like Hurok, van Wyck was trying to get as many engagements as possible, but Tchaikowsky grumbled that he had no time to take a holiday, a complaint that his future London-based manager Terry Harrison, one of the founders of Harrison Parrott in 1969, would come to hear often.

Playing the piano supported Tchaikowsky financially and enabled him to dedicate his summers to composition. But such a schedule hardly helped Harrison develop his performing profile. In order to achieve and maintain public success, an artist must remain in the public eye, but Tchaikowsky was not interested in 'success'. He always thought that concerts took away time from composition, and found it increasingly difficult to negotiate the two areas of his professional life. Harrison remembered:

> There were times when it was difficult to manage André […]. That was when he became obsessed by something, like a person he didn't like, a person connected with the concerts, or a conductor he didn't like. […] or he became obsessed that he was falling behind with his composing, and would turn down

things. Sometimes I had to persuade him that he shouldn't turn down these things, either because he needed the money, or because it was an engagement that he should do because it was important, etc. That usually took a long time to persuade him and usually I was successful. It used to take two or three discussions over two or three days to get through. […] He actually should have been busier and played more concerts. But he became more and more interested in his composing, and the time that he would give us became more and more restricted for concerts. […] These blocks of time he would give us were less and less. Also, he liked to do things for pleasure rather than prestige. He wasn't prestige-orientated, he turned his back on the whole star system in the early 1960s when he could have probably done very well. He turned his back on it because he felt it was, to some extent, anti-musical. He also felt that you had to put on an act and a face and not be yourself. He felt you couldn't be your own man in the star system. You had to be someone who would perform in a certain fashion. He felt he was first a musician and very, very second a performer. He thought the star system had it the other way. He also had to be his own private person a lot of the time.[63]

In spite of his reluctance Tchaikowsky was an outstanding pianist. His technical ability was extraordinary, his sight-reading skills legendary, and his interpretations of Bach, Mozart and Bartók are remembered to this day. He often improvised his cadenzas in Mozart piano concertos and David Zinman, who met Tchaikowsky in 1966 in the Netherlands, recalled two of them:

I met André in Holland in 1966. I lived in Holland and was the conductor of the Netherlands Chamber Orchestra, and André was recommended to me. On our first subscription concert he played a Mozart concerto. He was such a bright and funny guy, somewhat odd and eccentric, and he always loved to shock people. He was famous for improvising Mozart cadenzas, although on that occasion, he was fairly straight. André would improvise cadenzas, really improvise them. Nothing was written down. There was an occasion in Rotterdam where we played Mozart:
André: 'You know, I'd like to improvise my own cadenza. What do you think?'
David: 'Why don't you do it?'
André: 'I'll go my own way, but the ending will be as the Mozart cadenza.'
David: 'That's terrific, André.'
André: 'I don't know what it will be, but it'll be something fun.'
Of course we couldn't rehearse it because there was no rehearsal on Sundays with the orchestra. Then we were on stage and the first movement goes well. He goes to the cadenza and he starts to play. It's one of his usual fantastic sort of 'Fantasies on themes of Mozart'. The orchestra was really up for this

---

[63] Terry Harrison, interviewed by David Ferré, 25 June 1985, London.

Sharing a joke with Martha Argerich in London in 1966

because they knew André and what a joker he was. They're sitting there sort of giggling as he goes into foreign keys and sort of fools around and comes back. Finally, he gets into the end of the cadenza, which is the Mozart ending, but, to my amazement, he's an octave low. Well, I didn't know what he was going to do. He made a run up to the trill, and he starts trilling, and then, I course, I knew I had to come in. So we did, but just then he realised he was an octave low, and he went on playing. We had to stop, while André went on, and went on another three minutes or so, got back, ended this time in the right octave, and we came in again. I was absolutely furious, completely and utterly furious. I wouldn't look at him the rest of the concerto. He was like a sort of beaten dog. You could see it. He was trying to make me smile as if to say, 'It's all right, I didn't mean it.' So we finished the concerto and left the stage. I went directly to my dressing room. André comes in sort of whimpering and apologising. He said, 'I was an octave too low, I thought you knew that'. I told him, 'But André, how could you play the trill with the turn, and expect me not to come in?' He said I was right. André went to all the music critics and assured them it wasn't my fault and it was his own stupidity. That was typical of André.

Then there was his famous Mozart cadenza for the C major Concerto K467, which I'll never forget as long as I live. What he decided to do was to combine all the themes together. So he had something going in this hand, then with arpeggios with the other hand, and all this going on at the same time with sort of Saint-Saëns modulations into very foreign keys. It was the weirdest cadenza.[64]

Tchaikowsky's phenomenal memory meant that his repertoire was bigger than that of many of his contemporaries. During his two-month stint as an artist-in-residence in Perth in 1975 he played a cycle of all 27 Mozart concertos: three every night for nine evenings, all from memory.

[64] Telephone interview with David Ferré, 13 October 1986, Baltimore.

Tchaikovsky with his friend and representative Judy Arnold,
at the Darlington summer school in 1966

He could look at music and play from memory after only one reading. This ability made him something of a legend, and audiences flocked to hear him. But they had to pay dearly for his affection: if the applause was not an ovation, if people did not listen attentively, or if late-comers did not enter the hall quietly, he would unleash his wrath. One of many such 'revenge' stories comes from Spain, where the applause after one of Tchaikowsky's recitals was modest, and the punishment he chose was the entire 'Goldberg' Variations as an encore.[65]

Perhaps the tension between composer and pianist was not entirely related to Tchaikowsky's desire to compose. It was also a legacy from his grandmother, who always pushed him to perform, telling him that, as a composer, he would only become famous after his death. Tchaikowsky hated to be told what to do by anyone, and Celina's insistence could have set foundations for rejection of piano performance as a sole occupation.

One of the conductors with whom Tchaikowsky most liked to perform was Christopher Seaman, who talked about him as a pianist:

> It was superb playing. It was unusual playing. It was playing that made you think. If you were very 'hide-bound' or prejudiced, his playing was a threat to you because it called your own prejudices into question. In fact, André was like that. I think a lot of people were very threatened by him because

---

[65] Zamira Benthall, interviewed by David Ferré, 5 July 1985, London.

Terry Harrison, Tchaikowsky's agent, and his wife Eve, c. 1965. Eve was to become one of his closest friends

he would call your prejudices in to question just by being himself. And he enjoyed doing that. I think he got a real buzz out of doing that.[66]

But Tchaikowsky was not an easy pianist for a conductor to work with. Seaman continued:

> He had a certain spontaneous side to him. You couldn't just sort of get up and do it. You had to actually understand what he was doing. He wasn't the sort of chap you could accompany well on one run-through. And for him it wasn't enough for you just to follow. You had to actually be part of what he was doing. It wasn't enough to follow it, you had to like it. Anyone who didn't give him that upset him a lot. I think that did happen with different conductors who would just sort of follow or not wish to talk about it, or not wish to identify with what he was doing. It's a delicate area. And he was always so interested in colour, orchestral colour and balance. If you could colour a chord right by bringing out a certain part of the 'purple note' in a chord, the note that gave the chord its poignancy. If you could actually find that and bring it out he was overwhelmed. He absolutely loved that.[67]

Another story from a concert in Hamilton, New Zealand, in 1971 remembered by Seaman illustrates Tchaikowsky's spontaneity from a slightly different angle:

---

[66] Christopher Seaman, interviewed by David Ferré, 8 April 1987, Oxford.
[67] *Ibid.*

The second half of the concert was the *Siegfried Idyll* by Wagner, and then next came André with the Rachmaninov/Paganini. André said to me: 'I would love to hear the Wagner'. I told him: 'Well, you're always back stage warming up. Why don't you take a gamble tonight? Don't warm up if you want to hear it. Come and listen'. The *Siegfried Idyll* is one of my favourite pieces. It has a wonderful atmosphere at the end, very serene and tranquil.

[…] We've just finished the piece, and I suddenly heard, 'Bravo! Bravo!' I turned around and there was some lunatic in a dirty raincoat walking down the aisle. I focused my eyes – it was Tchaik. He'd been sitting right at the back. He made a real 'Is-there-a-doctor-in-the-house?' entrance through the audience in his raincoat and jumped up on the stage, knocking over some potted plants from the edge of the platform. I thought maybe he had been drinking, but he hadn't. The audience didn't know who it was until I removed this dirty, beige-coloured raincoat. They saw the man standing in his tails and they realised that it was the soloist. Then they all clapped and he sat down at the piano. I was furious, absolutely furious.

We then started the Rachmaninov/Paganini and after about five minutes, he started to play *staccato* where it was normally *legato*. I thought, 'This is a bit odd'. I looked around and he's sitting there: 'Chris! The pedal has fallen off the piano!' I thought: 'Serves you right, serves you right'. I said: 'Do you want me to stop?' He said: 'Yes, yes!' So I stopped and André stood up and said: 'Ladies and gentlemen, I'm afraid the pedal's fallen off the piano'. I said, 'Well, we'd better put it back, hadn't we?' So I got under his piano on all fours and put the pedal back on. It only took a minute or two. Then we got on with the piece.[68]

Tchaikowsky did not like showy, pompous music. He thought that 'heroic' Beethoven was vulgar; he could not stand music that was an obvious crowd-pleaser and was bound to succeed. Seaman noted: 'He could not stand music that set out to save the world'. Tchaikowsky also said: 'I cannot bear sentiment in music. The place for sentiment is life. That is where sentiment should be. In life. Not in music'. He disliked music that was harmonically simple: 'He loved ambiguity in music. In fact, he loved ambiguity in everything'.[69]

Ian Dando remembered him as an outstanding pianist, at his best in Bach, Chopin, Beethoven and the late works of Schubert. But he identified Tchaikowsky's one weakness: 'He did tend to linger over little subtleties and details at the expense of the overall rhythmic flow'.[70] When Dando told Tchaikowsky his opinion, he remembered that he at first 'got mad at him', then agreed.

[68] *Ibid.*
[69] *Ibid.*
[70] Ian Dando, *loc. cit.*

A promotional photograph from around 1964

Two Polish composers: Tchaikowsky with Andrzej Panufnik in 1967

As part of his professional activities, Tchaikowsky recorded for RCA Victor and Columbia Marconi. But he did not like the process, as Dando recalled: 'He hated recording. He disliked the pretension that went with recording and the retakes. He was essentially a spontaneous pianist who existed for a live recital. A very creative pianist'.[71]

Tchaikowsky performed with many leading orchestras and many eminent conductors in the world, which include the BBC Scottish Symphony, BBC Symphony, Berlin Philharmonic, Chicago Symphony, City of Birmingham Symphony, English Chamber, Hagen Symphony Orchestra, the Hallé, the Haydn Orchestra, Houston Symphony, The Little Symphony of London, London Mozart Players, London Philharmonic, London Symphony, National Orchestra of Belgium, National Orchestra of Ireland, National Orchestra of Mexico, Netherlands Chamber, New York Philharmonic, New Zealand Symphony, Northern Sinfonia, Pro Arte, Rochester Symphony, Royal Liverpool Philharmonic, Royal Philharmonic, Serenata of London,

[71] *Ibid.*

Swedish Radio and Television Orchestra, Tivoli Summer Orchestra, Toronto Symphony, Utrecht, Vienna Symphony, Warsaw Philharmonic and the Wren Orchestra, among many others. The conductors with whom he worked included Franz André, Karl Böhm, Yoram David, Sir Colin Davis, Arthur Davison, Antal Doráti, Anthony English, Lawrence Foster, Lamberto Gardelli, Carlo Maria Giulini, Luis Herrera de la Fuente, Dimitri Mitroupolos, Fritz Reiner, Albert Rosen, Christopher Seaman, Uri Segal, André Vandernoot, Heinz Wallberg, Jozef Wiłkomirski and David Zinman.

The Antipodes

Tchaikowsky visited Australia for the first time in 1968, immediately falling in love with the country and the way of life there. He even considered immigrating, saying as much in an interview for one of the national papers. For two years (1975–76) he was artist-in-residence in Currie Hall, in University of Western Australia, Perth. Professionally, his life there was a resounding success, but personally, it brought him the darkest of sorrows: he met and fell in love with an artist, a heterosexual who did not return his affection.

If an Australian man broke Tchaikowsky's heart in 1974, it was a New Zealand man who healed it in 1977. A teacher of transcendental meditation, J., whom Tchaikowsky met during his first visit to New Zealand, made him feel a part of this world, teaching him about belonging, and not isolating himself from the people around. This affair, too, was doomed: J. was also heterosexual and, shortly before they met, took a decision to become celibate. From heights of happiness, and feeling in love, Tchaikowsky plunged into despair: yet another person, probably the love of his life, had rejected him. J. nonetheless helped him to deal with the situation and to accept it, not without some success. Meeting J. in New Zealand was the basis on which Tchaikowsky could later 'meet' Israel and confront his past. This part of his life is well documented in the diaries written in 1980 and 1981.

Personality

To write about Tchaikowsky's personality is to write about a subject with no end. He was a complex man, who appeared in different guises to different people. But he had a number of traits that were visible to all: he was an eager conversationalist, he was eager to entertain, and he would at times shock people by saying controversial things. He was a considerate friend, and he liked helping people.

Tchaikowsky showed many symptoms of neurosis, including anxiety, depression, anger, irritability, low self-esteem, a tendency to impulsive, even compulsive, acts, cognitive problems such as unpleasant or disturbing thoughts, repetition of thoughts and obsession, habitual fantasising, negativity and cynicism, dependency, aggressiveness, schizoid isolation and socio-culturally inappropriate behaviour.[72] Many of these symptoms were also typical of other Holocaust survivors. Tchaikowsky tried to overcome them by practising meditation, and focusing on positive events in his life, but his sensitivity to his surroundings and to reactions of people around him did not always make it easy, or even possible.

His diaries show that he was always worried about something. Judy Arnold remembers that he would be anxious about not being able to decide what time to start his practice, ringing her for advice, and spending much time deciding or worrying about what to do when he could actually be doing it.[73] He was always preoccupied with how he would play at concerts, how he should behave with his friends or his lovers, and worried with equal intensity about small and big things. Mention of his performance anxiety permeates his diaries, as well as self-imposed torments about his reluctance to spend time with people he himself had invited over for dinner, or for a longer stay.

The house in Cumnor, where he spent the last six years of his life, was his refuge. Ian Dando visited him there, recounting his impressions of the place, and his surprise that:

> For such an asthetically switched-on person who was a tremendous expert on Shakespeare and drama, music, opera, and everything – he had very broad tastes – how very plain and unadorned his house was. He was certainly no homemaker, not at all. He showed me to my room, and it was just full of piano music all over the floor. Volumes of piano music. Whenever he wanted an edition of Mozart Sonatas to practice, he knew exactly where in all this disorganised pile the stuff was. There was nothing decent or decadent about the home. Then I saw all this huge pile of dishes, in the kitchen, not only covering his bench, but also on the floor. He said: 'Oh, I'm sorry, but this is the day my housemaid comes. I never do the dishes. All I do is cook. When I run out of dishes after three days, Pat comes across and cleans up'. […] André just couldn't look after himself. He was like Schubert once again. […] There were no great art works or anything much in the place. He had a little lounge there in which stood his three-quarter Steinway grand. The lid was always

---

[72] These and other symptoms are listed in C. George Boeree, *A Bio-Social Theory of Neurosis*, http://webspace.ship.edu/cgboer/genpsyneurosis.html (accessed 1 January 2013).
[73] *Loc. cit.*

Rehearsing with Christopher Seaman, probably in New Zealand in 1971

closed and on that were postcards and mail and all sorts of junk. It was like the top of Beethoven's piano really. And then this untidy kitchen. Generally, an untidy place. Disorganised, no colour scheme, no beauty in the house because he just wasn't a home-lover and he was away half the time anyway. Always full-on central heating. In fact, it was an oppressively hot place.[74]

Tchaikowsky had a rich inner life. He had imagination, he spent his free time reading, listening to music or going to the theatre, and walking. He was not concerned with how his house looked. An untidy house bothered him much less than an untidy score, or an untidy love-affair.

Friend and Foe

Tchaikowsky was a man who compartmentalised his life and the people he knew, which meant that many of his friends had never met, or even heard of, one another. For example, some of Tchaikowsky's closest friends had barely heard of Halina Janowska, Tchaikowsky's correspondent for the quarter-century between 1956 and 1982 (with a four-year silence in 1962–66, when Tchaikowsky decided to sever relations with Halina for her own sake).

People who had known or met Tchaikowsky have their own memories and thoughts about him, but with access to his diaries many of these memories need to be revised. For example, he made a show of Christmas, showering his friends with gifts and cards, and it was generally believed that he enjoyed this holiday very much. The diaries testify to the opposite: for him, Christmas was 'AFH', the Annual Festival of Hypocrisy, and he longed to 'do away with Christmas' altogether.[75]

It becomes obvious from Tchaikowsky's diaries that there were very few people he counted as close friends. The three people he himself felt closest to were Eve Harrison, Michael Menaugh and Stephen Kovacevich (then Stephen Bishop, later Bishop-Kovacevich).

Eve brought peace and calm into his life, and was probably the only person to have had a balancing effect on him. She listened patiently when he had to talk about his problems and worries and, as well as offering moral support, looked after his paperwork when he lived in London. Their friendship developed when they discovered mutual interests in music, theatre and drama in the late 1960s, and they often went to see operas, concerts, and plays in London and Stratford. Tchaikowsky liked listening to recordings with Eve in the same room, often pointing out interesting passages in the

---

[74] Ian Dando, *loc. cit.*
[75] Diary entries for 25 December 1976 and 13 January 1979 (not included here); *cf.* p. 327, below.

compositions they were hearing. Without Eve, Tchaikowsky's life would have certainly lacked the stability and balance that her friendship brought.

Michael Menaugh was born in England. He met Tchaikowsky at the Dartington Summer School of Music, while studying chemistry at Oxford. After graduating and completing a research year in electron spin resonance, Michael became an actor and writer, whose special love was Shakespeare. He played Hamlet, Richard III and Benedick in professional productions in the UK and was a member of the Young Vic Company. His play about Lord Byron was performed at the Folger Theatre in Washington, DC. In 1977 he moved to Brazil where he studied linguistics, publishing papers in *Studia Linguistica* and *Linguistic Analysis*. Michael is also a talented pianist; in 1970 he won an amateur piano concerto competition with Tchaikowsky playing the orchestra part on a second piano. Michael remembers:

> One Saturday morning back in the late fifties, I was listening to the BBC's radio programme 'Interpretations on Record'. The work in question was Ravel's *Gaspard de la Nuit*. When the presenter played an extract from André's performance of *Ondine*, I was totally mesmerized. There was something that just spoke directly and wonderfully to me. A few years later I heard André play the *Goldberg Variations* in a broadcast concert and again I was completely drawn in by his artistry. So when I decided to go to the Dartington Summer School of Music in 1964, I chose a week when André was scheduled to play. It was customary for the students and artists at Dartington to have morning coffee sitting and chatting together on the lawns. And on this particular day I joined a group which included André. Of course, I was in awe of him but I was immediately struck by his sense of humour which was as silly as mine and we found ourselves joking and laughing together. He said he was going to play Stravinsky's *Petrushka* in a recital the following week but since he'd added notes in some places and introduced his transcription of the bear dance in the last scene, he felt he ought to make an announcement before playing. So I said 'How about "Ladies and gentlemen, the performance you are about to hear is entirely genuine, only the notes have been changed to protect the innocent"'. And he loved it.
>
> A week later I had a phone call and it was André saying that the announcement had been more successful than the performance and that I deserved a part of his fee! He then invited me to his Chopin recital at the Festival Hall the following month. After the recital a group of us had dinner together and again André and I found ourselves sparking jokes off each other and laughing uncontrollably. Thereafter, André visited me at Oxford and I visited him in London. The rest is history.[76]

---

[76] Letter to Anastasia Belina-Johnson, 18 August 2013.

At Dartington Summer School
c. 1965 Tchaikowsky stood
in for a circus organist but
confessed that he failed to
rouse the elephants to dance.

When Menaugh moved to Brazil in the 1970s, Tchaikowsky always made sure he could visit him if his concerts took him to that part of the world. During one of those visits, Michael helped Tchaikowsky to go a step further with his self-acceptance, and feeling of belonging, and their conversation on that evening was recorded by Tchaikowsky in his diaries.[77]

Another close friend of Tchaikowsky was Stephen Kovacevich, an American-born British pianist, who at the age of eighteen won a scholarship to study the piano in London with Myra Hess,[78] and has lived in the UK ever since. Both Tchaikowsky and Kovacevich were managed by Terry Harrison. Tchaikowsky trusted Stephen's musical taste implicitly, and before important concerts he liked to play to him and discuss any musical or technical issues. Tchaikowsky left his Steinway piano in his will to Kovacevich.

---

[77] Diary entries for 25 and 27 February 1979; *cf.* pp. 247–49 and 250, below.

[78] Myra Hess (1890–1965) was a highly regarded pianist who studied at the Trinity College of Music, Guildhall School of Music, and the Royal Academy of Music. She gave her debut in 1907, performing Beethoven's Piano Concerto No. 4 with Sir Thomas Beecham. She toured worldwide, made many recordings, and was renowned for her interpretations of Mozart, Beethoven, and Schumann, as well as frequently performing works by her contemporaries.

Tchaikowsky by Milein Cosman, c. 1978

Throughout his life, Tchaikowsky met many prominent musicians, conductors, artists, writers and cultural figures. He was a quick judge of character, often too quick, and could take instant like or dislike to someone for no apparent reason. If he felt he was too harsh on someone, he would always apologise the following day, a trait often seen in his diaries.

Father and Son

Tchaikowsky grew up with a highly negative view of his father, as seen in his diaries and letters. His grandmother was the main proponent of this view, which did not begin to change until 1980, when he suddenly decided to meet his father. But he expected his father to be similar to himself and was gravely disappointed when he realised it was not the case. His decision to meet his father came to him by surprise, while he was visiting Israel in January 1980. His account is well documented in the diary entries of that year.[79]

---

[79] *Cf.* pp. 280–89, below.

Literary Legacy

André Tchaikowsky was a prolific writer of letters, kept a diary, wrote a short story (*The Fortune Teller*) and completed several chapters of an autobiography.

Letters

Tchaikowsky never kept any of the letters he received, and not all of his recipients kept his letters and postcards. But the letters that do survive show his astonishing command of languages, his sense of humour and an ability to tell a story. Tchaikowsky's most important correspondent was Halina Janowska, who published a selection of their letters under the title *...mój diabeł stróż* ('...my guardian demon').[80] (The title was chosen from one of Tchaikowsky's letters, in which he referred to Rimbaud as his guardian devil.[81]) This correspondence, which awaits publication in English (it has already been translated by Jacek Laskowski), naturally reflects the personalities of both writers, together with the strengths and weaknesses of their relationship.

Tchaikowsky met Janowska in 1953: she was a fellow student at the State Academy of Music in Warsaw and later became a criminal psychologist and writer. From the first meeting it was clear that they shared a very special relationship, characterised by love and mutual support. But it was doomed from the start by Tchaikowsky's homosexuality, and one of the men with whom he fell in love was a friend of Halina's called Peter. Halina remembers that one day, when Tchaikowsky and Peter had lunch together, Peter said that there is nothing more beautiful and wonderful than a woman's body. Tchaikowsky wanted to verify the truth for himself, and the last night before his permanent departure from Poland he spent with Halina. It is not known whether he found the truth as beautiful as Peter had suggested, but he was excited by the possibility of Halina becoming pregnant and fantasised about having a child with her.

The following excerpts were chosen by Janowska specifically for this book.[82]

---

[80] The first edition appeared as *...mój diabel stróz* (with a subtitle explaining that it featured 'Letters between Andrzej Czajkowski and Anita Sander'), State Publishing Institute, Warsaw, 1988; the second edition was published by Siedmioróg, Wrocław, 1996, with the pen-name Anita Sander changed to the author's real name, Halina Janowska.
[81] Letter to Halina Janowska dated 9 October 1979.
[82] Translated from the Polish by Jacek Laskowski in 1996.

Hans Keller and André Tchaikowsky, Dartington Summer School of Music, 1968

12 October 1956, Brussels

Halinka, my darling, why haven't you written to me for so long? Whenever I get a postcard from Poland, I always hope it's from you. Surely you don't forget so quickly! I beg you, write, sort me out a little – if I'm writing letters then things must be very bad. I love you like I've never loved you before, I cry like a baby, I don't so much think about you as sense you. The only memories I'm not afraid of digging up are our mutual ones. The only hope which doesn't seem nonsensical is OURS.

Don't be lazy, write – write quickly and make it long, and make it delicious and, at the same time, slightly foolish, as only you can. Most of all I'd like to bring you over here or go back to you myself. I'm not sure I won't even do that. Halinka, I am so sad here – how good that you're in this world.

Your Andrzej
Write at once!

21 October 1956, Brussels (radiogram)

We'll call our son Gaspard – what do you think?

Write soon, kisses Andrzej

26 October 1956, Warsaw

To the presumed father of our putative children!

Thanks for the touching radiogram, but where did you get GASPARD from? Are you aiming, creatively speaking, to compete with Ravel himself? I'd prefer Daniel because there's a prophet, and a writer, and a defender of the oppressed, and on top of that a biblical figure, so the heritage is right!

It's hard to believe that Daniel will leap out of your head like Pallas Athene from that of Zeus, so you'll have to come back, darling. One swallow doesn't make a summer [...].

25 June 1957, Warsaw

My dearest Andrzej, what's happened to you? Even Tristan did not conduct such a lively correspondence with Isolde as you're doing with me... If I join you for ever Polish literature will suffer irrevocable harm. I've read the letters of the great Prus[83] to Miss L. – they do not compare with yours! I am bewitched!

My broken finger has grown back and I'm preparing my diploma recital for September (the Bach *Partita* in B flat major, the Beethoven *Appassionata*, Schumann's *Childhood Scenes* and Prokofiev's Sonata No. 3). Just before the vacation, I played part of the partita for Maria[84] while my finger was in plaster. I thought she would be charmed, but she said: 'This, my child, is a conservatory, not a circus'. Next month I'm off to Malbork (accompanying at a choreographic summer school for young people). Yes, yes – you will be playing New York, but I will be playing Malbork.

Many, many kisses, Your H.

17 September 1957, New York[85]

Halinka! Help!

I'm at my wits' end. Maybe these are inauspicious times for old mythomanes but even so, it's hard to deny that you're hellishly, hellishly far away. And these last ten days I've needed you terribly. There are so many situations when no-one can help me like you can. Consequently, no-one did help me, or rather, which was worse, they all helped me as best THEY COULD....

I called John[86] in Los Angeles. 'I've finished the concerto and I'd like to know what you think of it.' This is what I heard: 'Oh, how charming. That's really nice. And are you dedicating it to me? Great! I'm very busy at the moment, but I'll have a look at it sometime. Is everything else all right? No news? Take care, old man'. [...]

HALINKA, I WANT YOU HERE! When you come over in the spring we'll buy a small apartment and we'll live together in Paris. Most important of all, we must have children. I so want someone who will always be mine – always. Then all this playing and everything else will have some point... [...]

Many long, passionate and matrimonial kisses.

Your Andrzej

---

[83] Bolesław Prus (1847–1912), born Aleksander Głowacki, was a leading Polish literary figure.

[84] Wiłkomirska, pianist, professor at the Academy of Music in Warsaw.

[85] This letter is addressed to 'Halina Czajkowski (Pianoforte)'.

[86] The American pianist John Browning, the winner of the second prize at the Queen Elisabeth Piano Competition, Brussels, 1956. *Cf.* also p. 48.

8 November 1957, New York

My poor little Funnyface,

I came back to New York the day before yesterday and found your three letters. I read them in the wrong order and got everything mixed up. Truth to tell I cried when I saw the muddle and 'what's become of us'. Then I picked my nose and drew some conclusions. Halinka, it's quite simple: you can't leave Marek now. You wouldn't have agreed to stay with me anyway – that's not 'real life'. Even if we spent fifty years together, had more children than Haydn wrote symphonies and made love in every possible position, it would still not be as good for you as one hour with Marek. You would feel that even more strongly now than you would have done earlier [...]. And Marek, too, would be very unhappy. Halinka, enough of this play-acting – it's time to start living. You're exceptionally lucky that you're succeeding to do so at last. [...]

PS. I was at Horowitz's. He's old, sick and sad. His wife's eyes follow him, and they're filled with love. They have not said a word to each other in four years.

I'd really like to die young. A.

March 1962, London[87]

Halinka, funnyface,

This is my saddest letter and my last. Although you asked me to reply immediately, I couldn't bring myself to do it for a whole week, and even now I'm finding it a great effort to write. Darling, we can't meet in Stockholm this spring. We can't meet anywhere, ever. The pain I'm causing you by writing this is nothing compared with the terrible wrong I've done you over the last seven years and which I became aware of only after your last letter. The most experienced sadist couldn't have done you more harm. For years I've been undermining your sense of reality for just one reason, apparently to ruin your life. Without giving you anything myself, I took away, or poisoned, everything you have [...].

Take care of yourself, Halinka, our friendship *was always real*, and so passionate, and so mutual, that it could almost, but not quite, have replaced love. A friend like you were to me is very hard to find in this world, and it's as that friend I shall always remember you.

But you must forget about me as quickly as possible.

Andrzej

19 October 1966, London

Unforgettable Halinka,

Many, many thanks for the consignment (I can scarcely call it a letter). Judging by it you're just as I remember you: imaginative, disarming,

[87] This letter, substantial parts of which were destroyed, was the reply to the proposition that steps should be taken to bring 'Daniel' into being.

entertaining, bewitching; and yet (or maybe therefore?) I still think we should back out of any correspondence. I don't even know if, after all these years, we still know, let alone like, one another! I've changed a lot, I've grown old, I've become selfish and a hermit – I live alone and cook for myself so as not to have to go out; I've limited my social life to a minimum and my sex life is close to non-existent. That's nothing like as sad as it might appear: I've got books, records, I'm never bored and I don't even feel lonely. I'm now living for myself and not for other people, and my friends have come to realise that 'you can't count on me', and they rarely write or phone. But the main reason why I prefer not to write to you is my present conviction that one has to live in the real world and not in an imaginary one (see now how much I've aged?). Not just because we can't run away from reality, or because we are condemned to it – that's a pessimistic reason, and I'm now teaching myself optimism – but because reality is a great deal *more interesting* than fantasy – it's changeable, it's astonishing, it's full of surprises. In your life I have always been the Imagination and thereby done you much harm; who knows – Marek might have treated you very differently if it hadn't been for our 'adulterous correspondence'. At least he entered your life, while I entered only your head. Am I still sitting there in your head? If we could *meet*, then I would agree to that despite the feeling that such a meeting would prove mutually disappointing (not because I would be disappointed by you or you by me, but because we would certainly have no point of contact). [...]

Halinka, I know that this letter will hurt you; but I will send it – one must write the truth.

All the very best.
Your old Andrzej

16 April 1982, Utrecht (postcard)

Darling Funnyface,

Everything's fine! I spent three days in the clinic in Mainz for tests and the doctors didn't find anything suspicious so there's no reason to cancel the tour. I had my first rehearsal of 1982 (Chopin's Concerto in E minor, the Rondo is still a bit wobbly), and the first concert is the day after tomorrow. Till mid-May write to: Bei Herrn H. Hermes, Wielandstrasse 29, 6200 Wiesbaden, West Germany, after that I'll be home.

No end of kisses. A.

A letter written by Basia Lautman, Halina's daughter, brought the correspondence to an end:

*Anita Halina Janowska, Tchaikowsky's most
assiduous correspondent*

6 July 1982, London

Darling, darling Mummy,

These last three days have seemed like a nightmare to me. I was hoping I'd
wake up. What has happened is so senseless I can't even think about it.

When I came back from Italy I thought I'd visit Andrzej. The telephone
was answered by Eve. I thought she was looking after him, but she told me
she had some very bad news. Andrzej [the line was left unfinished to express
Basia's inability to write about Tchaikowsky's death to her mother].

It's so horribly hard for me to write this letter, though you probably know
by now. I couldn't say anything to her. I just cried and cried. Now I'm taping
a record of Schubert's Quintet for you. They played the *Adagio* at his funeral.

It was only later that I phoned Eve. She told me that they were playing his
Trio Notturno the next day in Cheltenham. […]

Yesterday I phoned Eve again. Andrzej said you were one of the three
people he wanted to write a farewell letter to. He said he'd write them after the
chemotherapy, when he was feeling better. But he never did feel better.

Mummy, I'm so worried about you. Half my pain and sadness is because I
know how you must be feeling now. I can't forgive myself for not seeing
him again. And for not being with him.

I kiss you with all my strength and hug you.

Basia

Diaries

Part Three of this book contains previously unpublished excerpts from Tchaikowsky's private diaries. Frank, witty and at times overwhelming in their intense brooding, they do not always make for easy reading. As well as showing heights of happiness in love and work, they show the darkest depths of despair and excruciating, neurotic self-doubt and torment. Tchaikowsky kept diaries between 1974 and 1982, all of which survive, apart from one book (1975–76) left on a plane. He wrote up his diaries in all sorts of places: waiting for a plane, on trains, even at the barber; it becomes obvious that he often used the writing as a way to avoid contact with other people.

The topics covered in the diaries are wide: there are reviews of literature and poetry he read, theatrical works he had seen and operas he had attended, and critiques of musical works he played or heard. He was an avid reader, and had a phenomenal memory. He quoted extensively from books in many languages, and could hold his own in conversations with literary scholars.

Because he liked to embellish his own stories, many incorrect facts about his life were passed from person to person. Now it is possible to re-evaluate the stories and myths about him because his own diaries and letters shed light on previously unknown or misunderstood events.

Autobiography

On 13 October 1974, Tchaikowsky wrote in his diary:

> I may indeed give up this diary, because an interesting alternative has been suggested to me. Jasper, my agent's partner, asked me two days ago whether I'd consider writing a book. 'Whatever about, Jasper?' 'Why, anything you like. I could probably place it for you, as I am friends with a literary agent.' 'But what on earth made you think I might write a book?' 'Oh well, you are so well-heeled" [*sic*]. 'You mean I've been tossed about?' 'If you prefer.' And we agreed to arrange a meeting between his publishing friend, him and myself.
>
> At first, I felt entirely skeptical and uninterested. What have I got to say? I've always been extremely egocentric and consequently ludicrously unobservant; most of my life has been spent looking inwards, gliding somnambulistically through countries, times and circumstances without quite taking them in. Now some of those outward events were, so far as I can judge, of some intrinsic interest to the general reader, but I am in no position to report on them: all I could produce is a succession of my states of mind, and what general interest can I claim for that? I am no Gérard de Nerval.[88]

---

[88] Gérard de Nerval (1808–55) was the nom-de-plume of the French poet, essayist and translator Gérard Labrunie.

Since then, however, a technical approach occurred to me that has lent the task some interest, if only to myself. This would be to attempt an autobiography[89] constructed as a succession of separate scenes, taken seemingly at random at fairly wide intervals (nine months to a year), letting the reader piece out the intervening events from the latest situation described, without any explicit explanations that could only weaken the contrast. Film-goers are familiar with that kind of narration (I think it's called shock-cutting), but I haven't come across an autobiography written in this way: most of them are dutifully and often tediously continuous. I imagine a book in which chapters would be headed not by titles or numbers but by dates, and all necessary information would somehow be discreetly concealed within the current scene. It would call for a measure of craftsmanship more typical of a novelist than of a memoir-writer, and the difficulties of the presentation would make working on it more interesting than any of the subject-matter (which, after all, doesn't contain anything that hasn't been related ad nauseam). The first thing will be to select the most revealing incidents, the ones that can imply most of what has been left out.

On 18 October he started writing, and was so engrossed in the work 'and found working on it so exciting that it's already in danger of eclipsing my piano practice'.[90]

He kept writing the autobiography until 1980, showing excerpts to his friends and relatives, and seeking feedback and advice. But after his visit to Israel in 1980, he found what he had written contrived and false, and was ashamed of sensationalising the story of his survival and complaining about 'a nasty aunt'.[91] He decided that he would stop writing and did not want to see the work published. The complete manuscript and drafts are kept in Eve Harrison's private André Tchaikowsky archive.

The Last Joke

André Tchaikowsky complained in his diaries of intestinal problems in late 1981,[92] and in early 1982 his doctor (mistakenly, as it would turn out) diagnosed colitis.[93] Tchaikowsky documented the progressing illness and treatment in his diaries in 1982, presenting a bleak account of the last six months of his life. He died on 26 June 1982 in the Sir Michael Sobell House, an Oxford hospice, with Eve Harrison by his bedside. He was 46.

[89] What else can an egocentric write? –AT
[90] Diary entry dated 19 October 1974; *cf.* p. 134, below.
[91] Diary entry dated 3 December 1980; cf. pp. 309–10, below.
[92] Diary entry dated 20 November 1981; *cf.* pp. 325–26, below.
[93] Diary entry dated 2 January 1982; *cf.* p. 335, below.

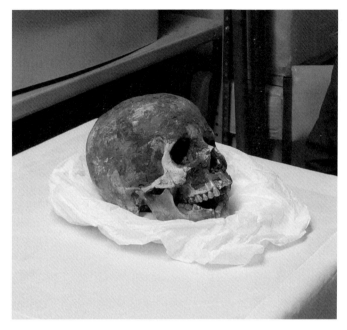

*Tchaikowsky's skull, caked in stage 'earth',
in the store-room of the Royal Shakespeare Company*

Three years before his death, on 10 October 1979, Tchaikowsky made a final will, in which the thirteenth and last paragraph stated that he left his skull to the Royal Shakespeare Company 'for use in theatrical performances'.[94] Terry Harrison knew about Tchaikowsky's bequest, and remembered there conversation about it. Tchaikowsky said that he wanted to know that after his death there will be a part of him left that was still performing. He also said that, if Shakespeare had indeed been an anti-Semite, 'it would give me a great pleasure to have a Jewish skull wandering around Shakespeare's *Hamlet*.'[95]

When the bequest was made public, there were two reactions: surprise, and lack thereof. Those who knew Tchaikowsky agreed that it was typical of him; the public at large found it gruesome.

The skull was used in a *Hamlet* production in Stratford in 2008, but audiences began 'over-reacting'[96] when it appeared on stage, and the

[94] The entire will is quoted in *The Other Tchaikowsky,* pp. 487–90.

[95] Terry Harrison, *loc. cit.*

[96] Urmee Khan, 'Royal Shakespeare Company to stop using "distracting" real skull in Hamlet', *The Daily Telegraph*, 2 December 2008.

Company withdrew the skull, reinstating it when the production transferred to London.[97]

But Tchaikowsky did reach new audiences posthumously. This short biography would not be complete without mentioning the world premiere of *The Merchant of Venice* (Bregenz Festspiele, 18 July 2013). Although the full account of its reception is given in the chapter on the composer's music,[98] it would be fitting to say here that at last Tchaikowsky's opera has been given the platform it deserves, bringing an opportunity to appreciate his wit, humour and perceptiveness, as well as his loneliness and continuous search for his own identity.

[97] *Cf.* p. 262, below.
[98] *Cf.* pp. 398–400, below.

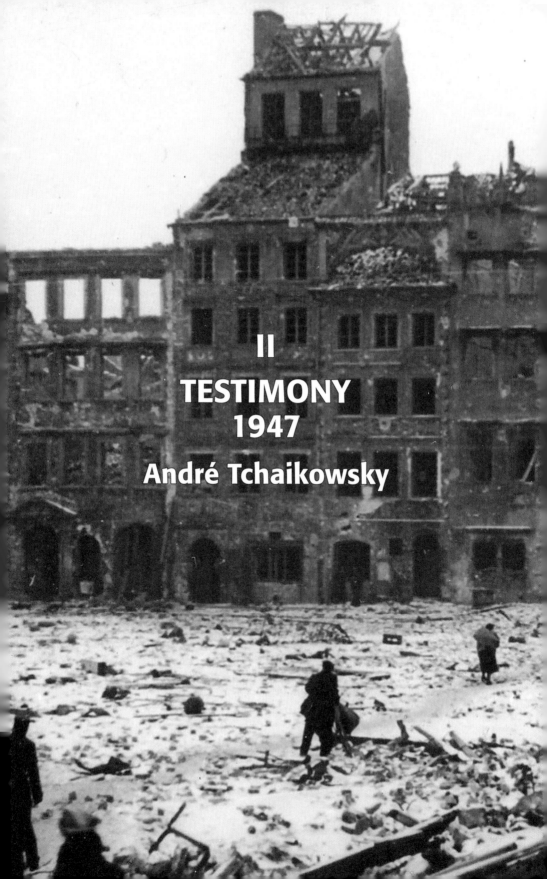

II
TESTIMONY
1947

André Tchaikowsky

Soon after the end of World War II, the Jewish Historical Institute (JHI) was created in Łódź (later moving to Warsaw) with the purpose of recording the experiences of Jews who endured the ghettos or otherwise survived the war. This testament was given by Andrzej Czajkowski (recorded as Andrzej Krauthamer [*sic*]), then aged eleven or twelve.

JHI Catalogue Number 301/3617.
Oral testament given to Genia Silkes[1] in 1947
Translator (Polish to English): unknown

Testimony

Andrzej Krauthamer born in Warsaw on 1 November 1935
Father's name: Karol Krauthamer – an attorney
Mother's name: Felicja Rapaport – a beautician
Place of residence:

1. Before the occupation: Warsaw, 1 Przejazd Street
2. During the occupation: 76 Aleje Jerozolimskie
3. Later: the Warsaw ghetto, 2 Leszno Street Warsaw: the Aryan side
4. At present: Łódź, 56 Piotrkowska Street, apt. 8

He was an only child.
At present he attends school number 68, the sixth form. He reads and writes in Polish, English and a little in French (he learnt it himself).[2]

The child's profile
A big boy with an open smiling face, with black eyes and black hair. Very gifted, intelligent and well-read. His intellectual level is many years ahead of his physiological development. He is talented and shows great written and musical skills. He composes and performs his own musical pieces. Very warm, good and childlike, and at the same time very reasonable, tolerant and serious. Extremely attached to his grandmother, the only person who survived the occupation with him. He is very absent-minded, nervous and

---

[1] Unknown.
[2] Tchaikowsky could read German, French and Russian, but it is not known if he could read English at the time of the interview.

impatient. He reads too much and associates too much with adults, which has a negative influence on his personality.

The child relates

When the war broke out and Warsaw was bombarded, I couldn't understand what it was all about. I thought it was the devil. But because I was surrounded by my whole family, I just hooted at this devil. My hoots were perhaps quieter than the bombs, but they were also more derisive. And suddenly we heard a crash. It got darker: smoke and dust filled the hall. I started shouting so loudly as if I wanted to compete with the crash and the rumble around. Our neighbour was dripping blood. I started screaming again, but something fell on my head and scared me and I ran away. My cousin Józek cried: 'The gas, the gas! I'm being poisoned!' Then he started running away but was hit by some stone or brick and passed out. I cried: 'Józek, wake up! We must go!' Granny cried: 'Grandpa, Mania, help!' Zosia: 'I knew it!' And our parrot cried: 'Stupid, stupid!' And I said to her: '*You*'re stupid!' (And I don't remember more.) A bomb hit the courtyard and demolished the house around and that's how we got out, since the gate was knocked down. Something hit the parrot, it cried 'Ra, ra!' and it turned out it was dead. But the canary and the starling survived. Józek was seriously ill. He had a high temperature. We had nothing to eat. There were eleven of us: Granny, Mania, Grandpa, Józek with mother, Zosia, Rzyket, Małgosia, Zosia No 2, Rommy, his wife, me. Józka was carried by Małgosia and Zosia No 2. The birds were hungry. I didn't want to eat, I had half a roll which I gave to them. Mum gave me – not a roll but a smack for it. We lived at Grandpa's at 1 Przejazd Street. I didn't know what was up and thought that it was all done by a witch. And then everything was normal. I don't remember anything else from that time.

I was in the country at Walercia's and ate noodles. Once I was beaten by peasants' children for being a Jew. Walercia gave them something very unpleasant for it – a hit with a brush. I had two friends: Anusia and Romcia. There were forget-me-nots there. One time I almost fell into a well. Anusia said: 'Get into the bucket and I'll lower you into the well!' I did it. She lowered it too early and I felt that there's nothing for me to stand on. Anusia lowered it because she made a mistake, and I fell further down, but my sleeve got caught in the bucket. Moving lower and lower I managed to get into the bucket. When I got out, I was drenched and had bronchitis. I was ill for a week, maybe more. And then I went in a wagon to a nearby village. There was a hotel or a guesthouse there, and Mum and my stepfather. Then we went to Warsaw. We lived in an old flat (7 rooms). Józek lived next door. Because of his carelessness Józek burnt a wardrobe. Then we had to move

Andrzej Krauthammer photographed in 1947,
at the time of his deposition to the Jewish Historical Institute

to Granny to 1 Przejazd Street. Mum told me that there, at Granny's, there were a lot of children and that it'd be very funny. First I lived at Granny's and then with Mum at Tłomackie Street. There was a square there and I played with children. Then it was cut off. Grandpa died of consumption, which developed out of flu. Mum moved in with us. Józek with mother and uncle Maurycy were taken from the Aryan side by the Germans. Granny went out to obtain papers for us.

I was playing with Dziunia Żelichowska in the square when a van with Huns came. The Huns got off the van and went to a nearby restaurant. They left it dead drunk. Dziunia ran away; I – the younger – stood by Granny. One of them caught a young Jew by the collar, turned him round and slapped him with his right hand on the face. The youngster's cap fell off his head, and a thin stream of blood trickled from his nose. The German slapped him again. He let the collar go, the Jew lost his balance and fell down. Did he pass out? I don't know. Then the German kicked him very hard with his heavy boot on the right side and the body rolled to a gutter. I thought it'd finish here. But no! The German lifted his leg and with a stamp crushed his face against the spring mud. A few more times the leg of the monster was lifted and then lowered onto the head, the belly, the legs. A nightmare. When me and Granny recovered from the numbness in which we watched that macabre scene, there was no one in the square. The van had gone. And there was a tangle of blood and meat in the gutter.

When the ghetto was established we had to move from our house to Granny's place on 1 Przejazd Street to a six-room flat. My Granny had a cosmetics factory and Mum had a shop. One day we stood for a long time during a blockade. Opposite us there were masses of Jews. One of the Germans pulled one small Jew. There was nobody to stand up for him. He had tripped the Hun up. The latter fell. The boy leaned over him and knocked him on the nose with his fist. 'Is it over?', I asked Mum. Yes, she said. I looked up. The boy was lying in a pool of blood. But one could tell that he had fought bravely, because the Hun was dripping blood in all directions.

When we moved in with Granny there was also my stepfather with us. It was still before the war that Mum divorced her first husband, my father, and married a dentist, Albert Rozenbaum – my stepfather. In the ghetto my stepfather became a Jewish policeman. I saw with my own eyes that he beat Jews. He broke the arm of one Jew. He beat a Jewish beggar woman because she was sitting on a step. She answered: none of your business. Look at him, how great he's become! I didn't like him. I was very small and stuck out my tongue at him (that's what Mum told me later). When he became a policeman and started beating Jews, Mum started hating him. She quarrelled with him, but we lived together. At that time Granny went to the Aryan side to obtain papers for all of us. After a month Mum sent me off to Granny. It was on 7 August 1942. She and her husband didn't manage to get out and I never saw them again.

I lived in the country at Chylice as Andrzej Bonguard from Paris. The reason for that was my look. I didn't know what a Jew was. As a result, the following dialogue ensued between me and the village children:

'Are you a Jew?'
'But what's a Jew?'
'It's Mosiek'[3]
'And what's Mosiek?' 'It's you!'
'It's me?'
'Mosie!'
'Really? I'll go and ask Granny if Mosiek is me?' I repeated everything to Granny.
Or:
'Are you from the ghetto?'
'From the *what*?' I asked in a naive voice 'From the ghetto.'
'What town is that?'

---

[3] *Mosiek*, also *Mosie* – a pejorative term for a Jew (a diminutive of the name Moses).

'You know very well!'
'What! You don't want to tell me? I'll tell Granny!'
'Wait a moment. Don't go! It's such a town where only Jews live.'
'You, Mosie, where're your balls?'
'Show me your balls!'
'Wait a moment. Must go and fetch them (and the end was the same)'

But then it stopped being a game. A woman asked me: are you a Jew? And I said to her: I was born in Paris, and my Granny was born in Łomza. My name is Andrzej Robert Bonguard, and so on. But all these personal data that I knew by heart did nobody any good. On the contrary. We had to run away. We went by train to Warsaw. On one of the stations there was a search. My eyes and those of a Nazi met. And I stared in his with my black Jewish eyes. Staring like that, I revenged the youngster who lay in the gutter, the boy who went on a wild-goose chase and lay defeated in the *Umschlagplatz*,[4] the victims of hunger, tuberculosis and typhus, the corpses I had seen in the streets. I took revenge for Treblinka, Majdanek, Auschwitz, for the gas chambers, and crematories and Pawiak, for my mother, for the whole Jewish nation. I said with these eyes: I may die, but you'll also die, you rotter. Will he kill me or not? But actually I was not scared at all. He took my mother. What else could he do to me? Kill me? Ha-ha! I'm sure the other world is better than this! And in fact – I thought – if he kills me, he'll remember my stare till he dies. What was in this stare? Anger? No. Hate? I'm not sure. It's only now that I really hate them. So what was it? Revenge... What does it mean? He knew, he could feel my stare, he understood... And then, for the first time in my life, I saw an expression of pity on a German's face. Oh, what hypocrisy! He produced a candy from his pocket and gave it to me. I spurned his hand. He grinned cynically, put the candy back into his pocket and went away. And only then I nestled against my Granny with tears in my eyes, as if I feared that they could take her away from me.

In Warsaw I and Granny lived at 39 Złota Street at an old hysterical woman's (a mentally ill thief Waszczenkowa). We were very uncomfortable there, because I and Granny slept on a very narrow sofa, and Granny is at least two metres large around her waist. Waszczenkowa stole my leather jacket with polecat-ferret collar, and a ring, and sent them to her son Karolek who was kept in German captivity. We found out about it when a telegram from Karolek came when Waszczenkowa was not at home. Granny opened the envelope and read what was there: 'Thank you for the polecat-ferret

---

[4] A collection point in the Warsaw Ghetto, from which Jews were deported to the Treblinka extermination camp.

jacket and the ring. I'll be back soon. Karol.' Granny always said that she
suspected Waszczenkowa was a thief.

One day Waszczenkowa went for a walk with me and met an acquaintance
who asked: 'Where're you taking this Jewish brat?' Waszczenkowa told my
Granny about it and added that she expected a search as that acquaintance
had already denounced a lot of Jews. After this conversation with
Waszczenkowa Granny went out. She left me at Aunt Irka's (Rega) and went
somewhere, I don't know where. Then she came back to Waszczenkowa's
place and met there a Polish policeman and Kobzowa, an old servant of
Waszczenkowa. Granny gave the policeman a bribe (I don't know how
much). The policeman went away. Granny quickly took our things and
without waiting for Waszczenkowa's return we quickly left the place.

Granny went to a new place where she stayed. At that time I was at
Irenka's on Świetojerska Street (I don't remember the number. I was led in
when it was dark, and I never went out of this place). There were nine of us
living in one middle-sized room. Among others there was Zosia, Granny's
close friend. As to Granny, she wandered from place to place, she didn't
have a steady address. She earned her money where she could. She paid
the Marciniaks three thousand (3000) zlotys a month, and she brought
my food herself. But the Marciniaks usually ate all that food, even in my
presence. Later Granny became more clever and brought me a parcel every
day instead of bringing it once a week, since the weekly parcel had been
gone after one day anyway. One day the caretaker of the house came. I was
sitting in the corner and reading a book that Zosia had obtained, and I
didn't understand a word of that book. The caretaker approached me, told
me to read a bit aloud (he himself was illiterate). And then he turned to
Zosia and said: Is this your 'gudłaj' (this is how Poles called the Jews)? Yes,
my little son. He nodded: Aha!, and went away. The next day I was already
at Międzylesie, at the Grzelaks.

The first week at their place was pretty pleasant. Nobody could suspect
that that was where my gehenna would begin. The Grzelaks had a neighbour
who hated Granny and me. Already at the beginning she carried on a nasty
intrigue. She told Granny that she'd been to Warsaw and that I'd been shot.
The result was that I didn't see Granny for a whole month. Meanwhile, Mrs
Grzelak with that horrid hag hatched a plot and put me in a cell which was in
the cellar. I stayed there for a long time. I ate very little. The air was horrible.
When after a month my broken-hearted Granny came to fetch my things and
when I heard her voice, I cried so loud as if I wanted to wake up the dead. Mrs
Grzelak fumed with fury. She said if I went on crying like that the Germans
would come and kill me, Granny and her whole family. She didn't want to
keep me any longer, unless I stay in the cellar. Being desperate, Granny agreed.

The Grzelaks gave her another condition – a surgery. All this was very good because it happened they had no ether so the whole surgery was carried out without anaesthesia. To make matters worse, I couldn't cry, so I bit my lips as hard as I could. After the surgery the doctor said I passed my exam. But the surgery was not successful. It had to be repeated and after that I went to the country with a man called Adam, whose surname I don't remember. I went to the village of Brześce, where he was a village teacher. He was as black as me, so he made me his nephew. His black look led to the following adventure. We were standing with Granny at a tram stop when a man started looking Adam in the eyes. We were going to Słuzewiec where we were to part with Granny and go to Brześce by train. Adam said:

'Why are you looking at me like that?'
'Because your hair's so black.'
'What, you do not like it, do you?' Adam said with emphasis.
'I certainly don't.'

We got on a tram. But there were people all around who blocked Adam's way. Then Adam said to Granny: 'I'll pretend that I run away, and you'll pretend you don't know me. They'll run after me and will get a good hiding.' He jumped off the tram which was running, and started escaping. Two men flanked him. And he took them by the collar and led them to a policeman. He showed his papers, admitted that he only simulated an escape to play a prank on them, and then entered a gate and gave these two a good hiding. The policeman beat them on his own part and put them in jail.

But I only spent a few days at Brześce. People recognised me there and I had to come back to the Grzelaks. I had my third [surgery] there. But all in vain. A week later I went to Kozłowice near Zyrardów. I had a feeling it was a passage from hell to paradise. I was free, could wander, run, bake potatoes with shepherd boys in the field, pick mushrooms, go to the cinema, play different games with children. The food was wholesome and tasty, the milk straight from the cow. The Adameks family were very kind to me, and I must admit I abused their kindness a bit. I was not always a good boy. I obeyed them unwillingly and went far into the forest, I played with boys I didn't know. I just wanted to make up for all that time in the cellar. Granny came to me from Warsaw only once a week, on Sundays. I had nothing to read, I read one and the same Bible a thousand times over and over again. And I also taught the old Adameks to read and write using a spelling book. (It's such an uncanny coincidence: where I was unhappy the houses are burnt and the people homeless and gone; the Grzelaks are in Łódź and they are very poor. The Adameks, on the other hand, are in good health and happy, because they help people.)

And then two small boys from a *Volksdeutsche*⁵ family tricked me into telling them part of the truth. They taught me anti-Nazi songs. And that's how it happened. One day, when I was picking flowers, I noticed two boys who were sitting on a hill, scowling at me and weeping. I asked them: 'Why are you crying?' And they said, because the Germans have killed our Mummy, and there's no Mummy any more. The elder one got up, and clenching his fist at invisible enemies, cried: 'Oh, those Germans, I'll pay them back some day!' And then he turned to me: 'Listen, do you know any anti-Nazi songs?' I answered: 'No.' 'Ok, so we will teach you', he said. And they taught me two songs. The first song goes like that:

Siekiera, motyka, bimber, szklanka,
W nocy alarm, w dzień łapanka⁶ (and so on)
The second song:
Pierwszy tydzień – sacharyna
Drugi tydzień – margaryna
Trzeci tydzień – nic nie dają
Czwarty tydzień – wysiedlaja⁷ (and so on)
And they said to me: 'just don't sing them when the Germans are by, it's forbidden'. Then I said: 'When the war is over, I'll sing these songs in German ears on purpose, and I think the war will be soon over'. The elder said to this: 'My father has an illegal radio and listens to foreign programmes. The Germans are being flanked: by the English on the one side, by the Russians on the other'.
'Has your grandmother got an illegal radio too?'
'Sure, even two!' I answered naively. (I just wanted to show off.)
'Oh!' the elder said, 'So let her bring one for you'
'Ok' I said, 'when she comes today I'll tell her to bring me one of them.'
I got a little confused, because I didn't want them to see through me.
I called 'Look! There's a bonfire. Let's go!'
A moment later we already stood by the bonfire.
'Let's play at pissing,' the elder said.
'Go ahead!' the younger cried with laughter.
The elder urinated and then said to me:
'Now your turn'
I said I couldn't, and that I've just urinated. And then the elder gave himself away and told me to show him 'what mine was like'. What could I do?

⁵ Ethnic German.
⁶ 'An axe, a hoe, drink hooch and be gay, At night alert, *łapanka* by day.'
⁷ 'The first week – saccharin, The second week – margarine, The third week – nothing at all, The fourth week – resettle us all.'

I said;
'Oh! Granny's coming'
And I ran home.
'Come back!' the elder cried. 'We'll go to the cinema. Come along.'
'No,' I answered.
I quickened my pace and then broke into a run home. (They didn't play too wisely with me. If I were in their position, I'd do something much more clever. I'd try to keep that boy – that's myself – in the forest as long as possible. I wouldn't be able to bear it too long, after all, and would have to wee at last. Then they would see 'what mine was like'. But they were fools.) I ran into the house and told Granny everything. I was upset, but I didn't cry. Granny took me immediately to Warsaw to Mr and Mrs Dębski, Mrs Adamek's relatives. We went there by train. An hour after we left, Mrs Adamek's house was searched. Her nephew, whose role I was playing, has gone to Cracow, has he?

I didn't do very well at the Dębskis'. Mrs Dębska didn't give me food, and her son, Mundek, who was 14, beat and bullied me as much as he could. I had nothing to do, and cleaning was not what I fancied to do at all. It's true I had a Geographical Atlas but the Dębskis didn't let me study it because it took up a lot of space when I opened it. But once when he was drunk Mr Dębski gave himself away a bit and I went to Mrs Balińska. It was the worst place I've ever been to. Why? I'll explain it in a few complaints:

The first complaint:
Balińska was mad and hysterical, and her daughter was a devil incarnate.[8] There were arguments between them every day. When I first came to them, Balińska was lying with her legs burnt because she had been making hooch. Myszka took advantage of her mother's situation and beat her and bullied her horribly. Still on the day of my arrival the following argument took place:
'Myszka, go to bed!'
'Pity you can't put a pamper on me and place me in a cradle'
'Róża, how does she talk to me!' Balińska was playing the role of somebody dying. 'God!' And she called God's name.
'I won't talk!' Myszka cried. 'I'll act!'
And she grabbed a siphon with soda water and sprayed it in her mother's face.

8 Presumably the Monica and her mother described with such distaste in Tchaikowsky's unpublished autobiography: *cf.* pp. 28–23, above.

'Somebody help me! Let somebody from the *Gestapo* come here!'

'Let them kill me! Let them kill me! I don't want to live any more!'

'Shut up, will you?!' – Myszka cried in rage. – And let a cat[9] catch her! She hurled the soda siphon at the hysterical woman. The madwoman shut up, but the consequences were tragic indeed. She passed out, and blood ran down her face onto the white pillow. White-and-red, I thought, and suddenly, instead of pity, I felt a surge of deep hatred towards Poles. As if by accident, I sat down on Myszka's gramophone records. The three on top got broken. I covered them with paper and then tripped Myszka. But the shrew didn't fall. When Balińska came round, she saw a strange view. Myszka was trying to throttle me and crying: 'Jew! Jew!' And though I was just being throttled I managed to add to each of her 'Jew' the ending 'ess', and the result was 'Jewess! Jewess!'. And then I came up with an excellent idea. I bombarded Myszka with insulting questions and escaped, leaving her confounded behind. Who did I go to? To Mrs Dębska.

But Dębska threw me out neck and crop. As the Balińskis lived on the ground floor I approached their flat from the backyard and peeped in through the window. There were Germans there, and I heard Balińska say: 'Don't you know that she is a Jewess?' Gesticulating, she started saying something in German. The Germans laughed, then took some money from her. When they left I tapped on the window pane and Myszka opened the window and knocked me on the nose. I fell and got a bit bruised. I sat there a little and then went to the front door and rang the bell as if I was just an ordinary acquaintance. Myszka opened the door and said: 'Ah! You scamp!' I kicked her and hid in the wardrobe. Myszka tried to lock me out of spite. But I managed to throw a shirt on her head and when she was trying to take it off, she tangled herself in that shirt.

My main hiding places were: the wardrobe, behind the wardrobe, the toilet, then a dustbin, behind the chest, the bathroom, and the made-up bed. The last on my list was the worst because one was in danger of suffocating. When I hid there first time I really thought I'd suffocate. In the other hiding places I sat all day. And I usually ate in the bathroom or in the kitchen. Though I spent there two months I couldn't get used to all those rows which were on an everyday basis. Before Christmas Granny peroxided my hair and it was typical 'clair blond' (silver colour). But in the middle of my hair there was a bald patch because she burnt my hair and it hurt horribly. Then Granny bought me a tuft of hair of the same colour. It stuck out like a real fringe and I looked like a Pole.

---

[9] A pun: the name *Myszka* means *mouse.*

Throughout Christmas I sat behind and in the wardrobe. When I was in the wardrobe I had a lot of peace to think. I thought that when the war is over I'll take revenge on the Germans and on all the evil people I had met. When I was behind the wardrobe, on the other hand, I could listen to talks. Myszka as usual butted in when her elders were talking. She offended the guests with her behaviour. She scared all the guests away and on the following day nobody came and I could go out for the whole half-hour. In fact it's not much, but for me to leave the wardrobe and be free for half an hour was a lot. But as soon as Balińska heard some steps on the stairs, she told me to go back to the wardrobe. She gave me a book to read despite the fact that Myszka was against, and she even beat her own mother. I threw that book away, though I was horribly bored in that wardrobe. I had no toys, I had to sit idly. But I wanted to avoid the row because the neighbours would come and everything would start again. And I'd had enough of it all.

Little by little my hair grew around the light patch and I became a guinea-hen, as Myszka said. Granny peroxided the hair and then, when my real hair grew under the artificial hair, she took off the artificial patch and peroxided my whole head again. I didn't know that the hair was black at the bottom. I gave myself a haircut with Myszka's huge scissors (she was a dressmaker). Balińska was terribly upset and locked me in the wardrobe. Were it not for Granny, it's a hundred per cent sure that I'd suffocate or ninety-nine percent that I'd go crazy. But I was already crazy anyway. If I'd stayed there longer they would have had to take me to a mental hospital.

Granny took me to Mrs Grodecka to Szustra Street. She had a seven-room apartment there. Her mother lived there too, a fifty-six-year-old woman. She had a friend, Mr Sawicki, and an eight-year-old son in my age, whose name was Andrzejek, like mine. So I was called Jędrek and he was called Andrzejek. (At present they live in their flat and they're doing fine. When I grow up I'll take my revenge on them.) Mr Grodecki was in German captivity. At the beginning I felt there like in paradise. I went out every day, I ate well, played with Jędrek. And the mother and her friend were as sweet to me as candies. But already after the first month the candies started tasting bitter. They must've been stuffed with pepper. At first she took seven thousand [zlotys], and then she wanted twelve thousand [zlotys], and Granny didn't want to give her that much. So they started to stint on my food. She gave everything Granny brought to Andrzejek. She didn't let me come up to the window. She didn't let me go out. She made me make up the beds and sweep the floors. I hate such things; I'd prefer to read books. They kept peroxiding my hair and I lost all of it. When it grew again, Granny dyed it black and said she won't do otherwise. Hearing this Grodecka said that if Granny doesn't peroxide my hair immediately, she'll go to the *Gestapo* and inform on me. So Granny replied that in this way Grodecka'll also inform on herself as she had kept me. So Grodecka went to Mr Sawicki, slapped him twice on the face and said that he was to blame for all that and now she has to suffer. And then Sawicki went to the police and informed on all of us. But when he came back with *Gestapo*-men, nobody was to be found in the flat any more.

Granny went to Mrs Walter, Granny's acquaintance who saved us from death and didn't take a penny for it, to 17 Kaliska Street. When I grow up, I'll reward her for it. But she may be dead by then because she is already very old. She's looking for a flat and is in a very difficult situation. She was very kind to me. She took me for walks and looked after me very well. And Grodecka, when there had been a bombardment, just took her son, climbed down to a shelter and never thought about me. At that time a bomb hit a neighbouring house. The plaster from our ceiling fell on my head. I fell off my bed, the bed collapsed because it was just a camp bed, but luckily nothing happened to me.

On 1 August 1944[10] the uprising broke out. The Walters were the party people and they had known about the uprising, and on hearing the first shots the lawyer Mr Walter played the Polish national anthem and the patriotic song *Warszawianka*. I don't remember anything from the uprising until the moment when a Hun entered the shelter and roared 'Raus!' They made us stand at the gate, our faces towards the wall, our hands up. One small child turned back and saw a revolver aimed at it, and they killed that child. I prayed. Then they drove us to a square and beat me with a truncheon and it hurt. They killed a lot of people and I saw such horrifying people who were burnt alive and I saw people burning and crying and jumping off windows and killing themselves that way. And I saw an even worse incident. A German took a woman's child and when she started to cry and beat him, he kicked her in the face and started to torment the child. He flayed the child, broke its teeth, broke its arm and nose and then threw it into fire still alive. Then the woman started from the ground and hit him on the face. She kicked him twice in the belly, broke two of his teeth, and then jumped into fire. There was a lot of money scattered on the ground, but when one man picked up a thousand zlotys, a German undressed him and killed him, and then burnt the corpse. But the worst thing was that that woman cried horribly when she was in fire. I couldn't look at all those atrocities, but Granny looked at them and she later told me.

---

[10] In the original: 1 July 1944.

They took us to a camp at Pruszków. I caught scarlet fever there. They took me to hospital. I was fine there and stayed there for six weeks. Granny was without a penny, she had no financial resources. We slept two days and two nights at Rada Główna Opiekuńcza. Then Granny went to her acquaintances, Mr and Mrs Talar. They took us in, but the conditions there were horrible. I was infested with lice, ate only dry brown bread. I slept in my clothes, Granny in her dress. Granny had only one shirt and one dress. When she wanted to wash her shirt, she slept in her dress. And when she wanted to wash her dress, she put Mrs Talar's coat on her shirt. The family of the caretaker was poor, but kinder to me than Mrs Talar. They gave me shoes and trousers, I got a dinner every day, and I made friends with their daughter Kazia.

Granny had to walk a long distance (45 kilometres) to trade and earn a living. She bought me two eggs, a loaf of bread and a big piece of back fat. All the time when the two small little girls didn't want to eat something and left it, I snatched it and ate. I licked candy wrappings, ate all the leftovers. And now I had my own food. She also bought me two notebooks, because Ewa and Kicia had torn mine. Then Granny met a man called Olek, a fur-trader and we moved in with him to Włochy near Warsaw. He was a rich anti-Semitist. He laughed at Jews, but he was good to me. He helped Poles very much. He arranged some clothes for me, gave us food, so much of it that we could burst from overeating. And it is at his place that we lived to see the Russians come.

I don't remember the moment itself of liberation that well, because I was at home. I was still sad and so was Granny, because Granny didn't have her children, and I didn't have my Mummy. At the very beginning there was still hunger, the only thing we had was potatoes. I was sitting at home and then suddenly I heard a noise and a scream. I ran out into the street and saw a mass of soldiers in the square and a lot of people around. I dashed into the house and wrote a poem 'To a Polish soldier', and I wrote in it that these soldiers are awaited and that they liberated the whole nation. (What would it have been like if I'd seen Polish soldiers and didn't write anything for them? I would've been the worst scoundrel.) I took that piece of paper, stuck it to a piece of cardboard: I still had a little glue left over from Christmas when I'd made toys for the Christmas tree, and I stuck it to the back of the car with drawing-pins so that nobody knew it was me and so that they had a surprise. I ran back home very fast. The first to see it was the chauffer. He started to read and after a few minutes a whole crowd congregated at the car and started reading the poem aloud. Everybody asked who wrote it, but nobody saw me and nobody knew it was my work. Only a few days later I said I'd written that poem, but the car was already gone. It went further on, to chase the Germans away.

And then a new life began for me. My eyes didn't see any more Germans. It serves them right, damn them! I didn't have to hide any more, I was free. I went where I wanted. I played outside with children, but nobody knew that I was a Jew. Granny said it's better not to say. We lived for two more months in our old flat. And then Granny packed our things and took me and we went to Łódź. In Łódź there were a lot of vacant flats. Granny moved in one of them and we still live in it. Then Granny started working and sent me to the school which I attend still. I learnt to laugh and smile at people. I unlearnt to be afraid all the time. And what's most important, I learnt to be a child. And this is one reason why I don't like war movies. They make me afraid, because the horrible fear which I'll never be cured of, because it's deep, and my laughter is only a cover. Even now I'm still thinking of what I went through at that place of Balińska's when I cried that I didn't want to live any more. I remember those sleepless apathetic nights very well. But under that apathy there was despair, and under the despair there was envy, and under the envy – hatred – and under the hatred – rebellion. I didn't imagine I would be able to live and write about it some day. But writing is not all. Writing is very little. I'd like to be big and take revenge for my mother, for that boy, for all the suffering I've seen. Even now at night I can see all those nightmares from the days of the occupation. Sometimes I wake up at night, sweating, because I can see the Germans and have an impression that they are coming towards me and Granny, and want to kill us. I also dream about all the rooms, the hideouts, and the people I stayed with. Now I want to learn, I want to play and write. I must work very hard now, to make up for all that time.

My strongest experience from the times of the occupation was when I parted with Mummy. Another, when I was on the Aryan side and looked at the burning city of Warsaw. And one more, when I saw the Jews being beaten. I can't forget the scene of the search at the Balińskis.

Now I am with Granny and I'm Andrzej Czajkowski, because this is what Granny wants. And I'm still too small to get my own way and disobey Granny.

Recorder's signature: Silkes Genia

Witness's signature: Krauthamer Andrzej

III

DIARIES
1974–82

André Tchaikowsky

André Tchaikowsky kept a diary from 1974 to 1982. (One notebook, with entries from November 1975 to June 1976, was left on a plane and never recovered.) The extracts published here have required very little editing – his writing is clear and his command of English exemplary – and so only a small number of obvious grammatical and spelling mistakes have been silently corrected. Tchaikowsky's own footnotes are indicated with a terminal '–AT'; the others are mine. His frequent underscoring of words for emphasis has been retained here as italics. His extensive quotations from literary works in other languages have been presented in their original languages, with an English translation given in the footnotes.

The diaries show Tchaikowsky's private world: that of a composer, pianist, music and literary critic, friend and son. Some of the entries, naturally enough, are explicit, and so any potentially problematic comments relating to people who are still alive, or whose close family members survive, have been removed for legal reasons. On the same grounds some names are represented by their initials only – a practise Tchaikowsky himself followed in his entries. All excisions are indicated by ellipses ('[…]'); other square brackets contain my remarks and explanations as appropriate. But rather than pepper the text with ellipses, where entire entries have been dropped, they have been allowed to disappear silently.

Anastasia Belina-Johnson

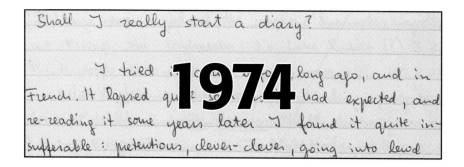

Shall I really start a diary?

I tried it once before, long ago, and in French. It lapsed quite soon, as I had expected, and re-reading it some years later I found it quite insufferable: pretentious, clever-clever, going into lewd intellectual contortion to impress a hypothetical reader, if not posterity. A *performance*, in fact – the only thing I had been trained to do. Can I now manage something simpler, then? Can I keep it up? And will it make me even more of a loner?

3 March

Perth

Let's try to catch up with the events of the last two days:

Arriving at Perth airport at 1.15 a.m. the night before last, I certainly didn't expect to be met by Prof. Callaway[1] in person. It was some moments before we noticed one another, and while I looked round the lounge in search of somebody I didn't know wearing that tell-tale lost look of waiting for somebody *they* didn't know who might be me (how I enjoy such moments! I try to mystify those people and go unrecognised as long as I can), the thought struck me that perhaps, after all, there would not be anybody, that Terry[2] hadn't let them know, or that someone at the university had got the date of my arrival wrong. This would pose the problem of accommodation, as I didn't know where they had arranged for me to stay, and I was just planning to solve it in the most enjoyable way by ringing David C.,[3] who never minds being woken up, and asking him for a night's hospitality. I was beaming with pleasure at the prospect and Prof. Callaway, who happened to look just then in my direction, thought I was beaming at him! He might not have recognised me otherwise.

---

[1] Professor Sir Frank Callaway (1919–2003), an influential music educator.
[2] Terry Harrison, Tchaikowsky's agent; *cf.* p. 57, above.
[3] Unidentified.

> 1.1.a
>
> Shall I really start a diary?
>
> I tried it once before, long ago, and in French. It lapsed quite soon, as I had expected, and re-reading it some years later I found it quite insufferable: pretentious, clever-clever, going into lewd intellectual contortions to impress a hypothetical reader, if not posterity. A performance, in fact — the only thing I had been trained to do. Can I now manage something simpler, truer? Can I keep it up? And will it make me even more of a loner?

He took me to my room at the campus which is pleasant enough, with a shower bathroom-and-toilet and a tea-kettle and wash-up basin in the room itself. There is no fridge and no cooking facilities, and a search for crockery through cupboards and drawers yielded two mothballs and three tennis rackets. Is this a leftover from previous tenancies, or a discreet hint of what they expect of me in my spare hours?

Yesterday I had lunch with the Callaways and dinner with David. The Callaways' guest at the moment is the Rev. Chad Varah, the founder of The Samaritans, at present on an extremely busy sabbatical year.[4] At first I thought him slightly ga-ga, merely because of his rather senile voice, but within an hour was ready to admit that *I* was. He is delightful company, full of wit, sense and energy, a prodigious memory and a keen interest in literature and music, a born raconteur, and broad-minded enough to put most agnostics to shame. He's read all of C. S. Lewis, is friends with Harry Williams,[5] but to my surprise had never heard of George Lyward.[6] I am delighted to find that we'll be on the same flight to Adelaide on Thursday.

Now for David. It's not easy to write about him, partly because I am waiting for him at this very moment, which had been undermining my

[4] The Rev. Edward Chad Varah (1911–2007) founded The Samaritans in 1953.
[5] The Rev. Henry Abbott Williams (1919–2006) was a Cambridge-based writer and priest known especially in the 1960s for his radical theological views. Chaplain and Dean of Chapel at Trinity College, Cambridge from 1948 to 1969, he then became an Anglican monk in a monastery in Yorkshire.
[6] George Aubrey Lyward OBE (1894–1973) was a British educationist and psychotherapist who founded and led Finchden Manor, a house for underprivileged boys in Tenterden, Kent.

concentration throughout this entry, partly because our relations are in a state of enjoyable flux, and every little event may be contradicted by the very next. Last night, whatever its eventual outcome, has proved a small but definite step forward not just in my relationship with him but in my general development: for the first time, in a situation which mattered to me enough to make me anxious, I ceased to be the ill-starred Question Man (Eve will know what this refers to).[7] Instead of humbly pleading for a kiss, I simply pulled him to me and kissed him. Had I asked for it as a favour, this would no doubt have been refused, or more, *granted* as a favour; as it was, it was returned, repeated, evidently enjoyed, and I had the completely unforeseen bonus of a spontaneous kiss he gave me on his own initiative some two hours later.[8] Will it go any further? do I want it to? I am not sure. And without knowing my own feelings, what hope could I have of influencing his life? It would be hard enough to try and push a free, thinking creature into a direction of my own choice (and not too moral either); it is simply impossible to push even a tennis ball in a direction one has not chosen, or in two different directions simultaneously. Moral: do not push!

Later – I've just had another evening with David, one that he seems to have enjoyed much more, and I less. No more kisses this time: he seemed to avoid bringing me back to his place deliberately, probably to prevent any further importunities – a distinctly humiliating thought. In other ways, however, he gave me every reassurance and kept on praising my value as a companion and possible friend, saying again and again how happy he was, how different this was from his other relationships etc. It may be that by not showing the least disappointment and falling in with his arrangements with willing good grace, I have at last won him over – that is, persuaded him that I like him for what he is, not for what I can get. But there he is wrong! He needs a friend, and I could be that friend, better perhaps than anyone he knows: but what can he offer me, besides the beauty and grace of his body and physical charm? I don't need another friend – indeed, I am the luckiest man alive in this respect and, as this entry shows, am getting spoilt! Tonight I was the Good Samaritan, spent nearly all I had on a lavish dinner, and didn't even let him buy the petrol for his car; I listened to rivers of talk, none of it memorable though all of it friendly, and was called a

---

[7] This refers to Tchaikowsky's habit of asking for permission for any act, however big or small, which was often felt to be off-putting, exhausting, and even embarrassing by his partners. Eve Harrison told him that impulsiveness can often work, but that he should be able to read the signals; he took it to mean that he needed to be more direct.

[8] 'He kissed her once behind the pigsty when she wasn't looking and never did it again, although she was looking all the time' [quotation from *Under Milk Wood* by Dylan Thomas] –AT

good listener; I enjoyably idled away time that could have been given to *The Merchant*.[9] All this is fine, and I don't regret any of it. But it would not be so fine another time. A friend is one thing, a sugar daddy quite another; and a *platonic* sugar daddy is just the part only a fool like me would accept.[10] The point of tonight was to convince David that all these pleasures were free, that he would never be asked to sing for his supper; at the time I was equally anxious to convince myself, which made it the more persuasive; but now I can see that very premise to be spurious. Had I been more conscious, it would have fitted into a plan of seduction as cool as Laclos:[11] David has been lured into the happy delusion of a friendship he is hungry for – a useful first step. But I am no Valmont and can never keep up a pretence. At least the real purpose of this little book begins to emerge: it will make me clearer to myself.

4 March

No, these comments are very unfair. Naturally enough, I used this book as an outlet for the only feeling I'd had to repress; but there were many more, equally genuine and far more enjoyable. As G. L.[12] told me at our very first talk, 'joy is made up of pleasure and pain'. And the words came back to me yesterday as I was sitting next to David in his car. Whatever else he may grant or withhold, he can't help looking beautiful, or prevent me looking at him when we are together; visually at least he is mine, and a joy every time I look. His presence is a *joy*; granted, it gives rise to more feelings than it satisfies, but then the very longing is enjoyable. That's what Baudelaire called poison, and he preferred it to opium and wine! No, it's today that I feel lonely, at any rate when I am not working. This is just what these lovely people do, make me aware of my own constant loneliness: perhaps that's what love is, an intermittent realisation of a constant state? We are just as lonely the rest of the time, but we just don't know it.

At any rate, there can be no harm in not ringing David again. Let chance bring us together, or better still, let him ring me: if he doesn't, he will prove me right. If, as I fear, it is hopeless, the sooner I get off the better; if not, surely it is his turn to miss that company he claims to have enjoyed so much? (And yet I am so superstitious that I was scared to write that last sentence, lest the doubt it implies rubbed off on D's actual attitude). Mais le

[9] Tchaikowsky had begun to compose his opera *The Merchant of Venice* in 1968.
[10] I did with Pip! –AT
[11] Pierre Ambroise François Choderlos de Laclos (1741–1803), a French novelist, official and army general, author of the epistolary novel *Les Liaisons dangéreuses*.
[12] Here and henceforth: George Lyward: *cf.* note 6, p. 102, above.

George Lyward by Milein Cosman

dessein est pris; rien ne peut m'ébranler:[13] if there is any wooing to be done, it shan't be done by me. Amen!

6 March

The power of words! I have had two days of fairly deep depression, merely because of reading a chapter in Varah's symposium book on The Samaritans, entitled 'Befriending the Sexually Frustrated'.[14] What he said was enlightened and tolerant; he described the condition as very painful, and so it is; but that condition had never depressed me so much as recognising it under this grim and brutal label. 'Sexually frustrated'! Is this what I am? I used to think of myself as being 'in love', 'infatuated', 'falling for so-and-so', words which lent my plight some romance and dignity, seemed to put me into the company of Stendhal, Baudelaire, Proust…. It was V., for instance, that I should have called sexually frustrated. The word made me think of women, repulsive middle-aged or elderly spinsters, some desiccated, some obese, mere courtesy to whom was an effort of hypocrisy. Am I, then, in their company? Is D. as nauseated by my advances as I am by V.'s? It's the humiliation that's hard to take, not the loneliness. Chad would probably say that Stendhal ranks with V. too, that we're all part of the same humanity: his genius lent him insight into his situation but that could only have increased

---

[13] 'But the plan is made, nothing can shake me': quotation from Racine's *Mithridate*, IV, 4 (1673).
[14] Chapter from Chad Varah, *The Samaritans in the '70s: To Befriend the Suicidal and Despairing*, Constable, London, 1973.

his distress. But since reading the words, I feel bitter about a state of affairs I thought I had come to accept.

Take a trivial incident yesterday. Passing the dining hall I heard, with surprise and amusement, a fragment of *The Virgin's Prayer*.[15] I don't regard either prayer or virginity obsolete, merely unfashionable which is a point in favour in itself, but I'd hardly expect this piece to have interested a young student of today. (That it was a female student could of course be taken for granted). Later, a girl came running towards me. 'Are you André Tchaikowsky?' I could as soon have confessed to stealing the china, but there was no denying my name. She chatted on. 'Are you happy to be recognised? How did you find my rendering of *The Virgin's Prayer*?' She was Chinese, plain, bespectacled; I was carefully polite, but was aware of a bitterness bordering on hatred. 'This is the kind of conquest I can make', I thought. 'I am the answer to the *Virgin's Prayer*!' And my indifference to girls turned to resentment, although my two reasons for hating them are both equally unfair and irrational: one, that no boys pay any attention to me; two, that the girls do.

10 March

Adelaide

Let's be honest: already when writing that last entry I was planning to show it to Chad. But I certainly couldn't know that his reaction will encourage me to show him the two previous fragments as well – including the one referring to his 'senile' voice! He is, in fact, adorable, and I doubt whether anything on this trip will equal, in durable value, his acquaintance and friendship. For we already are friends. It was particularly rewarding to be given that friendship in answer, not to the more obviously acceptable aspects of my personality, but to disclosures which normally bring me *at best* sympathy!

And since then he has helped me again. I had hardly arrived in Adelaide before I was struck down with a diarrhoea so severe that at least the first of the five concerts had to be put into question. A doctor came to see me and prescribed, among other things, Kaoline at the rate of 10 milligrams 'every time a loose motion is passed' (it says so on the bottle). Kaoline containing opium, and I being a remarkably conscientious patient, a day of continuous diarrhoea brought me to a state of near-unconsciousness. The following

---

[15] The best-known piano piece by the short-lived Tekla Bądarzewska-Baranowska (1838–62). As *Modlitwa dziewicy* ('A Maiden's Prayer'), Op. 4, it was published in Warsaw in 1856 and, as *La prière d'une vierge*, appeared as a supplement to *La Revue et Gazette musicale de Paris* in 1895, soon becoming immensely popular, selling hundreds of thousands of copies. It survives even today as a standard country-and-western number.

morning I got up and sat down to meditate, but felt so sick and giddy I could barely force myself to sit up for the minimal fifteen minutes. I collapsed back into bed and rang the doctor, who was not on duty; presently, though, his partner appeared in my room, he told me, to my relief, to discontinue Kaoline and wrote out a meticulous diet which had nothing to do with his partner's suggestions of the previous day.[16] No two doctors agree about diet. To my added relief, he advised me against trying to practise, although the first concert was only twenty-four hours away, but didn't give me the medical certificate that alone would give me legal ground for cancelling the concert. Altogether, a very wise man.

Now, this is where Chad comes in. Illness is helpless; convalescence depends largely on the will. I knew Chad could only come to the first concert, as he was off to Melbourne the next day, and his presence alone made the thing worth trying for. It was a date between us, an occasion for me to give him something in return, and I began to look forward to it. There were other considerations as well: for one thing I am down to play a cycle, not five random programmes, and a cycle only makes sense if it is complete; for another, *starting* with a cancellation would have made it psychologically harder to play the following concerts – the audience would expect an off-colour performance from a man they had known to be ill only two days before. But it's Chad that gave me the personal incentive, and for me it's the personal that matters!

Well, the concert took place this afternoon, and went very well. The fourth partita was as good as I've ever played it – perhaps the best. The first was not so good; I nearly always get most nervous in the pieces with the fewest notes, and the fear engendered by this piece is out of all proportion to its apparent level of difficulty. I noted danger signs in the *Allemande*, cut down my losses by omitting the repeats in the *Courante* and missed four obvious notes in the *Gigue*. Still, it was vastly preferable to a cancellation! It seemed to go down very well, the town hall was practically full and I got many curtain-calls and a bit of an ovation, though I was determined to play no encores.

Chad came backstage alone, although two tickets had been left for him. This was another sacrifice on his part, as he is very fond of pretty girls and knows how to find them! He asked me to tea and we managed to shed everybody else [...]. By that time the last signs of my illness has disappeared and we had a delightfully quiet hour at my hotel. He's a wonderful addition to my life.

---

[16] Tchaikowsky must have seen another doctor the day before.

All ears in Australia, with Sir Frank Callaway in the background

I've come to the conclusion that my diarrhoea is psychosomatic, just as my headaches had been in earlier days. Last Christmas it was due to my anxiety over P.; two years ago, to the suspense over the fate of my piano concerto. Then what, except sheer hypochondria, makes me go on taking those intestinal disinfectant pills?

20 March

[…] Last Sunday I. arrived. I found him at the reception desk of my hotel writing me a message. He wears his hair like Captain Gulliver's, is barefoot and puts nail-varnish on the toes of one foot. This produced in me a mixed feeling of revulsion and embarrassment, some of which may have shown in my face. I must have decided there and then not to have that holiday with him at the end of May: he is full of good-will, but our life-styles are incompatible. Somehow his taking acid doesn't bother me nearly as much as his painting his nails. Is it, once again, that I cannot disclaim kinship with that breed? Or is it that style, to me, means more than content? Taking LSD may be a tragedy, but paint on male toenails is a mere lapse of taste. I prefer tragedy – it's less cheap. But who'd have known me to be so *square*? I. has far more reason to be disappointed in me than vice versa. What a shock to find me siding with the parents! I had never felt any sympathy to their lot before. What does one do when one's child becomes, say, a tart?

Later – Chad rang and left a message; he's in Canberra. After several attempts, we managed to find both one another and a clear line, and what emerged was not one joy but two: in addition to talking to him, I've had the delight of an invitation to play for The Samaritans in London, and of course accepted at once. I'd sensed the immense value of his friendship nearly at once, but till now I couldn't see how on earth I could ever be of any use to *him*. And now an opportunity has appeared so quickly! No one can replace G. L.,[17] but Chad can come nearer than anyone I know: I love him already and have a feeling he's fond of me too. G. L., did *you* arrange it? You're perhaps the only person I could conceivably believe it of. Anyway, I know you'd be pleased!

23 March

Perth

Most of what I did in my spare time was read. Racine again, edited and ponderously annotated by a Mr Picard (why do people who admire Racine talk of him in the style of Victor Hugo? At least Picard can see differences between the plays, which could never be suspected from Thierry Maulnier's[18] grandiloquent book). Three novels by Graham Greene, including the masterly *The Quiet American*. The first two volumes of C. S. Lewis' SF trilogy[19] – isn't he grinding his axe rather hard? I started skipping towards the end of *Perelandra*,[20] which is something I only resort to in extremes. Finally, two books I tried to read and failed: *Eminent Victorians*,[21] smug, florid and unreadable, and Bertrand Russell's inquiry into the meaning of truth,[22] which is so clever that it struck me as wholly idiotic. It's obviously so far above my head as to make me wonder if I've got one. It partially reminded me of Molière's grotesque philosophers – especially the second one in *Le Mariage Forcé*.[23]

And now for Perth! I've got the same little room, which became home to me while longing for it in Adelaide, and they're going to lend me a fridge.

---

[17] George Lyward had died on 22 June 1973.
[18] Born Jacques Talagrand (1909–88), French journalist, essayist, dramatist, and literary critic. The book to which Tchaikowsky refers is *Racine,* Gallimard, Paris, 1936.
[19] C. S. Lewis, *Space Trilogy: Out of the Silent Planet; Perelandra; That Hideous Strength,* MacMillan, London, 1965.
[20] *Perelandra* is the second book in the *Space Trilogy* of C. S. Lewis.
[21] Book by Lytton Strachey, first published in 1918.
[22] *An Inquiry into Meaning and Truth*, Penguin, Harmondsworth, 1965.
[23] Moliere's *comédie-ballet*, written in 1664.

In fact it feels more homely than my own London flat: unlike at Waterlow Court, here I feel part of the community, and yet my privacy is undisturbed. The only threat to that has been David, and I've decided to keep at a distance from him from now on, both for safety and from self-respect. The little he'd be prepared to give me simply isn't worth the agonies and mortification it would no doubt cost.

To my delighted surprise, I have managed to dispense with Tuinal[24] last night and slept just as well on Valium. Let's try to keep it up – or down? And I've found myself more alert today: in Adelaide depression had made me quite stupid.

28 March

The idyllic life!

Today I committed a crime – a delightful feeling. My unsuspecting victim is Bob Cornford,[25] whose long-delayed variations degenerate into absolute rubbish in the last two movements. After some hesitation, composed equally of genuine moral scruples and sheer superstition (if I am bad, won't it bring my concerts down?), I went to Prof. Callaway and told him of a conversation with Bob on the 'phone, in which *he* had emphatically asked me to have the two movements removed. Callaway is not impeded by mere moral scruples, he soon sensed I *wanted* the stuff out (in fact he may have guessed the lie), immediately announced that it was obviously for the best and proceeded there and then to expunge all traces of the undesirable movements from the programme notes. In his reformatory enthusiasm he even changed the titles, first to *Diversions*, then, at my prompting, to *Contrasts*. I hope nothing of the sort ever happens to my own compositions! Having behaved like that myself, whom can I trust? But I feel no remorse – only relief of being rid of some of this amateurish, perfunctory and ill-written music.

Perhaps no kind of life would agree with me more than the one I am leading here. There is privacy in my room and pleasant company when I want it; the students treat me as one of themselves. The campus is most beautifully situated between the park and the river – there is even a small beach and a little sailing harbour with two jetties – and walking across it to the studio which had been put at my disposal is a joy in itself. The days are still hot and there are many sprinklers turning about on the lawns: I walk right through them, get drenched and the sun dries it up within one or two minutes. Walking barefoot is also part of the pleasure: it makes one feel free, even when one is

---

[24] A barbiturate sedative no longer in production.
[25] Robert Cornford (1940–83), British composer, pianist and conductor, and dedicatee of No. 4 of Tchaikowsky's *Inventions*, Op. 2 (*cf.* pp. 368 and 370, below).

walking to work! And that work, which had been such a drag in Adelaide, is positively enticing here. There are enough different programmes and brand new pieces to make it a challenge but not so many as to make the project unfeasible: at the rate of three hours a day, I should be able to assimilate it all. True, I haven't done any writing for over three weeks; but perhaps this is just as well, considering the ten different recital programmes I am to play within the next seven weeks? I shall not make an obligation of it.

My room is now furnished with an enormous fridge, prone to masturbatory tremour and likely to frighten me at night, and that unprecedented luxury: a telephone which I can switch off. Now, wouldn't this alone make emigrating to Australia worthwhile? I am really considering it.

The first concert went very well and today there is a rave review – a pleasing coincidence. (Again, superstition nearly prevented me putting the last three words down). Although the presence of a fellow pianist in the audience usually paralyses me, having David Bollard[26] there actually helped. I played the whole thing to him, knowing he'd appreciate whatever music I manage to bring out, and forgive the rest. [...] I feel real affection for him, as opposed to fancy, though with the least encouragement I could no doubt fancy him too! David C. was there as well and I realised the only satisfaction this man can provide me: that of snubbing him. As he came in, radiantly conceited, as spoilt as Bosie,[27] my only wish was to put him in his place. 'You've got to buy me another dinner soon', he announced. 'Who says so?' 'I do; and you promised.' 'I see you are still at the innocent stage of taking my promises seriously.' 'What are you doing now, anyway?' 'I am taking David B. out to dinner.' Will this have proved sufficient, or is he insensitive enough to count another snub?

6 April

'Perhaps, like families, all happy days are alike?'[28]
It would take a good writer to describe happiness without making it appear like boredom. In fact, boredom is far the more eventful of the two, as the restless mind keeps trying out new ways of escaping it. So I shall merely mention my continuous happiness here, so that it may comfort me in less

---

[26] New Zealand-born Australian pianist, at the time staff member of the University of Western Australia, and later Senior Lecturer and Coordinator of Keyboard at Monash University in Melbourne; he is currently an adjunct professor of piano at the Conservatorium of Music at the University of Tasmania.
[27] 'Bosie' was the nickname of Lord Alfred Douglas (1870–1945), writer, poet and corrosive personality best remembered as the lover of Oscar Wilde.
[28] Play on the opening line of Tolstoy's *Anna Karenina*: 'All happy families are alike; each unhappy family is unhappy in its own way'.

lucky days, and to avoid the example of these who never realise their own contentment until they have lost it. Mine is made up of such small simple things – sunlight, the comfort of my room, the choice of privacy and good company, the rhythm of leisure and work. At the moment it seems to me that I could live this way indefinitely. Perhaps even this could be arranged?

After the second of the Bach recitals, I found myself alone and used some of the yet unspent energy on orchestrating, enjoyably and I think quite successfully, another page of the *Prince of Morocco*.[29] I'll try to do the same next Wednesday. There are still three score pages to be done, and then I shall have run out of sketches and shall be faced with the task of fitting in some real composing! How much of that can I afford to do without harming my work as a pianist? This has always been my main problem. It's not a question of time but of concentration: composition devours all you've got. You start by dabbling in it, experimenting with a harmonic turn or a basic contrapuntal combination, and suddenly you're hooked – it rages on in your brain and leaves room for nothing else. The last movement of my first string quartet came to me one day in Göteborg when I was due to play a Chopin recital; apparently I really did play it, but I never heard a note of it. With so many different programmes to play here, and so many new pieces, can I afford this kind of risk?

11 April

Well, 'it' has happened. I gave a really awful performance last night. And several concerned comments have since confirmed that this time it really was as bad as it had felt to me at the time.

For once, however, I am not depressed: almost relieved. It was due to come for some time and now that I've fallen down I can set about picking myself up in the next performance or two. The consistent good luck of the last few performances has begun to scare me. The obvious danger was that of seeming better that I really am and setting up expectations that no later concerts could have satisfied; it was time to establish my essential fallibility. But the true cause of my comparative lack of remorse is that the recital went wrong for the best possible reason – the only one perhaps that my conscience can fully accept. I had thought of a new composition.

It came to me the afternoon before, in an idle hour on the beach. I had been looking over Anne Hodgson's programme notes on my cycle of keyboard variations, wondering why there had not been a really good set of them since the Copland (which are truly great) and thinking with dismay of the inevitable debacle of the variations (or 'contrasts') for which I was personally

---

[29] *The Merchant of Venice,* Act II, the Casket Scene.

responsible (the programme notes state specifically 'commissioned by André Tchaikowsky'). Why had I made that idiotic mistake? Of course, I couldn't possibly have rounded off the cycle by a set of my own – I simply couldn't write keyboard variations. What harmonic sequence could have carried the piece through in today's world of tonal dissolution? At that point I realised I was in fact groping for the very conception I had dismissed as impossible. More than that, I was already composing: thinking in notes, not words.

The first few notes were clearly a mere by-product of the Copland variations, which I had played only the night before:

It would have been fraudulent to call an original theme that was so obviously derived from the first variation of the Copland. But wasn't there another, more distant antecedent? Why did the themes sound so much like Bartók? It wasn't only the interval that recalled him, it was the symmetry of the two phrases – the falling answer to a rising question, the inversion that is so central to the construction of his themes. As in the *Andante* of the 1938 violin concerto…

I've got it! It's the viola concerto! The very opening in fact:

I couldn't remember any more of it, but this was enough to get my imagination fully mobilised. What a peg to hang my thoughts onto! And there is no shame in needing a peg: what about Racine? Is a whodunnit better than *Le Rouge et le Noir*[30] or having an original plot? Now, calm down, I thought, you're not writing a masterpiece as yet! In fact, isn't there something old-fashioned in writing variations on another composer's theme? Yes, there is: and fuck fashion. The reason why the practice had been discontinued is that most links with the past had been deliberately broken. But what if a link did exist? And in this case it was more than a link, a filial bond: I shouldn't have written a note without Bartók. At least, that is, a note I'd care to preserve. And suddenly I realised the almost unique value of this theme as a subject for variation treatment: the fact that it was *unharmonised*.

And all this time the actual music went on in my brain. I duly practised as I planned, but composition took over from practice, and I found myself experimenting with the theme at the piano! I soon found the pedal bass

---

[30] A historical psychological novel by Stendhal, written in 1830.

note I needed – D flat, in relation to the theme at its original pitch – and in the next twenty-four hours found the beginning and the end of the work, the first four variations and a fast, climactic, fugal one that may prove to be the best but one. Could Bach withstand such an invasion?

I went on doing 'all the right things'. I resisted the temptation to borrow the Bartók score from the library to see how the theme went on and did all I could to master the obsession. I fell back on all the little things I normally avoid as 'distraction' on the day of a concert, hoping they would defend me against the far more dangerous distraction that was robbing the concert of all its importance. I read; I tried to force sleep by drinking far too much over lunch; I even played with myself, despite total reluctance, as it were for medical reasons! None of it helped – it never does help to try too hard. I began to panic. At 5 I played through the entire programme – far too much – and only left the stage in time to let the audience find their seats. There were some twenty minutes left, and I went for a walk. Perhaps the direction of the walk was the final mistake: for it brought me, of all places, to the very beach where I first conceived the idea. It took renewed possession at once, and I lost what little concentration I had managed to gather in my warm-up on stage.

I cannot describe the performance – I only half heard it. My first act on completing it and taking the final bow was to run out of the theatre, fearing recognition and pursuit by well-meaning hangers on and 'friends'. I was lucky in escaping them.

Only one member of the audience found me: a real friend. B. was the one person I had really wanted to see. I had tried to ring him at lunch-time to warn him of what was coming, but hadn't found him at home. And now I was touched, but not altogether surprised, by his coming to my place, gratifyingly alone, soon after the concert. It was just the kind of thing he would do: no pressure, no officious commiseration, no hypocrisy, simply 'Are you all right?' It says a lot for our relationship that I can make a fool of myself in front of him and not feel in the least humiliated. Most often colleagues would have hurt me by their mere presence.

And today it was wonderful to see D. B.'s own artistry so abundantly revealed. He and Graham Wood played op. 96[31] at a lunch-time concert, preceded by Tartini g-minor sonata.[32] [...] B. [...] showed a mastery for which I had been completely unprepared. Everything was there: beautiful tone, exquisite sensitivity, complete continuous control. I couldn't quite

---

[31] The Sonata in G major, Op. 96 (1812), the tenth and last of Beethoven's sonatas for piano and violin.
[32] Possibly a sonata by Giuseppe Tartini (1692–1770), B. g5 (1713) also known as 'The Devil's Trill', or Sonata for violin and continuo B. g10, 'Didone abbandonata' (c. 1731).

suppress the hateful and patronising thought: What is this kind of artist doing at a University Music Department, teaching people scales?

12 April

It would have been deliciously ironic if the idea that wrecked my recital proved in practice to have been a hallucination, or a dead-end. But I prefer less stoic satisfactions to that of admiring the ironies of Fate at my own expense, and am eager to record the, for me, almost unbelievable fact of having written three variations in one day! When did I last work so fast, or so easily? Not since October '66, when the introduction to the piano concerto took shape in, I think, two days – or was it four? What is certain is that it took four years of intermittent agonies to finish that work, and today's luck may be similarly followed. This doesn't worry me: what does is the danger of a new piece swallowing me up and making a mess of all the remaining concerts. Already I've let two days go by without practising: yesterday by design, today because only my own music was compellingly real to me. But from tomorrow I'll make a point of not writing until my daily quota of piano work has been done – and it had better be a fair chunk!

Today's harvest can only call for a thanksgiving prayer. But there've been other joys too: I am really popular with the students here at Currie Hall, and the affection in the air makes up for any closer relationships I might wish to have. In fact, I probably prefer it! I am free to like everyone and be compelled by none; they show me more unsolicited marks of appreciation and fondness than a lifetime of servitude on my part would get out of C. A Chinese boy called Patrick Tso, with whom I played bridge last Tuesday night and to whom I took immensely, gave me today a metal sculpture as a souvenir and was quite emotional about it. Another favourite of mine, Hamish, told me yesterday of his brother's 21st birthday; the brother is also a resident here and though I've seen little of him, I find him perfectly charming. I bought a bottle of champagne and a 21st birthday card which was passed round and signed by most of all of the house; then the two things were left in his room, for him to discover when he came home at night. I asked for my contribution to be left unrevealed, but I am ashamed to say that it gives me pleasure to know that this request could hardly have been complied with! This way I get both the credit for buying the champagne and originating the whole project, *and* the credit for seeking no credit.

And, of course, I expect full marks for the frankness of such entries as this – including this last sentence.

20 April

A free day at Currie Hall.

A new block is under construction and the builders have left behind an electrical cable roller on the lawn. The boys jump on it, spread their arms to achieve a balance and struggle to maintain it as the roller begins to move forwards. The secret is to keep stepping backwards at the exact pace of their mobile platform; the position is precarious, and soon three boys strive for space on the moving roller. One of them, C. W., can even play ball at the same time; he catches it with his hands, with his head, avoiding all superfluous motion, which gives his posture a cool elegance. I, from the ground, send it to him, and often fail to catch it back, while he never misses: but soon the fun of the game gets the better of my self-consciousness and I no longer mind being clumsy. At the same time, of course, I'm beginning to catch the ball more often! But that's by now irrelevant. I've got the point: let us learn to enjoy also the things we do badly. How would this maxim work in the field of sexual activities?

26 April

Oh, never has this little book been more necessary! Never, since starting it, have I felt more vulnerable and confused. Perhaps by setting out the events I can clarify my reactions to them?

C., after all, has repaid all my earlier attention, although unwittingly, and by proxy. Or should I give him the credit for more subtlety and concede that he may have known what he was doing? At any rate, he's introduced me to a man who eclipsed him at once – not by looks, but by a most original and fascinating personality. The difference between him and C. is like that between late Beethoven and Mendelssohn, or Bartók and (at best) Ravel.

Among the many objects d'art accumulated and displayed at C's house the one that captivated me was a hand-made chess-board in Australian aboriginal style (assuming that today's aboriginals do make chess-boards). It is fascinatingly asymmetrical, with all the squares uneven in size, shape and texture, and seems mobile, *alive*, like a Van Gogh cornfield or those Modigliani portraits where the eyes are on different levels. C. had long wanted to introduce me to the man who'd made it, and did his best to make him sound interesting. But that was at a time when I had eyes for C. alone, and any other presence would have struck me as a mere illusion. Two days ago he invited both of us to dinner, and we met.

His name is D. and he is 31. I cannot describe his appearance, because my memory of it is distorted by the emotion it gives rise to. I don't know if he is beautiful; he does not need to be. He is intense, misanthropic, *tragic*; in direct contrast to C., he doesn't do anything to please, and has no use for small talk. He has every conceivable talent, but only one vocation: to FAIL; and he pursues that grim vocation quite relentlessly. Can it be hoped that he will fail at *that*?

His house, to which he ended by admitting me after great reluctance, is as messy as Beethoven's sketch-books, and in exactly the same way. The reason for his hospitality was that he has some five recordings of the Diabelli Variations, the very work I am to play here on Monday! On my side, of course, this was only one of the reasons, but he was too innocent to realise that. The demon that inhabits him and wrecks him from inside by eating away all his self-confidence has long persuaded him that no one could possibly find him attractive. It took me some time to realise that the long handshake I had taken for a green light was in fact nothing of the sort. We sat, listening to the Katchen[33] recording, amid a jumble of cups, pictorial and musical sketches, stereo sets made by himself, in working order but not quite finished ('Don't touch that', he warned me, 'you'd get a nasty shock'), books, records, clothing… The total aspect of the room seemed at once creative and destructive, and perhaps I can *only* describe D. by describing his house, though either subject is beyond my power. D. is completely self-taught; he paints, sculpts, plays the piano, composes; some of his music was lying on the floor but it seemed to me too indiscreet to examine it. (I ended up by being even more indiscreet in other ways). An early self-portrait happened to be lying by: that face looked haggard and haunted, the face of a man who has watched his own collapse. One couldn't determine its age, but D. told me he'd done it at sixteen or seventeen.

This brings me to his conversation. At dinner, we were discussing transcendental meditation which C. had introduced both of us to, and D., who had taken it up quite recently, told us the reasons which led him to give it up. The phenomena that occurred while he meditated were too uncanny to be dismissed as 'release of stress' or else the stress in question was beyond human endurance. At first, D. explained, he would feel a physical twitch in his ears. Then, some thirty seconds later, he realised that the twitch had in fact been a word, usually a pun, and some of these puns were cleverer than anything D. would have been able to think up consciously. The subject matter was always the same: parting, divorce, conflict; and though D.

---

[33] Julius Katchen (1926–69), an American pianist.

described it disparagingly as merely unpleasant, 'frightening' would not seem to me too strong a word. It fact, what crossed my mind was nothing less than daemonic possession, though C. and I both discussed repression as the main possibility. What struck me almost as much as the startling subject-matter was the frankness with which D. revealed such experiences to a total stranger. What had I done to deserve such confidence? What could I do that would justify it in retrospect? I was being treated as a close friend by a man obviously jealous of his privacy, and I felt giddy at the privilege.

Sex, of course, raised its ugly head (I blush at the vulgarity of the euphemism) and there D.'s integrity and honesty kept us out of the usual humiliating tangle: he told me, clearly and frankly, that he didn't feel drawn to me that way – what man would? – but that said, he showed the astonishing generosity of letting me go to bed with him for most of the night. I had forgotten how keen those joys can be – darkness, the heady tang of cigarettes and sweat, the feeling of knees against knees, feet against feet, the smoothness of D.'s back under my hand (his skin ranges from gravel to silk), the desultory whispered conversation... And yet what most people would call sex did not take place: every time my roving hands extended their licence below a certain point, he would gently remove them, and the same restrictions applied to my lips. Perhaps in my younger years I should have found this situation intensely frustrating; now, nearing forty, I am discovering separate and exquisite joys in what I used to consider mere means to an end. For I'd much rather let it have *no* end: have the orgasm, like the horizon, always in front of me. This was the happiest night I've had this year.

As I was leaving, about six, D.'s face was cold and stern and his voice laconic. I contrasted it with his affectionate smile while we were playing chess before dinner at C.'s and thought I had pushed my luck too far: he may never forgive this sudden intrusion into his life and may, partly through sheer fatigue, come to resent his own earlier generosity! I decided not to contact him till after the Monday concert and only hoped he wouldn't be too angry to come to it as planned. Meanwhile, despite shortage of sleep, I found myself fertile and stimulated, and discovered new details in the Diabelli, which weren't due to Katchen's performance! This was in the evening; in the afternoon, I'd had an interview with Margaret S[eares] and was again surprised by my own vitality and enthusiasm. It will also be good to have *her* in the audience: she offers the ideal blend of admiration and discerning criticism. I couldn't wish for a stranger incentive to work that I have this weekend; will I, then, wreck the concert by trying too hard? Lord knows, it has happened enough times...

I just rang D., overcoming shyness and misgivings and am glad I did. He did sound cold at first ('This is André.' 'Yes, I hear.'), but cheered up when I had mentioned the two Mozart records I bought him this morning. Or was it because he realised I wasn't trying to invite myself over to his place? Anyway, we had a long friendly talk, happily free of the excessive intensity that made our evening together so remarkable, but that no relationship could possibly have sustained. Love must learn to be quiet sometimes.

I shouldn't have had the courage to ring him but for Chad's advice six weeks ago: 'Put *your* cards on the table, but don't try to play both parts at once. You can't know how anyone else feels until they have told you, but you can make sure they know how you do.' Indeed, how was D. to know that for all my forwardness of the night before last I hadn't by now forgotten his very existence? He sees nothing worthwhile in himself.

1 May

I scarce discern the filaments
Which from your glance gleam out,
Not in your shade cheek more discover
Than the wispest glimmering;
Yet had I means wherewith to paint
In words, what scratches render there
I should in speech sketch shadows, faint,
Or write your wraith in air.

These lines are by D.: and it is once again of D. alone that I can write, if indeed I can write at all. No doubt I am still too near to the tremendous inner events of last Thursday night to be able to write of them clearly, or without letting past pain impinge on the present joy. In fact most of that night was too intolerable to dwell upon; but if it was a poor man's Gethsemane today it's Easter (It is, in fact, Sunday). To set it out just for the record, I confessed my servitude and misery to D., let him know I was in love with him; and his reaction to that was unparalleled in all my experience. He showed the most acute concern for my state of mind, which proved, far more than any erotic gesture could have done, just how much I mattered to him. Truth however, as always with D., mattered even more, and nothing could interfere with his concern for THAT. He showed me, with the kind of unsparing factual clarity no infatuation could survive, why he could never think of me as a lover; his make-up is such that the very affection he feels for me would alone preclude any sexual attraction, and he referred to sex as 'an act of contempt'. […]

At first I experienced nothing but a sense of loss. It was as if I'd gone to sleep on some fragrant tropical island and woke up in a provincial hotel room in Sweden! Life had lost all its intoxication and there seemed nothing left but futilities. On coming home I took both Valium and Tuinal, but 3 hours later I was again awake and quite disconsolate. [...] During the afternoon, however, I started, for the first time in months, to write music again – not to compose, merely to continue the interrupted fair copy of the first movement of the Second String Quartet. And this occupation, which I had long avoided as boring, gave me the crucial proof that my mind was once again my own. No more running about like a decapitated chicken! After over an hour of work, I rang D. to tell him how much better I felt, as I knew he'd be apt to worry about me almost more than I did myself. He had asked me, some twelve hours before: 'Will you now drop me?' I had protested I wouldn't, then suggested that the question made it sound as if *he* might miss me; 'Well', he said beautifully, 'I'd like to think I had been a valid person to you in my own right, not just a peg to hang your dreams on'. I could now reassure him on that count, but in my awareness of having already trespassed abundantly on his time and life, I kept the call very short, and he mistook my tenseness for a kind of dismissal.

Yesterday he rang me. He didn't know my private number, so he had to find Currie Hall in the 'phone book and ring me on the 'public' 'phone in the foyer. He had been very worried, he said, about the money I had paid him for his painting: would I take it back? By that time, overflowing with newly rediscovered joy and energy, I had been on the point of ringing him myself. The work had gone well, I felt free, I was a man in my own right again: D. could now have a friend, not a slave![34] I went over to his place and spent a perfectly beautiful evening. No, I told him, of course I didn't want the money back. It's true that I had been acting under compulsion ever since I met him, but now I freely *wanted* to do that before I had *had* to do it. And no, I wouldn't buy it more cheaply: it had been a fair price. I admitted the selfishness of my earlier motivation, the frantic desire to play a part in his life, to be useful, to matter, to count: well, I did matter! He had proved that point beyond all doubt. But I had always disliked do-gooders, and how I was glad my career as a do-gooder had been cut short. Those kindly middle-aged ladies who visit prisons and slums *need* prisoners and tramps, not vice versa! And yet they want credit and gratitude for acting out their own compulsions and using other people in the process. What about J., W., my grandmother? As G. L. said, we all become what we resist. But surely I can get one stage further now?

---

[34] God knows, he has earned it. –AT

Oh bless you, D.! I love you, truthfully and unashamedly, as you've taught me to. Like G. L., your own insecurity actually helps you to reassure other people! Are you alone to be debarred from the fruits of this miracle? Are we to have the bread and you the nails?

27 June

It is exactly a month since the last entry, and I've been using the second fortnight to recover from the aftermath of the first. Some day, perhaps, I shall try to describe what took place between me and D. between my return from Auckland and my battered departure from Perth; but I should have to understand it first, and that is still a long way beyond me. He did a lot for me, on his own terms, more than that, he had cared a lot. Why then, on our last night, did he refuse to admit that he loved me, putting it all down to mere compassion, and why did I set such a stake on a verbal admission that I couldn't have? It was absurd of me to ask for it in the first place, though his generosity had been such that it never entered my head I could be refused; but to insist, protest, *haggle*, only to have to leave in exhaustion and utter defeat… No, that way madness lies; let me shun that.

No more of that; no more, that is, unless a merciful letter from D. should re-open the questions. Meanwhile, let's use this diary to get over the recent upheavals, to learn to live in the present again, to notice and re-act to my environment, which for the past fortnight I was utterly unable to do. That was in Israel, where I had a much needed holiday with Eve and the Segals;[35] I am now on the plane back to London, and in two days shall fly on to a summer music course in Finland. This is more hopeful, as in teaching I shall be forced to respond to the challenge of the present moment; in Israel, though I obediently admired whatever was being pointed out to me, my friends lost no time in seeing through my mediocre and half-hearted act.

Essentially, my state of mind is that of a convalescent. I eat, drink, sleep (no Tuinal since the arrival in Israel), feel depressed in the morning and merely numb the rest of the day. Life has wrung me out and left me drying on the clothes-line. It is perfectly bearable – most people spend their entire existence in a similar state – and I am not impatient to be alone again. I've re-opened this little book as one takes up knitting…

---

[35] Uri (b. 1944) and Ilana Segal, Israeli conductor and his wife, Tchaikowsky's friends.

2 July

Jyväskylä, Finland
And now for some occupational therapy!

After three days, I can already see that it can work. I am teaching six hours a day, with an office clerk's one hour lunch-break, and there have been long stretches when I've actually attended to what I was doing. Except for one Norwegian, all the students are Finns, all very young, and the standard is astonishing. As far as sheer piano playing is concerned, they really ought to be teaching me! There is a 14-year old boy called Juhani Lagerspetz,[36] who can do anything he's asked before one's had time to finish the request, with ease and evident pleasure, and a smile of joyful discovery that I find immensely gratifying. He's the most amazing of the nine or so I've heard, but most of them are impressive, both in their latent musicianship and actual accomplishment. As for Juhani, I'd like to drag him off to London and go on teaching him! The Norwegian student, Gunnar Sama,[37] is also exceptionally rewarding to teach. He is older – early twenties – and there is little left to show him by now (at least for me), but he seems eager and grateful for whatever I may suggest. In fact, after a while I might find him somewhat ingratiating, whereas Juhani is a gem of modest spontaneity. There have been hours at a time when I haven't thought of D. at all! and when I do, it's without the earlier bitterness. Obviously, work is the answer.

Other musicians here include Szymon Goldberg[38] and the Dvořák String Quartet. Obviously the former must have put in a deft word with the latter, for they asked to see my string quartet, which is just out in print, and might even play it! I doubt it though; the middle movements are hard enough to discourage any quartet not brought up on Bartók and/or Webern. (I only mention Webern because of his difficulties, as he has never been an influence.) At any rate, I gave them the score and parts, and shall try to get a tape from the Lindsays[39] to give the Czechs an idea of what it sounds like. I am impatient to get back to London and some writing, especially *The Merchant*. If I could finish the second act this summer! No, this approach doesn't work: it freezes me up. No self-imposed deadlines. But let's see how much *can* be done…

There's hope for me yet.

---

[36] Finnish pianist, now a lecturer at the Sibelius Academy.
[37] Norwegian pianist (b. 1949) who now teaches at the Norwegian Academy of Music.
[38] 1909–93, Polish-born American violinist and conductor.
[39] The Lindsay String Quartet was a British string quartet active from 1965 to 2005. The members were Peter Cropper (first violin), Ronald Birks (second violin), Roger Bigley, followed by Robin Ireland (viola) and Bernard Gregor-Smith (cello).

9 July

Waterlow Court.

I was, of course, quite mortified to find no letter from D. either at home or at the agents! Then this morning he rang! The conversation was only half-audible and less than self-satisfactory (at some point a third person found himself on the line and wouldn't get off), but the fact of his ringing was immensely gratifying. Why, only yesterday I forcibly restrained myself from ringing him! I'm so glad I didn't.

The reason he hasn't written is that he can't bring himself to say what I have asked him to say in our last talk and in my first letter: namely, that he loves me. Since then, I wrote again to let him off that tricky request, but in my third letter I had to confess that I found it difficult to know how to write till I'd heard from *him*, as there was no telling what kind of correspondence he'd prefer. Perhaps it's the threat of silence that did it, or simply remorse at denying me; anyway he took the trouble of ringing to say that he'd tried to write and found it difficult, as he couldn't comply with the request and was afraid of upsetting me.

It took most of the day to write him a letter. No work got done, and tonight I'm taking a step back: sleeping pills. This disappoints me, as I've been doing very well without them (and probably would tonight), but I want to put a double-bar after the strain of that long and increasingly self-pitying letter, and start afresh tomorrow with work in the foreground of my mind. Yes, I *am* worried about my relations with D.: he couldn't make me durably happy, but he has got the power to undermine all I do and even all I am. No conscious evil could be more harmful than his good intentions. I haven't yet sent the letter, as I'm dining with Chad tomorrow and may show it to him before posting it – he will no doubt wince at the end bit, and I am almost blushing at it myself but I'd rather not have to rewrite it…

15 July

An exciting and happy week-end!

Work, of course: what else? I remember S.[40] saying that work and life are mutually exclusive; he eventually gave up both, or did they give him up? Anyway, I should hardly call him *alive*, and his aphorism, however witty, now strikes me as spurious. Rubbish! Work *is* my life. It is the only field of life I may ever be any good at.

---

[40] Possibly a reference to Tchaikowsky's piano teacher Stefan Askenase.

The last three days, though, were exceptional. Were I less superstitious about counting my chickens, I should not describe them – as it is, I'll merely say that I have done a fortnight's solid writing in a few hours, spread over two days: Saturday and Sunday.   (It's Monday now.) I sketched (admittedly, I had most of the elements before) and today I went on to the next session – the arrival of Lorenzo, Jessica and Solario. The drudgery, of course, is still to come: I haven't even got the *vocal* parts complete. But I've got the shape and continuity, and the kind of impetus that tends to bring the next phase into mind while I am still writing the last one. My mind is alive, my life full…

I sent the letter to D., and followed it by a shorter one, amending a sentence I had regretted very much in the first. By the time he answers (when?) I may be free of most symptoms of that particular meningitis, though I will keep the correspondence up as long as he does – if he should lapse, I shall still go on sending him books and records (I sent another book today). He's been neglected all his life, and all I can do to make up for it will be too little. But it will prove neatly ironic if I end up doing it all entirely for his sake! It's composition I am now hooked up on, and this is just as well, as it greedily takes all I've got and keeps asking more! Fortunately, it provides the very energy it needs, and leaves me with a surplus of vitality that takes several hours to abate – last night, after playing through five violin sonatas, I still had to resort to Tuinal.

16 July

Another improbable harvest: about six pages sketched through in a few hours. This is a state I've known only by hearsay, or at least forgotten since my teens; by the time I'd turned twenty a growingly anxious perfectionism had begun to undermine my spontaneity. After such a day, all I can do is offer a thankful prayer, and this act is as spontaneous as the rest.

At times like this, I need nothing else to make me happy. D. once called it 'withdrawal into work'. As an artist, he ought to know better: what relationship could be more absorbing, more rewarding than this kind of work? I hope he is using his own time to some purpose: I once made him a fierce little speech about his standing on his independence, when in fact he was enslaved by objects (TV, cigarettes, brandy). And noxious objects at that: were I his worst enemy, I still couldn't saddle him with lung cancer, or destroy his brain cells one by one, as the bottle does, or make him stare in front of him all day, like a spastic in a geriatric ward, the way the box does. D., I am working, are YOU?

5 August

Well, it's happened: today I broke off relations with D. He doesn't know it yet – the message may take a week or more to reach him. It's not a letter, merely a copy of T. H. White's *Farewell Victoria* (he'd asked me to get him all by T. H. White that I could) with the book-shop's card paper-clipped to the inside cover, inscribed 'Farewell D.' and signed. He may, at least at first, think it a bluff, an attempt to blackmail him into a reaction. But he'll be wrong: I mean it.

It is now nearly four weeks since I wrote him that long, painstaking and exhaustive letter, and the satisfaction of having at least tried my utmost spurred me on to an almost unprecedented burst of composition. I had no idea what the answer would be – 'Fuck off' struck me as a definite possibility – but I felt I could accept and cope with even that. The one thing that never did occur to me is that there might be simply no answer at all. A week after posting my letter, I grew expectant; three days later, restless; then agitation gave way to an irrational but overwhelming certainty that the answer would infallibly *arrive the next day*. I watched out for the postman's step, which I had grown to recognise, heard the rustle of paper as he pushed mail into the neighbours' boxes, and sometimes into mine. That disappointment over, I'd immediately begin to wait for the next day delivery. I no longer composed, practised, lived: I postponed the mental deadline till the morrow, which was Saturday, and on Saturdays there was only one delivery, at 11 a.m.

I was meditating when it came. The box gave a sharp click: something had come. I forced myself to stay still, eyes shut, thinking the mantra whenever I remembered it, for the prescribed time. I opened the eyes, got up, went up to the box, and sure enough there was an Australian stamp on the envelope. More than that, the postmark said actually 'Perth'. But why had it been addressed c/o Harrison and Parrott, and merely forwarded to me? and the handwriting didn't seem familiar. I opened it and found an insipid, well-meaning letter from some woman who had come backstage after one of my Perth recitals. And now I knew there'd be no further mail till Monday at the same time: 48 hours to kill.

And kill them is just what I did. Now you cannot, except as a figure of speech, kill time, only yourself; at any rate, you can take a holiday from life and consciousness. I took five pills, then a further five, and duly passed out. O bliss! And when I came to, it the evening, I was in a state of drowsy, herbivorous indifference. I lay in bed, equally free from pain and happiness, without any incentive to open the book that lay on the floor, let alone get up and switch the radio on. I didn't want a drink, or food, or even a pee. Had a letter from D. been put into my hand, I might not have bothered to open it. Later on I took another five pills.

This, obviously, was the answer: it erases all questions. I neither could not wish to work, and spent the next few days relishing, if so strong a word can be applied to so pale a sensation, the daily dissolution of my mind through pills. I had never taken them in the daytime; there were now no more days, and time was obliterated too. But my supply was running low, and I rang my G.P. to ask him to send me a prescription. Instead, he asked to see me.

I couldn't go to the surgery drugged, or he'd never let me have what I wanted, so two days before the appointment I went down to two double Tuinals at night. The days were again unendurable, and the chief feeling was that of indignation. Surely, whoever the sender, a letter such as mine did deserve some kind of a reply? I remembered the time when the bloated old she-blob next door wrote to ask me if we were 'still friends'. No, I replied, we were not, but I spent that very evening drafting and copying my letter, and pushed it through her letter-box the same midnight. It's not a question of love, friendship, or even compassion: it's a matter of sheer humanity, when the other person has put his or her head on the block for you, to let them know if the axe is going to fall. 'Fuck-off', by comparison, would have been positively gracious, an acknowledgment of my bare existence, and a definite fact to adjust to instead of the corrosive non-fact of waiting for a letter that might yet arrive any moment (by special delivery), the waiting that consumed, undermined, poisoned and jeered at every hour I lived.

Such life as my mind still led was focused solely on revenge. But how could I do even that, unless he put himself in my hands in any way? 'Too late, D.', I wanted to say, 'you have had your chance.' But he was not pleading for a chance: it was my letter that had been pleading, and it had gone unanswered. Heaven has no rage like love to hatred turned.[41] Did Longreve know Racine? But I also knew, of course, that any letter from D., however inadequate, however belated, would overturn all my teeth-clenching plans of sending it back unopened, with 'TOO LATE' on the envelope. I should *have* to have seen what he said. And having read it, what would I become? 'Hangdog and subservient?'

My charming G. P., Peter Asher, cured me with a few words. Having asked what the matter was, he interrupted me after a couple of sentences with: 'But it's a classical case, André! Your man is a typical psychotic. That's the whole knack of hysterical behaviour: they always appeal to you and reject you at the same time, and never commit themselves to any clear decision. I'll be

---

[41] William Congreve (1670–1729), English playwright and poet. This quote is from *The Mourning Bride* (1697), spoken by Zara in Act III, scene viii.

very surprised if you ever do get the letter you are waiting for, and even if you did, and even if it said everything you wanted to hear, you'd be a fool to trust it.' 'But there's more to it than that, Peter – the man has got genius. His house is full of his own paintings' 'Unfinished ones?' 'Well, mostly...' 'Typical again. It's easier, isn't it, to start 60 promising pictures than to finish one?' 'Is such a man curable?' 'No.' I've never heard him so positive. 'Then there is no point in being angry?' 'Anger, André, is a luxury; can you afford it?' He was really on the ball every time that day. His master-stroke came at the very end. 'Tell me, André, why do you seem to pick out lame ducks? Is it that you feel only lame ones would ever look at you? You are wrong there.' Most head-shrinkers could have envied that.

Since then, I've been on the mend, I can write, play, laugh. I still have fantasies of snubbing D., but they will subside. (A very funny idea occurred to me, mercifully too late, after David C. rang me from the airport, where he was changing planes on his way back from New York to Perth. I gave him a message for Jody,[42] hoping he'd notice the omission, and neither of us mentioned D. Then it occurred to me, after ringing off, that I could have asked David to give D. a totally unexpected and perplexing message: 'David, would you please ask D., as gently as you can, not to floor me with letters all the time? This is getting beyond a joke. Why, sometimes he writes twice a day, and I am getting persecution mania!' What would D. have made out of that? Would he think I've gone crazy, or that he had – to the extent of writing to me, in a trance, without knowing it! –or that David and/or I were pulling his leg? I almost wish I had done it.)

16 August

I am neglecting this diary: neglecting my work, and my life. True, three days ago I reached the long-coveted, long-retreating final double-bar of Act II of *The Merchant*, and Hans K[eller],[43] who saw it that same evening, thought the ending 'smashing'. But it was reached in the sketchiest possible

---

[42] Jody Fitzhardinge first met Tchaikowsky at the beginning of his first visit to Perth, when he approached her for help with his Transcendental Meditation practice. They instantly became close friends and confidants, and maintained correspondence when Tchaikowsky left Australia. Jody also visited him in London. Jody's partner at the time, George Haynes, painted a portrait of Tchaikowsky now kept by Eve Harrison, who inherited it after the composer's death. Throughout her academic career, Jody taught Italian language, literature and art history at a number of universities in Western Australia. She now works in an art gallery specialising in contemporary Australian Aboriginal art, and dedicates some of her time to painting.
[43] Hans Keller (1919–85), Austrian-born Jewish violinist who, arrested and beaten by the Nazis after the *Anschluss*, managed to escape from Vienna to London, where he became one of the most influential broadcasters, writers and teachers of music in Britain.

way: not even the vocal lines have been completed, and sometimes not even established. What I've got is the general drift of the final third of the act, its duration, shape and impetus, the overall harmonic direction. At times there's only the base, or only the tune, without always a clear idea of who is to sing it or play it. And twenty-four hours later I had lost all interest in it.

It's not D.'s fault. True, it is his withdrawal that is the immediate occasion of my near-collapse; but things had to be going wrong for a long time for me to have become so dependent, for my very life-force, on another person. He is a symptom, not a cause. No, it is my withdrawal I've got to acknowledge, my long, stubborn, continuous refusal to join battle in a field I have always known to be particularly dangerous to me, where I am at my weakest and silliest, and which yet cannot be indefinitely by-passed. For all my spurious well-being, at the time I met D., I was probably due to collapse anyway, simply under the weight of my own pent-up sexual yearning; had he not had the foresight to withdraw, I'd have collapsed onto *him*. Why didn't I? Isn't this what happened? And now, when half-crushed by my weight he frees himself in the only way he knows (by ignoring me), I hate him, hate him so much that I should gladly watch him die of cancer, and derive some small comfort from the probability of his own unhappiness. The letter he hasn't written will, I hope, bother him much longer than me. Will it though? There are far fewer events in his life to form a distraction, and he's less mercurial and slower to forget; but then he may be right in saying that he had never loved me in the first place, and he has powers no sane man could. All right then, let him withdraw into a haze of brandy, smoke and schizophrenia! I don't mind his memories of me being destroyed, provided he has to destroy most of himself as well to achieve it. Aren't I a lovely soul-mate?

25 August

I am on the mend.

The turning point came last Thursday, at a dinner-party given by Chad in my honour (as he put it) and for that very purpose! For the first time since my return from Australia, I've found myself really responding to another person; interested in him, not yet exactly attracted, but *willing* to be that as well, should the situation ever develop in that fraught direction. His name is once again David, and he's an actor and a novelist – just the combination of activities that is bound to appeal to my curiosity. His second novel is, in fact, due out tomorrow, but it has already been reviewed by [the] Sunday Times and The Observer, the former being quite enthusiastic. I am eagerly looking forward (a state I had long forgotten!) to reading that novel, and perhaps also be able to see him act. […] The rave reviews have immediately made him appear less accessible: as a successful author, what use can he find for my appreciation, what time for my company? It's almost as if I had preferred him to have bad reviews. Perhaps it will take some success on my own part to enable me to face him. At any rate, the obsession is broken! I have returned to London and the present time. And I've been pushing ahead with the score of *The Merchant*, undeterred by the pressure of early instruments in the Casket Scene, or even by David Munrow's[44] obvious contempt when I asked his advice yesterday. This week I'll experiment with early keyboard instruments at Fenton House (assuming they let me) and find a lute-player to advise me on the scroll-reading song. John T.[45] will no doubt help me there. It's so much easier to live *forward*!

I love Chad more than any of his guests.

31 August

Fatigue and boredom! I've been living above my means for too long and am mentally and emotionally in the red. An earthquake in my front room would hardly interest me. I haven't the energy even to *want* anything, and if sometimes I am lonely, it is only myself that I miss. I still try to keep the work going, three hours a day at the piano, a page a day on average on *The Merchant*. One day – how long from now? – I'll notice I've somehow finished the act, scoring and all, and that will give me all the boost I need. Keep working through the drought and you'll enjoy the rain when it comes.

Company is a waste. I cut a sorry figure at Chad's party, nine days ago now – tongue-tied, tired, *dull*. Why have I been so slow and stupid recently? Is it depression, or the cumulative effect of sedatives? As long as I have nothing on my side to offer, any get-togethers can only be a charity on my friends' part. And we know all about *that* word, don't we? The stingy rat.

An obliging lute player has promised to look in tonight on his way to John Thomson's party and give me some practical information on his instrument. This, and a look at some modern harpsichords will have completed any special research I need to have done for the act. This work is the only thing that still interests me – apart from ever grislier revenge fantasies about D. (e.g. setting him and all his works alight). Of the two, and it's just as well, *The Merchant* is more likely to be finished!

---

[44] British musician and early-music historian (1942–76).
[45] Tchaikowsky's neighbour at Waterlow Court, John M. Thomson, at the time music-books editor for Faber and Faber.

12 September

Calvi, Corsica
I am getting better.

Are those tennis-balls really green? Either that or they're reflecting the surrounding pine trees (in the evening light almost any miracle is possible), or else the game is being played with Granny Smith apples. I am watching it from my fourth-floor balcony, and this is the third of my nine days here.

Another particularity of the place (i.e. besides green balls) is that the girls seem consistently more attractive than the men. Certainly the chamber-maid that looks after me is worth the entire male personnel in this respect – though that's a tepid enough compliment for so delicious a creature, at once merry, beautiful and kind! Just *how* kind? Let's not try to find out. For all I know she might turn *my* balls green.

Anyway, I am utterly sexless at present. This makes the beach a more restful place than usual, free of the nagging temptation to steal surreptitious glances at my fellow bathers, and I was happy to keep my eyes shut and feel the sun on my face. Today I took my first pedal boat since Mauritius (this diary may prove to be in ABA form). The waves did their job and all the money and papers in my wallet are drenched and glued together with corrosive water. I must find some other arrangement.

As a change from horror stories, I bought and devoured my first P. G. Wodehouse! This promises to be a new craze. I can't get any more here, so today I've started *Middlemarch* which I've brought with me. It shows my present determination to regard everything as light entertainment that I've had several laughs over the early chapter! To my surprise, George Elliot seems to get more fun out of Mr Brooke than Jane Austen out of Mr Wodehouse, and she's *wicked* at Causaubon's expense (I've only just noticed the pun in that name now that I wrote it down!). She even ironises about Dorothea's naiveté, which is far more than I ever expected of her.

The light has left the pine trees and taken to the mountains, and the tennis-balls are now white. These are different players though, and I still think the previous pair played with green balls – how could the light effect *follow* the ball, and leave the players' clothes looking white?

So much for my range of interests, and this entry at any rate, *is* in ABA form (this sentence is a coda).

17 September

After the first few days in Calvi, I've relapsed into the most complete apathy. Yesterday, despite the fine weather, I spent most of the day lying on my bed, feeling cross with myself for thus wasting my short holiday, yet unable to summon up the initiative to move. The most unpleasant thought that's been nagging at me is the fear that I might be turning into another D. – the same reluctance to act, to meet people, to take an interest in anything outside myself (or even myself, for that matter). *Am* I turning schizoid? This would be a hideously ironic way of granting my wishes – I had wanted to share D.'s life and I'd be made to share his fate instead! ('… craignez que le ciel rigoureux Ne vous haïsse assez pour exaucer vos voeux'[46]). I now see what folly it was of me to have plunged for an obvious psychotic! And yet, while I was drawn toward 'the tragic type', it was bound to happen. I hereby vow, if I yet manage to recover from my present crippled condition, to avoid anybody who appeals to me through his pathos or frailty. Indeed, it will be a long time before I can really respond to anyone. I used to doubt the possibility of my feelings ever being requited: now the capacity to form the feelings has gone. O God, do not let my soul die! I'd so much rather die altogether.

The other thing that disturbs me is not a mere fear but a fact. I have been taking sleeping-pills for much too long, over twenty years on and off, and I can't help noticing the extent of my mental deterioration. I am losing my memory, intelligence, sense of humour and repartee, am slower in recognising even pieces of music that I've always known, and what would take me two days to learn a few years ago now takes several weeks. I have started to forget people's last names, and can no longer remember the author or context of disconnected remarks that come into mind. Perhaps, by discontinuing at once all sedatives, the process might yet be reversed. But I have no guts for that. I get panic-stricken when I can't sleep at night, and even here, on holidays, couldn't help taking Valium the last two nights. On tour, dispensing with sleeping pills would be simply out of the question. Perhaps, in some two or three years, I could arrange to dispense with touring? But I see no other way of making a living, and anyway, by then I may have too few brain-cells left to be worth preserving. Once again, I can only wish for an early death…

Such thoughts can only lead me to take more, not less, sleeping-pills.

25 September

Ilkley, Yorkshire

I am here to play the first concert of the season, and it is my first performance in four months. I am not nervous, though I am aware of not yet being back in proper technical form and the programme includes a Schubert sonata

---

[46] 'Be fearful, my Lord, fearful lest heaven's rigour/Hates you enough to execute your desire.' Racine, *Phèdre* (1677), Act V, Scene iii.

which I've barely learned (the D major, op. 53[47]). But immediately after writing the preceding dirge, my state of mind clicked back into working order, and since then I've been free of anguish and depression. Certainly there is no question of my developing any form of psychosis and no need to consult a psychiatrist. As for my mental deterioration, yes, that's true – my memory, in particular, is far more sluggish that it used to be. But people live on with one lung or kidney, and there is probably no adult human being with all teeth intact, they get on as best as they can, and so will I. Let's then see what I can still accomplish. If it takes me longer to learn a piece than it used to, perhaps the result will be more thorough? My youth was spoilt by excess of facility.

Why is it that one only has to stop desiring a thing for it to come true? Two nights ago D. rang. Eve was with me at the time, and I was not inclined to pick up the 'phone, especially as the answering machine was on. 'Shall I answer it?' I sad doubtfully, and Eve suggested that it might be something to do with my trip to Ilkley. I picked it up and heard: '458-6625? I have a call from Perth, Australia, for you.' 'From whom??' I asked urgently, meaning to ask the operator not to put the call through if, as at that hour was most likely, it did come from D.; but meanwhile he was already on the line. Now this had been one of my revenge fantasies, along with sending back his letter unopened, and by now I was too well rehearsed to need thought or decision. It was an utterly automatic reflex action to say: 'Good night, D., I don't want to speak to you. Good-Bye!' And to put the receiver down before he could answer. Two months ago, such an action would have been unthinkable; one month ago, a triumph of proud retaliation. At this time, practically all I was conscious of was the urgent desire to cut off all contact with that receiver as if it burned me. It was so spontaneous that I cannot possibly repent it: this *was* my genuine reaction, and at the time, taken unawares, I couldn't have acted differently. Later, I wondered whether I shouldn't have added 'too late!' or something to this effect. D. is probably totally unaware of the anguish and mortification his long silence had inflicted on me, and must have taken my reaction for a mere gratification whim, and a proof of the falsity of all my earlier passionate vows and protestations. But would he have understood whatever I said, when he had obviously misunderstood all my letters? And is it a subject to discuss on the 'phone at 8000 miles distance? It would have taken all night to elucidate it, and we'd have ended in a yet thicker tangle. Besides, I can't help being misrepresented in D.'s mind; what I want is to keep him out of mine. I am only beginning, after a long summer

---

[47] D850 in Otto Erich Deutsch's catalogue of Schubert's music.

of futile obsession, to feel complete within myself and function normally –
can I afford to jeopardise that? At any time during the past five months (it
feels like five years) he could have had my head on a plate if he'd asked for
it, and he couldn't be bothered to ask. *Now* nothing he could ask or say can
make any difference. The D. dossier is closed.

6 October

London
If, in the last few months, I rather lost interest in this diary, it's because
I had lost it in myself. Ever since the preposterous folly of allowing an
evident lunatic act as the supreme arbiter of my value, I've been unable
to regard myself as a worthwhile person. Till then, all I thought and did
had seemed to me interesting – even, or perhaps especially, my failures.
But in submitting myself to D.'s judgment, I had left myself no alternative
to endorsing it; and his verdict, if that's what it was, was more severe even
than my aunt Dorka's. She'd found me hateful, and tried to blackmail and
bully me into what she considered morality and goodness; he simply looked
away. And, since I obviously didn't matter to him, I ceased to matter to
myself and found myself dragging a limbo-like, posthumous existence.
    [...] Recently, though, I've found myself reacting to people and
circumstances much more, even if I still feel too lazy to put my experiences
down in correct English.
    I've played four recitals this week and my playing seems to be improving.
One very welcome change is the almost total absence of stage-fright: indeed
I've now been playing *better* in public than I do at home. This is because
recent events have forced me to see things more in perspective, and I no
longer regard a bad concert as a 'disaster'. One of the characteristics of a
disaster is that one has to live with its consequences: an earthquake may only
take a few seconds, but, assuming one survives it, nothing will change the
pile of rubble back into one's home; or that dismembered corpse into one's
mother or daughter. Having barely escaped total personal disintegration, I
can afford to view a bad performance a good deal more lightly…

13 October

I may indeed give up this diary, because an interesting alternative has been
suggested to me. Jasper [Parrott], my agent's partner, asked me two days
ago whether I'd consider writing a book. 'Whatever about, Jasper?' 'Why,
anything you like. I could probably place it for you, as I am friends with a
literary agent.' 'But what on earth made you think I might write a book?'
'Oh well, you are so well-heeled' [*sic*]. 'You mean I've been tossed about?'

'If you prefer.' And we agreed to arrange a meeting between his publishing friend, him and myself.

At first, I felt entirely skeptical and uninterested. What have I got to say? I've always been extremely egocentric and consequently ludicrously unobservant; most of my life has been spent looking inwards, gliding somnambulistically through countries, times and circumstances without quite taking them in. Now some of those outward events were, so far as I can judge, of some intrinsic interest to the general reader, but I am in no position to report on them: all I could produce is a succession of my states of mind, and what general interest can I claim for that? I am no Gérard de Nerval.

Since then, however, a technical approach occurred to me that has lent the task some interest, if only to myself. This would be to attempt an autobiography[48] constructed as a succession of separate scenes, taken seemingly at random at fairly wide intervals (nine months to a year), letting the reader piece out the intervening events from the latest situation described, without any explicit explanations that could only weaken the contrast. Film-goers are familiar with that kind of narration (I think it's called shock-cutting), but I haven't come across an autobiography written in this way: most of them are dutifully and often tediously continuous. I imagine a book in which chapters would be headed not by titles or numbers but by dates, and all necessary information would somehow be discreetly concealed within the current scene. I would call for a measure of craftsmanship more typical of a novelist than of a memoir-writer, and the difficulties of the presentation would make working on it more interesting that any of the subject-matter (which, after all, doesn't contain anything that hasn't been related ad nauseam). The first thing will be to select the most revealing incidents, the ones that can imply most of what has been left out.

19 October

Well, I did start the autobiography last night, and found working on it so exciting that it's already in danger of eclipsing my piano practice. That would be a pity, especially as I've been at last giving signs of getting back into form. On Wednesday I played K. 482[49] in Bristol, and though a few of the runs were admittedly fluffed, most of the fingerwork showed some sparkle as well as control, and the performance as a whole was lively and confident. Perhaps the débâcle with D. will have been of some use after all. One of my

---

[48] What else can an egocentric write? –AT
[49] Mozart, Piano Concerto No. 22 in E flat major (1785).

curses as an artist and as a man was the pernicious dependence on outside approval, the habit of seeing and judging myself on other people's behalf, evaluating and usually dismissing what I did at the very time of doing it. Every concert was an exam, a trial, and the presence of a knowledgeable friend whom I was anxious to impress would increase my nervousness quite beyond control; unlike most of my colleagues, I used to beg my friends to stay away whenever I played. Well, this is where the D. experience may prove to have helped. As never before, I had put all my strength into winning his admiration, his respect, his love, and he didn't show any sign of being impressed. It was too decisive a defeat to need repetition: the lesson sank in. From then on, I haven't been concerned with anybody's approval – not even my own. Of course, I still try to play as well as I can, because doing something well is more *fun*: but it's the performance I am concerned with, not my *rating*, or any marks I may get for it. I shall play in London, where I've already been at my most neurotic, and we shall see if this attitude holds.

2 November

Well, no, it didn't hold. I was paranoiacally aware of Ilana Segal's presence in the audience and couldn't relax for a moment. Nothing could be taken for granted, the simplest ornament was the object of a separate struggle. Except for the finale of the Chopin sonata (which Ilana, to my amazement, singled out for special praise) I managed to stay in control throughout the long programme, but the effort has left me exhausted, and even now, four days later, I still don't feel that I have quite recovered. The day after tomorrow I'm playing a lunch-time recital at Smith Square, broadcast live and repeated by the BBC next Friday; what will that be like? This time my bogey will no doubt be Stephen Bishop, who made a point of telling me he'd be able to listen. I am feeling really disturbed that he should have taken the trouble of telling me that: he knows me quite well enough to know it could only increase my nervousness. Of all my friends, Stephen is the one most likely to make me nervous, the least apt to overlook technical mistakes in favour of the general conception; he has a way of saying 'oops!' after each wrong note, whether his own or another's, which, though good-humoured enough, strikes me as ironic and unforgiving in its cumulative effect. His attitude is thus in league with that of my super-ego, and he makes it all the harder for me to absolve myself. He registers every slip and reports his findings afterwards. He gives no marks for an interesting interpretation unless its instrumental realisation has been flawless. At my last QEH recital, he was the only friend to be totally unimpressed by my attempt at *Petrushka*, which others agreed in finding colourful and interesting and which to Stephen was merely a mess.

Of course I can't stop him coming to hear me. But why does he have to warn me of his presence beforehand? It's hardly like him to be so unperceptive.

I must stop grumbling. Tiredness makes me irritable. Today, moreover, I've brought upon myself a slightly ridiculous situation: a girl from the Problem cleaning agency who's been here once before, developed some kind of fascination for me, rang me several times and finally prevailed on me to have her clean the flat again. She's arrived 1½ hours late, talked non-stop and bombarded me with loaded questions, all of which I answered. The work was obviously a pretext, and got very perfunctory treatment. Now, mercifully, she's going away.

Later – I talked to Stephen and feel much better. He had simply forgotten my hypersensitivity on that subject.

12 November

If I am to go on with that temporarily discontinued attempt at an autobiography, the only profitable approach is to jot down, loosely and artlessly, whatever memories come to my mind. *Then*, not before, can I confront the one really interesting task of letting events filter through the shutters of my consciousness at the time. Till I know what the events *were*, I can't select among them, and it's futile to look for any special way of presenting them. It's too early to decide what to let my putative reader know, or how to let him know it: first of all I must know it myself, in far greater detail than I will eventually use. Selection, at this stage, is precisely cutting the branch I am sitting on, or spending money I have not yet earned. But doesn't the same apply to the sterile perfectionism of my attempt at musical composition? I begin to prune and fuss long before I've let myself go, before the work has had a chance to acquire any spontaneous impetus. Why can't I write BAD music, as I did, joyfully and spontaneously, in my student days?

My next step in the book will be a cast of characters – a catalogue of all the members of my family and household whom I can remember.

26 November

Travelling from Cumberland to Stratford took nearly six hours, one of which I used to start a new chapter (probably the second) of the autobiography. It may mean nothing, but I really enjoyed doing it: the sense of DISCOVERY is easily my favourite sensation. The first sentence that occurred to me and prompted the attempt is still the one I like best: 'care was taken to choose colours into which the required yellow badge would blend tastefully'. I am quite sure this is factually wrong, and cannot even remember whether such badges were in fact worn in the Warsaw ghetto[50] (why should they have been, since *everyone* was Jewish anyway?). But it does seem a concise and valid presentation of my family's blindness to the apocalypse, and the absurd way they clung for comfort to their gentile ways. Poor souls, they had never before seen a situation in which money couldn't make any difference. What comfort from her knowledge of five languages, or her ability to play the piano, did my mother derive in the gas-chamber?

[…]

6 December

Well, I've finished the *Allegretto giocoso* (at least I think I have) and should be able to orchestrate it in Lanzarote. The four soloists' parts are very difficult to sing and may require occasional doubling. Now there is only the finale left, admittedly a long one, and I hope to put in a few hours' work on it before leaving home (i.e. in the first 3 days of next week) and again on my return, before the piano practice has built up to a full-time daily rate. When that is finished, I shall try to go on with the string quartet, though that could again develop into an obsession and a threat to my work as a pianist! Perhaps it requires a longer stretch of free time. Although an opera is of course incomparably longer, it's also looser, and I can dabble in it – a *recitativo* here, an orchestral interlude there – whereas a close-knit construction like a sonata movement or a passacaglia leaves no respite till it is completed. I remember what the first movement of that quartet demanded of me! At 3 a.m., after 400 mgms of Tuinal, it nagged at me till I got up and sketched out the development section. This is what I love most, and yet I'm afraid of it, afraid of being possessed, cowardly counting the cost and deciding I cannot afford it, and using my piano work as an excuse (though as such, it's plausible enough). And then I complain that I have lost my talent! All I've lost is the courage to bring my imagination to the boil. An hour a day on the string quartet for a fortnight, and I'd be in that state of compulsive obsession that outsiders call inspiration – at any rate when the results are good.

Peter Frankl wants me to write a trio for himself, George Pauk and Ralph Kirshbaum, and though I'd like to try very much, it would be tidier to finish the string quartet first. How long is it since I last completed a piece? Over three years, when the piano concerto was finished. And the boost that gave

---

[50] Inhabitants of the Ghetto were required to wear armbands with yellow stars.

me! I could do with another such boost, and it will be many years, if ever, before *The Merchant* provides it.

Chad came and saw my two autobiographical fragments. He was impressed with the first, critical of the style of the second, and offered some detailed and helpful linguistic correctives. I certainly don't think I shall give *that* up! But it hasn't got to the stage of drawing me in – I write a page or two now and then and have no urge to fill in the gaps, which shows that there at least the overseer has been kept at bay! Easy does it.

It's a very different task from creation: after all, I already know what's happened to me, and all that's left to decide is what to select and how to describe it. This means at least there I'll be free of that anguish of the total void that often makes me avoid composition. A blank page and a blank brain – no one who hasn't experienced that particular failure can guess how helpless and humiliated it can make one feel. Impotence is a joke compared with that.

23 December

In my books, a good day is a productive day, and yesterday was outstandingly productive. For one thing, I've managed to score two pages instead of one, so from now on I can hope to complete the *Allegretto* section at the usual comfortable rate of one page a day. But what was far more important, and totally unexpected, was the sudden breakthrough in my book. Even in sheer quantity, seven pages in one day is well above my standard. But the special quality of the occasion comes from my sudden, unified conception of the 1945 chapter, bringing together the end of the war and the distasteful episode of the poem for Mother's Day and making them interrelate. At the same time, with tremendous excitement which I am very tempted to call inspiration, I heard the imaginary, violent dialogue that alone could give the incident all its meaning and make it palatable – without which, indeed, I could never have brought myself to relate the matter. It is one of those early actions that spread a slimy trail of shame and self-disgust over the rest of my life, and for which I had never been able to forgive myself. (Perhaps I shall now, having made a public confession of it). Not to have missed a murdered mother may be callous enough, but children *are* callous and need to be, in sheer self-protection. So far I am excusable. But to write glib tear-jerkers about her loss, *to order*, for other mothers, alive and well-fed, to sniff sentimentally into their fancy handkerchiefs! How little real grief I must have felt to make this tart's performance possible! Or, rather, how deeply repressed it must have been! It was a double hypocrisy: I first had to pretend to myself that I didn't miss her, so I could pretend to others that I did. I am still nauseated at the sheer cynicism of it.

When I discussed this with M[ichael] M[enaugh] a few weeks ago (the only person, apart from my two psychoanalysts, who's ever heard of it) I said I couldn't bring this act of mine to the public knowledge, and he said I should try. Since then, I had not thought of it and on this holiday, till yesterday, the whole book had been lying fallow. Then, about noon, while I was waiting for some friendly neighbours I had invited for a spell at the hotel beach, the vicious phases of my inner dialogue with my mother burnt into my consciousness. I was aware of their importance and decided not to work on them till my visitors had left, as it was the kind of activity I should have hated to have to interrupt. At first, I didn't know where or when the dialogue would take place; as a reaction to Mother's disappearance, it was most likely to take part during my reflections in front of the end-of-the-war poster. It wasn't even yet a dialogue, just bitter reflections about Mother choosing to die with Albert rather than try to save her life with me ('…il me sera plus doux/De mourir avec lui que de vivre avec vous'[51]). Then, 'she' changed to 'you' and immediately the tension increased. The next step was to think of Mother's answer, which, as she was a product of my memory and imagination, couldn't include anything I hadn't known of her fate at the time. Just as Racine had helped me to frame my reproaches, Shakespeare gallantly handed me out a line that could sum up her most probable attitude: 'No longer mourn for me when I am dead'.[52] There was a third literary reminiscence, Oswald Alving's 'I did not ask you for life',[53] which I recognised in my own 'I didn't want a chance; I wanted YOU.'

Then came the brain-wave. Why not make me talk to Mother in my head in this way *while* I was writing that wretched sentimental poem? True, at the factual level, I had done nothing of the sort at the time. But what does my share of the talk express but the very real grief and resentment that had been bottled-up ever since her disappearance? Are feelings only less real for being suppressed?

I wrote that whole scene at one sitting, in under two hours.

28 December

Back to the cage at Waterlow Court where all my habits join forces against me and every wall is saturated with my old neuroses! All the symptoms

---

[51] 'It will be sweeter for me to die with him than live with you.' Racine, *Andromaque* (1667) Act IV, Scene iii.
[52] Shakespeare, Sonnet 71.
[53] From Henrik Ibsen, *Ghosts* (1881), Act III. The line Tchaikowsky refers to in fact belongs to Oswald Alving's mother, who tells him: 'Oswald, I never asked you for life'.

are back: causeless fatigue and irritation, constant tug-of-war between the urge to escape from friends and pseudo-friends and the guilty attempts to conciliate them, the pending insomnia. (Fear of insomnia already *is* insomnia, just as fear of impotence brings on impotence.) I have no guts to say: 'Look here, you're a charming person, but I simply can't see you' (or even 'don't want to see you'). What I say instead is 'I can't see you till next Tuesday.' I know it will only ruin my Tuesday, but for the moment three days' freedom from, say, John T. is as much grace as I dare beg. 'Tuesday, then?' he says eagerly. I beam 'This will be *lovely!*' And, amazingly, this tired, pointless old act still takes them in. [...]

When will I learn to say no, to stop making polite offers in the hope that they will be refused (and which are, needless to say, almost invariably accepted) and wearing friends and acquaintances round my neck? [...]

31 December

So, what was 1974 like?

Emotionally, of course, it was awful – the worst year for a decade since M[ichael]. R[iddall]. and I split in 1964. It's good to see that one can survive such a year and see it, with puzzled wonder, from the other side.

Musically, it was very much better. Last summer, despite really pathological depression, I got far more writing done than at the corresponding period in '73. Most of the concerts were decent too. In fact, last season was probably my best to date (the present one has been nothing like it so far).

And haven't I been happy some of the time? Yes, I have! The first four months of the year were a delight. It says something for my enjoyment of the Perth set-up that *despite D.* I have never ceased to look forward to my return there! Jyväskylä is another place I'd like to re-visit. And as holidays go, Lanzarote was one of the best.

What should I like to see happen in '75?

My greatest fault in my own eyes is laziness. If only I didn't make such a fetish of sleep! And why is it so natural and easy to get up early on holidays, while it takes hours of ludicrous inner conflict every morning at Waterlow Court? Why can't I just get up as soon as I'm awake? I'd actually be less tired on less sleep. Why is my first impulse on awaking to look at my watch, as if there was a set hour before which it was a sin to be awake? Shall I try putting my watch outside my reach, so that I have to get up to get to it? But then wouldn't I simply drag myself back to bed? It still sounds worth trying.

I'd like to write so much more! Finish Act II of *The Merchant* (I am in fact disappointed it's not finished yet), do at least one more movement of the string quartet, perhaps start on the piano trio. I had hoped to write the epilogue of *The Merchant* next summer mid-July, and everything takes me so long, so bloody long… And now there's the BOOK!

Is it a fallacy to think I could accomplish more away from London, where there would be no distractions – no friends? Shall I try to sell this flat and get myself a place in the country, whether I do eventually emigrate to Australia or New Zealand or not? Wouldn't a fresh environment give me a boost? Somewhere on the seaside or at least a river. Or perhaps Cambridge? It would also be Eve's weekend place, and an *occasional* visitor would be welcome. But enough of this city of ten million, nine and a half of which seem to be forcing themselves on me! A house in a village with one grocer's shop which sells everything and doubles up as post-office, some lovely scenery, and a 'phone I could plug out. No contact with the neighbours. The hordes of friends I've met everywhere on my tours all converge on London and make a point of looking me up, but would they follow me to Backwater-on-Sea?

Let us start with a fresh set of habits!

1975

13 January

Can I be so incredibly lucky as to finish the draft of Act II tomorrow? There is so little left that I can barely resist the demand of my super-ego to *force* the work through tonight. But at last I am learning from experience, and I know such convulsive, self-coercing efforts to produce nothing but dismay and exhaustion – and today I have done quite enough. In fact I am surprised, for the weekend was distracting and tiring enough to make any results improbable! On Saturday, after an absurdly early start and a day trip to Oxford, I still *made* myself work for nearly an hour before supper, and sure enough next to nothing got done. I went to bed early, without pills of any kind, and drifted off quite easily. At 3.15 the 'phone rang; it was MM,[1] sobbing and inarticulate with distress. I told him to come over, gave him whisky and a large dose of Valium, and kept him here throughout yesterday and last night. At first I thought he might recover enough to be sent out to the cinema, so that I could write for a couple of hours, and he himself was quite anxious not to be 'in the way'. How glad I am that he didn't go! By 9.30pm he was giddy and nearly passed out. Had he gone out, this might have happened in the cinema, in the street, while *crossing* the street; he could have been run over. He is emotionally and nervously exhausted, psychically run down, and yesterday was the only free day he had in many weeks, and his nearest approach to a rest after a catastrophic personal upheaval. I ended up by giving him the spare keys, so he can use this flat as his own whenever he chooses, and come and go whether I'm here or not. He probably won't sleep here tonight, but he's promised to ring tomorrow and report on his general condition. I'd feel easier if he had a medical check-up.

And this morning did away with two of my long-standing assumptions: one, that I can only work efficiently if I've had enough sleep, and two, that I cannot write a note away from the piano. I woke up at six, meditated,

---

[1] Michael Menaugh.

had a lemon tea, and took the score into the bedroom 'just to have a look'. Within an hour and a half I'd harmonised the entire coda (strictly speaking, the middle part of it, as the beginning and end were already there), and checking it at the piano found it quite all right! I also filled in the harmonies of two earlier pages (at the piano, when MM had left) so that now there are at the most two pages to compete – possibly one, as the first of them may prove to be quite full enough as it stands. Even tiredness is a pleasure for such a good reason.

There are two reasons why I had long set my heart on finishing the draft by tomorrow: firstly, I am showing it to Hans[2] in the evening and secondly I've got to get back to practising the piano on a full-time basis – i.e. with undivided concentration. Whether I finish the Act or not, I have *got* to shelve it. I shall try not to give in to the usual sense of failure if it's not *completed*, just as I am now trying not to make, as so often before, this self-imposed deadline a 'fetish'. If I had obeyed my super-ego and sent my ailing friend out last night, I shouldn't have had anything like the spontaneous play of invention that took me by surprise this morning. If I obeyed it tonight, I'd produce either nothing at all or the dreariest dutiful homework. So let's enjoy the well-earned fatigue!

Much else has happened this week, most of it interesting and rewarding (except, of course, for the inevitably disappointing sequel to the Steve episode, which I shan't bother to report). There was the dinner with David Cook[3] and John Bowen,[4] who gave me a copy of his *A World Elsewhere*, a rather self-consciously intelligent and well-written book; the visit to the Redcliffe-Mauds[5] at Oxford; the Young Vic's production of *Rosencrantz and Guildenstern Are Dead*, which is not a play I expect to survive, despite the brilliant idea![6] But the one event I *must* record is Tony Rooley's[7] help with the lute part in 'You who choose not by the view'. After checking the playability of the chords, he said: 'Aren't you rather wasting the lute? It will look good on stage, but the little that will be heard could as well be played by *pizzicato* strings in the pit. The lute is basically an *obbligato* instrument. It

[2] Keller.
[3] British author, screenwriter and actor (b. 1940).
[4] British playwright and novelist (b. 1924). *A World Elsewhere* was published by Faber, London, 1965.
[5] John Redcliffe-Maud (1906–82) – raised to the percentage in 1967 – was a British academic, civil servant and diplomat; his wife Jean Hamilton (1904–93) was a pianist. Benjamin Britten's *Young Person's Guide to the Orchestra*, Op. 34 (1946), is dedicated to their four children.
[6] An absurdist tragicomedy, first staged in 1966, by the British playwright Tom Stoppard (born Tomáš Straussler in Zlín in Czechoslovakia in 1937).
[7] Anthony Rooley (b. 1944), a British lutenist, a founder of early-music ensemble the Consort of Musicke, and from 2008 a Vice-President of York Early Music Festival.

13.1. – Can I be so incredibly lucky as to finish the draft of Act II tomorrow? There is so little left that I can barely resist the demand of my super-ego to force the work through tonight. But at last I am learning from experience, and I know such convulsive, self-coercing efforts to produce nothing but dismay and exhaustion – and today I have done quite enough. In fact I am surprised, for the weekend was distracting and tiring enough to make any results improbable! On Saturday, after an absurdly early start and a day trip to Oxford, I still made myself work for nearly an hour before supper, and sure enough next to nothing got done. I went to bed early, without pills of any kind, and drifted off quite easily. At 3.15 the 'phone rang; it was MM, sobbing and inarticulate with distress. I told him to come over, gave him whisky and a large dose of Valium, and kept him here throughout yesterday and last night. At first I thought he might recover enough to be sent out to the cinema, so that I could write for a couple of hours, and he himself was quite an-xious not to be, "in the way". How glad I am that he didn't go! By 9.30 PM he was giddy and nearly passed out. Had he gone out, this might have happened in

6

can contribute more than mere chordal accompaniment! In fact, unlike the guitar, it's not an instrument that sounds at its best in chords. What it excels in is single-line ornamental tracery. Listen…' and he played an example. After he left, I wrote non-stop till nearly 11, and finished the scene in full score, *obbligato* lute and all, at one sitting. Perhaps I am finally learning to think less and do more?

Later – why am I so tempted to take some Tuinal tonight? It will be the first time in over a month. It is particularly silly because I no longer *need* it: I should sleep just as well on Valium, and often go off on nothing but whatever I drink with my meal, and I've found myself both more relaxed and more alert on whatever amount of sleep I get these days (admittedly less, but without Tuinal I *need* less). Why, of all times, tonight, when my only chance to complete the draft in time to show Hans lies in my being wide awake tomorrow? Perhaps this is just why. Perhaps I instinctively fear that feeling of being 'on duty' under my ruthless super-ego's orders, which would no doubt wake me up absurdly early and drive me to work. Perhaps it's that 'must' attitude I seek to avoid. Instead, the delicious alternative of almost instant and complete oblivion, a slothful, long, groggy morning, a suspension of self-imposed responsibilities… Yes, I shall take them. They may harm tomorrow's prospects less than all this mental standing to attention. Yes, but will it make me slip back into taking them again night after night? Will they be even harder to resist tomorrow? There is, damn it, always *some* reason to take them, once one's set on proving it to oneself… Still, I'll take the chance. I've been almost *too* good recently, and am growing smug. Don't I need that feeling of moral abdication after the various efforts of the last few days?

14 January

To the best of my belief, I've finished the draft of Act II.

P.S. –Hans shares my enthusiasm for it.

30 January

I am on my way from Oulu to Tampere, two small Finnish towns. If Oulu is anything to go by, only a fool would be patronising about Finland. With a population of 80,000, they have a university, an opera, and a symphonic orchestra giving 25 concerts a year (as opposed to 4 in Hemel Hempstead). Playing Prokofieff III with the latter must have seemed foolhardy, but they gave a very competent account of it, and their American conductor, Stephen Portman,[8] clung to me whatever I did like a keen rider to an unruly colt. Socially, Stephen took up most of my time, so there was none for any of the innumerable solitary occupations I had planned to go ahead with (correspondence, proof-reading of the piano concerto, this diary, even

---

[8] Portman (born in Mount Vernon, New York, on 1 January 1935) studied piano with Paul Wittgenstein and Paul Nordoff, and conducting with Pierre Monteux, George Szell and Sibelius' son-in-law Jussi Jalas. In a career spanning 25 years, he conducted the Cleveland and Royal Philharmonic Orchestras, the Finnish National Opera and the BBC Singers, among others.

possibly working on my book). But it was so enjoyably spent that I couldn't possibly begrudge it.

Stephen, whether he knows it or not, is a comic character. For one thing, he looks strikingly like Charlie Chaplin, which alone would impart unintentional humour to whatever he says or does. For another, he seems to suffer from intermittent amnesia, which drives him on to talk ever more, and ever faster, in an attempt to catch the drift of his own elusive thought. 'What was I saying? Oh yeah – I did this piece – I mean conducted it – what the hell was it, it's on the tip of my tongue – you know, by the same guy who wrote whatitsname – anyway, as I was saying, there was this piece and I was doing it – now, why the hell am I telling you this?' 'Stephen', I said, 'are you sure you did conduct this piece?' a pause, while Stephen frowns and tries to think. 'Er…ah…I *may* have'.

We soon discovered, amid torrents of disconnected talk, that we have many mutual acquaintances from his New York days; indeed he even claims to have met *me* there, and though I don't remember it, anything Stephen actually *remembers* should be treasured, let alone believed. Another pleasure was meeting a friend of his, a delightful German teacher called Frank Merkel, who flew with me as far as Jyväskylä this morning, and may come on to Tampere and hear me tomorrow. Having lived abroad for many years has made him speak language slowly, clearly and with unusual care, and I find myself understanding everything he says! He is intelligent and full of gentle humour, and though between him and Stephen I've hardly had the chance to be alone (which I normally find indispensable), I didn't for a moment regret it. I ended up giving him my address, as we got on so well that it seemed a pity to lose touch; normally I only give my address when specifically asked for it, and my 'phone number not even then.

Letter-writing will just have to wait!

4 February

Lahti, Finland
The conductor in Gävle[9] was also called Czaikowski![10] He is Polish and married to a lady who claims, no doubt rightly, to have studied with me at the Warsaw conservatory. He showed me her photograph, but she is not embalmed in my memory. Needless to say, I also pretended to remember her.

---

[9] A historical city in Sweden, the capital of Gävleborg County, and the oldest city in Sweden's Northern Lands.
[10] Renard Czaikowski (1934–2000), Polish conductor.

Hans Keller and Milein Cosman at Dartington in the mid-1970s

He is insecure, nervous and given to bragging, and his conducting is a series of jerks. This was particularly noticeable after Paavo Rautio's[11] masterly ease and flexibility two days before Tampere. A flexible beat can accommodate anything unforeseen, but Czaikowski's is as rigid as the tick of a metronome. When he does try to follow one, it is a series of desperate mini-emergencies – one for every beat.

An embarrassing thing happened just before the end of the rehearsal. I farted! Fortunately, I remembered Mozart's correspondence,[12] which gave me the nerve to weather it (though not to look at anyone, of course). Later, a memory came back to me after decades of repression, and I immediately used it in my book. It is one of my earliest, and concerns my grandmother farting at dinner, and accusing mother of it. Mother would simply apologise, and my grandmother would point out to me how much her daughter loved

---

[11] Finnish violinist and conductor (b. 1938). He was principal conductor of the Tampere Philharmonic Orchestra from 1974 to 1987.

[12] Mozart referred to bodily functions freely in his letters to his family. *Cf.*, for example, the letter to his cousin Maria Anna Thekla Mozart, dated 5 November 1777 in Robert Spaethling (ed. and transl), *Mozart's Letters, Mozart's Life: Selected Letters*, Faber and Faber, London, 2000, pp. 86–88. Benjamin Simkin dedicated his *Medical and Musical Byways of Mozartiana* (Fithian Press, McKinleyville, Ca., 2001) to discussing scatological passages and remarks in 39 of Mozart's letters. Tchaikowsky will have known Mozart's letters in the edition by Emily Anderson, *Letters of Mozart and his Family*, 3 vols., Macmillan, London, 1938.

her. (This is all she was trying to prove by laying the blame on my mother: everyone knew the fart had come from herself, and she didn't mind it.)

All yesterday was spent travelling. I had lunch in Stockholm and dinner in Helsinki, with my respective agents. Mrs Wide, who represents me in Sweden, is a well-meaning, chatty, Jewish-mother type; her Finnish counterpart, Mr Groundström [*sic*], impressed me much more – I was polite with her and merry with him. The morning and evening were both spent on trains, the afternoon on a plane. One might call it a full day!

I bought some Doris Lessing novellas, and read one of them – a substantial one, *The Temptation of Jack Orkney*. She seems to me a thinker and a moralist rather than an artist, but I'd say the same of George Eliot! Some people are both, either at once, like Constant,[13] or alternatively, like Tolstoy. Anyway, the novella is very impressive…

15 February

I am sitting opposite Stefan Askenase in his dining-room. He is writing letters while I am idly chewing over the impressions and events of the past few days. The Helsingborg programme yielded some unexpected fun, as I had learnt the Badura-Skoda version of the Mozart A-major rondo (most of the original has, of course, disappeared)[14] and the orchestra, despite several insistent requests, got the score and the parts of the Einstein version. I was told this by Uri the evening before the concert, on my arrival from Joensuu; there was a single rehearsal the next morning. Uri then left me with the score, which proved far more different from the version I knew than I had expected: even the distribution of solo and *tutti* passages was often different, so that I had to shut up where I had expected and learnt to play and vice versa. Some of the obviously orchestral passages Einstein put into the piano part struck me as quite unacceptable, but it was too late to write them into the orchestral parts, so I had to work out, or improvise, equally long alternatives! I had two hours at my disposal that evening, but a good hour and a half went in fact into the K. 595,[15] which was the main work on the programme, so that I only *thought* about the rondo. I went to bed quite exhausted (I had, after all, been on two planes, a train and a boat

---

[13] Henri-Benjamin Constant de Rebecque (Benjamin Constant; 1767–1830), was a Swiss-born French politician, writer on politics and religion, and author of the partly autobiographical psychological novel, *Adolphe*.

[14] The Rondo for Piano and Orchestra in A major, K386. The German-American musicologist and music editor Alfred Einstein (1880–1952) believed it had been composed in late 1782.

[15] Mozart, Piano Concerto No. 27 in B flat major (its dates of composition are unsure and are estimated to be somewhere between 1788 and 1791).

before starting work, and had to walk with all my luggage from the landing-place to the hotel, as there were no taxis!); aware that I had hardly covered the ground but without the energy to worry.

Well, it all went without a hitch. Uri, conscientious as ever, devoted an even hour to the 7-minute piece, and the concerto, which we had played together before, and which he had carefully rehearsed with the orchestra on the previous day, for once took good care of itself. Not that I shall let this encourage me to take any piece for granted in the future! In fact, my attitude at the concert was wholly serious including, in the concerto, some nervousness as well as concentration. In the rondo, I was too amused by the aleatoric elements of the performance to be nervous, but the necessity of alertness was of course obvious enough! This was, then, a good concerto, and it concluded a very pleasant and on the whole successful tour. Tchaikopath rides again!

Stefan, who at 79 is still one of the liveliest and most amusing people I know (and, of course, one of the most civilised) told me of his visit to a sex-shop in some small German town. They sold, among things he was perhaps too well-bred to mention, aphrodisiac chocolates. He asked 'Haben Sie diese Pralines für Diabetiker?',[16] a question which may have created a new branch of the industry.

Another of his stories: in the twenties, when Paderewski was Prime Minister or president of Poland,[17] Stefan went back from Cairo and arrived eventually in some Polish border town. On arrival at the hotel he was asked to leave his passport with the receptionist, and a few hours later heard that the passport was being held by the police, for reasons unknown, and that he was to pick it up at the police station. Unwillingly enough he went, asked for it and was told to wait. Then, from the next room, he heard the following exchange:

– Have we got a passport of some Askenase?

– Yes, I took it to check on his military record, but the chief said you must give it back to him for he is a concert pianist and will certainly be a minister soon! You cannot be too careful with *that* bunch.

And the policeman was all smiles and compliments when he brought back the passport.

---

[16] 'Do you have these pralines for diabetics?'
[17] Paderewski was Prime Minister (and concurrently Minister of Foreign Affairs) from January to December 1919, whereafter he was Polish ambassador to the League of Nations. He retired from politics in 1922, re-emerging to head the Polish parliament-in-exile in London in 1940, although he died soon afterwards.

Opening of the Piano Concerto, Op. 4

11 March

[…] Carlisle tomorrow; Newcastle on Thursday; our own London QEH on Friday! There is of course a rehearsal before every performance, as the three different halls will present different acoustical problems (there was to be one today, but they *noticed* a few hours before I was due to set off from London that they didn't have a piano at their rehearsal centre in Newcastle!). And the journeys – to and from Carlisle tomorrow, down from Newcastle to London on Friday… And then the nerves.

How nervous shall I be this time at the QEH? Have I practised the Schumann adequately? Hardly, though I did make a determined effort to weed out the accumulated mannerisms that had gradually distorted my interpretation of the piece and made me avoid it for the last four or five years. Yes, it's at least that long since I last played the piece, and even longer since anyone had enjoyed it! (Except for Larry Foster,[18] who seems to *prefer* messy performances, and who conducted my last attempt at it.) Certainly I should never have chosen the piece, if there was a choice. I have little to offer in it; I no longer even *like* it. But given these circumstances, I shall do whatever I can.

27 March

I am on my way to Houston, where I am playing the Liszt II with Larry – a very welcome new addition to my repertoire. This is the beginning of a long and wide-ranging trip, including a stopover in Tahiti, nearly two months at my beloved Currie Hall in Perth, a very crowded 4-week tour of New Zealand, and two concerts in Mexico City on my way back. I expect to be away for at least four months.

Away from where? For by the time I get back to England, I may no longer have a home of my own: I've decided to sell it. Eve will take care of all the arrangements and will also try to find me a secluded cottage in the country, where I can at last become what I have so long desired to be: a recluse. It will free me of the seemingly innumerable friends, pseudo-friends, well-wishers and acquaintances who smother and exhaust me whenever I return to London; and who knows, perhaps it will also free me of my own stale habits? The habit of lying, due to cowardice, which makes me say: 'I can't today, but perhaps next week' when I really mean 'Never', a lie the other person is nearly always obtuse enough to take at face value! The habit of laziness, of long hours spent chatting on the 'phone or reading horror-

---

[18] The American conductor Lawrence Foster (b. 1941).

stories in my rocking chair, so that it takes me all day to fit three hours'
practice into a flaccid, bloated out, distorted schedule (Dali's soft watches
seem to have been invented for me), of whole mornings in bed, prostrated
with chronic fatigue and oppressed by guilt, hating myself for not getting up
but hating the thought of work even more; the tedium of chores, shopping,
cooking, looking for mislaid objects in a cramped, claustrophobic flat,
littered with far too many ever-accumulating possessions; the persistent
fears of interference on the part of well-meaning neighbours and friends, as
if I didn't interfere with my own plans myself![19] How much of this can be got
rid of through a simple change of environment? I shall still, after all, be the
same person. But yet aren't I freer almost anywhere else, and above all, don't
I get more *done*? Even on this flight, I've already managed to complete the
proof-reading of the second instalment of the piano concerto. Again, this
entry is the first in over two weeks, and the last one was also written on a
trip, and also on the way out, not on the way home. Home, with its incessant
petty distractions and preoccupations, takes away all my initiative.[...]

30 March

Houston, Texas
Who shall be here but Horowitz! No other name could have excited my
curiosity to such an extent. Although I have met him and played to him in
'57 (an episode which, after many revisions, has become part of my after-
dinner repertoire),[20] he then had already gone into the long retirement from
which he re-emerged only recently, and I had never heard him play except
on records. Judging from some of these, his 'monstre sacré' status did for
once seem based on some reality and his most fanatical worshippers include
some particularly hard-bitten pianists (for instance Stephen [Kovacevich]).
Yesterday I easvesdropped on him from the wings while he practised on his
own piano in the concert hall, and the snippets I heard made me want to fall
at his feet. The sound, in particular, was enchanting in a thousand different
and unexpected ways, and even though in the abstract I might not always
have liked *what* he did, the *way* he did it was breathtaking in its artistry. This
morning, while looking for a piano stool in the empty auditorium before
my own daily session on the remarkably heavy resident piano, I couldn't
resist sneaking in and taking a look at this fabulous animal Horowitz takes
around whenever he goes, *by air*, at his own astronomical expense. The
first surprise was to find it unlocked, the second to find it a Baldwin: in

[19] And what about the supremely noxious habit of barbituates? –AT
[20] *Cf.* p. 54, above.

Working on the orchestral material for the Piano Concerto, Op. 4,
to be premiered in October 1975

'57 H[orowitz] was certainly a 'Steinway artist' and it was a Steinway that I played at his home. Under my fingers it sounded very unremarkable, light in action, brilliant in treble, but without the depth and vibrancy I heard it yield to its owner.

Now that the concert is over, I recognise that preliminary anticipation to have been the most exciting part. (Isn't this what happened to Marcel with La Berma?[21] I wish I had the Proust here to re-read the relevant passage). For once in my life I was early, panting with impatience, and the recital started 15 minutes late. He got a tremendous ovation before playing one note, people yelling 'bravo' at what they hadn't yet heard, so instead of beginning directly he was forced to get up and bow again. He then produced a careful, sophisticated and totally unspontaneous Haydn sonata (No. 52) and followed it up with a cloying chi-chi performance of *Kinderscenen* (a piece I detest anyway, with its continuous *gemütlichkeit* – how much did Schumann really remember from his own childhood? It's the musical equivalent of little Nell! The lady on my left whose snores made me giggle was giving the valid comment on the work and performer alike. He only came into his own with an apocalyptic rendering of Scriabin's Fifth sonata. After the interval he played the Liszt E-major Petrarcha sonnet and *Au bord d'une source*, Chopin's a-minor waltz and b-minor Scherzo, and four encores; the first three of these at one sitting, barely stopping to announce the next piece. They were an enchanting Scarlatti sonata which I didn't know (in A major – I could look it up),[22] a horrible early Scriabin etude, and Moszkowski *Etincelles*.[23] Then he walked off-stage, re-appeared and made a show of going back to the piano at a sudden impulse, which brought the public to the point of orgasm. (But I had heard him try out 4 encores the day before, so I knew there was still one to come). This time he played some unidentifiable monstrosity, phenomenally difficult and phenomenally vulgar; it would be plausible but unkind to attribute that aberration to Rachmaninoff, and I am more inclined to believe it one of Horowitz's own transcriptions. The playing was, of course, unbelievable – it had been that throughout the second half.

The thought that moved me most was that here was a man who had, for twelve or fifteen years, given himself up as finished, and yet, judging

---

[21] Reference to an episode of Proust's novel *À la recherche du temps perdu* (1913–27), where the Narrator's excited anticipation of seeing the actress La Berma in a play turns to disappointment.

[22] Horowitz played four Scarlatti sonatas in A major over the course of his career: κ39, κ101, κ322 and κ533. During this period it was κ322 that he had in his repertoire.

[23] *Étincelles*, Op. 36, No. 6, is the sixth piece from Moritz Moszkowski's *8 Characteristic Pieces*, published in 1886. It was one of Horowitz's favourite encores; he even composed his own coda to the piece.

by present results, must have spent each day of those apparently barren years, working hard and lovingly at his craft. What integrity! And what courage to re-appear in public at 72, after over a decade's silence, and with a mythological reputation to uphold! Can this be learnt?

Of course I didn't go backstage to try and be re-introduced to him. Whatever for? He surely doesn't need *my* praise. As for myself, I had already had the best he can offer: he plays as only he can, but he'd no doubt say hallo just like everybody else. That's a point snobs will never understand: they get a kick out of any triviality that passes between a famous person ('a big name') and themselves. Oh Judy Arnold, will you never learn?

What did give me a kick is cutting out part of the front page of his programme, pasting it on a piece of paper and sending it to Terry Harrison with the laconic comment 'The competition is quite tough in Houston'. I was so pleased with this little joke that I sent it to two more friends – carefully chosen, so that they shouldn't meet and find me guilty of repeating my jokes!

2 April

Well, it was a very pleasant six days. Houston itself is a dehumanised nightmare, but the orchestra, apart from being excellent, proved appreciative, warm-hearted and companionable. Coming one day after Horowitz (and playing moreover, pretty sloppily, even by my own erratic standards) I didn't expect any success at all either with the public or the critics. I am not, of course, as monstrously conceited as to regard H[orowitz]'s visit as in any way relevant to the efforts of someone like me, but I rather expected the critics to use his name as a weapon against me, just as they once used my namesake's. Well, they didn't, and what's more they received me very favourably. The second performance was more relaxed and on the whole better, despite a catastrophic wrong note at the climax of my solo in the central section that drew a startled gasp from the audience. Larry Foster, one of the most dependable conductors around, later told me my *accelerando* before the first cadenza is impossible to follow ('you simply must get to know the orchestral part better'), but he's invited me to come back all the same and I accepted with sincere alacrity. [...]

One of the reasons of my present good mood is that I have been determined to keep it this way. I blush to acknowledge it (snobbery again!) but I was very impressed with a booklet entitled *How To Be Your Own Best Friend*[24] which I found at the hotel newsstand and read through at

[24] Mildred Newman and Bernard Berkowitz, Ballantine Books, New York, 1971.

least twice. Embarrassed as I may be at finding wisdom in an American *bestseller*, I have to concede that it says a lot of things that I particularly needed to hear, and phrases the advice in a way that makes it particularly easy to implement – or is it that I've read it at a time when I'm ready for it? Anyway, for once good advice is as tempting as the most picturesquely sinister promptings, and I am going to try following it.

The points I shall particularly try to keep in mind are:

Stop trying to please other people.

Make a point of noticing what I've done right (very important at concerts).

When things have gone wrong, forgive myself as quickly as I can – it makes it incredibly easy to forgive others. […]

Stop depending on will-power – especially as I've hardly got any! To begin with, I may not start on my autobiography this evening, although I had long decided on the two long flights to Los Angeles and Tahiti as offering the ideal opportunity. It looks too much like a decision 'from above'. Instead I'll start writing it when I happen to be thinking of it, which may or may not be tonight. In any case, I've done two pages of orchestration in the last two days, which I had not expected as I was playing a concert last night, and in obedience to a genuine impulse. Often deciding *not* to do something creative frees such an impulse, which no amount of self-nagging could have brought about! It was after I had made up my mind not to work on the book in Lanzarote that the Mother's Day episode[25] came to me and took me unawares! It's by far the best thing in the book.

It is a long flight, though: three hours to Los Angeles, and about 8½, if my calculations are correct from LA to Tahiti, so boredom may yet drive me to work on the book. Or shall I get drunk and try to get some sleep on the way? If there are 3 empty seats in a row, it might prove feasible. In either case, having nothing to read is an advantage (I did look through the Houston airport bookstall, but found nothing of compelling interest).

Later – I've already managed to lose my raincoat, almost certainly at Houston Airport – not that I mind. But my gloves were in one of the pockets, and I must remember to get a new pair along with a new overcoat.

9 April

Apart from the inevitable fatigue, a very pleasant 24 hours in Sydney. The jet-lag phenomenon has increased my usual absent-mindedness to an absurd point, and the first thing I did on arrival was to lose my ticket. By the time I had reached my hotel and noticed the loss, it had been found (in the

---

[25] A reference to Tchaikowsky's unpublished autobiography; *cf.* pp. 78–79, above.

customs' hall at the airport) and the information on it duly computerised, so all I had to do is to pick it up today before flying on to Perth.

Although I could barely keep on my feet when entering my room, I couldn't resist just checking on what was on at the famed Opera House. The newspaper I bought didn't yield any information, so I walked over to find things out on the spot. This is what I found:

Opera hall: no performance. The Australian ballet will start something at the end of the month.

Concert hall: no performance. The eternal van Otterloo[26] is conducting there tonight, but not last night.

Music room: a festival of adventure films.

Theatre: 'A funny kind of evening with David Kossoff'.[27]

The only musical event in the grand building was taking place at something called The Recording Room. It was a recital by a pianist called Stephen MacIntyre (have I got the name right?) As he was starting with Beethoven op. 101, he had to be either great or really foolhardy, and statistical probabilities favoured the second hypothesis, so I decided to give him a miss.

But oh, the glorious building, the incomparable, spacious and intricate harbour! Sydney may not be the city to live in, and it can be infuriating if one's got anything urgent to *do* there, but for sight-seeing it must have few if any equals. I found myself wishing for a week or longer to explore it, take every ferry and get off at each separate stop, get to know how the various innumerable bays and peninsulas relate… One day I'll make a point of staying over and treating myself to Sydney.

Meanwhile, Perth. How shall I fare this time? A second visit is notoriously dangerous, especially when the first has been such a success. Shall I disappoint them, have they come to expect too much? Is there any danger of my getting tired of them? This has happened many times, notably at Dartington, but I find it hard to believe of Perth, when everyone is so good at leaving me alone. In any case, a second visit is a far subtler challenge than the first. I'll have to keep very alert, and I am feeling anything but that at the moment.

David Bollard will meet me off the plane […]. Does it mean Frank's[28] too ill to come? There'll be several changes. Margaret's husband is back, which means I'll have to win *him* over, if the friendship between me and his

<hr>

[26] Jan Willem van Otterloo (1907–78), Dutch conductor, cellist, and composer, chief conductor of the Sydney Symphony Orchestra from 1971 to 1978.
[27] British actor (1919–2005), who became known for a series of monologues based on the Bible.
[28] Professor Sir Frank Callaway; *cf.* p. 101, above.

wife is to continue; the Tunleys[29] are away, which *may* mean Frank being in charge, unless he is positively bedridden; David C. is out of the country; D., of course, out of bounds where I am concerned. The subject change may be in my relation towards the community at Currie Hall. At my first visit, I knew no one and set myself the special task of winning them all over; this time the problem may be how to keep them at bay without offending them. Till I've got over the fatigue of the journey (3/4 of the way round the globe, after all), got adjusted to the change of time and got back into my stride pianistically, till I've set up a working routine and am beginning to notice some results, there can be no question of bridge-and-lager parties, long chess sessions, or using my 'fridge to play Father Christmas to the boys (if I still have a 'fridge). Later, yes: not now. I must return *casually*, without any welcome-back parties or mutual effusions, without any attempt on my part to regain my former popularity. If I don't try, no doubt I *shall* regain it, and they'll respect me all the more for not courting it.

A footnote to the activities of the Sydney Opera House: one show that filled it was '*Les Girls*, the world-famous all-male revue!' How could Mozart stand a chance after that?

16 April

Perth
Yes, the old charm still works!

For all my cautious resolve [...] I couldn't resist the pleasures of popularity. The merry student crowd at Currie Hall all but staged a festival to welcome me back, the older student and staff members saying 'We've all been waiting for your return', the newcomers introducing themselves and saying 'I've heard so much about you'. A particularly charming specimen, called Dawson Johns, came up to me with the words 'Hallo André, whom I don't know yet know!' and within half an hour we had got a bridge game organised. Chess got played too, with Joe Lam, and a trip down to the beach yielded, beside a swim in the salty and deliciously mountainous Indian ocean, the unexpected discovery of a nearly all-male, and obviously homosexual, nudist colony! Joe Lam drew my attention to a part of the beach that was about five times as crowded as the rest, and said it was a nudist colony (though he assumed it to be a mixed one), so I went out to investigate. It proved unsurprising: flabby middle-aged gentlemen, ostensibly engaged in a laborious slow-motion mimicry of keep-fit exercises, ogled some genuine

---

[29] Professor David Evatt Tunley (b. 1930), Australian musicologist and composer, now Emeritus Professor at the School of Music, University of Western Australia.

young athletes who never gave [more] than a glance in return. Both sides were equally self-absorbed and therefore equally unattractive. I'm not tempted to go there again!

What did prove fun was the Sunday afternoon event. The students had bought huge rusty-looking vats of some cheap and really rather foul wine and made a great occasion of bottling and labelling it. As I didn't trust my skill with the large and to me unfamiliar corking-machine, I joined the crowd that was engaged in finding labels for the bottles and contributed several ('Dracula's Kiss', 'Pink Mia' and, in a fit of candour, 'For external use only'). At the same time, a three-boy band treated us to ever louder and faster renderings of the never-on-Sunday tune and similar finds, the authentic touch being provided by a bazouki [*sic*] (along with an electric guitar and a set of drums). Some of the students danced, a few of them quite beautifully; others, shamelessly but predictably, helped themselves to the red vinegar they were supposed to bottle. It's been the most enjoyable episode of my stay so far.

[…] Despite the flurry of social and peripherally professional activities (correcting programme notes, setting up the teaching schedule, getting interviewed, and of course visiting half the members of the Music Dept, I've managed to keep practising three hours a day and orchestrate the *accelerando* which leads to the second *Allegro con Brio*. The latter task, however, can no longer be continued on a daily basis, and today I'd decided not to practise either. As it happens, I've also scratched my right middle finger with the top of a beer-tin (how Australian!), but I had reached the decision before this happened. Now I'm off to give my first lecture, on the Mozart Fantasy and sonata and Op. 106;[30] shall I be able to play the illustrations?

23 April

Well, no, I could barely play the illustrations, hampered more by my nerves than by the plaster on my finger; but despite that, the lecture was a great success. I did it off the cuff, which suits me best, and found myself saying things I hadn't been aware of knowing; two hours elapsed without any effort, padding or fatigue, and I could have gone on much longer if Frank [Callaway] hadn't stopped me. My first recital, two nights ago, was more debatable. I had prepared it carefully, with a diet of at least three hours practice a day and early nights, which helped me to avoid panic and futile self-reproach: it didn't quite manage to ensure an accurate performance, and the outer movements of the *Hammerclavier* were full of loud and noticeable

---

[30] Beethoven's Piano Sonata No. 29 in B flat major, Op. 106 (1818, known as the 'Hammerklavier').

clinkers. The other piece, Mozart's *Fantasy* and Sonata in c-minor, was in my own opinion, almost uniformly excellent, the exception being a rather hasty and occasionally untidy finale. My good impression of it was confirmed by a girl graduate I had taught here last year, who slipped backstage at the end of the interval and said: 'Fantastic! You are better than last year'. What perfect timing! Just when the imminent opening of the 106 made me most need encouragement. Her opinion, however, was not shared by David B., who, as I've noticed before, has the reluctance to accept another man's interpretation of any work from his own repertoire (not out of jealousy, but because he's so identified with his own conception that he's come to believe the piece cannot be brought off in any other way. I have exactly the same problem with the Mozart c-minor concerto and the Schumann and Chopin fantasies). I had expected it, just as I know in advance he won't enjoy my performance of the Schubert B-flat sonata, *however* I play it, so it doesn't really worry me. […]

I am anxious to hear Margaret's[31] reaction: David has hinted that she also hadn't liked the Mozart, and no doubt the 106 disappointed her even more, for she didn't even come backstage.[32] She is at once honest, sympathetic and discriminating and even her criticism may somehow prove reassuring (mine did to Stephen over the Diabelli).

[…]

11 May

A crowded week, both with people and minor events. It would take many hours to describe it all. To begin with, I shall briefly skim over my third sonata recital, which was successful 'on balance', ranging from first-rate playing through various shades of hard trying to downright disaster. Beethoven's op. 90[33] was fair, but no more; Schumann's op. 22,[34] played *so rasch wie unmöglich* with the *schneller* and *noch schneller* not merely observed but often anticipated,[35] was unintelligible even to myself. Things improved after the interval: the Haydn No. 23 was excellent, and most of the Mozart K. 333[36] well in control – calm, expressive, varied. The exception was the semiquavers in the rondo which tended to end faster than they had begun

[31] Emeritus Professor Margaret Seares, now Chair of The University of Western Australia's Perth International Arts Festival.
[32] She did in fact like the Mozart, but not the Beethoven. –AT
[33] Piano Sonata No. 27 in E minor (1814).
[34] Piano Sonata No. 2 in D minor (1831–38).
[35] The first movement bears the indication *So rasch wie möglich* ('As fast as possible') – qualified later in the movement with *Schneller* ('Faster') and *Noch schneller* ('Even faster').
[36] Piano Sonata in B flat major (1783).

(a typical failure of mine). As I sat down to play the encores, a male voice boomed out: '*The Moonlight*'! 'Well no, not quite, but almost', I answered, 'here are two pieces by Schumann called *In the Evening* and, predictably, *In the Night*.' I had only meant to play *In der Nacht* but threw *Des Abends* in on the spur of the moment.[37] By now, though, I had very little concentration left, and *In der Nacht*, although duly practiced beforehand, was an unqualified mess – a tachiste[38] exhibition by untrained monkeys would have made more sense. While splashing through it, however, I thought: 'Suppose I *could* play *The Moonlight* after all? Wasn't it cowardly of me to refuse the challenge?' I finished *In der Nacht* as worst I could, came back for the curtain call, sat down at the piano again and, sure enough, heard '*The Moonlight*'! This time it was a girl's voice, softer more tentative and full of suppressed laughter, which in turn gave rise to a few titters. 'All right!', I roared, 'you've asked for it, you shall have it'. Of course I was determined to play it by then, even without the second request: I had to rescue the evening after the flop of *In Der Nacht* and show myself a sport in the process. *The Moonlight* was what I'd sat down to play.

As I began, there was a collective gasp of recognition. This time I concentrated very hard   I *had* to, in order to get through the piece at all – and produced a really intense, committed and surprisingly controlled performance. The evening was saved!

Margaret Seares, who had heard me prepare most of the programme and got emotionally so keyed up that I resolved never to involve her in this way again, came to my room afterwards for a detailed post-mortem. There was, however, a less serious reason for her visit, and here it comes:

HOW LOVE CAME TO GRAHAM HAMISH PEARSE:
(A romance in prose).

When Hamish apologised for raiding my 'fridge, I suggested that we go for a walk. We reached the Broadway Fair and Hamish stopped in front of the pet shop and pointed lovingly at a white cockatoo, saying: 'I am going to get one of these before I go home.' Then seeing the thought that came into my face, he added quickly: 'No, not you – *I* am buying it!'

A few days later, another student told me that Hamish had decided to leave Currie Hall, go home and try to 'straighten himself out'. It wasn't

[37] 'Des Abends' and 'In der Nacht' are the first and fifth of Schumann's eight *Fantasiestücke*, Op. 12 (1837).
[38] *Tachisme* was a school of 'action painting', originating in France in the early 1950s as a reaction against Cubism, using drips and blobs straight from tube (*tache* is French for 'stain') and spontaneous brushwork to eliminate a sense of form.

certain whether he'd suspend his studies or follow the course from home. Then on Sunday, the 4th of May, the students in the dining-room greeted his entrance with 'Happy Birthday to you'. He sat down at a different table from mine, and I didn't join in the congratulations. Instead, I thought:

'The cockatoo! Of course! It will combine as a birthday and a farewell present. How tiresome that it should be Sunday and the shops are closed! What fun though – even a day late! This will establish me as part of the Currie Hall legend ("Remember the day André let loose that cockatoo?"). It will have to come with a birthday card. Shall I attach this to its neck, or will it then eat it?'

And so on. Poor Hamish was, of course, the least of my preoccupations: I saw a dashing gesture to make, a figure to cut, and if he had changed his mind about the bird, this would only make it even funnier. That evening I composed a limerick:

> Many happy returns, me old mate!
> May grog flow in your life by the crate,
> And since by what I've heard
> All you want is a bird,
> Here is one – take it out for a date!

I was very pleased with this effort, my début in English poetry. I rang my ally Margaret S, and she immediately offered her car to transport the bird (saving me the task of walking with it right through the campus looking like Papageno). We hesitated between three alternatives for our next step. What would be funniest: let Margaret leave the bird at the office, saying, in her most poker-faced manner that it was a gift for Mr. Pearse, she being merely an employee of the pet-shop? take it into the dining-room, where the students were just having lunch? or take advantage of that same lunch to leave the cockatoo, complete with cage and limerick, in Hamish's room? We decided on the last course of action, one of the tutors innocently lending me the pass-key, and this is why Margaret and myself were so eager to come back in the evening and see the general reaction.

These wasn't any. No one seemed to have heard any special news. We knocked at Hamish's door and got no answer. This made us anxious for the parrot: if Hamish hasn't been back, won't it be hungry, thirsty or incontinent? We did feed it when we brought it in, but neither of us had any idea of its daily needs. We ran into another tutor and asked him to open the room, still without saying why (all tutors have pass-keys). By now there were quite a few of us, and though no one but Margaret and myself knew what to expect, everyone sensed something unusual afoot and was pent up with curiosity and latent amusement.

The sight that confronted us was no less of a surprise to the two conspirators than the rest of the crowd. On one side there was the parrott, well-fed and content, with plenty of seed and water left in its cage; on the other an unconscious figure lay motionless in bed. The unopened limerick lay on the table just where we had left it, next to an empty brandy bottle. The others chuckled; Margaret and I exchanged a look of concern and shock.

[…] A surprisingly alert and chirrupy Hamish re-appeared at breakfast. He sat down opposite me and said:

'It was you, wasn't it?'

I should have liked to mystify him, but there was no chance: I was the person he had pointed out the parrot to. I nodded and smiled.

'It was the poetry that gave you away. When I got back last night, I didn't really see the bird for some reason (sic!), or perhaps I just thought I was seeing things. But this morning it was still there, and once I noticed and read the verse I knew it was you: you always call me mate.'

'Must be my mating urge.'

'Do you know, I'm really pleased to have it? I have called it George. It doesn't say anything yet but in a month or so it should get really friendly. Thanks a million, man!' (Hamish is MATE and I am MAN).

The next time I called on him, he was reading a Mickey Spillaine novel[39] aloud to George, who didn't show any signs of suspense. Hamish looks after him beautifully (I also gave him an instruction booklet with the faintly alarming title *Enjoy Your Parrot*), and many people in the hall have commented on the general improvement in his state of mind and behaviour. As a joke, my idea misfired; but to my own surprise, it actually seems to have *helped* the boy, which is just what I had been trying and failing to do. Perhaps this is the only kind of relationship he can maintain. Here is someone perfectly dependent on him but whose demands will never increase; who'll never walk out on him, or snub him, or answer him back (for a month, at any rate). With gloves on, he can paw George as much as he likes. The formula for helping people is 'STOP TRYING!'

1 June

[…] The last movement of the Beethoven was a shambles last Thursday; I simply can't play the semiquavers. There is just one more programme, consisting of the Schumann Fantasy and the Liszt sonata, due to take place

[39] Mickey Spillane (Frank Morrison Spillane, 1918 –2006), an American author of crime novels, many of which featured his signature detective character, Mike Hammer. It is not known which of Spillane's novels Tchaikowsky is referring to.

at lunch-time next Thursday; the same evening I am to give a lecture on the Mozart c-minor concerto and the next day I am due to leave for Sydney and New Zealand. This is what I regard as a 'cluster' and such clusters always fill me with panic. Some comfort can be derived from the thought of cancelling the first date in New Zealand, which is a whole week earlier that the rest of the tour; if necessary, I'll see the local doctor when the time comes and try to get a medical certificate letting me off. Meanwhile, tomorrow is a cluster in itself: practice all morning, taking out the whole Music Department to lunch, meeting the Samaritan lawyer in the afternoon, *and* giving a concert to the Currie Hall crowd after dinner! I'd do better to go straight to bed.

P.S. – George Haynes, Jody's boy-friend who is a painter of some reputation, had done an oil portrait of me at my studio a few days ago. And now he's given it to me! This must be one of the most generous presents I've ever received: it's like being given a grand piano. It's the more generous as George and Jody are by no means well-off…

7 June

Yes, I am going to appear in NZ on schedule! I am on the 'plane to Sydney via Adelaide, and shall spend most of tomorrow completing the journey to Dunedin (which includes a long transit stop in Christchurch). There is a particular ironic satisfaction in thus meeting the appointed day and confronting an audience unaware of my hectic activities in the last few days, or how close the concert came to being cancelled. It's like a Mozart coda!

My stay in Perth had a natural stretto-finale. I have never lived more fully: though in love there have been stakes of greater intensity, here intensity was combined with variety, ceaseless and challenging activity, and humour – a quality that only happy love-life allows to come to the surface. Once, long ago, Shura Cherkassky[40] asked me 'What is happiness?' and I improvised back 'Living with the whole of yourself'. By that definition, which I still think valid, I have never been happier than now. There was hardly a cell, nerve or drop of blood in me that hasn't been brought into action: sex, that facile substitute for really exciting things, was the only form of action that didn't come my way, and I never missed it. (I never do miss it in the abstract, unless a particular individual is concerned). […]

Thursday – Have I ever had a busier day?

After many attempts, I got up in time to have a shampoo and a sandwich before warming up for the concert. The latter was billed for 12.45, an earlier time than usual due to the length of the programme and the doors would

---

[40] Ukrainian-born American pianist (1909–95), based in London from 1961 until his death.

have to be opened at the latest by half past twelve, so the warm-up would have to start within minutes of noon – and duly did. But almost immediately there arose the following disturbance:

The ABC had asked to film part of the concert as a sequence in a programme on University life, and I had replied that they were welcome to it as long as no TV lamps were used. While I played myself in, they put up a microphone, cameras and other apparatus. As I got up and turned around to walk off the stage, I noticed that a lamp had in fact been installed and switched on.

'This must go off', I said.

'We cannot film in here without it', said the producer.

'That's as you like: either the light or myself will go off. It was the only condition stipulated when letting you film.'

I went into the dressing-room and a minute later the producer came in after me. From the door he said bitterly:

'We have wasted two hours of our time.'

'There must have been a failure in communication', I began mildly, unaware that the man I was speaking to was the very man who had promised the Music Dept. not to use the light. However, my comparatively conciliatory manner was due more to the need to protect myself from my own anger, within minutes of playing, than to any desire to spare him.

'We've wasted two hours of our time and ruined the story. Thank you very much!'

'You're most welcome', I said in my haughtiest voice.

It later turned out that the man had already been rude to Prof. Callaway and actually swore at the secretary of the Music Dept.!

The programme consisted of the Schumann *Fantasy* and the Liszt sonata.[41] It is not a good combination: the demands of the Liszt reduce the Schumann, which though much less difficult is emotionally nearly equally high-powered, to the status of a warm-up piece! My mind, obsessed with the tour de force awaiting it, could only react to the Schumann as something else to be played before the Liszt, thus robbing the first movement of all its intensity, while the second was, of course, a mess. The last movement, which I had always played in four, emerged alla-breve this time,[42] and alone proved to be a success. The tempo wasn't faster than usual, but flowed better, especially in the bridge-passage with irregular rhythmic groups; there was

[41] I preceded it by an announcement: 'Ladies and gentlemen, we've all heard of unrequited love, but there is no such thing as unrequited friendship. The Schumann *Fantasy* is dedicated to Liszt and the Liszt sonata to Schumann'. –AT

[42] That is, played in two.

no need for any changes of gear, so the over-all atmosphere produced all the cumulative effect I was aiming at.

Now for the Liszt – a very different experience. It is lucky that its sphinx-like introduction is easy enough to dispense with practice (I'd been a fool to practice the Schumann), so its dark threat took me unawares; I was gripped, indeed scared, by its very first note. In what followed a good deal went amiss – the left-hand octaves in the coda were, of course, a foregone conclusion – but the emotional response was there in all its intensity, and variety, and the audience was as hooked as myself. After the end there was a long, long silence: I was too exhausted and awed to get up, the crowd to applaud. It's a most welcome encouragement, as I have committed myself to play it in London in November! Obviously the experience I provide in it is sufficient to 'absorb' the mess, just as it was in *Petrushka* two years ago.[…]

17 June

Tauranga

And on Saturday I did an excellent K. 491[43] in Wellington! One of the best. One of the factors that helped it came from the local meditation teacher, who gave me a check-up two days before the performance, and on hearing my usual claim that nothing noticeable has happened to me, said:

'In this case we'd better go into it a bit, for you're the only one. No one has ever meditated regularly for more than two years without deriving *some* benefit from it: whether you notice it yourself is irrelevant. Has nobody among your friends remarked on your being more relaxed than before?'[…]

Yes, I am getting better at everything except dealing with people. Last night, I wasted an hour and a half with two kindly bores because I felt it would have been rude not to invite the local manager for a drink after the concert. It's true that he'd been very kind, but I could have spent that time writing letter to my *real* friends…

29 June

In flight

'O, how shall summer's honey breath hold out against the wrackful siege of battering days?'[44]

In fact, this particular honey breath is holding out quite well! Five concerts in six days, with as many trips in between, and I am still in working order. True, I take ludicrous amounts of sleeping pills (400 mgms of Tuinal + 20 of

---

43 Mozart, Piano Concerto No. 24 in C minor (1786).
44 Shakespeare, Sonnet 65.

Valium), but during the day I feel well up to things. Of these five concerts, only the last one was poor, not so much from fatigue as from having no one to play *to*: it was the only recital of the week, no conductor or orchestra to relate to, and nobody I knew in the audience.

For it seems that my nearly life-long phobia of colleagues and discriminating listeners at my concerts is at last disappearing! London will prove if my hopes are justified. Only a week ago I reproached the Radio NZ concert manager for telling me that the outstanding young Kiwi pianist Michael Houston would come to hear me in Timaru as well as Dunedin, but the latter's presence in fact proved a stimulant. It has occurred to me, *for the first time*, that only the listener discerning enough to detect my mistakes will notice and appreciate any good ideas I may have, especially the sophisticated and subtle ones I am most proud of. It's the experts, not the bumpkins, that I should aim at! (Stephen is an exception: he's far too preoccupied with technical perfection. But Radu is the last person to be kept away from my concerts, and I shall positively play *to* him the next time he comes – so far, I've been silly enough to beg him to stay at home and made him miss, among other things, my best K. 491! What does he care about my mistakes? It's my idea of the piece that interests him.)

My conductor here was Brian Priestman.[45] He's extremely accomplished at holding the orchestra together, as he showed in *The Rite of Spring* and in following most of my rhythmic vagaries in the Chopin f minor [...].

Personally, he's charming, a born raconteur and has a wit of lightning repartee. For instance:

I: Is sex really all that important? I can go without it for months on end, like a camel without water.

BRIAN: You must have a very big hump.

[...]

26 October

Now, at last, is the time to re-open this long abandoned diary! In two days time my piano concerto is to receive its first performance at the Festival Hall, with Radu Lupu as soloist and Uri Segal conducting. Radu has been working as never before and plays it like a fiery angel! Sometimes he does the opposite of my dynamic markings and every time the result is better. For the last week, ever since Uri's return from New Zealand, we have been

---

[45] English conductor, born in Birmingham in 1927. After holding positions in Canada, New Zealand, South Africa, the UK and USA, he retired in 2003.

practising the piece every day but one and today a run-through proved all but sufficient (despite my making an awful mess of the second piano part).

The orchestral rehearsals start tomorrow. This is the danger, for the piece is almost impossible to prepare within the four hours the Royal Phil. [harmonic] put at our disposal tomorrow; there'll be a general rehearsal on the day, but that can hardly be more than a run-through, with three hours, minus, the break, for the entire programme! The Franck symphony alone takes nearly an hour, and there is also Mozart's D-major Concert Rondo. No, whatever work the piece demands must somehow fit into tomorrow's schedule.

A more serious fear is this: how much of what I have written is unplayable? How much will I be asked to re-write? This may lead to sheer panic, for any necessary alterations will have to be made *and copied into all the relevant parts* between 4pm tomorrow and 10 o'clock on Tuesday morning. It took me at least 50 hours just to correct the parts… However, we shall see – I'll just do whatever I can. At any rate, there seems to be very little chance of my finding time for this diary in the next few days!

My chief feeling is intense curiosity. *Can* orchestration be learnt just from books? To what extent have I learnt it?

27 October

Well, unbelievably, nothing has had to be re-written! The horns did, as I expected, complain towards the end about having not enough time to insert or remove the mute, but the general laughter that followed Uri's answer to them was not at my expense. Uri said simply: 'Use your hand', an infallibly popular old joke. Bars 149 to 161 of the Finale will be played by solo strings, and this is, so far, the *only* alteration. Chris Seaman had suggested this very change on first seeing the score years back in Wellington! Otherwise, the orchestration is of course not perfect (too many secondary details which can't be heard, especially in the *Agitato* section of the *Passacaglia*), but often very effective, at times striking, and the general effect should prove worth the effort. John Schofield,[46] who was sitting with me throughout the rehearsal (and to whom I soon hope to devote a separate entry) said to me: 'I did not know you were such a romantic'. How good to have my music speak for me!

6 November

And this entry is being written with John Schofield's ball-point, part of the Parker set he madly and wonderfully sent me on my birthday. As I had

---

[46] John Schofield of Josef Weinberger Music Publishers.

*Radu Lupu (left) and Uri Segal, soloist in and conductor
of the first performance of the Piano Concerto, Op. 4*

foreseen, there was no time to continue this diary in the past ten days: it can prove almost more strenuous to survive a success than it is to prepare it.

That it *was* a success is undeniable. Virtually every musician in London was there (some, but not many, as my guests) and most of them were far more impressed than they had expected. This was above all due to Radu, who gave one of the greatest performances I've ever heard of anything (comparable, say, to his Brahms I, or Beethoven III). From his very first entrance, he held me spellbound, and I listened to every phrase with incredulous awe. It's truly amazing how often he would take me by surprise, sometimes by his exquisite timing, sometimes by a subtle departure from the indicated dynamics, which every time proved an improvement on what I had written! Perhaps I only provided the notes and Radu the piece? He was also intensely aware of his share of responsibility for the ensemble, and the first two movements were virtually flawless – not merely accurate, but uninhibited and exhilarating. The first sign of fatigue came in the first *tutti* of the finale, which Uri, who had been living on nerves for over a week, had never had time to rehearse properly; it sounded slow, cautious and limp, a bedraggled survivor of the *Capriccio*. Again, Radu's first entrance brought fresh authority and urgency, but the movement as a whole didn't seem to cohere very well – not at any rate as an *Allegro*, which should indicate an attitude as well as a tempo! Most of it was way under full speed, and the RPO strings obviously haven't acquired the knack of plucking with alternate fingers, which put a frustrating brake on Radu's *Piu veloce*! Radu again brought matters to a clinching pitch of intensity in the final cadenza, which was played so hauntingly that at times I barely recognised it! This was just as well, for immediately afterwards the orchestra fell apart in the *Molto allegro* and kept only approximately together in the Tempo I; Uri, by his own admission, is not cut out for this kind of work.

Of the many compliments I received through that evening and the following week, the most surprising was the rave review in The Times, written by Joan Chissell, who'd hardly ever found a good word for me as a pianist! Now, however, she suddenly referred to me as 'the eminent pianist' and described the concerto in the most amazing hyperboles. But the one that gratified me most was a 'phone call from Tamás Vásáry,[47] who had never rung before and spent the first five minutes apologising for ringing me now ('I know you don't like being called, but Peter Frankl said he assumes the entire responsibility for this call'). Coming to the point, he then said:

'Since Bartók died, there has not been a piano concerto on this level and I had come to believe that it was no longer possible to write one today. Your concerto has proved me wrong. It is definitely a work in the great tradition and I am sure it will eventually become part of the repertoire.'

If only I could agree! For what Tamás said corresponds exactly, not to my achievement, alas, but to my ambition. I *had* set out to write the best piano concerto since Bartók. I did think of it as a contribution to the repertoire, in relation to it, feeling all the weight of that long tradition that has now nearly spent itself out. I was never content merely to write another piano concerto!

Have I succeeded? Not quite. The Concerto evolved while it was being written, and it's now the earliest written parts – the Introduction and Finale – that satisfy me least. I had set out to write an austere, neo-classical concerto, void of all irrelevant virtuosity, with every note derived from the main theme. Then, by the time I reached the cadenza, I felt the need for something different – freer, more fluid, more singing, and I thought of the glorious cadenza of the Schumann concerto. This was what I now needed – something in deliberate contrast to the rest of the movement. I had already made up my mind to work out my first movement as a Passacaglia, and now I tried out the first phrase (i.e. the climactic phrase of the *tutti*) against the *ostinato* bass. It worked!

Later it proved a lot of hard work to expand this cadenza into a passacaglia polyphonic enough to introduce most of the instruments one by one, and now it really does sound as if the cadenza, which had in fact been done first, was a condensed recapitulation of the earlier movement. But its romanticism spread itself all over the passacaglia, and the macabre scherzo, written last, only intensified the effect. Where was my neo-classical concerto?

---

[47] Hungarian pianist and conductor (b. 1933).

What I have got is a deliberately arid introduction and a predominantly four-square fugal finale framing two movements of far higher emotional intensity. Hans Keller doesn't agree that the finale is ill-suited to the work – on the contrary, it enriches it according to him, whereas a more romantic last movement could have made the whole work sound hysterical; in any case the cadenza and coda bring both aspects of the piece together, so all is well! But he does agree with me that the introduction is too long and monotonous, the original idea sounding too bare when it re-appears shorn of its counterpoint (the *ff* dialogue between trumpets and strings-cum-woodwind after bar 30 or so). I also find bars 85–120 of the finale an academic, thick, laborious bore; the capriccio, on the other hand, couldn't be better, and little need be done to the passacaglia – I was a fool to limit the number of violins to sixteen, which is too thin for the climax, as Andrzej Panufnik[48] pointed out in his orientally polite way! Also, the flute in bars 126–132 or so needs to be marked up. Shall we call it a 90% success?

---

[48] Polish composer (1914–91), based in Britain after his defection from Poland in 1954.

Isn't it fitting that I should have lost my diary on the flight from Johannesburg two weeks ago, just as I was retu... ...ossession of my new home? For from no... ...past is to be considered irrelevant. Never mind what I have wanted, suffered, feared, achieved: I have that rare chance,

1976

25 June

Cumnor

Isn't it fitting that I should have lost my diary on the flight from Johannesburg two weeks ago just as I was returning to take possession of my new home? For from now on, all my past is to be considered irrelevant. Never mind what I have wanted, suffered, feared, achieved: I have that rare chance, a new start, and I don't want it weighed down by obsolete habits (feelings also are conditioned by habit).

I am not even sure whether I shall continue this diary at all. There is something tiresomely self-conscious about keeping a diary, like living under one's own anxious supervision, the Catholic examen de conscience. I may jot something down now and then, but will not let it become another self-inflicted duty. And yet this is precisely why I'm writing now! For days now, I've been feeling positively guilty at not inaugurating this note-book, as if an examiner were awaiting it.

At any rate, I have laid aside the famous autobiography: I am heartily tired of wallowing in my own retroactive bitterness. People and circumstances did me a lot of harm at one time; granted, but the time isn't now, and they can only go on hurting me if I let them. Let's outgrow them instead.

One part of my past that will stay with me, I hope, is work. If Act II of *The Merchant* had been left on that plane, I'd have been in a very different state! As it is, I've started on Act I; perhaps here, with a peaceful environment, a detached house in which I can make what noise I like, and no interference except the occasional visit from well-meaning friends, I shall at last learn to combine piano practice and composition.[1]

It's a fair chance, for several things here have proved easier than I had expected. The biggest surprise was Tuinal, which I haven't taken for 3 weeks and am not tempted to! I was determined not to take it at Cumnor, seeing

---

[1] I'm making it a rule to practise 3 hours a day before any writing. –AT

172

it from the first as the-chance-of-a-lifetime to break free of the habit, but I did expect to have to revert to it on tour. Well, I took them with me when going to play a recital in Durham, and forgot to take it! I had wine with my dinner on the eve of the concert, lay down for an hour's rest, and woke up in the morning. Perhaps I'll be lucky enough never to take the hateful things again. The milder sedatives, Dolmaine, Valium, do get taken occasionally when I wake up after three hours' sleep, but I no longer swallow them as a matter of course, without giving natural sleep a chance…

Many other things have proved easier than expected, and several misgivings unfounded. The neighbours, while kind and helpful if necessary (and they already *have* proved necessary when I locked myself out within a week of my arrival) show no intention of thrusting themselves upon me and killing me with kindness, and the practical business of running a house is actually easier in the country where plumbers, builders etc. are less overworked than in London and easier to get. Also, from being the filthiest slop of my own acquaintance, I am developing into Mrs Ogmore-Pritchard![2] I wash up (not the Siberian martyrdom I had expected), wipe the floor when I've spilt something, remember to put the dustbin out for collection on Tuesday…

In brief, I am all aglow with the quiet content of my new rural life. How did I ever stick it out in London (a very strange sentence, that) and for so long? Sixteen years infested by tedious irrelevances, an unweeded garden. Talking of that, a gardener is coming on Sunday…

Personal life? There is none, and I do not miss it. I doubt if I shall seek out – if anything is to be it will have to come out and find me. How sincere am I writing these words?

And I am developing a possibly dangerous weakness for the local cider.

1 July

In flight from Zurich to London
Fun!
I had just come back from my sunset walk on Monday, and was sipping inevitable cider when the 'phone went. It was Terry:
    'I have a rather nice engagement for you.'
    'Oh yes? Hold on, I'll get next season's diary.'
    'You don't need your diary, it's on Wednesday.'

---

[2] A character from Dylan Thomas' 1964 radio drama *Under Milk Wood*, who endlessly nags her two dead husbands.

Cumnor, 25.6.76,

Isn't it fitting that I should have lost my
diary on the flight from Johannesburg two weeks ago
just as I was returning to take possession of my new
home? For from now on, all my past is to be considered irrelevant. Never mind what I have wanted,
suffered, feared, achieved: I have that rare chance,
a new start, and I don't want it weighed down by
obsolete habits (feelings also are conditioned by habit).
    I am not even sure whether I shall continue
this diary at all. There is something tiresomely self-
conscious about keeping a diary, like living under
one's own anxious supervision, the Catholic examen
de conscience. I may jot something down now and
then, but will not let it become another self-inflicted duty. And yet this is precisely why I'm writing now! For days now, I've been feeling positively
guilty at not inaugurating this note-book, as if an
examiner was awaiting it.
    At any rate, I have laid aside the famous
autobiography: I am heartily tired of wallowing in
my own retroactive bitterness. People and circumstances

                                                          1.

    '*This* Wednesday? You mean the day after tomorrow? But Terry, tomorrow
I've got appointments in town right through the day: Weinberger's in the
morning, lunch with my bank manager...'
    'It won't be so very tragic to cancel them, will it?'

'Not tragic, but *rude*. I invited the bank manager for tomorrow some 3 weeks ago...'

'He'll be far more pleased if you put some more lolly into your account. If you like I shall ring him myself. Now will you listen? It's the Zurich Festival and they want you to play the K. 271[3] and the 414.'[4]

'OK., let me play through the 414 and see how it goes. I'll let you know in 25 minutes' time.'

'No problems with the 271?'

'There shouldn't be.'

Among my innumerable virtuous resolutions on my arrival in Cumnor, was that of playing through one Mozart concerto a day, in chronological order, just to consolidate the inevitably hasty job I did of the series in Perth. I had begun to implement the rule, and got as far as the Double (which I am soon to play with Stefan[5] on his 80th birthday), thus including a session on the 271, which I had often played before anyway; the 414, a recent addition to the repertoire, had been untouched since Perth. I played it through now and was surprised to find it so well in my head and fingers. I was now glad of having done the complete series, so that I should be able to play any Mozart concerto at short notice, and even gladder of having stuck to my resolution of practising regularly, whether I had any concerts or not. How often in my 'writing periods' I had to refuse such sudden engagement, not just because it would make a dent in the time allotted to composition, but because I was too out of fingers to play 3 consecutive notes evenly! The trick is to be *always* on form, at least technically; mentally the process of writing may at times still prove too obsessive to leave much concentration for anything else. But I hope, at any rate, to dispense with the biannual wrench of practising myself back into form from absolute bottom, and the sheer terror of public performances for which I know myself to be unfit!

While I was inspecting the K. 414, Terry was checking rehearsal time, flights etc. he also had to make sure that the Zurich Chamber Orchestra had not meanwhile engaged anyone else! For he had already rung me before, about 9 p.m. (I was just going out when the 'phone rang, but decided not to answer it as I was anxious not to miss the sunset!); receiving no reply, he had to ring Zurich and tell them he had not found me, so they immediately started looking elsewhere. However, I was in luck: the deal was made. Suddenly I realised that I was looking forward very much to going. For once, I felt reasonable trust in my fingers and wanted to show them off; the

---

[3] Mozart, Piano Concerto No. 9 in E flat major (1777).

[4] Mozart, Piano Concerto No. 12 in G major (1782).

[5] Askenase – *cf.* p. 45, above.

fee would no doubt be considerable and help to pay off the mortgage; and a day in Zurich sounded more fun than one in London. I was also glad to be able to show Terry that I am more 'professional' than before, or, as I'd put it, more sporting. Eve promised to ring all the people I had committed myself to seeing in London.

It all went very easily: the local taxi took me to the airport, a pre-paid ticket waited for me there, and as I meditated on the flight (and fell asleep) I wasn't even tired on arrival. This was as well, for I had barely reached the appointed hotel when I had to rush off again to meet the conductor (Edmond de Stoutz[6]) and play both concertos to him. Once again they went well and we got on very amicably.

But the evening was not over yet: another kind of success was to come my way. Admittedly, it's a trivial one, which by now can satisfy nothing but my vanity, but I have reached an age when I can't help feeling pleased, and surprised, and amused, when anyone chooses to treat me as an erotic object. It is, of course, only gratifying when the person in question is young and presentable, and this was the case.

He stared at me as he passed my bench, walked on a bit, turned and gazed, then walked away more slowly, glancing over his shoulder two or three more times. The invitation was so obvious, and my opinion of my own looks so poor, that it occurred to me he might be a tart. If that was the case, there would still be time to withdraw; I got up and followed. There were two empty benches in the shade, he sat down on one I on the other. More stares, in an increasingly embarrassed silence finally he got up again, leaving me uncertain whether he'd decided against me or was merely looking for somewhere yet more secluded; I followed once more, just in case. He stopped against some monument, so did I. More silence. 'Nun' I finally said, 'was tut man weiter?'[7]

He answered in French, it turned out he was from Geneva. The banality of his conversation soon extinguished the charm of his looks. But the ball was rolling by now, and soon we arrived at the stage of what Emlyn Williams[8] calls 'a casual fraternisation', performed discreetly in a clump of trees. He was not a tart.

That night, for the first time in over three weeks, I took some Tuinal and woke up at the 8 a.m. alarm-call with no ill effects. The rest of the day went almost monotonously well: no mishaps, no nerves, the rehearsal finished half an hour ahead of time and the concert found me concentrated, alert and

---

[6] Edmond de Stoutz (1920–97) had founded the Zurich Chamber Orchestra in 1946 and conducted it until 1996.
[7] 'Well, what shall we do next?'
[8] Bisexual Welsh playwright and actor (1905–87).

relaxed – a sadly rare combination. The only drawback was the piano, a new Steinway that has already drawn complaints from Rubinstein[9] and Arrau,[10] and which has been described to me as hard. It was not hard, it was dead: I was playing on cotton-wool, no amount of pressure seemed to make any difference. Perhaps in Mozart this uniformly dull and muffled sound was received as a proof of my own masterly restraint? At any rate, I received an ovation and was asked by the conductor to play an encore; knowing not when to stop, I played two. Afterward the manageress of the restaurant I misguidedly chose recognised me (no great feat, as I was still wearing my tails), stood me the dinner and treated me to a solid hour of her conversation as an added bonus. Fat but soulful, she is an ardent concert-goer and attends Menuhin's festivals at Gstaad. I was visibly drunk by the time we parted.

11 July

In flight from Stuttgart to London
Obviously the 'plane was invented so that I could keep up my diary! Let's see what happens in the next three weeks – I have no flights in my schedule till October. This time I am coming back from Baden-Baden, where Stefan Askenase celebrated his 80th birthday in the grandest style. The ceremonies included two concerts, at one of which I played the Mozart two- and three-pianos concertos, two receptions, a special morning ritual, not unlike a religious service, at which speeches in Stefan's honour alternated with orchestral music, an official lunch, and a late-night party. I couldn't avoid any of it; Stefan relished it. The concerts were admittedly enjoyable, especially Stefan's performance of K. 466 – I had never heard the Romance played so originally and beautifully, and the first movement was also quite striking. The Double and the Triple also went reasonably well; I played the first piano in the former, second in the latter. The social part of it I merely endured. Man may be a social animal (who said this?[11]) but I am just an animal; certainly there is no fun that I can see in 120 people painstakingly congratulating one another for several hours…

At one point, one of those coquettish elderly ladies to whom I never fail to develop an instant aversion noticed my listless silence and said 'Herr Tchaikowsky, sagen Sie auch etwas Nettes!'[12] As I didn't even know her name, 'Wer sind Sie?'[13] would have been an appropriate answer. I didn't say

---

[9] Arthur Rubinstein.
[10] Claudio Arrau, Chilean pianist (1903–91).
[11] First Aristotle, and then Baruch Spinoza.
[12] 'Say something nice!'
[13] 'Who are you?'

it for two reasons: one, because such rudeness would have spoilt Stefan's birthday; two, because it didn't occur to me.

Still, I didn't waste *all* my time. In between the rehearsals, I managed to orchestrate the first two pages of *The Merchant*; it went well and proved fun, and I am looking forward to doing some more in the coming days (the sketches are ready for orchestration till the change of tempo). And I only took Tuinal on two nights out of four. A partial success…

But how relieved I had been when it turned out that I can come back one day earlier that I had expected!

18 August

Waiting for Godot – 'une oasis d'horreur dans un desert d'ennui'![14] Its inflated status seems to me a typical case of the emperor's new clothes. Beckett has contrived just the right anti-plot to make his lack of invention seem inevitable: it's like the impotent man's claim to chastity. Anyway, why should facile nihilism be any more 'profound' than glib comfort?

Alas, I am writing this to avoid a more personal and painful subject: my friend Michael M[enaugh] has walked out on me after a totally senseless row that was entirely of my doing, so the fault is mine![15] I have deserved his reaction: in a way, perhaps I needed it. The trouble is that my recent personal progress – giving up Tuinal, combining composition and piano practice on a daily basis, breaking free of a sterile and half-hearted sexual infatuation, learning to keep more to myself etc. – has made me abominably smug, and totally oblivious of the fact that none of these achievements can in the least benefit anyone else. My friends may be glad of it all for *my* sake, but my capacity for relating to them, caring for them, seeing them in their own right rather than as objects of my own feelings is as it was: nil. If Michael's break and the resulting shock can teach me that it will have been worth it, *provided* that the break is not permanent: nothing could make up for the loss of both my closest friend (unless Eve be that) and the most remarkable, gifted and sensitive individual I know. I shall gladly serve the sentence I've deserved, but oh, let it not be a life sentence! Let me yet have the chance to be a friend to *him* for a change…

The work is going well: three hours of piano practice every morning plus a short but usually intensely concentrated session on *The Merchant* in the early evening. Shylock, so far, has proved less intimidating than I had

---

[14] 'An oasis of horror in a desert of boredom' – a quotation from Baudelaire's *Le Voyage*.
[15] In fact, Michael did not walk out: he was expelled by Tchaikowsky, late in the evening, which meant that he had to spend the night at a bus stop, waiting for the first morning bus.

expected, but then I may of course be writing shit! I like the ominous bare octave I've just reached, at his 'I think I may take his bond'. Am I giving him too much too soon? And is he getting too much like Golaud?[16]

19 August

Emlyn Williams' autobiography[17] threw me into a trance of hero-worship, and ten days ago I wrote him a fan letter; I said in it that I had tickets for his Dylan Thomas one-man show on the 5th September, and announced my intention to visit him backstage. Today came the reply. I feasted on his few lines like Malvolio on Olivia's supposed letter[18] (perhaps I've also been fooled and it's not from Emlyn?). Everything about it is gratifying: his starting 'Dear André' (I had written 'Dear Mr. Williams, I have never met you, yet I nearly started, Dear Emlyn? This is what comes of your treating your readers as intimate friends!'); his using a personal stationery with his address and 'phone number, which I greedily copied into my address-book; the fact that the letter and my address on the envelope were in his own hand. Fancy his surrendering his 'phone number to an unknown admirer who might turn out to be a crank and plague him everafter! I'd never be capable of that; it's real generosity. On the other hand, I'd never have the face to send my reply by second-class post… This is because I *am* mean and have a horror of being found out! As Michael said to Eve, I'll give anything except myself. Expensive gifts are in fact so much cheaper… Emlyn may have spent twopence less, but he put his home address and 'phone number at a stranger's disposal, called me André (thus implying I *may* now call him Emlyn), welcomed me backstage after the performance[19] and called my letter 'the sort of present that makes two years of pen-work worthwhile'. You shouldn't do it, Emlyn: once unleashed, I may become a real menace. Who shall I write to next – Patricia Highsmith,[20] to ask her not to use the phrase 'reach a crescendo', or the American poetess who made so many boobs in her translation of Rimbaud? She renders 'ici-bas' by 'here on earth', when the TITLE is *Une Saison en Enfer*! I think her name is Thodes.[21] Bless you, Emlyn!

---

[16] A character from Debussy's opera *Pelléas and Mélisande*.

[17] Published in two volumes: *George: An Early Autobiography*, Hamish Hamilton, London, 1961, and *Emlyn*, The Bodley Head, London, 1973.

[18] In Act II, scene v, of Shakespeare's *Twelfth Night*.

[19] I hope he remembers this when we do meet, but I have a feeling he might – there are occasional advantages in having an unusual name. Perhaps he's even heard of me as a musician? Would the Pope like a word from me? –AT

[20] American writer of novels and short stories (1921–95).

[21] Her name was Enid Rhodes Peschel, and her translation of Rimbaud's *Season in Hell* and *Illuminations* was published by Oxford University Press, New York, 1973.

6 September

Emlyn's show was excellent; our meeting was a disappointment for both sides. It started off well: I was just going through the stage-door, when a silver-haired lady asked:

'Are you Mr. Tchaikowsky?'

'Yes, are you Mrs. Williams?'

'No, just a friend. Emlyn, *here* is Mr. Tchaikowsky!'

Emlyn popped out of his dressing-room and started shaking hands with the first man in the queue.

'Not, *that's* not him', said the lady.

I was too shy to laugh. Once Emlyn saw me, he was quick and almost perfunctory; it was obvious he had not heard of me and his charming letter and readiness to meet me had been due to a misapprehension. He had expected a precocious schoolboy, or a student, young and fuckable. There was an almost ridiculous discrepancy between his attitude until we met and afterwards. Nor did my conversation help: all I provided was starry hero-worship only forgivable in a schoolboy. I had expected him to put me at ease, but almost all he did was to ask whether I was related to P. I. Tchaikowsky. And he *still* doesn't know I'm a musician!

7 September

A sample of Chad's [Varah] conversation:

'The woman said she could tell anyone's zodiac sign after talking to them for five minutes and of course I agreed to the demonstration. Actually, nearly an hour elapsed before she announced she knew mine.'

'And did she get it right?'

'She did…'

'You see?' said Eve triumphantly, 'and you say you don't believe in astrology.'

'…at her twelfth go', finished Chad.

A graffito at the Turf Tavern gents':

'I thought cunnilingus was an Irish airline till I discovered Smirnoff'.

Playing at Dartington c. 1976; Hans Keller sits in the front row

28 October

I am going to see Michael.

Tomorrow.

[…] I didn't sleep much that night. The next night was worse. Not since the D. débâcle, two years ago,[22] had I been in such a state – weeping, sobbing, shaking. The prospect of having all my friends gathered round me, except the one I was most desperate to have, was intolerable. And I would have to be merry, welcome the friends, express astonished delight at their presents and laugh at their jokes! I had gone to bed at eleven, as the next day I was playing a lunch-time recital in Birmingham; by the time I looked at my watch to ring Eve, it was too late – 12.15. If she lived alone, I'd risk waking her up; after all, I'd do as much for her if she were in distress. But I wouldn't do it for Eve's flat-mate, and what if she answered the 'phone? Whom else can one ring at this hour? (By this time, it was one o'clock). I thought of calling the local branch of the Samaritans, but I had just enough pride left to prevent that, and after all I was not considering suicide, just desperate to talk to someone. In my mind, I went to addressing Eve. 'No,' I cried, 'you can't make me sit through a fake ceremony and pretend joy, it would take no one in, I don't want your presents, I don't want any of you if I can't have

---

[22] 'D.' was the Australian man with whom Tchaikowsky had a traumatic love-affair in 1974; *cf.* pp. 117 *et seq.*, above.

Michael!' Five Valium pills (25 mgms.) did nothing to subdue the distress. I took a beer, then another. By three I was asleep.

I had asked for an alarm call at 8.30, but was awake by seven or soon after. My mood had changed; I was calm and firm, I could cope. I started the day quite casually by trying to ring the National Theatre and book some tickets for the TNP[23] production of *Tartuffe*;[24] it was engaged, I meditated and tried again, it was still engaged. The taxi was coming in half an hour's time. Suddenly I rang Michael. It was early enough for his flat-mate not to have left for work, but I recognised my friend's voice when he gave the number.

'Michael, this is André. I am sorry – I couldn't help ringing.'

'What's the matter? You sound awfully depressed.'

I told him. He suggested a meeting. 'What are you doing after Birmingham? No, wait, my flat-mate is going out on Friday evening – can you come on Friday?'

'Anytime. Anything. I know I used to want everything on my own terms – I no longer have any terms.'

'What are your plans for…'

'I no longer have any plans.'

He asked me to ring today to finalise arrangements, but his 'phone is out of order; Eve suggested that I cable him, but I preferred to give him a chance to call me himself, and presently he did. I'll see him tomorrow evening at his place, and perhaps spend the night in London if it turns out that I've missed the last train.

Who, after reading this, would believe the astonishing fact that we weren't lovers?

Now for that spot of farce that used to follow high drama in Greece.

I was having a sherry at the Turf Tavern when I noticed a poster announcing 'Love and Hate' by the Dionysian Society, at Jesus College. I looked at my watch: it was just about to start. The name 'Dionysian' seemed to promise a certain abandon – there was just a horrible possibility that it might turn out to be a pop group. But in that case I could slip out straightaway, and still be in time to catch the 8.35 bus back! There was no risk of being turned out either: they wouldn't have advertised the event unless it was open.

I went, found the room, took a seat and timidly surveyed the pleasant young faces round me. There were no microphones or electric guitars; some of the people had books. Presently a slightly older man came in and

---

[23] Théâtre National Populaire (TNP) was a French dramatic theatre in Paris that continued the traditions of the theatre founded in 1920 by the actor and director Firmin Gémier.

[24] Play by Molière written in 1664.

apologised for opening the proceedings in English! A madman? Not at all: the entire discussion that followed was in ancient Greek. My seat was in the furthest corner from the door, so I couldn't make any but the most conspicuous exit. I stayed on, struggling not to laugh, increasingly in need of a pee, and terrified lest anyone asked *me*, in fluent Greek, my own precise views on love and hate. I tried to look as if I understood; when others laughed I managed to put on a shy smile. No one, o relief! paid the slightest attention to me; perhaps my white beard disqualified me automatically. And yet somehow I didn't feel excluded, or bored, merely prodigiously amused. Pop group! It just showed how much I knew my Oxford.

And I ended up as a subscription member of the Society! For just £1, gentle reader, you too can have ancient Greek pamphlets pushed through your mail-box. It would have cost Socrates more to learn English

31 October

Michael: complete reconciliation. No heavy weather, practically no post-mortems, an atmosphere of instant and almost casual ease. This was his doing, from the moment he opened the door with the warmest of welcoming smiles, saying: 'Would you mind popping across to the Off Licence Shop for some dry white wine? You know, those Nicolas one litre bottles…' 'Michael, I *have* lived in Paris!' In the shop I also found a bottle of Aquavit, a favourite of Michael's. 'Cor' said the cockney lad who was doubling up as assistant salesman and chief attraction, 'what's this stuff like?' 'Try it, just have a sip.' He liked it; I was amused by him and quite carefree.

For once, I hadn't tried to evolve a scenario beforehand: I went to see M. trustingly and with an open mind, and he knew how to reward trust. This *is* perfect happiness. I love him.

2 November

It was as if God had wanted to make me a present on my 41st birthday! Yesterday was a landmark. Firstly, I have completed the interminable scene of Shylock's bond, which had been oppressing me for some three months; admittedly, some secondary details are still missing, but the vocal parts are complete and the development of the prelude which I used as a link between scene (rather like Mussorgsky's *Promenade*[25]), grafted now onto the rising bass that underlay Antonio and Bassanio's earlier discussion of the loan and

---

[25] Many of the movements representing the paintings in Musorgsky's *Pictures at an Exhibition* (1874) are connected by a varied interlude entitled 'Promenade'.

culminating in the same two chords, is there. Now for a short transition to Jessica's first entrance…

Secondly, after nearly a year of neglect, I've suddenly found a way of continuing the autobiography. The new idea is to write the '47 chapter from *Grams'* point of view. She also had her tragedy, infinitely greater than mine, as after inhuman efforts and griefs she had nothing whatever to look forward to; she had looked to me for consolation, but had no idea how to elicit the love she was desperate for (can one *elicit* love in any case?) and all she did only antagonised me further. A recent dream has proved to me that I am now at peace with her, and knowing that how could I find patience to masturbate my own stale grievances? But the main reason, as always, is not moral but artistic: the story of my own predicament had come to a natural climax in the previous chapter, and nothing further about it could interest the reader; it is time for a readjustment. Of course I shall spare none of her absurdities and contribute my usual amount of sneers (Hans K.'s 'Beware of the danger of continual irony' is still the most helpful comment I've had on the piece), but now the reader will hate *me* and sympathise with her, wincing at my total callousness. With the final chapter introducing Father and being treated almost farcically, it means that the book will continue changing as it goes on right to the end and that's a great improvement. How could I hope not to bore my readers when I was bored by it myself?

This means of course, that the fragment I wrote last January will have to go, as I'd suspected all along; it will be replaced by a long lament by Grams (she was rather given to those). Also, I shan't be able to go back to the book till *next* January, when the long flights of the round-the-world trip give me time for it. But what a joy to see that the book needn't be an abortion after all!

Later – I think I might treat myself to an evening off. I have reached my target for this year by bringing Act I of *The Merchant* to the half-way mark, and seem to have a fairly good chance of getting beyond it; my head is still ticking. But it is also aching, and after the combined practice, writing and socialising of the last few days I am very tired. I'll take a bath and see how I feel then. Butler's advice to writers: 'Never consciously agonise'[26] has helped me to get more done on the average, not less. I only wish it had come from someone whose own achievement I could admire more!

---

[26] 'Never consciously agonise; the race is not to the swift, nor the battle to the strong. Moments of extreme issue are unconscious and must be left to take care of themselves' – from 'Agonising', one of the ideas that Samuel Butler noted down and preserved in a series of five loose-leave folders, edited after Butler's death in 1902 by David Price and published by A. C. Fifield, London, 1912.

Later still – I did after all, I think, manage to write the transition to Jessica's entrance. But is it any good?

27 November

A.m. – I have just woken up from a rather peculiar nightmare.

In it I was Racine, or at least someone sufficiently obsessed by Racine to have become thoroughly identified with him. I had written all my secular plays, and now intended to make my exit from the theatre with a supreme technical tour de force which would take the three unities to their extreme. The time would be not just any 24 hours, but these very next 24 hours which I should spend writing my last play; the place, this very room, which no excuse, no pretext, or physical necessity could make me leave. I had created an abstract universe in which no character had ever gone to a meal, except to be poisoned; now, for the duration of the gageure,[27] I'd have to live in it and abide by its rules.

And the action? Why, there'd be no action. Hadn't Pascal said that all man's unhappiness consisted of being unable to stay put in a room?[28] If he was right, here's my tragedy: it will put him as well as me to the test. If he was right, if Jansenists are right, there is nothing but tragedy throughout the universe; and I've been suspecting for some time that they might be, that there is no salvation for the likes of me, and that long before being accused of poisoning men's souls I had irretrievably poisoned my own. But in that case why should staying alone in a room be more tragic than anything else? 'L'homme qui n'aime que soi ne hait rien tant que d'être avec soi'.[29] He could have meant me: I've never loved anyone but myself. For some time now I haven't even managed that... let's get some light, I am getting morbid.

The candle won't burn.

This is ridiculous: how am I to write in the dark? I could dash off a tragedy on any subject, without a subject ('toute invention consiste à faire quelque chose de rien'[30]), but I can't be expected to write without seeing the paper, or compose 1600 alexandrines at one session purely in my head. If I give up and go out, though, the world will laugh: they've been waiting for me to fail for some twelve years. Besides, if the light won't come on, how do I know

[27] Impossible task or challenge.
[28] He had, in his *Pensées* (1670).
[29] 'The man who loves only himself hates nothing more than to be alone' – another quotation from Pascal's *Pensées*.
[30] 'Any invention is based on making something out of nothing' – Racine, Preface to his tragedy *Bérénice* (1670).

the door will open if I try the handle? And if it didn't, I'd feel frightened. Better not to try.

Let's face it, I am frightened anyway. I am afraid the door *will* open of its own accord. Who would come in? Nero? Roxane? I have released enough malevolence to be destroyed if it ever came home to me. Anyway, in the real, day to day world I have nothing but enemies. I have been too good at my craft, have known it, let them know it. Without the King's patronage they would long ago have destroyed me; as it is, they hate me for the royal favour more than for all my successes.

Look, here is Agrippina, shaping her fury into flawless verse. 'Ne crois pas qu'en mourant je te laisse tranquille.'[31] Is she addressing Nero, or me? Theseus destroyed monsters; I created them. It would make a fine show indeed if they now crowded in on me! It's a mercy the window is barred.

If this is a tragedy, it is a particularly relentless one; no intervals, no curtains. No one will be murdered: Bérénice has proved this unnecessary. No need for blood and corpses, I had said; but I had also asked for grandeur of action, heroic characters, and my own tragedy is not a bit like that. Here I am, cowering alone in a dark room, eyes glued to a door I can't even see. Perhaps it has opened already? That fool Pradon[32] could have managed better than that.

What am I waiting for? I cannot write; I shall never write. From now on it's obviously my job to live my last tragedy, not to write it, and this time there will be no applause. What was that soft, soft click just behind me? I daren't look around.

Pull yourself together, man; pull yourself together. Pull what together? Is there still a self left? All my life I had emptied my soul to make room for imaginary passions, let them invade me and blow gales inside me. Jealous, tyrannical, blackmailing they ravaged whatever self I had once possessed, spat and shat in my brain, to emerge from it in immaculate decorum and tragic dignity. No one but me has watched Phèdre masturbate. Only I know the exact tortures Roxane inflicted for fun on her slaves.

If I survive this night, I'll take a steady, respectable job and calmly wait till the curtain comes down.

---

[31] 'Do not think that by dying I will leave you alone' – Racine, *Britannicus,* Act V, scene 6.
[32] Racine is reputed to have said of his playwright rival Jacques Pradon (1632–98): 'The only difference between Pradon and me is that I know how to write'.

6 January

In flight to Colombo, where I am to play a charity recital for the Befrienders (nées [sic] Samaritans)

A postscript to the Birmingham concert, which was broadcast live:

Jonathan Ward, 7, two doors down from me, meeting me in our street:

– We heard you on the radio the other night!

– Thanks. A friend of mine has recorded it, so I am going to listen to it tonight…

– Didn't you listen while you were playing it?

[…]

6 March

Christchurch

On Friday the 4th I became a conscious member of the human race.

I had always been an outcast – or a prisoner. At first the confinement was quite literal, whether in the Warsaw ghetto or in a wardrobe; released from that, I actually sought confinement (which I then probably regarded as security) in claustrophobic relationships or the larger ghetto of the homosexual community (if that is the right word for a group whose members have so little else in common). The trouble was my *mind* was still in prison: I had been trained to forge my own handcuffs. As for being an outcast, that also started in its most literal and drastic form: who can be more cast out than one whose very right to live has been denied? Even after the war, I had been physically bullied for being a Jew. Then, in my teens, came the discovery of my sexual inclinations, which I supposed to be extremely rare: I regarded myself as a monster. Grams' comment when I'd told her was: 'They'll be pointing their fingers at you' and I had heard enough lewd jokes on the subject to share that grim view. Unable to merge, I undertook to stand out, and succeeded. Even *I* didn't at first suspect that the solitary position of a 'star' performer was not of my own choice. I performed

187

Christchurch, 6.3. – On Friday the 4th I became
a conscious member of the human race.

I had always been an outcast – or a prisoner.
At first the confinement was quite literal, whether in
the Warsaw ghetto or in a wardrobe; released from
that, I actually sought confinement (which I then
probably regarded as security) in claustrophobic relationships or the larger ghetto of the homosexual
community (if that is the right word for a group
whose members have so little else in common). The
trouble was, my mind was still in prison: I had
been trained to forge my own handcuffs. As for being
an outcast, that also started in its most literal and
drastic form: who can be more cast out than one
whose very right to live has been denied? Even, after the war, I had been physically bullied for being
a Jew. Then, in my teens, came the discovery of my
sexual inclinations, which I supposed to be extremely
rare: I regarded myself as a monster. Grams' comment
when I'd told her was: "They'll be pointing their fingers
at you" and I had heard enough lewd jokes on the
subject to share that grim view. Unable to merge, I
undertook to stand out, and succeeded. Even I didn't

97

on stage and in conversation, as an artist or as a clown: I might get no
one's love, but I knew how to force their applause. I even performed when
alone – was that because I couldn't love myself? I often courted dislike as
much as admiration, and that proved even easier to get. What did it matter
which reaction of the two it was, as long as I was *noticed*? I was making up
for years of hiding.

It took me a long time to notice the strain of that perpetual display. I didn't connect it with my intolerable headaches, with my fits of exhaustion, with the seemingly unaccountable rebellions of my nervous system. Nor did I see myself as a simple 'ham': my act took myself in, whomever else. But what I was conscious of was an overwhelming need for *love*, and though this was in fact repeatedly granted me, I could never accept and believe it. To see oneself as an outcast is quite as damaging as to be one; perhaps more so, since a real one may yet eventually find acceptance, whereas I kept rejecting whatever was offered.[1] To my suspicious and black-and-white mind, it always seemed based on spurious grounds: I was accepted as a fellow Jew, a fellow queer, above all as a pianist: that made me interchangeable with any other specimen of the same group. It never felt enough just to be me.

How could I break out of that, reach out to the Others? I couldn't: they would have to reach out to me. To be complete, the acceptance would have to include sex – that controversial aspect of my make-up was the greatest barrier. How could I believe others to accept it, when I had never quite managed to do so myself? And yet it had to come from the *other* side: a heterosexual would have to love me. This was a ludicrous event to expect, and I had never consciously expected it, or even wished for it; it was outside the laws of nature as I knew it; and nothing else could rescue me. I was learning to accept defeat.

It has happened now. J. did precisely that, met me in my own cell, freed me, led me out. Nothing could take it back: I now *belonged*. That realisation, however, was but a prelude to the overwhelming revelation that now followed, with the suddenness and irrevocability of a gun-shot. *Everyone* belonged, and always had; they just didn't know it. I burst into tears.

How could anyone be outside, when they were in the world? How could one be confined, when the world was open and free? One cannot be alive and not belong; but one may not know it. Webster's summer bird-cage[2] was the product of Blake's mind-forged manacles.[3]

I told all this to J., of course. He shared the joy, but refused any credit for it. I was no longer dependent on him, but loved him only more rather than

---

[1] For expecting a door to slam in my face, I was slamming it myself to get in first! –AT
[2] A reference to a line from *The White Devil* (1612) by the English Jacobean dramatist John Webster, (c. 1580–c. 1634): "'T is just like a summer bird-cage in a garden, – the birds that are without despair to get in, and the birds that are within despair and are in a consumption for fear they shall never get out'.
[3] The second verse of William Blake's poem 'London' (published in 1794) reads:

In every cry of every Man,
In every Infants cry of fear,
In every voice: in every ban,
The mind-forg'd manacles I hear

less; I recognised Plato's description of Love widening beyond its sole initial object. It *was* solid, as J. had said, and it *was* forever; it included everyone and everything. I remembered the TM team of Cosmic Consciousness, which had seemed so ridiculous and pretentious when I heard it first (just as their use of 'The Absolute' had). It seemed perfectly natural now. J. held out his hand.

'You wouldn't think I love you less now I am free?'

'Of course not', he replied, 'the two are the same.'

The World is Home. _

19 March

In flight Auckland–Papeete

[…] The next morning I felt so well at peace that I could be entirely casual: it was no longer a parting. J. now had a close friend, which was something he had always missed; I had had an experience that had put me at peace with the world. How could we lose any of that again? The only possible danger was that of my being still in love with him next time we met, but that seemed unlikely. We both felt sure we'd meet again, but made no plans: the ticket I had given him is to Zurich, not England, and he will only visit me if he particularly wants to. My love for him is by now as unconditional as his trust in me: nothing further needs to be done. (This, incidentally, was what he had prematurely assumed on Tuesday, the basis of the entire misunderstanding! He took the joy in my face to be that of a freedom already achieved, whereas I was merely rejoicing in *impending* freedom. A prisoner about to be liberated would have felt the same kind of happiness, but the handcuffs would still need removing…)

Well, I AM free now.

24 March

Tahiti–Los Angeles

My five day's stay on Tahiti was filled entirely by J. And not just memories, either: he took care to add fresh supplies. First came a Telex message which I've clipped into this book. It runs as follows:

DEAR ANDRE HAPPY DAY HOPE YOUR HAVING A MARVELLOUS TIME AND WISHING I WAS THERE BEST THOUGHTS AND BEYOND J. BLISS.

'Best thoughts and *beyond*'! He's certainly apt at finding substitutes for his taboo word. But more was to come.

It was good I had extended my stay by one day, or I'd have missed a cascade of presents. J. could have lived for at least a week on what he spent on them and the 'urgent, air-mail' postage. It consisted of two novels by Hesse –

Gertude and *Damian*, a funny-card with an affectionate message, a letter written at the post-office on a cable form and, best of all, the following message, bashfully hid among the pages of *Damian*:

'This gift is to tell you – best at a distance: thanks for coming along. As a teacher, I had got rather depressed and weary of nothing to live for, to use my abilities in, and they have no purpose and no joy quietly sitting unexercised… So I have thanks to say too.'

'This', I thought reading that reticent and rather clumsy admission, 'is the happiest I have ever been.' All my suffering with J. came from a feeling that there was nothing I could do for *him*. Now it appears I have!

'Best at a distance'. Dearest J. It gives so much more value to your message that it should have proved so difficult to deliver. Anyway, I can't see that there is a distance! It's as impressive for us to be distant now, wherever we both be, as it was to achieve contact on our penultimate meeting, while we were lying on one bed and in different worlds… I wrote that to him, and now intend to maintain a steady flow of letters, whether he reply to them or not! At first the tendency will be to write too often, then possibly too seldom as I get back into the stream of work, but I'll make a point of keeping it fairly continuous. I am the only person he's ever regarded as a close friend, and it's for me to prove him right.

12 June

I am at last recovering from the ghastly experience of the TM course; it should not be described but forgotten and will no doubt find its way into the lumber-room of obsolete nightmare as soon as the asana-induced[4] pain in my neck, shoulders and back has subsided. No congress of the Bolshevik party has ever produced more rigid and doctrinaire fanaticism, and the Catholic dogma of papal infallibility will not be necessary among Maharishi's followers: a fart of his would immediately become a dogma. The lectures and discussions at the continuous, interminable and very nearly compulsory meetings are as futile and far less ingenious than the theological debates of the middle ages: should Shakespeare, for instance, be dismissed as 'negative' or can he be rescued by providing that he had Cosmic Consciousness?

At present the Absolute is pleased to announce that the impending new Age of Enlightenment will last ten thousand years. In order to speed up its arrival, everyone is to breathe through alternate nostrils, do the prescribed number

---

[4] An asana is one of a range of yoga postures that allows the practitioner to sit in the same position for an extended period.

of exercises the prescribed number of times a day in the prescribed order and attend the meetings. (The first time I left a meeting half-way through, I was searched for, found in my room and gently rebuked.) How long will it be before insufficiently enlightened people are burnt or buried alive by kindly inquisitors who explain to their victims that it needs to be done for their own good? And before there is an Avignon Maharishi or a TM Luther? Everyone except me seemed ready to die for the cause if necessary – isn't killing for it the usual next step? Today's martyrs are tomorrow's executioners. But leaving aside melodrama, what will happen to all these complacently naïve people when His Holiness' predictions (including such easily verifiable ones as the immediate end of all wars) fail to come true?

One good joke, though: 'Harry, would you mind levitating while I do the carpet?'[…]

31 August

[…] This morning I have finished Act I.

At least I think so – I can't see what more needs to be done except the orchestration, and that, of course, is the one stage of composition that can be continued in between the concerts. (I shall try yet a third pen.) As the first engagement of the new season is tomorrow week (Ravel left-hand with the BBC Welsh), I had decided to put composition aside by the end of August, *whether the Act was finished or not*, so as to leave myself at least a week's undivided attention to my piano-playing. I was determined to abide by that decision, but as the date grew nearer and the work progressed, realised with increasing concern what a wrench it would prove to leave it unfinished! It would have been like giving up smoking.

So I worked at it more everyday ever more anxiously and compulsively, unable to stop even at times when I knew a rest might do the work itself good! Alcohol, Valium, Mogadon[5] were all combined to make me sleep a few hours, but the effect wouldn't come for half the night, or wear off early the next morning. Then an extra composition session would be added to the usual evening one and it was only by eleven, after some hours' intense work and a light breakfast, that I'd make a point of practising, at any rate, two reluctant hours. Till yesterday, I didn't know if I could meet the self-appointed deadline; I had the last page, but not the orchestral crescendo leading up to it; then I woke up with the idea for that in my head, but though a good morning session made me feel confident in the afternoon, the evening proved sterile – I'd got the bare outline, but couldn't find the

---

[5] A brand of sleeping pill.

secondary counterpoints. By 10.30 I broke off in despair and started getting some dinner, and it was just that momentary respite from my own nagging that my brain had needed. It was in the kitchen, cutting the ham, that it struck me I needed no more *instrumental* counterpoints: what I did need was another brief sign of the street-urchins, that had been inexplicably good through the climax of Shylock's lament, whose continued presence on the stage needed to be accounted for, and who would combine particularly well with the high flute and clarinet interplay I'd just written. This would in turn motivate Shylock's reaction to them in the sudden *ff* of the next bar: he'd ignore all their jeers, how could he notice them now if they were silent? Full of cider by now, I yet went straight back to the piano and fitted them in, wondering whether the bit would stand up to sober judgment! This morning I looked at it again and found it all right (I think, I'm not sure), so there was nothing left to do but fit in a few inner parts earlier on and an extra bar on the penultimate page. By a quarter to nine I was through, went to bed and slept until twelve. No doubt I'll be exhausted in the next few days, some reaction is bound to occur; perhaps I'll even play terribly in Cardiff. But who cares? What *timing*! To end the job on the last day of the appointed period! Perhaps I shall yet make a professional composer after all.

4 September

And talking of thanksgiving, now that this book is coming to an end, hasn't it been the best year of my life so far? J.'s contribution alone would have made it that, but there has been so much more – I now have a congenial environment to live and work in, a measure of solitude without loneliness, a feeling of being part of the place which I had experienced nowhere else: I have found a house. This, of course, is part of the larger realisation which I owe to J., but even before that I'd felt related to Oxford, where I knew nobody, as I never had to say, London, where all my friends lived! Work could now occupy its true position at the very centre of my life, and last season, on the while, was the most consistently successful yet (now, for a change, I'm playing terribly but this is quite natural in the wake of the Act I effort, which made me practise less and more absent-mindedly everyday! Also, I hope to play myself back into shape before long). Act I, although more complex than Act II and equally long, took two years as opposed to three and seems, as far as I can judge, more successful. But the greatest progress has been in myself – I am steadier, more at peace with myself and therefore the world, capable of long stretches of happiness and not merely brief flashes of joy, more responsive in true relationships and more deft at avoiding fake ones. I find it easier to be frank with people, now that I've gained enough self-acceptance to dispense with theirs! All this makes me thank J., and Whatever it is that has healed me through him and that is till at work within me and the world – what does it matter what one calls it, as long as one opens oneself to it?

Bless you, J. Hail to Thee, Nature, God, Life – I could go right through the dictionary…

8 September

The last notebook opened with my move into Cumnor and ended, as neatly as if it had been planned, with the completion of that first Act of *The Merchant* which I had started at the same time as the notebook! I hadn't realised that coincidence before: it means that, except for the orchestration of its second half which is still to do, the act took only one year and three months. For me, this is not bad going!

And the present diary opens with the first pianistic engagement of the new season. I am writing this in the train from Cardiff, where I have just recorded the Ravel Left-Hand concerto with the patient BBC Welsh orchestra and an imperturbably polite young Japanese conductor called Hikotaro Yazaki.[6] Alas, they needed all that patience and politeness. I am ashamed of that long, repetitive demonstration of impotence (there were several retakes, some of them even worse than the first attempt, which yet will be used!). I blush to think of people who will hear the transcript, especially the long final cadenza where no cut could be made and of which the first take was spoilt by mechanical noise – and the second by me. I hope they will all have the tact to keep silent about it. And I can't help wondering how many more performances I'll have to screw up before I get into my stride again…

6 October

London

Tomorrow is a special occasion: the first performance of my *Ariel* song-cycle, with Margaret Cable[7] and the Melos Ensemble, and myself playing the piano and the celesta. I had to wait eight years for this, and did nothing to bring it about although I've always believed it to be my best piece; certainly nothing written since had come to me with equal joy, and spontaneity. I still remember how it first took shape: in '68, while I was touring Australia and using the odd free hour or two to orchestrate the little there then was of the

---

[6] Born in Tokyo in 1947.
[7] Cambridge-born English mezzo soprano.

piano concerto, I was taken by surprise by wisps of music that obviously weren't relevant to my conscious efforts. The first thing to appear was the clarinet phrase that now opens the second song. At first I took it to be a piano miniature, then I heard a voice coming in, but could think of no text it could fit, and tried for a while to force it into the more convenient medium of a piano cycle. It rebelled. Not only I kept hearing the voice, but presently (not on that first occasion when I was lying on the grass in Adelaide, but within weeks) wood-wind instruments appeared, equally unsolicited and, I thought, unwelcome. The tour ended in November, I went to New Zealand for a holiday and fell in love with R. E. in Christchurch. The feeling was mutual and frightened us both equally; we agreed at once that I should leave. The next morning I flew down to Queenstown and settled seriously in conceiving the finale as a double-fugue: the two themes, with their attendant counterpoints, kept locking themselves into a confused tangle. But at other times, when I was relaxing or day-dreaming over the daily letters from R., the other, unforced, transparent music kept appearing of its own accord. Soon various disparate bits began to cohere. I realised that I had to follow my instinct in music as well as in life. To hell with that super-ego stuff! At that time, I was sure I'd never finish the concerto. But here was something that I could not have planned or predicted, any more than Robert: it was *true*, it was Life; I gave it to both. I tried various texts to fit the music I already had, notably *Ode to a Nightingale*. I don't now remember when *Ariel* occurred to me, but once it did I could never doubt it as the ideal text. The work went on in my mind during my brief but intensely happy holiday with R., and on returning to England I settled down to it in earnest (much to the detriment of my piano-playing). *Where the bee sucks* was finished in full score in about a month: that's very quick for me. The other two songs gave more trouble in different ways: *Come upon these yellow sand* (how happy R., had been with the melismatic setting of the first word, when it occurred to me in his presence!) forced me to imitate dogs and crowing cocks when all I wanted was an ethereal sprites' dance, and *Full fathom five* started so well that I was scared to go on lest I spoil it (I still love that song best of all). Six months' later all was ready but the epilogue. At that time Halinka was staying as my guest in London, but I refused to see her or anyone else and locked myself in for a week in order to finish the piece. Predictably, nothing happened. Then, just as the new season was about to start, I went down with Bornholm's disease[8] and was seriously ill for three weeks. As I began to get up and about, I went to the piano, expecting nothing of myself

---

[8] Bornholm disease is a viral infection of the intercostal muscles.

in my weakened state, and *for that very reason* got the epilogue ready in, I think, three days! And I *still* love the work. Oh God, shall I ever again write anything so unforced, so euphonious and so different from my other works? It puts to shame all I've written later (namely, the piano concerto, the Second string quartet and what there is of *The Merchant*). There are many good things in these works, but the difference is that *I* wrote them, whereas *Ariel* wrote itself though me…

8 October

The performance has come and gone. What a disappointment! Not with the work though: it sounds exactly as I had imagined, and the only two alterations I made were forgoing the bassoon mute in the first song (since it makes no difference) and lengthening the flute harmonic at the end of the second, since the celesta was virtually inaudible! Even in the closing bars, where it is unaccompanied, half the notes didn't speak. Now this is not my fault, as I also tried parts of *Die Zauberflöte* on it and they didn't sound either. But this was not the real disaster. Through both the rehearsals, predictably, I was the only one to make mistakes; all the players were impeccable and Margaret [Cable] sang as if she'd lived with the piece for a year. Last night, in the vital and long clarinet solo that precedes the 'sea-change' of the first song, Thea King[9] found herself playing the wrong line and the shock struck her altogether. The horn and bassoon dutifully continued with the interminable procession of sustained notes that were meant to sustain Thea; it did seem to go on forever and the effect was nightmarishly grotesque. Stunned and incredulous, I half expected Cecil Aronowitz[10] to stop conducting and start afresh (in retrospect, I realise that would have been the real disaster), but Margaret came in and sang with admirably sustained control. Other people were not so unshakeable, so that this proved the first of many mishaps. The harpist forgot the final chord of the first song – a very improbable mistake! The other two songs went far better, with most mistakes being as usual provided by me, and I was the sole offender in the epilogue. I had arranged to have the performance recorded, but of course I shall not be able to use that tape: 83 more pounds wasted.[11]

It's reassuring to see that even such a partial rendering conveyed some of the work's atmosphere. Everyone seemed impressed – with the exception of the *Times'* music critic who, incidentally, had asked the manager beforehand

[9] English clarinettist (1925–2007), appointed a DBE in 2001.
[10] South African-born British violist (1916–78), a founder member of the Melos Ensemble in 1950.
[11] The interview with Chad Varah quoted on p. 376, below, makes it clear that it was not Tchaikowsky's own money that was wasted.

who'd written the text! He started off by giving Mozart and Debussy a much-needed plug, praising them as innovators (they may, of course, have been new to *him*). Then he informed the public and myself that '*Ariel*, although obviously much more recent, seems far more conventional' – did he realise how flattering the very idea of such a comparison was? – called my imagination 'astringently romantic rather than modern' – quite right, thank God – and summed up by calling the piece well crafted, agreeable, but not at all memorable. I sympathise with Max Harrison's amnesia.

The public was attentive to the point of absolute stillness, received the piece warmly, and several strangers told me how much they liked it. The Melos said they'd like to do it again (especially Thea King, perhaps to make up for the lapse), but I don't know to what extent they meant it. Of my friends, Stephen said he liked it very much and loved the first song (of all things!), Eve found it weird and disconcerting but full of atmosphere and Ilana said it was great. I had no way of judging beforehand whether my fondness for the piece could be shared by anyone else; but even if nobody at all had like it, it would still be my favourite among all my works.

9 October

This is being written at Didcot station; I am on my way back from Cardiff, where Eve and I went especially to see the Prospect production of *Antony and Cleopatra*. It was well worth the journey, partly because a new stimulus was needed to refresh me after *Ariel,* mainly because Dorothy Tutin's[12] Cleopatra is perhaps the most sublime creation I've ever seen on stage. But there were disappointments.

To me, the main of these was Timothy West's[13] absence. He is my favourite English actor, and one of the very few people who can no doubt make sense of the inexplicable part of Enobarbus. (It's a wonderful, part of course, but enigmatic: cynics are hardly given to melting rhapsodies on another man's mistress, let alone to dying of a broken heart!) I was also personally sorry not to have seen him again after he'd proved so approachable and natural in Oxford, and after he answered my request for the company's itinerary with an invitation to come and talk to him after the performance. To make things worse, his place was taken by an incompetent nonentity who couldn't even be heard and whose face was less expressive than the average arse.

---

[12] English actress (1930–2001), made a CBE in 1967 and DBE in 2000.
[13] English actor (b. 1934), who made his breakthrough in the Associated Television series *Edward the Seventh* in 1975; he was created a CBE in 1984.

The opening page of Ariel

If Alec McCowen's[14] Antony was less disappointing it's because I had believed him to be badly miscast from the start. He's also one of my favourite actors, but he'd never been a heroic one, and a failing hero is still a hero! Antony is a man who can drink and make love all night and every night, and in the morning lead his soldiers into battle; till Actium he's adored by all his followers, and his behaviour there is in direct contrast to everyone's expectations, including his own. He has inexhaustible vitality and energy, can live with a woman who'd exhaust anybody else – and would Cleopatra love anybody who was not a hero? If she merely loved power, she'd fall for

---

[14] English actor (b. 1925), awarded an OBE in 1972 and CBE in 1985.

Octavius instead of mourning for Antony, and that's simply inconceivable. His part needs Nicol Williamson's physique (though Timothy West would do just as well), a ringing voice undaunted by rhetoric and a larger-than-life presence. Alec McCowen understates nearly everything, speaks realistically as if it were prose and generally flattens the whole part.

The production was perfunctory, no alarms, no noises of sea-fights, no army on either side and, worst of all, no contrast between Rome and Egypt. Who'd have known that the maltreated messenger was Egyptian? They all wore much the same costumes as they did in Hamlet. The soldier pleading with Antony not to fight by sea was fully dressed like a well-to-do Elizabethan courtier, so that the scars he mentions had to be taken on trust. The cuts also suggested perfunctory hurry – no Seleucus! The greatest trouble was taken with the drunken dance on Pompey's galley and they were so pleased with their effort there that they placed the interval after it (i.e. before anything decisive had happened).

All I can say of Dorothy Tutin is that she did full justice to the part. *Can* one say more? But there was an unexpected minor triumph as well and that was Derek Jacobi's Caesar. I'd have expected that to be a singularly unrewarding role, but with him every detail spoke: 'Welcome to Rome' or 'Poor Antony!', both delivered with icy contempt, drew an uneasy laughter from the audience. I preferred this to his Hamlet.

14 October

Last night I played my first concert in Oxford since moving in here – a Mozart-Schubert recital in aid of the local TM branch. From their point of view, it was a success: sold out well in advance and crowds turned away at the door. From my own, it was a double disappointment: firstly, because my anxiety to play well made me play badly (I am particularly ashamed of the rushed first movement of K. 310[15]) and secondly, because I had expected that night to mark my entry into Oxford's musical and social life, and nothing of the sort happened. I hoped students would come backstage – e.g. Hugh S., whom I'd invited to *Falstaff* and lent the score and record of *Wozzeck* to, Chris Muris, who'd written to me on behalf of the OUMCU (Musical Club and Union) to ask me if I'd give them some master classes. The only person, or almost, who did come backstage was a notorious bore from Currie Hall at the University of Western Australia; I'd managed not to let him know that I now also live here and vaguely assented to his invitation 'next time I'm down this way'. At first, anticipating an instant success, I'd borrowed a Mus. Doc.

---

[15] Mozart, Piano Sonata No. 8 in A minor (1778).

gown and cap to wear at my last curtain call, but the applause after the second encore had died down before I could make the joke, and on second thoughts it's just as well: it would have been premature and might have looked as a gesture of ingratiation. But I ended up with the too familiar feeling of being admired and thanked rather than befriended.

Just heard *Carmen* again, and it never fails to reduce me to tears. It's the most Mozartean opera outside Mozart: it's equally satisfying to the laziest man-in-the-street and to the most demanding connoisseur. On the first night of my recent German tour, I had a concrete image of what I want most: I saw a dark-blond young man in a grey-blue suit, in tears, to his own surprise and embarrassment, at something of mine he'd just heard. A middle-aged man, just like me, was ogling him greedily at the interval, but the boy didn't even notice: he was too full of music. Unlike my usual explicitly erotic fantasies, it was my *absence* that gave the scene its value: the music had become autonomous and might survive me. By definition, I'll never know if this dream comes true…

3 November

Liverpool

I do hope my 43rd year does not continue as it had begun! My birthday, two days ago, was the most ridiculous flop since Eeyore's.

To be sure, I played badly – all three evenings, in varying degrees. That in itself would have been enough to depress me, but though the bitter after-taste of the messy finale is till with me and will no doubt remain till I've proved myself afresh in some way, it was only part of the trouble. There was a violent row between the rehearsal and the first concert.

What happened was that the leader started being grossly rude to the conductor at the very beginning of the rehearsal. The latter being Japanese and consequently super-humanely patient and polite, it was all too easy for the bully to get at him again and again. Michi Inoue[16] having stopped the orchestra twice in the first eight bars to voice a request, the leader shouted: 'For Heaven's sake, let us play till we have got our fingers warm at least!' Michi and I exchanged a look of startled concern and he went on without a word. But now the leader began to interrupt *him*. He accused him of being unclear, of missing a beat, of adding a bar, all, as far as I could see, for the sake of harassing him; Michi, imprisoned by his own politeness and further handicapped by jet-lag fatigue and scanty knowledge of English, did nothing to defend himself, but looked increasingly tense and

---

[16] Michiyoshi Inoue (b. 1946), Japanese conductor.

distressed. I was fuming, but contrived not to show it as I couldn't be sure whether Michi wanted me to intervene. The only effect of my anger was to undermine my concentration and make me play worse by the minute (I had badly underpractised the f-minor in any case). At the break I found Michi puzzled and distressed, and his inarticulate way of expressing it made it more pathetic. 'All the time, all the time. And why?' was all he could say.

I asked him if he'd like me to speak on his behalf and got a hesitant assent. The leader was not to be found, but the deputy manager was and I protested with increasing and no doubt exaggerated vehemence. (I can now see that my over-reaction must have been due to my lifelong habit of identifying with the persecuted.) I used words like sabotage and scandal and ended up by refusing to shake hands with the leader unless he apologised to Michi. It was very unfair to the manager, who hadn't seen the rehearsal, and who was now in the notoriously invidious position of the man-in-the-middle who gets shouted at by both sides! Michi, *in his own case*, was far more conciliatory than I on his behalf.

I now see that my quixotic 'rescue action' was ridiculous. But remembering the intensity of my indignation, I also know that I could not help it. It's a mistake I'll no doubt make again.

Meanwhile, I had produced an atmosphere in which it was almost impossible to work. In the evening, the leader and I didn't acknowledge each other's presence, I didn't shake hands after the performance, and at the break he insisted on a direct set-to that I cut short in sheer disgust. The man is of the kind who can't admit the bare possibility of having been in the wrong, and I can only bully back a bully.

To my regret, Simon Rattle heard that scatty and shabby performance, and Terry a very similar one tonight – the rondo was, if anything, even worse. Terry's comments scribbled on the programme, were: 'orchestra too thick – beard; tone – swallowed; notes – not clean', all of which was true. Well, I can trim my beard easily enough, but it will cost much more work to satisfy him on all the other counts.

I feel far more guilty at the performance than at the row – after all, I *could* have prepared this concerto and played it much better. All my efforts went into the e-minor. The row was unforeseeable and, at the time, beyond my control, so I can plead temporary insanity!

Also, I'll never see the man again, but my fingers are always with me and a potential source of humiliation when they aren't working…

And now for a couple of Bertie Wooster[17] stories to cheer myself up!

---

[17] Bertie Wooster is one of the two central characters in the *Jeeves* novels by P. G. Wodehouse.

2 December

Farewell, November! I shan't miss you.

Perhaps the best experience in that difficult month was the beautiful production of *Così* I saw in Bath (Kent Opera, in a very witty English translation, directed by Jonathan Miller who for once left well alone and conducted incredibly well by Roger Norrington). For once the second act didn't seem too long, because it wasn't being played for laughs! It made me realise that the function of the two acts is quite different: the first spins out the story to the point where the outcome is a foregone conclusion, the second is a close-up of the four characters caught up in a joke that has got out of control (hence all those consecutive arias). The result is far more painful and the damage more irreparable than I had realised. The final reconciliation, in the very key in which the Countess forgives Almaviva, is perhaps even more moving here because of the underlying bitterness: the two girls are far more humiliated than the incorrigible count who will no doubt start again the next day, and the lovers' reply to their vows of faith ('I believe you, my beautiful joy, but I'll no longer put it to the test') which had always struck me as merely neat and amusing, implied so clearly 'How I wish I never had!' It was a bit like an *Othello* in which Iago would have been proved right. Despina was suitably sordid, a bawd rather than the usual soubrette, and 'Fra gli amplessi'[18] made me weep as never before: I could have emerged from a washing-machine by the end of it. Ferrando started *pp*, which together with the change to the minor made me as incapable of resistance as Fiordiligi. (The entire thing was beautifully acted.)

And I had only gone because my friend Margaret Cable was Dorabella! It was most impressive to see her act so subtly and look so well on stage. One thing I never noticed before is the similarity of her second act aria to both of Despina's: Mozart is just as much of a moralist as Jane Austen, consciously or not, but his touch is so light that the point has escaped me till now. Once noticed, it speaks for itself!

The last few days have brought a marked improvement, especially in my relation with my friends – I saw Stephen and Ondine,[19] Radu and Terry and felt great encouragement from them all. And at last, a letter from J!

---

[18] 'In the embraces': the duet in Act 2, scene 3, where Fiordiligi succumbs to Ferrando's charms.

[19] Stephen Kovacevich (then Bishop) and his girlfriend Ondine, daughter of the French-Venezuelan violinist Maurice Hasson (b. 1934), London-based since 1973, and his first wife Monique Duphil (b. 1936), also a distinguished musician who is now professor of piano at Oberlin College and Conservatory, Ohio, USA.

24 December

My first free day, completely and shamelessly idle. No practice; no composition or orchestration; no work on the autobiography; no travelling; no social life. I've become so conditioned by guilt that I have to *restrain* myself from orchestrating the virtuous daily page, which I normally do at home as one says one's prayers! But I will not: now that the depression is over, I want to get rid of the fatigue, and one totally vacant day is as healthy as an occasional fast – it will make me work with eagerness and joy, not mere sense of duty. Practice has been abandoned for a week, and only today have I felt the first faint tingle of interest for it; I'll probably leave it for another day, who knows? The neighbours might find it strange to hear me practice on Christmas Day, and though I don't really care *what* they think, it might do for an excuse if I want one…

The BBC obliged by furnishing my time with both the Brahms B flat sextet (alas, quite indifferently played) and a compete and beautiful performance of The Italian Song Cycle[20] – Janet Baker, John Shirley-Quirk and Steuart Bedford. I followed the Brahms on the score and the Wolf on the text (they changed the order of the songs, so it was quite difficult to keep track of them).

Another wonderful leisure occupation: Jadria[21] sent me Troyat's enormous and fascinating biography of Pushkin![22] It arrived yesterday, I devoured the first three chapters last night and will no doubt spend most of tonight over it. But let's face it, I do feel guilty at the amount of work that still remains to be done just on putting Act I in full score, just as I do worry about my overdraft and debts… Perhaps, like last night, I'll start by treating myself to that long-promised free evening, only to find myself orchestrating after all at three am?

---

[20] That is, Hugo Wolf's *Italienisches Liederbuch* (1890–91, 1896), settings of 46 Italian folk-poems in German translation.

[21] A diary entry for 5 January 1978 (not included in this publication) reveals that Jadria was 'the only friend of my mother's to survive the ghetto'. No further details about this person are known.

[22] Henri Troyat, *Pushkin*, Victor Gollancz, London/Pantheon, New York, 1950.

At rehearsals, David combined enthusiasm with frank criticism, a most stimulating mixture, and I was equally grateful for both. Also he *isn't* like talked like a publicity agent. He called my *second* — *my* technical problems imaginary, and capp— up calling me one of the greatest pianists he knows – me, who keep wondering whether I am a pianist at all! He even forgot himself so far as

23 January

London

No man who is just being married to the woman he loves can be happier than I've been today.

Being impressed by a performance shows indeed that it's a good performance. Being impressed by the work that is being played denotes an immeasurably better performance and an entirely different attitude on the *players'* part. But there is something yet better than that and this is the total unthinking experience of the work, a flood of emotions that makes all evaluation impossible – except of course in retrospect, when one realises that one has participated in a *great* performance (I say participated, not witnessed, as the commitment of the players forces that of the audience and eliminates any gap between both sides). This is what happened today when the Lindsay[1] premièred my second string quartet.

The greater including the lesser, I did occasionally gasp at the beauty of some of the music (quite forgetting it was my own) and ravishing touches of imagination on the Lindsays' part. For instance, while the last page of the first movement had always struck me as the work's 'ace of trumps', that of the *Passacaglia* took me quite unawares – I knew it to be carefully crafted, of course, but it's sheer luck that at times so few notes can sound so well. And I remember how diffident, almost *bored*, I was while writing it! Perhaps *Ariel* is not my best piece after all? It was certainly the one I was happiest writing, but this in itself may prove nothing whatever. When I said, in this very note-book, that it puts my few late works to shame, I may have meant the process of writing rather than the result. Perhaps I am the last person to be able to judge the latter; however it may be, this coolly conceived, calculated, meticulously executed quartet moved me today as it might any innocent listener. I have fallen for all my own tricks!

[1] The Lindsay String Quartet.

I hardly needed Peter Cropper[2] to tell me that he considered this the best piece they'd ever premièred – their love for it was apparent in the way they played. In a way, the most encouraging comment came from the producer, the phenomenally intelligent and knowledgeable Misha Donat,[3] when he compared it famously with the piano concerto. 'This is terrific!' he exclaimed excitedly as I arrived, late as ever, for the balance test. 'Do you like it as much as the piano concerto?' 'Yes – even better. More invention...' I don't know what they all mean by invention: Hans [Keller] also compliments me on my invention while I can spend a year or two without getting any new ideas! But it's lovely to know that a recent work is an improvement on an earlier one (it may be silly to compare a string quartet to a piano concerto, but these are the only works of mine Misha has heard), that everyone except Eve prefers the second quartet to the first, and that a medium of which I know so little is yielding to repeated efforts. Another reason for valuing Misha's praise is that he had booked the première of the work without having seen the score or asking to see it (much as Radu had committed himself to the piano concerto entirely on trust), that he never at any point felt any doubts or anxiety, so it was wonderful to prove his touching vote of confidence right!

I have wonderful friends. I really do. Stephen and Ondine were there and Ilana, and two Israeli friends of hers who care for me more than I know (Uri is away but will hear and record the repeat broadcast on Saturday), and Simon Rattle, who'd only met me three times and heard two erratic and messy performances, but was impressed enough this time to make me feel I'd made up for them! And Lisa Lupu (Radu is in America), and Milein Keller – Hans could only listen on the radio, but he's been my chief adviser and probably knows the piece by heart, besides taking a lot of the credit! And Eve, who hated it, and Alan Golding,[4] and Angela K[okoszka]. and Kaarina [Meyer], both escaped from the office... Levon Chilingirian[5] (an acquaintance rather than a friend) was interested enough to come, though maybe more on the Lindsay's account. [...]

No doubt the word will get round, and many who have missed it today will hear Saturday's broadcast – e.g. Imogen Cooper,[6] who didn't know it

---

[2] First violin of the Lindsay Quartet.
[3] Head of Classical Music for BBC Radio 3, and composer, now freelance writer, lecturer and producer.
[4] Tchaikowsky's accountant.
[5] British violinist, born to Armenian parents on Cyprus in 1948; his family moved to London in 1960. He is the founder (in 1971) and first violin of the Chilingirian Quartet.
[6] English pianist (b. 1949).

was on, Chris,[7] Nicky Braithwaite...[8] (This page looks like Who is Who in Music!)

The thing to remember is that inspiration or the lack of it proves nothing! As I wrote to Jacek, the point is not to express but to elicit emotions. I may have yawned while writing that slow movement, but it moves me now (especially the coda, from the sudden simplicity of the second violin solo, which seemed so insignificant at the time).

Trust yourself, Tchaikopath. Love yourself. Other people do.

2 February

London–Toronto, the start of my American tour

The first engagement is a recital at the McMaster University in Hamilton (Ontario), with the programme I've played every night last weekend: Beethoven op. 10 No. 1, Brahms op. 76 and the Chopin four ballades. I play it badly – indeed I've been playing well below standard ever since November, and the only positive sign is my increasing concern. I don't practise any less than I did last season, but until now it's been mattering to me a good deal less, and perfunctory, daydreaming practice, done merely to appease one's conscience, has never yet produced results.

What I need is some outside stimulant, something to get me interested in my piano-playing; the solitary set-up at Cumnor is ideally suited to my composing side, which is now catching up at the expense of everything else, but precludes the help of a colleague's advice and any fertilising influence. Luckily, this is just what I am likely to get at my second American engagement, which is a set of 4 concerts with David Zinman and his orchestra at Rochester, N.Y. – K.453[9] and Bartók III, twice each. David is the most inspiring conductor I know, full of ideas and responding to them, the best partner for bringing out one's own latent creativity. Already, I *want* to play well with more determination than I have felt for a long time!

(Merely wishing for it is not enough).

5 February

Hamilton, Ontario.
Much of my time on the flight to Toronto was spent writing to Hans. It was a difficult letter: Hans had given me his recently published book *1975*

---

[7] Christopher Seaman.
[8] Nicholas Braithwaite (born in London in 1939) who has held positions of principal conductor or music director in orchestras in Australia, Europe and New Zealand.
[9] Mozart, Piano Concerto No. 17 in G major (1784).

(1984 – 9)[10] and, while I agree with a lot of what he says in it, I hate the way he says it. The whole tone of the book is a downright assault on the reader: dogmatic, arrogant, shrill, precluding any possibility of there being any valid counter-argument. The syntax is often impenetrably obscure, but never fails to clear up in time for him to blow his own trumpet. Now Hans has been a friend as well as a teacher to me, and I've come to feel at home in his house; affection, gratitude, admiration, have all combined to make me feel rotten for hating his book. I first rang him at home, and found myself speaking to Milein (whom I like, if anything, even more); she heard my objections and said she felt sure of my finding a way to put them to Hans without causing offence. The next day, as the subject wouldn't leave me alone, I rang him at the office. It was the more embarrassing as he immediately congratulated me on my Second quartet, the success of which is partly due to his own advice! This, and the admirative [*sic*] inscription in front of the book, made it a real wrench to tell him what I had rung to say. His reply was astonishing: 'Well, I can tell you you're the only one to feel this way, as all the reviews I've had have backed me up'. For Hans, of all people, to hide behind the critics' back! His conscious quest is for truth; his unconscious craving for praise. He is just like the rest of us – more vulnerable than most, if anything. Always expecting to be beaten up, he hits out first, and this is what makes his prose so aggressive: once he *knows* a person, he is patient and gentle. The inherent contradiction in *1975* is that the whole book is devoted to the threat of spiritual collectivisation; is conceived as a defense of individual judgment – and on every page of that same book he tells the reader what to think, admire or despise! And it's a related inconsistency that Hans, who gleefully sneers at critics like the rest of us (e.g. 'we know all about the pleasure which minor minds derive from having their own thoughts, if thoughts you can call them, confirmed by an outside source: the craft of criticism itself would at once cease to be a going concern if such pleasure were to dry up'), invokes the praise of the press the moment a book of *his* is criticised!

In the difficult circumstances, I think I wrote a reasonably good letter, though I had to work in some flattery in order to enable my reservation to reach him at all: it's never easy to dismiss a flatterer, whatever else he says. But this is the only part of the letter I am ashamed of. I wonder if I've fallen between two stools, cheapening myself by hyperbolic compliments, only to alienate him after all by home-truths that were the real reason of the letter? I do hope not: I'd greatly miss his friendship, far more than his advice on composition. But I trust him to accept them from me, if not to see their

---

[10] Dennis Dobson, London, 1977; republished by Toccata Press, London, in 1986 as *Music, Closed Societies and Football.*

validity – and was there ever anybody like Hans to prove himself in the right when he was wrong?

This is where Hans' insecurity shows most: he daren't be wrong. He lives in a world where a Jew can only survive by being chronically right and always brighter than anyone else: one failure or hesitation, and he'll be back on the train to Dachau. Those chimneys are still smoking for him, but a temporary respite has been granted to outstandingly clever Jews. Shall I one day have the guts to show him this entry?

A book that will compensate for a year of Hans Keller's prose is Troyat's tremendous and breathtaking biography of Pushkin, which I finished just before leaving England. Like most writers who write in an adopted tongue (Conrad, Nabokov), he can't always resist showing off his mastery of it, and I needed Larousse to help me cope with a vocabulary as rich as Flaubert's. But at least the mastery is there, and he holds the reader's conviction even when established fact must perforce give way to conjecture. And what story-telling, what insight, what wit!

15 February

Curaçao

The week in Rochester was nothing less than a breakthrough. It would be little to say that it was the high point of the season, for God knows the season has been nothing to brag of so far. But it almost seems as if it had been one of its highlights for David [Zinman]. And, since he's always been my favourite conductor, the pianist in me could get no greater boost.

At rehearsals, David combined enthusiasm with frank criticism, a most stimulating mixture, and I was equally grateful for both. After the concerts, he talked like a publicity agent. He called my Mozart sensational, my technical problems imaginary, and capped it all up by calling me one of the greatest pianists he knows – me, who keeps wondering whether I am a pianist at all! He even forgot himself so far as to call my Second string quartet a masterpiece (I always carry that cassette in my pocket, as luggage at airports goes through an X-ray check that might damage tapes), so, since he wants me to come back with 'something unusual' as well as more Mozart, I might suggest my own piano concerto – I play nothing more unusual that that.

As for more Mozart, we've already had more than we'd expected! Just the kind of thing I love most happened in Rochester. David noticed last Wednesday that his Sunday all-Mozart programme came to barely 55 minutes, and asked me to play an encore; I suggested another Mozart concerto, and after much merry discussion, which included my playing to him the whole of K. 414,[11] he decided on K. 467[12] as being both a neat contrast to K. 453[13] (which was already in the programme) and a work the orchestra was familiar with. He put the suggestion to the orchestra and they all voted in favour! Extra work for, as far as I know, no extra money. I can't see this happening in England…

Bartók III being played on Thursday and Saturday nights, we found time to rehearse both concertos *twice* in between the two concerts: two rehearsals on Friday, with a practice session in between the two on my part, and one on Saturday morning. The Mozart programme was played twice on Sunday, and went well both times. Oh, I do love a challenge, an emergency (within limits, as the destruction of *The Merchant* would not stimulate me at all) and I did my best in both concerts, especially the G-major. In K. 467, the chief progress lay in the slow movement, which I had asked David to teach me, and played it, as it were, to order, just like any orchestral musician. Oh, the joy of obeying, when there is someone worthy of one's best obedience! Even I, an old chronic rebel, must acknowledge that. David's Mozart makes one believe in reincarnation. He is also superb in French music, of which I heard *Nuages et Fêtes* (with whisper mutes on the trumpets in the trio of the latter) and the Second suite of *Daphnis and Chloë*. And his opening of the Bartók created a hush I was almost reluctant to break.

Somewhat later – This is the note from Hans I found on my arrival here:

'Dear André,
The journalist writes for the reader whom he wants to interest; the writer addresses the ideal reader who's interested. If he finds him on a representative scale, he has succeeded; if he doesn't he has failed.
But if he doesn't find anybody substantial who objects, he has failed too – so many thanks!
Kindest regards,
Yours ever
Hans.'

This answers none of the points raised so painstakingly in my own letter, throws me a perfunctory bone in the word 'substantial' and converts all my objections to further praise of himself (on top of all those reviews?) in the slickest way.

---

[11] Mozart, Piano Concerto No. 12 in A major (1782).
[12] Mozart, Piano Concerto No. 21 in C major (1785).
[13] Mozart, Piano Concerto No. 17 in G major (1784).

Curaçao, 15.2. – The week in Rochester was nothing less than a breakthrough.

It would be little to say that it was the high point of the season, for God knows the season has been nothing to brag of so far. But it almost seems as if it had been one of its highlights for <u>David</u>. And, since he's always been my favourite conductor, the pianist in me could get no greater boost.

At rehearsals, David combined enthusiasm with frank criticism, a most stimulating mixture, and I was equally grateful for both. After the concerts, he talked like a publicity agent. He called my Mozart sensational, my technical problems imaginary, and capped it all up by calling me one of the greatest pianists he knows – me, who keep wondering whether I am a pianist at all! He even forgot himself so far as to call my 2$^{\underline{d}}$ string quartet a masterpiece (I always carry that cassette in my pocket, as luggage at airports goes through an X-ray check that might damage tapes), so, since he wants me to come back with "something unusual" as well as more Mozart, I might suggest my own piano concerto – I play nothing more unusual than that.

As for more Mozart, we've already had more than we'd expected! Just the kind of thing I love most happened in Rochester. David noticed last Wednesday that his Sunday all-Mozart programme came to barely 55 minutes, and asked me to play an encore; I suggested another Mozart con-

39

All right, Hans; I'll trouble you no further on the subject, or myself with you. There is a waste paper basket under this very table. But I wonder how you *really* felt?

14 March

Mexico–London

This was altogether a very pleasant tour. For one thing, I played well every time except the duo recital with Monique[14] in Guadalajara last night (having made the usual mistake of congratulating myself too soon and taking the programme for granted). After a very doubtful season, this sudden progess would of itself have been enough to raise my spirits. True, I have done little orchestration and no work whatever on the autobiography, but I had decided that beforehand, so as to avoid any strong interests which would compete with my concentration on piano-playing, and even so I did more work on the score than I had planned, including some actual composition in Caracas (filling in the somewhat sketchy accompaniment to Gratiano's 'Ay-ya-yay' etc.)

There were other pleasures as well. The greatest was by far my luck in meeting an unusual number of exceptionally nice people – or could it be that I am at last learning to relate to them? Wherever I went, except for Curaçao, I found myself welcome and in good company. And it just might prove that I've earned enough money to get back into credit and pay all my debts! Well, almost: I didn't cancel a single concert and most were well-paid (including Guadalajara, which makes me feel all the guiltier). And in most places I am wanted back.

3 May

I am on my way to London, with the finally completed 1947 chapter[15] in my luggage. It is much longer than I had expected, longer even than 1939; it has also taken longest to write, and further revision will no doubt prove necessary. But Eve and myself are both very pleased with it. Indeed, Eve's enthusiasm for the first two-thirds of the chapter made me apprehensive for its conclusion; I couldn't think of a 'crunch' that would cap Grams' clash with Dorothy and the break-up of my parents' marriage. I knew that only an open row between Grams and myself could provide a climax, so I engineered one, using some of her later imprecations (e.g. her vow not to forgive my mother for giving me life) and putting into my own mouth lines that I'd have been glad of at the time: there is such a thing as staircase venom, and I've now used all of it. The scene was difficult to write, because I really no longer hate Grams, and some of the lines surprised and shocked me by their nastiness (the suggestion that Grams welcomed her daughter's

---

[14] Duphil.
[15] From Tchaikowsky's unpublished autobiography.

death still strikes me as downright monstrous); but on the whole I do think it works. Tomorrow I shall show it to Chad.

London threatens to be as tiring as usual, and for the same reason: I've committed myself to see too many people. Tonight I am staying with Lisa Lupu (Radu is on tour) who rang me and sounded depressed; from tomorrow I'll be at Terry's, who'll no doubt expect me to have supper with him on Friday night after the recital in Chelmsford. So far, so good; but I have also promised to see Stephen and Ondine, the Frankls, and for my own sake I'd be sorry to miss Eve… It all looks like an unwholesome cluster.

Recently, though only since my half-successful Birmingham recital last Friday, I've been feeling tired and morose, more averse to company than at any time since November. […] By now I am tired, lack concentration and interest in anything, sleep badly, play badly.

11 May

I am on my way to Birmingham, to give a master-class. As the train is late, let me jot down a few of the last events:

Chad loved '1947' – for once, there were no reservations whatever, not even stylistic ones (Eve had proved of great help there) and he sees no need for cuts or further revision.

Owing to an epidemic of depression around me (Chris, Lisa L., Stephen and even Terry) and to my incurable propensity for being everyone's problem page, I lost a lot of time and energy and my playing deteriorated to the point of amateurishness. It was vital to play to a colleague and get some advice, which, whether followed or not, would at least focus my attention back on its rightful object. At Terry's suggestion, I chose Peter Frankl rather than Stephen (Radu, who would be my first choice, being away), as Stephen's exacting meticulousness and ever-vigilant perfectionism could, I thought, only discourage me further. For the past few months – to be exact, ever since our row over Ondine – I had been feeling uneasy about our relations. Thinking over the commandment 'thou shalt love thy neighbour as thyself', it struck me that this is indeed the only way one *can* love anyone: not merely as much as oneself (that, alas, is very seldom the case), but in precisely the same way. Now, how does Stephen love himself? He's full of self-doubt, and since he doesn't always believe himself worthy of love, he's prone to suspect his friends of going 'off' him; and just as he's always driven to test and prove himself, he keeps testing his friends, not only in their attitude towards him, but in their intrinsic abilities. Am I, for instance, still as alert as I was last time? Why don't I get better at chess? Games loom large in Stephen's life, not only for their sheer enjoyment, but as a bout of friendly rivalry. He's apt to remember that he'd lost our last game of chess, or even two (though generally he's better at it) and will sit down at the board with a playful: 'Let's see if we can win back our lost honour', which, though a joke, still seems to me to indicate the symbolic value he attaches to games. I fairly licked everybody at 'categories' and I doubt if he'll suggest this particular game to me again.

Now this attitude carries over into music with daunting results. No musician is more dedicated than Stephen: he loves music, as I do, more than anything else, but with him the price of love is eternal vigilance, and he will not forgive himself anything. The results, in his case, are staggering: while Radu seems at times to give mere 'repeat performances', while Alfred[16] has ossified into a Herr Professor, Stephen shows not just a development but an ascension. I, on the other hand, have been going downhill as a pianist (it takes a talent like Martha's[17] to survive without a vocation) and I can't help feeling that Stephen, who loves me, is sad and disappointed when he hears me play. The more he likes my ideas, the more frustrating it is to him to hear them misfire through sheer lack of practice, or absent-minded practice, so that only on stage I become aware of difficulties and defects I have overlooked.

Thus Stephen gradually became an incarnation of my super-ego. And while I've never envied his achievements – indeed, I rejoice in them! – I grew to envy the very pains he was taking, the intensity of his dedication, the willingness to take on the dirty job of scales and exercises, and while he's always been too tactful to reproach me, I would upbraid myself on his behalf. He was no longer just a friend: he was someone who had believed in me and whom I had failed.

This was why I found it impossible to play to him, and rang Peter instead. What followed was a grotesque non-event: although I had made my request quite clear on the 'phone, and had been told that Peter would be thrilled to hear me play, neither he nor his wife showed any sign of remembering the purpose of my visit, and I spent three mortal hours making small talk with that sedate, perennially middle-aged couple, that had as much originality as a garden gnome. I had not eaten; I had not meditated; I had not practised, since Terry who had put me up has no piano, so I had counted on the session with Peter to make up for that particular loss! And all along I was aware of Stephen and Ondine waiting for me, of my promise to spend the evening with them, and of that evening dwindling into almost nothing.

Finally I went on to Stephen, over an hour late, with barely enough time for us to have a much-needed meal before my last train to Oxford. From earlier

---

[16] Brendel (b. 1931), Austrian, Briish-based pianist.
[17] Argerich (b. 1941), Argentinian pianist.

hints, Stephen already knew my perplexities, and his reaction was altogether admirable. First of all, he offered to stay away from my next London recital; secondly, he offered me help with some of the programme; and he was even willing to take the trouble of coming down to Oxford to hear it!

He came the next day, and his very presence made me aware of defects in my playing that I hadn't noticed before. Every chord was uneven, with many notes missing altogether; the tone was uncontrolled, the phrasing stifled and the pace unsteady. From the outset, it was obvious that my fumbling attempts at Chopin's first ballade couldn't by a long way be called a performance, let alone an interpretation (there is, of course, no such thing as art without craft). Stephen heard the mess through, was noncommittally sympathetic and suggested that I go on to the second ballade, which, however strained and untidy, certainly went better.

Then came the real event. Warning me that these were merely his personal views, Stephen took me back to the first ballade and right through it, rehearsing me as a conductor does an orchestra and demonstrating not only an infallible ear, but an infectious enthusiasm and an over-all *vision* of the work. I had always complained of the lack of cohesion of the first ballade, in which pretty but sentimental tunes seemed to alternate with gratuitous bursts of virtuosity; I had always feared that Stephen would prove a rigid, pernickety and generally restrictive task-master. All at once I was proved wrong on both counts. Stephen was inspiring and incandescent, and as quick to notice and encourage any improvement in my playing as he had been to point out its shortcomings; he quickly showed me that subtle restlessness of the first theme that makes the later agitation sound inevitable (I had taken all the themes too slowly, in six rather than two, and overlooked the unsettling off-beat accompaniment of the first). And, while he was careful never to mention the dread word 'technique' which had always bored and repelled me, the emotional demands of the piece inevitably brought physical demands in their wake, and once again I was faced with my impotence. But not discouraged; Stephen's approach was too vital and ardent for that; the difficulty of the piece was revealed as inseparable from its beauty, and only added to my excitement the romantic beauty of a challenge. Stephen has that best kind of understanding that comes from love, and for which no intellect will ever find a substitute. But he uses his intellect to communicate that understanding, and there his articulate and precise eloquence gives him a clear advantage over Radu, who perceives things instinctively but cannot always put them into words… We ended up the session happy, dizzy and exhausted, with a thrilling sense of achievement and mutual response, and love-making is my only word for it.

18 May

Zurich–London

The K. 246[18] in Zurich went well, and I love the city! I took an evening walk
through the town, starting at Bellevueplatz, then ambling along the quays
on either side till I reached the station. At one point I made a detour to the
right, which brought me into a fascinatingly shady old district; finding my
way back to the cathedral, I stumbled upon a giant chessboard painted on
the pavement, with suitably huge pieces. I wondered how heavy they were
and what they were made of, but a game was in progress, so I sat down on
a thoughtfully provided bench to watch it. Another kibitzer was already
settled there and I had some hope of being able to play him afterwards;
alas, the incompetence of both present players soon put paid to any hope
of a quick conclusion. It was amusing to watch them actually walk onto the
board (the only way to get at the centrally placed pieces), but there was little
other interest, so I got up and went as the cathedral clock struck eleven,
catching a positively shocked look from the two players. A huge green case
stood by, obviously meant for storage of the pieces; I thought the whole idea
charming, and well in keeping with the academic tradition of the city. (The
day before I'd stumbled onto Docent Büchner's grave in the Zürichberg
woods.[19]) If ever I realise my old dream of spending six months or so in
a German-speaking town to learn the language, it is even more likely to
be Zurich than Munich – certainly not Vienna, that taxidermist's paradise,
which regularly starved great composers and bragged of their achievements
afterwards! (They always used the one they'd just killed as a stick to beat
the new one with.) I love the Zurich lake, the bridges over the Limmat as
numerous as those over the Seine (and far less chi-chi), and the somehow
preserved feeling of a medieval university town.

This is the frantic week that leads up to my QEH recital (Schubert
C-major sonata, Brahms op. 76 and the Chopin ballades). I worked on this
programme very seriously last week; this week I might do better to let it go,
with tomorrow's small-town recital as a try-out (I've asked Janice Williams[20]
to come and hear it so as to have a candid post-mortem afterwards) and a
thorough revising and tidying-up session on my last remaining day. I do
hope I have the sense not to practise this evening, though anxiety may drive
me to it!

---

[18] Mozart, Piano Concerto No. 8 in C major (1776).
[19] Eduard Büchner (1860–1917) was a German chemist, awarded with the 1907 Nobel Prize in
Chemistry for his work on fermentation.
[20] Janice Williams, a student of Stefan Askenase, became a friend of Tchaikowsky.

Die Plebejer proben den Aufstand[21] is the third Günter Grass I've left unfinished. How can a man be at once so clever and so deadly boring? Perhaps cleverness, like sex, needs an emotional charge of some kind to avoid boredom. For my part, I'll avoid Günter Grass.

I've read quite a bit lately, mainly biographies: Ernest Newman on Wolf,[22] Hingley on Dostoyevsky,[23] Berlioz (I still prefer his prose to his music)[24] and *two* biographies of Ivan the Terrible, both inadequate in opposite ways: Graham makes him into a demon, Ian Grey into a martyr, and neither can write.[25] Now I'm on to Boris Godunov...

What a subject for Dostoyevsky Ivan would have been! Ivan IV, I mean, not Karamazov. Only D[ostoyevsky] would have sensed what went on in that month between Ivan's abdication and his return, suddenly aged, as a bloody tyrant.[26] It was like the crisis that made Rimbaud give up poetry – as tremendous and as enigmatic.[27]

An unintentionally comic book was Schlegel's comparison between Euripides' Hippolytos and Racine's Phèdre,[28] entirely to the former's advantage! It sounded very much like Thomas Rymer's attack on Othello.[29] Schlegel's moral disapproval of Phèdre was particularly enjoyable – as if *she* was so pleased with herself!

---

[21] 'The Plebeians Rehearse the Uprising': a novel by Grass, written in 1966.

[22] *Hugo Wolf*, Methuen, London, 1907.

[23] Ronald Hingley, *Dostoyevsky: His Life and Work*, Paul Elek, London, 1978.

[24] This parenthesis suggests that the book Tchaikowsky had been reading was either a new French edition of the *Mémoires* (ed. Pierre Citron, Flammarion, Paris, 1969) or the translation by David Cairns (*Memoirs*, Victor Gollancz, London, 1969).

[25] Stephen Graham, *Ivan the Terrible: Life of Ivan IV of Russia*, E. Benn, London, 1932; Ian Grey, *Ivan the Terrible*, Hodder & Stoughton, London, 1964.

[26] On 3 December 1564, the paranoid Ivan IV left Moscow, ostensibly on a pilgrimage, and from Alexandrova Sloboda, 75 miles to the north-east, announced his abdication. Split between the two places, the court was unable to function and so asked Ivan to return; he agreed to do so only if he were granted absolute power. He then founded in effect a police state, the *Oprichnina*, which unleashed a ferociously cruel wave of repression against the boyars, Russia's landed aristocracy. (The eponymous *Oprichniki* of Pyotr Tchaikovsky's opera were Ivan's secret police.)

[27] Most of Rimbaud's poetry was written between 1870, shortly before he turned sixteen, and 1874; after the age of twenty, he abandoned writing and travelled the world – to Java as a soldier in the Dutch Colonial Army, then Cyprus, where he worked as a foreman in a stone quarry and, after joining a trading company in Aden (he spoke Arabic), running its operation in Harar in Ethiopia. He died (of cancer) in Marseilles on 10 November 1891 at the age of 37.

[28] August Schlegel, *Comparaison entre la Phèdre de Racine et Celle d'Euripide*, 1807; Tchaikowsky probably read the reprint issued by A. L. Pollard, Old Marston, Oxford, 1962.

[29] In *A Short View of Tragedy* (1693) the English literary critic Thomas Rymer (1641–1713) criticised *Othello* as a 'Bloody farce, without salt or savour', pointing out from a neo-Aristotelian position what he saw as weaknesses in the plot.

The best bit of intentional humour was Berlioz's story of the lady singer's performance for the sultan of Constantinople.[30] But this will have to do me till after the QEH – if I read anything at all, let it be boring, like Ian Grey's biography of Boris Godunov.[31] And for the last fortnight I have abstained from both autobiography and orchestration... I'll soon catch up when I'm a free man again.

27 May

Cumnor

I must have improved, for the QEH recital which was a great disappointment to myself, has impressed all my friends more than anything I have done for more than a year.

My previous high-water mark had been the Birmingham concert with Uri at the end of '76, and certainly this was nowhere near so good (or at least so clean). But the encouraging thing is that while the previous concert had found me in good form and aware of it, this time I was well below form – at first timid, then shaky, then messy. It seems that even my second best, after a period of intense concentration and strenuous practice is better than what I think my best in laxer periods.

Since then, all the delight of pure laziness. It's now nearly a week, and I still haven't started practice or composition (except for a page of orchestration each of the last two days); the autobiography still lies where I left it; and, best of all, I don't feel the least qualms about it. One side-effect of work is the joy of a holiday, and I have worked long and hard enough to authorise myself to make the most of my present freedom. Nor have I set myself a back-to-the-mines date! The term ends on June 17, which makes me anxious to give it priority: the wonderful weather has brought the students out en masse and I spend deliciously idle hours watching then punt, many of them as naked as my diary. The anti-climax of their departure will no doubt force me to fall back on work, which will then be as welcome as they are now. This, of course, would mean that I have granted myself a four-week holiday! But why not? It's the only time of the year when I can do it; it's the place where I enjoy it most (four weeks in an hotel would drive me insane). Once under the inner pressure of composition, or the outer pressure of the coming season there'll be no escape from my own demands. And when else will the students be there with so little on?

---

[30] The reference is to a story in the 'Deuxième soirée' of Berlioz's *Les soirées de l'orchestre* (1852).
[31] *Boris Godunov, the Tragic Tsar*, Hodder & Stoughton, London, 1973.

South Bank Piano Recital Series 1977/78

Presented jointly by
Harrison/Parrott Ltd and
Ingpen and Williams Ltd

Photograph: Sophie Baker

André Tchaikowsky

Schubert	Sonata in C, D840
Brahms	Eight Klavierstücke, Op 76
Chopin	The Four Ballades
Chopin	Trois Nouvelles Etudes

Sunday 21 May 1978 at 3pm

Greater London Council

Queen Elizabeth Hall
Director : George Mann OBE

Tickets: £2.00 £1.50 £1.25 £1.00 75p
available 21 April from Box Office Royal Festival Hall
(01-928 3191) and usual agents.

An exclusive Harrison/Parrott artist

South Bank Piano Recital Series 1977 / 78

Gelber Vesmas Pollini Zimerman Browning Brendel Ranki
Frankl Zeltser Rogé Tchaikowsky Berman Eschenbach

Pollini (2 recitals) and Berman at the Royal Festival Hall
Brendel (4 Schubert recitals) and all other recitals at the
Queen Elizabeth Hall

*Poster for the Queen Elizabeth Hall recital 'which was a great disappointment
to myself [... and] impressed all my friends'*

Besides, nothing on holiday is taboo, not even work. If I find myself at it, well and good. If not, let the holiday be as wholehearted as work at my best – which so far it has certainly been.

It is good to have time for my friends. It's good to make new ones. It's good not to be just a music-producing machine.

2 July

[…] This was a packed weekend! I am punch-drunk.

First, there was the experience of *Total Eclipse*, the Christopher Hampton play about Verlaine and Rimbaud, which I had long ago heard on the radio, missed on stage and TV and now read as a painfully truthful revelation.[32] There is no more daunting character than Rimbaud; everyone has tried to solve the enigma of his sudden silence, and all have failed; the murderous integrity that isolated his life still frightens off biographers, poets, readers, anyone who would attempt any intimacy with his thought and work. And isn't it significant that, while half of the greatest French songs are settings of Verlaine, only mad dogs and one mad Englishman have tackled Rimbaud? (And personally I wish he hadn't; the Britten cycle[33] is nice enough for Britten, but bears the same relation to R. as a Hollywood Bible-epic to Jesus – and W. H. Auden's poem[34] is a timid fiasco).

Now the impossible has been done: Hampton has got as near to Rimbaud as Racine to Nero, or as near as any man can without getting radiation-sickness or being turned to stone. I'll never again ask why Rimbaud stopped writing – H. has made it feel inevitable, though still enigmatic. But the most miraculous achievement is the unity of tone between the phrases he adapts from R.'s prose and correspondence and those he invents (or, at any rate, those I can't trace). I ended up feeling convinced R. must have spoken virtually every word of that play. It's a downright uncanny experience – like reincarnation. I wish I could base my next opera on *Total Eclipse*, but it's just too good – I could only spoil it. *The Merchant*, over the years, has acquired a degree of unreality in which music may be a help rather than just an intrusion, but Hampton's play is only too true.

---

[32] It was published by Faber and Faber, London, in 1969.
[33] *Les Illuminations*, Op. 18, for high voice and strings (1931).
[34] 'Rimbaud', published in *Shorter Collected Poems 1927–1957*, Faber and Faber, London, 1966.

The other outstanding event was Alec McCowen's[35] reading of St. Mark's Gospel. All those hackneyed lines, that have come to sound so smooth and smug, suddenly regained the original awe and urgency, as if the miracles and the passion had only just happened and were related by a stunned and breathless eye-witness. Often the emphasis would fall on the most unexpected word, but the effect was never arbitrary – in fact, none of it was done for effect, and all for meaning. I nearly decided to leave at the interval, fearing a total breakdown once it came to the harrowing story of the Holy Week. But I got away with just a few tears, none of them in the obvious places (there was nothing *obvious*, anyway). Never had Jesus struck me as so admirable and lovable, with his sense of isolation, of being constantly misunderstood, his human vulnerability. Sometimes, in a parable, McCowen seemed to be searching for words so as to bring a transcendental truth within the reach of Jesus' first hearers, and though we all knew the lines in advance, we still felt all the awe of their being made up while we watched.

3 July

I've just written a letter to Christopher Hampton, asking if he'd object to my setting *Total Eclipse* to music! It's not *entirely* sincere, because I don't feel remotely equal to the task (Verlaine would be within my range, but not Rimbaud). But it's true that if I believed I could do it, nothing in the world would stop me. It would involve a drastic development of my traditional and over-civilised musical style – why, so much the better! I do need shaking up, and this might do it. How much easier is *The Merchant of Venice*! The difficulties are purely technical, not spiritual. I know how it feels to be Shylock, but only Hampton knows Rimbaud in the same way…

10 July

This morning, along with a business letter and an essay in officialese, came an anonymous-looking white envelope, which from the top of the stairs I took to be from England. The English 9 p. stamp was of course unmistakable, but the writing, though equally small, was neater than his, and it bore an Abingdon post-mark! Chilled at the thought of a fan-letter from some housewife (what else could it be, coming from a small town where I know nobody?) I opened it first to get it over with.

---

[35] McCowen's solo reading of St Mark's Gospel opened in London at the Riverside Studios in January 1978, shifting to the Mermaid Theatre and Comedy Theatre in the West End before touring to New York.

'Dear Mr. Tchaikowsky', it started, 'I was very pleased indeed to receive your letter.' MY letter? Since when have I been cultivating pen-pals in Abingdon? This is no good: I must stop taking even mild sleeping pills.

The penny dropped with the next sentence:

Total Eclipse was the least successful of my plays in terms of reviews and numbers of performances, but it's always been my favourite, and curiously enough, I still receive more letters about it, even though it's ten years since it was performed in London and it's now out of print, than about any of my other plays.

By all means go ahead with your project, and if it looks like coming to anything, let me know and I'm sure we can make the necessary arrangements. You don't say whether or not you would need a librettist but no doubt all those bridges can be crossed when the time comes.

Thanks again for writing: I'm delighted the play has made such a lasting impression on you. It was my first really serious piece of work, and I'm glad I charged in when I was so young: I don't think I'd have dared tackle the subject if I'd waited much longer.

There was a postscript telling me about the RADA production on London this week ('I don't believe I can face seeing it, but I thought you might be interested to know'), so I rang them, arranged to join the club and asked them to save me two seats for Thursday (not that I know whom to ask to it, if anyone). I'll write a thank-you note to C. H. afterwards.

What has happened is a repetition of the way I fell in love with John Browning during the Brussels competition in '56. Then I left a signed love-declaration in his room, half as an experiment and half as a joke, to see how he'd react; as he didn't react at all, I was puzzled, piqued and alarmed (suppose the note had been picked up by someone else?), and by the end of some three days I *was* in love. This time I've trapped myself in the same way, for I must admit that I only wanted to hear from C.H., or at the most meet him, when writing the letter and I wanted to have something more than congratulations to offer. He's called my bluff!

But I *knew*, several days before getting the answer (though it was his promptitude that threw me off the scent this morning, I had only posted my letter on Tuesday morning and that to his publishers) that, whatever I had meant in writing the letter, I was truly hooked on the play and wanted to give my obsession free course. I'm awfully glad to have an outside spur to go through with a project that only timidity and laziness may deter me from. As for meeting him, this has now become a secondary interest, especially as it is virtually bound to happen: *he* will want to meet me soon, no doubt, though he doesn't yet. I wanted to enter his field of vision, not his house, and now I know I have. Indeed it would be wiser not to hurry, since I am now as anxious to impress him as I was to please Edward! Let him, then, be the lighting-conductor for such anxieties, so that I can enjoy friendship with E. without neurosis…

This has been a wonderfully happy day.

15 July

The 48 hours I spent in London were so packed that I shall only record the salient events. […]

Pelléas et Mélisande at Covent Garden proved only a partial success: both baritones were excellent (Thomas Allen as Pelléas, Thomas Steward as Golaud) in beautifully contrasted ways, but Anne Howells is both too tall and too forceful to portray a strayed waif lost in a grow-up world – Mélisande should sound like a flute, not like sixteen first violins – and Colin's[36] thin and monotonous sound, which would be out of place even in *Ein Deutsches Requiem*, positively butchered this exquisite and elusive score. Everyone came in with a *sforzato*, and it's the only time I've heard the singers swamped in *Pelléas* – I should have thought it impossible. For once I was almost tempted to agree with all those philistines that find the opera a bore!

The next evening I saw *Total Eclipse*. I had some misgivings about a student production, but apart from some slight clumsiness in the changes of scenery (due, no doubt, to primitive stage equipment), no allowances needed to be made. The boy who played Rimbaud, Hamish Reid, will no doubt be 'discovered' in a big way soon, and Stephen Tiller as Verlaine was equally good. I went with Kyung Wha,[37] who knew nothing about either poet, not even their names, but the play gripped her immediately. The daring and dangerous ending was perfectly done: it was quite clear that it was Verlaine and not the playwright who was sentimental, and to watch Rimbaud kiss Verlaine's hands was even more painful than the stabbing had been (Kyung Wha felt the same).

On my return I wrote as follows to C. H.:

Dear Mr Hampton,

Hurray! You've given me several years of active play. But I'll express my gratitude in notes.

---

[36] Sir Colin Davis (1927–2013) was principal conductor at the Royal Opera House, Covent Garden, from 1971 to 1986; he was knighted after a decade in the post.
[37] Kyung-wha Chung, Korean violinist (b. 1948).

I didn't reply immediately, because I went to RADA's production of the play (for which I owe you additional thanks). Seeing it confirmed my conviction that I shall not need a librettist – you can trust my ability to ruin your great play single-handed. But I wonder if you would allow me to consult you sometime about such cuts as would damage it least: it seems a crime to suggest any whatever in so taut a play, but it would still take about five hours, set as it stands! Also, I doubt if there is room for *two* operas starting with the prelude to *Lohengrin*, and the first one might prove harder to dislodge…

Please forgive my troubling you again. You have troubled me for a long time and I am glad.

Yours etc.

From now on I should be careful not to talk about it, or the impact will spend itself in words. Let the project go inwards, not outwards.

1 August

Hampton hasn't answered my second letter, and by now I doubt if he will. After all, I had told him at first that I couldn't start work on his play for at least three years! This puts my request for consultation 'sometime' in almost astrological perspective.

But there are other reasons for joy:

[…] Michael M., having at last found peace and stability in Rio de Janeiro, has answered two bitterly reproachful letters from me with admirable calm, affection and dignity. Having given up everything (home, work, the one environment he knew) he discovered that what is left when all has gone is Michael! The very tone of every phrase in his letters shows how much he's gained. It's wonderful to have such a correspondent.

The next reason for joy is somewhat doubtful:

For years Peter Frankl has been nagging at me to write him a trio. Last year he came here and took me up on what I had thought were safely evasive assurances of 'trying', and asked to see the sketches. I told him my handwriting was illegible, so he asked me to play him some of it at the piano. I produced two chords out of *The Merchant*, which he likes (in telling the story I say I played a whole scene). When my Second string quartet was premièred last January, Peter rang Misha Donat, who had produced it, and assured him that he'd heard my trio, that it was better than the quartet, and did so well that Misha gave him and co. a date for its first performance! Of course I rang Misha and confessed that my trio had every virtue except existence (being, no doubt, too good for this world) but he still exhorted me

The opening of the second movement of the Trio Notturno

to try, and so did my publisher, aware of the number of performances that might result if that indefatigable threesome liked it.

Well, I don't like it. For one thing, it's too obviously a by-product of the piano concerto: both the themes of the first movement stem from it. For another, the agitated central section of the second movement (there are only two, I'm making it as short as I can) is blatantly pilfered from Bartók – it would only need to be better to sound like his first violin sonata. I hoped Hans, to whom it is to be dedicated as a thank-you and farewell present, would pinpoint its shortcomings in a way which would stimulate me into writing that real trio that may yet be latent in me! But, alas, he likes it: he says I've so far managed to avoid all the pitfalls of that difficult texture, but refused to tell me what these were so as not to inhibit me (nor did I insist).

24 August

Well, the trio's ready! What a relief. I have no idea if it's at all tolerable – indeed I doubt it – but it's so good to be a free man again, not to have to rush back home every evening for another usually frustrating and sometimes futile session… Never again shall I write anything to commission or outside persuasion – it takes genius to afford routine attitudes, routine talents do need inspiration.

Bartók's influence pervades the first movement no less than the second; in both cases, it's most glaring in the middle, the *pizz. accelerando* in the *Allegro*, the *agitato* part of the *Andante*. To confuse critics, I might put Schumannesque F. and E. initials after each movement. Or shall I forestall them by calling the piece Trio Hungarico?

Oh, to go back to *The Merchant*! I've already got the chord that will open Act III and other ideas are looming up. But of course this is not the moment: for the past two days I've given practice a miss altogether, as I no longer heard what I was doing! And my concerto is of course miles off.

That's the effect of composition: it undermines all interest in other activities, just as fatal diseases mercifully sap the will to live. Like being in love, it makes all else unreal. Shall I ever hear from J. again?

28 August

From Chad's[38] latest world tour:

'I devoted all of my live TV appearance in Hong Kong to a defense of homosexuality; but I only realised how successful it had been when, before I knew what was happening, the announcer got up and kissed me on the mouth!' This in front of several thousand viewers – the most public outrage since the murder of Lee Harvey Oswald.

I had a wonderful weekend in London, especially the performance of Mozart three great string quintets at Uri's last night! I had to conduct some of it, as the 'cellist was prone to get lost. But the first violin, a guest from Israel called Ilan whose surname I missed, produced the most breathtaking performance of the g-minor I have ever heard. And he was sight-reading it!!

---

[38] *Cf.* p. 102, above.

The Frankl-Pauk-Kirschbaum Trio for whom the Trio Notturno *was written:
from the left, György Pauk, Peter Frankl and Ralph Kirschbaum*

19 September

I spent last weekend at the Lupus', partly to watch the finals of Leeds competition in their company (*and* Murray's[39] for good measure), mainly to go over my piano concerto with Radu. The first time he let me play it right through, a shapeless mess including several breakdowns; then he spent two hours or so coaching me in it, beating or shouting time and correcting innumerable inaccuracies. 'But this is not what is written!' he'd shout, 'you are ignoring the composer's instruction.' The strangest thing was that not only Radu but I had quite forgotten who the composer was.

[...]

---

[39] Perahia (b. 1947), American pianist based in Britain.

1 October

Dublin

At last it is my turn to play my own piano concerto, here in an hour, in Cork tomorrow. I say 'at last' as if I couldn't have waited longer for the occasion, but indeed I should much have preferred Radu or Stephen to have taken the job: my own playing is far too erratic for so intricately polyphonic a work, which is apt to go to pieces if the soloist doesn't follow the beat.

The conductor, Albert Rosen,[40] has been patient, competent and conscientious, and the orchestra, while neither brilliant nor enthusiastic, shows the resigned dogged obedience of an infantry battalion in a muddy field. Much of it is out of tune, an occasional wood-wind solo turns into a downright mess; but nobody complains: it's all a job to them, and they pride themselves on having ploughed their way through more difficult things. No one so far has ventured a comment on the actual quality of the piece – I don't think they hate it, they merely think it none of their business.

This is being jotted down in the dressing room of Dublin's notorious Gaiety Theatre, a shabby, dirty, overcrowded place where I've been warned not to expect to hear the orchestra: no one ever has. In such cases the only chance is to keep looking at the conductor, and this is one thing I've never learnt to do! It will be my fault if the whole thing is a shambles… Cheer up, Tchaikopath!

The best comfort is to take the long view. However it goes tonight, tomorrow night and on the next twelve occasions, this is still a concerto I am likely to be asked to play more often than anyone else. It may take a certain number of utter disasters to teach me the piece; well, let's start and get them over with! I used to be just as much at sea in Prokofieff III.

This indeed may yet prove to be a good 'instructive' piece for me. It will force me to develop some muscles; it will help to discipline my wayward rhythmic impulses; it may even yet teach me to regulate my supply of adrenaline. And the day I at last get it right, how happy I'll be! Ten to eight, it's time to stop scribbling.

19 October

Mönchengladbach

The other event was my afternoon with Annie Fischer.[41] I'd barely dared to invite her to lunch – ever since hearing her in Warsaw when I was sixteen, I'd always felt towards her like the Notre-Dame juggler towards the

[40] Austrian-born Irish conductor (1924–97).
[41] Much-admired Hungarian pianist (1914–95).

Madonna – but it's good I did, for she treated me to a feast of generosity and encouragement. She had liked my first quartet some years ago, and now wanted to hear the second; I'd brought the cassette and the score. Annie does nothing half-heartedly – even her concerts are either great or downright awful, but never routine – and she studied the quartet as if she had to write a thesis on it. She kept asking me to re-wind the tape and listened to the same fragment now with the score, now without; she concluded that it was better than the first (though she insisted on praising that too). Her only criticism was that the *drammatico* passage in the *Passacaglia* came too early and too suddenly; I don't agree, though I had to admit that it sounded far from transparent and resolved to mark the accompanying parts down. (Two days later I heard it on Radu's excellent equipment and it sounded perfectly clear, so perhaps even this is unnecessary). My own doubts all concern the last movement, which sounds a bit too sectional for cumulative effect: as Stephen would put it, there are too many full stops.

Now it so happened that Bartók III, one of Annie's great specialities, was on the other side of the quartet. It was the Rochester performance with David, my favourite conductor, and he had been very pleased with it. Of course Annie wanted to hear that too, even though by that time I'd been with her some 3½ hours and was afraid of outstaying my welcome! She warned me, however, that she never enjoyed anybody's performance of it but her own, and asked me in advance if I objected to free criticism. This was not long in coming: 'Too slow', she said, before I'd even had time to come in. By the second theme, however, she had got used to the slow tempo (I hadn't realised it was slower than average) and begun to enjoy it. Now and then she'd acknowledge some unusual stroke by a wink and a smile, and soon we found ourselves exchanging almost conspiratorial glances ('Naughty, but fun'). At the end she announced that at last she'd found one performance of the work she could praise: all the others played it like Prokofieff, whereas Bartók needed a more rhapsodic treatment. 'But darling', she concluded, 'aren't you a little *too* free?'

Radu, who put me up on Saturday night, was greatly taken with the first two movements of the quartet but said he couldn't follow the finale (he had no score, as I'd given my copy to Annie). Of course I can defend and explain every note of it, but surely the very need of explanation, to so perceptive a musician as Radu, indicates that something is wrong? Music should work at the instinctive level. Perhaps one ought to work from the finale backwards, as Mahler did in the Fourth symphony; though this proved little help in the case of my piano concerto! I wonder to what extent my new two-movement trio works if at all, for I am full of doubts about that piece.

The night before lunching with Annie, I saw the ENO production of *Die Entführung*,[42] and the one element of it I must record was Valerie Masterson's Constanze – a transcendental performance. No flute could have been more agile than her coloratura, but there was far more to it than virtuosity: she moves and acts with supreme grace and dignity, the g-minor aria was subdued and utterly melting, and though no singer or producer will ever quite make sense of the interminable introduction to 'Martern aller Arten' (in this case she was made to kneel down and pray, which might have worked but for the infuriatingly inappropriate *rococo* grace of the music), it was a triumph from the moment she was at last allowed to open her mouth. She'll be the Countess in Jonathan Miller's *Figaro*, and I must make a point of seeing that: she is a born countess. And what a Queen of the Night she will make one day!

All this is being written half-way through a four-concert series of the Bartók III with the Niederrheinorchester (I *think* that's what they call themselves) and my friend Lothar Zagrosek.[43] He is as charming as ever, but not quite as good as I'd thought: his Beethoven VII seems to me an explosion of sheer adrenalin, without any attempt to regulate the energy. The result is monotonous, relentless and, to me, exhausting. The public adores it: a more discriminating performance would excite them less.

As for me, I am not doing as well as in Rochester. Once again, I can't control the supply of adrenalin, and a lot of it goes faster than I mean – especially the bridge-passage in the first movement and most of the finale. I have two more attempts, tonight and tomorrow: perhaps I shall have learnt something over the four evenings.

Otherwise, I do virtually nothing but sleep… On the way out, I started revising the opening fragment of *1948*, but I daren't go on till the concerts are over lest I get too involved (or am I once more rationalising the old laziness?). On Monday night, I read a German translation of *An Inspector Calls*,[44] which I find far too obvious. Whoever the figure is, he can no longer command the least credence as a policeman once he starts moralising, and no family would have been taken in.[45]

Nor have I found time for Vincent Cronin's biography of Catherine II,[46] which I've got out of the library and must soon return! It's the same fear of

---

[42] Mozart's opera *Die Entführung aus dem Serail* ('The Abduction from the Seraglio'), premiered in Vienna in 1782.

[43] German conductor (b. 1942).

[44] Play by J. B. Priestley first performed in the Soviet Union in 1945 and in Britain a year later.

[45] In the plot of *An Inspector Calls* an Inspector Goole who accuses members of the Birling family of complicity in the death of a young woman is revealed not to be the policemen he claims to be.

[46] *Catherine, Empress of All the Russias*, Collins, London, 1978.

getting too interested, so that the concert is no longer the uncontested event of the day. Ah! *that's* the word I wanted: Father's *uncontested* authority. This will be my sole contribution to the book today, but I may give it two sessions on Saturday, if I don't have my post-concerts headache…

I saw a poster of Christopher Hampton's comedy *Herrenbesuch* which I take to be *Treats*.[47] By the time I come home, it will be exactly a month since posting him that draft of the libretto: will he have replied? It's very difficult for someone of my temperament to be reduced to a passive position: all I can now do is wait, and the virtue I lack most is patience. For all I know, he may not even have got the letter! I should have sent it to the publishers, so as to get at least some note of acknowledgement. Now, of course, I can do nothing whatever: if he did get the draft, any further move on my part would be nagging. The most unpleasant thought is that he may be a friend of Emlyn's who would have told him of my fan-letter to himself, and made our meeting sound as funny as only *he* could (imitating my accent, no doubt). This, of course, would convince Hampton that I am a stage-struck leech and nothing more… But won't the draft counteract even that impression?

22 October

Cumnor

Emlyn Williams on Ian Brady's[48] Nazi interests:

'For the proud ego faced with sickening failure and determined to shy away from the sight, the only medicine – the one efficacious flattery – is the reiterated assurances that one is born out of one's time. A fascinating misfit…'

Uncannily neat and true. I know this truth at first hand, and so must he: there is no other way of discovering it. One of the things I most admire about Emlyn is his honesty. He's always had the guts to know himself.

24 October

Hampton did reply:

Dear Mr Tchaikowsky,

Thanks very much for your letter and the enclosed outline. By all means go ahead.

---

[47] Love-triangle play premiered in 1975.
[48] One of the two 'Moors murderers' who killed five children in and around Manchester in 1963–65, Ian Brady (b. 1938) counted *Mein Kampf* and books on Nazi atrocities among his reading matter.

The device of interspersing the scenes in the play with poems by Rimbaud and/or Verlaine has been tried in various productions of the play (I believe they did it at RADA), notably the New York production, which consequently lasted three hours. I don't think it works as a theatrical device, although I see the reasoning behind it: in practical terms, though, it slows down the play.

However, for an opera, it seems a far more logical idea, and the only danger I can foresee is, again, one of length. You'll obviously have to edit the play quite savagely and that's fine by me. As to translations of the Rimbaud – somewhere among my papers is a battered old notebook containing translations of large chunks of *Une Saison en Enfer* which I did for my own amusement more than ten years ago. If you're interested and haven't already settled on a translation, I'll see if I can root it out.

All best wishes,
Christopher Hampton.

I replied:

Dear Mr Hampton,

Why, if I may have your own translation of the relevant fragments, I will certainly look nowhere else! Not that there seems to be anywhere much to look: the latest version manages to translate 'ici-bas' by 'here on earth' when the *title* is *A Season in Hell*… Also, I'd be greatly relieved not to need anyone else's permission: they might not prove nearly as helpful as you have been, and their presence would only complicate the legal arrangements.

So, if you do find that notebook, please let me have it for a day or two; I shall return it by registered post. If not, let me know and I'll think again. What's the English for 'Jadis'?

Thank you for being so patient,

Yours,
André Tchaikowsky.

But I shan't post this yet. Not for at least a week. This is also Eve's advice: 'it would look as if you had nothing else to do in life.' He didn't post his letter till the 17th, nearly four weeks after getting mine, and I can't help noticing that the tone is markedly unenthusiastic: it's practically 'Do whatever you like with my play, but leave me alone'. I hardly think it fair to equate my outline with 'the device of interspersing the scenes in the play with poems by R. and/or V', as if I had chosen the fragments at random. In fact, I took particular trouble to make every selection as poignantly relevant to the previous or following scene as the Indian legends in Hampton's own

Savages.[49] (I may not have succeeded, of course.) Again, 'You'll obviously have to edit the play quite savagely and that's fine by me) seems expressly designed to forestall any further attempts at consultation on my part. Am I once again being too touchy?

But this is only half the letter. It's typical of H's dramatic flair to produce his one revelation so quietly (much as the mother's death comes out in his first play[50]). To think that the one person in England capable of translating *Une Saison en Enfer* has already done so – and that I may have it! Actually, he is doing quite a lot for me he's letting me have some of his private papers, and he's volunteered the privilege. What he doesn't want is any personal contact with me. Fine, Christopher – let it be your way. Indeed, once I do get the notebook (if he finds it, but I doubt if he'd have mentioned it unless he was pretty sure he could), I'll return it with thanks and something like:

'Now that I've got all I need, you may not hear from me again for a long time, but please don't take it to mean I've lost interest in the project. I am, indeed, determined to do my honest best by your play.'

This, of course, makes it sound as if I had to apologise not for having troubled him, but for terminating the correspondence myself! or, at any rate, suspending it. Eve agrees that it's an excellent face-saving device. Will it miscarry like most of my pride-dictated projects?

28 October

Well, it all went off very pleasantly.[51] The occasion gained a certain piquancy from the German agent's attempt to hide or hush up my Polish origins, although every Russian in the orchestra knew them without asking and was clearly careful not to ask! There were at least two members of the secret police, the second oboist and a young man with a moustache who hung about without even pretending to do anything except watch. But people are people and I felt a warm contact with many of them.

Despite a tinny baby grand, K. 271[52] went reasonably well, and I amused the orchestra by playing a *Vision fugitive* as an encore (they play most of them in Barshai's orchestration). Afterwards they played nine of Shostakovich's piano preludes, arranged for chamber orchestra with tremendous flair and imagination by one of their second violins! *And* the Bartók *Divertimento*.

---

[49] Play premiered in 1973 dealing with the extermination of Brazil's native Indians and the plight of its landless farmers.

[50] *When Did You Last See my Mother?* (1964).

[51] Tchaikowsky is writing about a recital he gave on 27 October, with the Moscow Chamber Orchestra in Salzgitter, a city in Lower Saxony, Germany.

[52] Mozart, Piano Concerto No. 9 in E flat major (1777).

The German agent, a delightfully jolly fellow called Hörtnagel who is a musician himself,[53] told me within minutes of his arrival that he couldn't take me onto his list as he was too busy. As I had never asked him to, I can only conclude that Terry has. He gave me my fee in a comically informal way ('it's not supposed to be you, so I don't even need your signature and you may keep the income tax part'). Normally they deduct 15% in tax, so obviously this does not affect Russians! I'll check this with Terry, the explanation might prove quite amusing.

As for the other two concerts, the one in Leverkusen has already gone to a strikingly handsome Russian viola player[54] whom Hörtnagel also represents (naturally he'd rather keep all he can in the family) and I am rather relieved for Halinka's sake. The one in Frankfurt might come off, if the Russian lady pianist I've replaced last night does not recover in time (apparently a genuine illness, not a passport virus), so we've agreed to keep this open and I shall not tell Halinka unless it occurs. Let her enjoy my company and see me enjoy hers. If I'm suddenly called away, she'll share the excitement; meanwhile I shall have given her a week of my attention. If not, I'm no worse off than before

This morning I did some work on the second fragment of *1948*. It's still not complete, but what there is seems far better than the earlier version (in which I had completely overlooked aunt Ida) and I am a whole page further ahead. Now I'll see if I can sketch some programme notes for op. 110…

14 November

Derby
From Michael's last letter:
'…your feeling of not being part of a group. I can tell you that everyone was longing for you to be just ordinary and a part of whatever society you were in your own nervousness about being an outsider made them react by treating you as the honoured guest. I think people would have loved you just to arrive (without a present), take your shoes off and relax and be boring. It has always been the problem: we manage to forget your brilliance and talents and deeply want to take you to us as ordinary André. But somehow your fear of being rejected made you too anxious to please and by reaction we did our best to please you: not a natural situation.

---

[53] Georg Hörtnagel (b. 1927) is a respected double-bassist and played in the Orchestra of the Bayrische Staatsoper under Georg Solti from 1948, founding the agency Konzertdirektion Georg Hörtnagel with his first wife, Elisabeth, in 1966.
[54] Probably a reference to Yuri Bashmet (b. 1953).

'André wouldn't like x so we can't invite them both together' or 'We better ask someone brilliant otherwise André will be bored'.

But the world is home – has always been home for you if only you had let it. You are special, without having to try. In fact trying creates an artefact and hides the person.

You rather, I think, enjoyed people saying 'Oh André's brilliant but difficult' – it gave you an excuse for being possibly rejected.'

Once again I find nothing to add to this fragment. What can be more valuable than a friend who sees all your faults so clearly and loves you all the more? It's love, in fact, that has enabled him to know me so well. And I had wanted to break off with him!

26 November

Halinka's letter was like Tatyana's: what on earth could poor Onéguine *do*? She offers me love, I offer her friendship, the two don't dovetail and we end up with neither. Now I understand her irritatingly masochistic, fawning, poor-relation-who-can-at-best-hope-to-be-tolerated attitude to me here, which easily got the better of the little patience I have, with tricks like 'I'll go out so as not to disturb you' to make me protest that I want her to stay, or 'pay no attention whatever to me' to ensure the exact opposite. Once again I had been too obtuse to realise what she was trying to hide (probably because I really preferred not to know) and all I felt was a vague guilt and unease, which of course made me treat her with increasing ill-temper and brutality. Now that it's all come out, I feel very sad, but glad that the pretence is over. In my reply I appealed to her to cure herself of me so as to make room for our friendship, but I doubt if she can: by now she needs the craving, indeed the pain, more than she does me. It's not her demands or expectations – she has none – but her very needs that preclude the friendship. Who could be friends with the person whose deepest need he constantly refuses? I can feel compassion, embarrassment, guilt – anything but friendship. But this very admission, which she had found so humiliating, the open request that she knew would be refused and might have made me refuse to see her again that has won her my respect and admiration. 'What irritated you before was my lifelong attempt to bungle your life rather than knock at the door.' Poor Halinka, who could blame you? I usually behave very much worse when I'm in love, and I have nothing like your constancy… But don't, please don't volunteer to be my slave! I want friends, sometimes lovers, not slaves.

1 December

I am on my way from London to Liverpool, having just combined a celebration of Radu's birthday (which included this time the fourth recital of his Schubert sonatas cycle) with a crash course in op. 110.[55] I played it to Stephen yesterday afternoon, and he found my approach to it altogether too uncongenial to be of much help; Radu also plays it quite differently (and, of course, differently from Stephen) but he found enough affinity with me to see at least what I was aiming at and to show me where and how I failed to achieve it. I played the first part of the recital (Bach Sixth partita, Bartók studies and op. 110) before lunch; that proved somewhat too opulent for subsequent concentration, but I tried to complete the programme and found myself utterly unable to play, of all things, *Davidsbündler*. The lunch could have accounted for some of the mess, wrong notes, etc., but surely not for the innumerable mannerisms and rhythmic distortions that have insidiously overrun the entire piece. It took us the one remaining hour of my stay to do *some* basic straightening up of the first six pieces, so I've begged Radu to let me come back the day after tomorrow and go over the entire cycle before the vital concerts at Lancaster and Birmingham (the latter broadcast live!). It was quite a shock for me to realise how much I have slipped. But, of course, it's just the shock I need…

18 December

(Mother's birthday). The last five days have been so packed that it will no doubt take me as long again to jot down the salient event. I bet most diaries are written by people with nothing to relate: otherwise, when would they find time for it?

Last Thursday (today is Monday), I got six pages of recrimination from Halinka. She simply won't believe that I don't need her as much as she does me, accuses me of faking sincerity to conceal my lack of self-knowledge and of provoking her into repeated declarations so I may reject them. I didn't exactly defend myself, but wrote roughly as follows (I am translating this from a rough draft for the letter, it being the kind of answer that definitely requires one):

Halinka,

Since your departure I've had three letters from you. The first, as I've told you, aroused my respect and admiration, for at last you had put your cards on the table. But it transpires that it was just the first pack.

---

[55] Beethoven, Piano Sonata No. 31 in A flat major (1821).

Each time you pick out of your well-stocked interior different curiosities that unfortunately no longer make me curious. Nor does it disturb you that all those wonders contradict one another. In the first letter you write 'at the bottom of my attitude towards you hides some absolutely insane desire' and in the third 'even if I loved you Heaven knows how, I could never feel any desire, for fear kills all lust'. Your third letter starts with 'All we tell each other is far from the truth', forgetting perhaps that in the first you twice dramatically assured me of 'speaking, provoked by you, the truth you never wanted to hear.'

Halinka, I don't know why you need this gradual hara-kiri, but I don't feel like watching it. And I thoroughly oppose any attempt on your part to draw out my own insides as well. You say your behaviour here was 'exemplary' because you didn't pick at my flies, but now you try to pick at my soul! I have never authorised either. Even if you knew enough psychology to be competent (of which I am by no means sure), in my case you could never be objective: you'll always find in my subconscious just what suits your needs. That kind of analysis may indeed harm the doctor, but will never cure the patient.

Your accusations are the easier to set because, of their very nature, there is no way of answering them. For instance, you accuse me of faking sincerity and lack of self-knowledge. Since no one knows the extent of his own self-knowledge, never mind proving it, no discussion is possible here. You ask me if I could 'afford' to admit that your 'unhappy marriage declaration of ten years ago' was provoked by myself. Again, I can hardly either admit or contradict, since you yourself consider the provocation to have been unconscious. Within subconsciousness everything is equally likely: I may be in love with you, or with Mickey Mouse, but perhaps my deepest wish is to be Dalai Lama?

Luckily there is one very simple test to show us the truth. Let us simply stop writing. If, as you insist, you are indeed indispensable to me, be it only to provoke, reject and subject you to my sadistic 'psychogames', sooner or later I shall come to miss you, especially as no one else treats me to so literary a kind of love, and tearfully beg you for a letter. You'll gain from it the satisfaction of your diagnosis being proved correct, and I that 'self-knowledge', that, according to you, I now so pitifully lack.

Farewell and greetings,
André.

It sounds horribly callous in its cool logic, but in fact she had managed to make me obsessively angry; and the fact that the very next night I was to play my Birmingham recital, broadcast live, only increased my anger at being disturbed, though I was still sane enough not to blame her for that unhappy timing. But the recital certainly suffered from actual lapses of concentration, as opposed to mere technical slips, and was a great disappointment to me. It may, for all I know, have been an improvement on the trial run in Lancaster; it bore no relation to my hopes for it, or to the extremely strenuous preparatory work beforehand (six hours on the day before, after Halinka's letter) and it seems to me that the inability to relax engendered by my compulsive marshalling of counter-arguments can't be irrelevant to the many mishaps that occurred in the Schumann.

That was on Friday. On Saturday, I returned from Birmingham in the early hours and immediately started writing my answer to Halinka. I had vowed to send her a gentler answer if the recital managed to withstand the occasional strain; it hadn't, and I took some pleasure in calling her bluff. It took till 4.15, so I must have gone to sleep about five. And that very evening I was going up to Stratford to see Clifford Williams' production of *The Tempest*!

19 December

That, however, proved an experience to wake up the dead. I had bought the tickets prompted by the memory of Williams' *As You Like It* at the National Theatre some ten years ago, but perhaps even that, though a complete triumph as *The Tempest* can of its nature never be, was eclipsed by the magic of this infinitely deeper and more elusive play. I had never quite loved *The Tempest* because of my inability to love Prospero: that pig! I preferred Caliban. And though I knew my reaction to be a deliberate misunderstanding of Shakespeare's intentions, I took heart from the fact that my whole score of *The Merchant* was another such misunderstanding, and from the knowledge that his works could be trusted to survive my mistake as they have all others. The complacent, sermonising Prospero, with magic powers and spirits at his command and an insufferable superiority to every other member of the cast, with all dice loaded in his favour, seemed to me a loathsome emblem of all authority.

And what an adolescent reaction that was! I had overlooked Prospero's loneliness, the double loss of his only child and the very part of himself he needed most externalised as Ariel, the painful necessity of his consciously bringing that loss about himself. Michael Hordern showed all the strain his exercise of magic had cost him in his very first gesture of taking the cloak off ('Lie there, my art'). But whatever effort and exhaustion it cost him, giving it up would obviously kill him: such, of course, is the way of all art.

By far the two greatest moments were Ariel's first appearance and final exit. I don't know how good an actor Ian Charleson is (he is certainly a fine singer, and I was very impressed with Guy Woolfenden's music): it was the very conception of Ariel as part of Prospero, obvious in reading but seemingly impossible to convey in the theatre, that was such a triumph. Prospero invoked Ariel without looking anywhere but into himself; not, in the suddenly darkened stage, was there anything to be seen; but a sound as if a sea-shell was held to one's ears gradually turned into a whispered delivery of Ariel's first speech. Still nothing could be seen, till suddenly, the speech concluded, a stern, remote figure was standing uncannily close to Prospero, right behind him, without any clue as to how it had got there.

And the end! At his dismissal, Ariel repeated the sea-shell sound and retreated backwards, while Prospero suddenly sagged with age and weariness: it wasn't just a spirit but *his* spirit, his very life-force that he had surrendered. And throughout the performance, Ariel's eerie impassive stillness, his dissociation from all the human activities surrounding him, had a cumulative effect that made his 'Mine would, sir, were I human' positively chilling.

I went to see Michael Hordern afterwards, little hoping he would remember my playing in a Poetry Reading at Cambridge a decade ago at which he was one of the four readers; but he remembered me at once, was warm and comradely, and called me André! To my surprise there were no other guests in his room.

The piano having proved an ungrateful bastard, I decided to treat myself to a week's holiday from it, but in other ways I made myself exceedingly and pleasantly busy. On Sunday I finished the fair copy of the piano trio, doing the remaining four pages at one sitting; yesterday and today I've done a double dose of orchestration, which I had started already on Sunday night; so that in the last three days I've orchestrated the whole scene of Bassanio's departure and have just reached Shylock's entrance. It would be just wonderful to finish Act I within this holiday, but I'm afraid it would ruin in advance that the Oxford recital for one will be a fearsome wrench! Edward has never heard me live yet, nor has Herbert whom I taught at the OUMCU master-classes last June. Those are the people that make me most nervous…

Going back for a moment to Halinka, isn't my attitude towards her uncannily like D.'s to me? The same refusal to admit the least need for the other person, the same cold reasoning in the face of desperate emotion… And how well I remember *that* torment!

But at least *I* answered. And will go on answering: of course she'll never accept my proposal to stop our correspondence, nor had I meant it to be anything but a proof of my independence from her – the only proof I could find, as she claims my dependence to be subconscious and accuses me of lacking the honesty to acknowledge it even to myself!

All the same, I have little hope that our friendship will quite recover after this exchange.

1979

29 January

I am on the plane to Glasgow, where Chris[1] and I are doing K. 456[2] at a lunch-time concert on the 31st. This is one of the Mozart concertos I have played relatively little, and thought, on hearing that I'd been invited by the BBC Scottish, that it was just one of those safe studio recordings that are such a help in consolidating an unfamiliar piece! Since I was already scheduled to play K. 456 in Malmö a fortnight later, I actually insisted on it in Glasgow – only to find out, on the occasion on my recital at Kilmardinny,[3] that it was a public concert already advertised all over Glasgow! I am never so foolish as when I've tried to demonstrate my wisdom, foresight and powers of organisation: I have the wisdom by my wit to lose.

I had expected to be unusually nervous at my recital in Oxford, but hadn't realised anything like the utter panic and dejection that befell me just before the performance; if I had, I'd have cancelled the concert. That would have been a pity, for in the end I turned out my best recital this season: intense, impetuous, and utterly 'committed' throughout, though occasionally far from clean in the second half. And even in the occasional showers of wrong notes in the *Davidsbündler* (usually in repeats of passages that had been immaculate the first time round) I felt free from guilt: I couldn't have cared more, practised longer or concentrated harder, and I was sure that my dedication was somehow bound to show through whatever happened. The Rachmaninoff op. 39 no. 5, which I played again as the first encore, was untidy in a less honourable way: I had spent myself before reaching it and it proved a mistake to choose so 'athletic' an encore. Learning from defeat, I added the tenth *Vision fugitive* to round off the evening.

[…]

---

[1] Christopher Seaman was the chief conductor of the BBC Scottish Symphony Orchestra from 1971 to 1977.
[2] Mozart, Piano Concerto No. 18 in B flat major (1784).
[3] Kilmardinny House is an arts centre in Bearsden, a northern suburb of Glasgow.

31 January

Glasgow–Heathrow
Apart from a few fluffs, this was quite a pleasant performance of K. 456. From Chris, it was a great deal more than that – his ear for refined detail of harmony and scoring made me realise how much in that delicious piece I had overlooked, and the first *tutti* set a standard of elegance and precision I could not always maintain. Now that I've got some idea of this adorable, angelic and exceedingly sophisticated work, all I need is more practice to feel at home in it, and I am particularly glad of an occasion to consolidate it a little in Malmö. (It will also be interesting to see how near Oskamp[4] can get to Christopher's achievement.)

[…] Today I felt that Chris' Mozart is as good as David's – and there's surely no better Mozart. But I still play better with David myself, for he demands more of me: Chris would regard his attitude towards a soloist as interference, but coming from a friend I find it a definite help. Next time I'll ask Chris to place me under orders, just like everybody else!

2 February

Cumnor to London and Worthing
A most impressive letter from Halinka, breaking off all relations in two pages of cold dignity. It made me pensive, sad at first, then glad to see that at last she's shaken off that disastrous spell, and even happier that she's proved herself so much more of a person than I thought. (I had expected frantic pleas to have me on whatever terms.) The joy of being able to admire her far outweighs the sadness of the loss.

My reply proved far easier than anticipated. No rough draft this time! She may of course tear it up unread, but this would be a pity as I managed quite a decent letter. It went somewhat like this (I can't be sure, having already posted it):

> Dear Halinka,
> It's sad to say goodbye to you. But I can see that you really need the break: you must free yourself. Your very letter proves it – it's full of that dignity and independence that I continually undermined in you, and then accused you of lacking them! I now see that the accusations were unjust, but I admit, sadly and shamefully, that you couldn't have proved this to me in any other way.

---

[4] Gerard Oskamp (b. 1950), Dutch conductor.

But don't burden yourself with any more anger towards me. Enjoy the freedom you have so painfully acquired, and find that happiness of which you've had so little, with someone who will love and understand you.

Of course 'it wasn't your fault': it was I who have treated you like a brutal boor, but this only made me hate myself in my mind and you in my letters. No wonder you have had enough!

But now it's your turn to believe (Halinka had written 'But believe that it wasn't my fault') that I will always think of you with tenderness, for few people want to form new and totally different relationships with me, free of all old grudges, it will give me quite exceptional joy.

Be well and happy,
Yours,
A.

How easy to it is to write 'noble' letters in this situation! Admittedly, I took the last sentence from Michael's letter to me, after I had threatened breaking off with him. The calm dignity of his letters melted all my resentment away, but nothing I could write would have that effect on Halinka: at last I have penetrated to her timidly hidden pride, and after years of enslavement she'll have to loathe me if she's even to find her own feet, just as I've had to hate away all the people who had enslaved me. Still, now she has a future!

3 February

Worthing
I've just written another letter to Halinka! Here it is:

Dear Halinka,
It will no doubt surprise you to get two letters from me (which will perhaps arrive simultaneously) when you no longer wish even for one. I realise that you may tear them up unread, or send them back unopened. But my answer of yesterday, written and sent immediately after receiving your farewell letter, strikes me as so superficial and inadequate that I must try once more.

Since yesterday I've re-read your letter many times and I give you my word that few things have ever impressed me so much. I was surprised by my own increasing joy. You may think: 'he's glad to be rid of me'. It's just the opposite – I feel I have not lost but won a friend in you, regardless of the fact whether we'll meet or whether you'll answer (I may not see J. either, but he's still the most important person in my life).

Before I had in you not a friend but a slave. Always in our relations you kept losing the feeling of your own value and your own rights; always what I felt, thought or did was more important than your own experiences, and that even in your own eyes. Somehow I finally had to wound your pride, just to make sure of its existence. And to you I wanted to prove that you're stronger than you think, that you can dispense with any inaccessible, hopelessly desired idol. It was not you or our friendship I wanted to destroy, but only that altar on which you had spent a quarter of a century burning candles in front of my image. Or rather I wanted you to destroy it yourself, to rebel and confront me, as you now did with such incredible dignity. You have long wondered what exactly I wanted of you; now you know it's happened.

But you know yourself what a brutal job this has been. And since I am by nature an artist, and not a butcher, I was repelled by it and by myself. Someone else would no doubt have managed it differently, without violence and freaks of temper: I couldn't. Your determination to have me 'at whatever price' struck me as unworthy of you – I had to find a price you will refuse.

And whom did I humiliate? Only myself: unprovoked hysterical scenes humiliate only their perpetrator. But for the first time in my life humiliation has the upper hand. What does matter is that all my life I have liked you, still do and always will, that I'm ever at your disposal, and that I respect and admire you as never before. I daren't ask you to reply. But I hope that you'll understand why I inflicted such torments on you and that it wasn't a game on my part.

I also doubt if you'll allow a hug but I assure you that no other consideration could restrain me.

Your devoted

A.

This represents far more what I really feel; the former letter was merely conventional. Halinka tried every possible way to win me over, but she could only accomplish that in this one way: she had to give up trying. It's only now that we could be friends, and indeed in my mind we are; but could she ever consider it after the supreme effort of rejecting me? It's not a question of mending what has snapped: what was never friendship anyway, can't be mended and is not worth mending. But is she flexible enough to start a new relationship with the same old person? I never could – all my emotional habits would prevent me. Still, I've re-opened my own door, and I am glad. If I cannot do both, I'd far rather like her than have her. But how ironic that she could only prove herself worth having by putting herself out of my reach! And how wrong my conceited assurance that she'll take any insult from me, that, as I put it in this diary, I had called her bluff! Why, she's called *my* bluff.

20 February

Rio de Janeiro
About Rio one can only gush. Whatever travel leaflets say about it is an understatement: they won't tell you, for instance, that the varied splendour of the scenery is matched by the different kind of beauty, no less varied, displayed on the beaches – and no amount of TM will ever make me so spiritual as to ignore *that*! In the street, someone starts beating a drum, and before you know the crowd is dancing a samba; a middle-aged gentleman, bliss on his face, is dancing nearby all by himself. Perhaps he's just arrived from a country where such behaviour would look ridiculous; here the thought of how he might look doesn't cross his head, and so his inner beauty, that of joy, shows through and gives him a natural dignity he's never had at home in a dinner-jacket. The Cariocas are not just friendly, they are positively affectionate (this, of course, is all the more noticeable after the contemptuous hostile rudeness of most caraqueños).[5] The language that sounds so harsh in Portugal acquires here a soft singing inflection that reminds me of Russian.

I found Michael at the first attempt. He looks fit (partly perhaps because he no longer agonises over *keeping* fit), settled, confident and happy. He's introduced me to many of his friends, who all have a way of dropping in unannounced […].

By a stroke of luck I daren't yet quite believe, my hotel, which had accepted me for just two days, is now ready to let me stay right through the carnival! By all accounts, this is achieving the impossible: in hotels and travel agencies I was repeatedly told that there was no hope of finding an hotel room anywhere in the city till the 1st of March. Finally I asked the receptionist here if he could advise me what to try and he said 'Why don't you simply stay here?' The room is very small, too small for instance to orchestrate in, but I've already developed an affection for it, and anyway it would be mad to underestimate my luck.

The sea here puts Debussy to shame: it rapes one, knocks one over, tumbles one about, plays with one like a tiger with its prey, almost like Rimbaud's precocious vision of it (though now I do exaggerate, Rimbaud's sea is a world on its own). It is just dangerous enough to be exhilarating. No wonder I don't feel like working! I brought mountains of work down, but I shan't force myself to do anything: this is too wonderful a holiday.

---

[5] The Cariocas are the inhabitants of Rio de Janeiro and the Caraqueños, logically enough, of Caracas, the capital of Venezuela.

23 February

I may just have finished the suit episode from *1948*.[6] I say 'may' because I can't decide if it's any good. But I'll copy it out, make whatever corrections occur to me and show it to Eve on my return.

If it *is* good, there is only one more scene to write, the final one! I have no idea how long it will take, or even how long it will *be*: all I've thought up so far is my reaction to being hit (relief) and the very end. But both the piano scene and the suit scene have ended very differently from my previsions…

Not a sound from Michael all today. I've realised that what hurts me is that realisation of having become unnecessary to him (though when he did need me I found it an intolerable burden and let him down). I also realise that his aggressive and arrogant attitude yesterday has been due to nervousness on his part. This of course makes it forgivable, but not acceptable, and I shall still not have a session on such terms.

I hope this time I can manage to avoid a row. After all, I no longer need him either and one thing one must learn is to accept and bear the inevitable sadness of leaving anything important behind… We have developed in different directions. Perhaps he was so provocative just to cause a break?

24 February

I have just had the following adventure:

Going out for my afternoon walk along the beach, I saw Michael in a gay café.[7] He asked me to stay but seeing me anxious to be on my way, he merely advised me to return to the hotel and deposit my watch and wallet before the walk.

'But, Michael, it's broad daylight!'

'This makes no odds.'

I followed his advice. Then minutes later I was walking on the beach near the water line admiring the waves. One of these splashed me up to my waist, so I took my shorts off and carried them on in my hand to let them dry. (I had swimming-trunks on , of course).

Presently a tall coloured young man asked me the time. I pointed to my bare wrist, with a visible paler stripe where the watch had been. He then asked for a cigarette and I told him truthfully that I don't smoke. In between his attempts I went on looking at the waves, and couldn't disguise some irritation the third time I was interrupted. All this time I kept on walking,

---

[6] From Tchaikowsky's unpublished Autobiography, an episode about his father buying him a new suit.
[7] It was, in fact, a 'regular' beachside bar.

with him slightly behind me and inland, and a black mustachioed pal of his slightly ahead.

After a while he got tired of asking for things, and I was allowed to walk on undisturbed. I assumed he had gone away. Two minutes later I saw the pal, who had stayed ahead of me walking at about my pace, turn round and laugh at someone I couldn't see. I thought he had run into somebody else he knew.

The cause of his amusement became obvious within a few seconds. Passing me at a pace that would have won him an Olympic medal, the tall young man whizzed my shorts out of my hand and went on running. The companion took off at a spring as well. It had been quite a near professional job.

But I was allowed a certain final satisfaction. Safely outside my range, the thief turned to watch my anger or dismay. But he saw me walking away calmly on (I had never stopped) with, I am sure, an expression of pleasure and amusement. All he would find in my shorts was some 80 or 90 cruzeiros (about £2), not the watch, wallet, cigarette lighter or whatever he had hoped to find. His practical joke had misfired, even though the theft had succeeded: I looked for all the world as if I'd *expected* him to grab my shorts. To some extent the joke was on him: what a poor catch! On the way home, I found Michael at the same café, told him the story which caused more laughter than concern and thanked him for the well-timed advice that luckily I'd had the sense to follow. £2 and a pair of shorts is a small price to pay for learning at first hand how such things are done

But of course it's only the first day of the Rio carnival and it will be very lucky if I manage to lose nothing more. In a way it adds spice to the holiday to have to live through a four-day battle of wits with Carioca thieves, and I've already wondered where to carry my Diners Club card (I shall buy all my meals and drinks with that and carry no cash whatever); Michael suggested the inside of my bathing trunks 'so that if they do rob you it will at least be fun' and I shall presently experiment. The thought of pulling it out in a posh restaurant would alone make it a temptation!

The only thing I do dread is physical violence. Losing my watch today would have been bad, but nothing comparable to what could have happened if I had done anything to defend it! And I wonder if it wouldn't be wiser to carry some really trifling sum on me, so they don't push my face in just out of spite: I'll ask Michael about that as well, he's just rung and asked himself to dinner. I haven't shown any dissatisfaction with him yet, which gives me a definite advantage…

What I have done instead is a small revenge. Last night he rang while I was out and the message was quite undecipherable: the only clear thing in it was '10.30 AM' and his name had been changed to Marcos. I got the night porter, who couldn't make it out either, to ring the receptionist who had taken it, and it turned out that M. would expect me at his place at 10.30 today. Well, I had no intention of going, especially as I suspected this was the time he'd chosen for pulling my book apart! It was his time to be stood up. I kept the message, started the new page of orchestration after breakfast and calmly waited for the 'phone to ring.

He rang at 11.15.

'What's the matter?' he asked. 'Didn't you get the message?'

'Of course I did, and I've been waiting for you since 10.30. Yes, here: that's what it says, I'll show you the message…'

He arrived here in a foul mood: Eduardo had been moody and neurotic, all his local friends had stood him up… I concealed my satisfaction, and realised how much I could gain, and not only with Michael, by merely teaching myself how to *wait*.

25 February

What happened last night is the most important event in this notebook.

I don't know how much of it I can jot down, I am quite exhausted. Perhaps I'll only write about it on the way home. Tonight all I've done is sleep, wake up with a mild headache, go to sleep again. I'll forego dinner for an early night.

I don't remember quite what started it, something to do with my confession of inability to understand the word 'spiritual'. M. and I were having an aperitif in one of the innumerable sidewalk cafés. Michael started rather diffidently.

'You're so spiritual, André, if only you would let yourself. You are so loving, but you won't let yourself. You've got an ice barrier in front of you and an emotional volcano inside you…'

And over dinner, melted by his concern, I told him of the crisis I had silently experienced in the last few days, of the bitter conviction he no longer loved me, and how the only satisfaction left to me was the pride at not having let on, not having protested or tried to put him under any pressure. His attitude in reply was more loving than it had ever been; I've forgotten the actual words. Soon I was fighting tears and begging him to wait till we were safely out of the restaurant. Michael didn't try to fight his. I invited myself to his place.

This was some of the ensuing conversation:

'Why don't you love yourself, André?'

'Of course I do. I'm quite fascinated by myself. I…'

'That you are. You confuse fascination with love. You confuse sympathy with love. You confuse need with love. Once you saw me standing on my own feet you thought I cannot love you because I don't need you… Why don't you love yourself?'

A trap-door opened in my mind and I fell through it.

'I do not think I'm lovable' I said miserably.

'Why not?'

'Well, there are faults and faults. I am vindictive. I have a horrible sadistic twist. In a quarrel I don't say what I mean, though that would be quite harsh enough; I say whatever will hurt the other person most. And I am treacherous: I don't express my grievances at the time, I brood and let them fester and then, when they've swollen and grown venomous, I overwhelm the unsuspecting victim with recriminations…'

He'd been nodding assent through all this.

'You are all that. You're horrible. And yet we all love you. Judy did; Vera did; you rejected them both and they loved you no less afterwards. I've loved you fifteen years, longer than any of your other friends. Why do you think that is?'

'Well I'm interesting, I'm complex…'

'You are not a novel. Can't you see that we just love you for yourself?'

'That's just a phrase!'

'No, it's not. We don't love you as a concert pianist. We don't love you for your brilliant mind, that only stands between you and real experience. You intellectualise everything, try to explain love, try to explain it anyway… Why not just accept it?'

'Because I can't return it. *I* can't love. I thought I loved you, possibly best of any of my friends, but when the stakes were down I gave you away to the police…'[8]

And suddenly we were in full storm.

'André, you still hate me for that night, don't you? You've never stopped resenting it, you never will. Why?'

'I hate you for having shown me what a shit I am. Do you know that it was only because of Christmas that you weren't carted away to a mental home? They couldn't find the health official who was supposed to authorise the incarceration…'

---

[8] Tchaikowsky is referring here to an incident at Christmas 1978. In the summer of that year Michael had a nervous breakdown, and was suffering from nightmares. Spending Christmas with Tchaikowsky in Cumnor, he had a panic attack on Christmas Eve. He told Tchaikowsky to just leave him alone but Tchaikowsky thought he was going to get violent and destroy the manuscript of his opera *The Merchant of Venice*, and so called the police.

Now at last he was shocked.

'God, André, there are friends of mine who would have *shot* you for allowing that!'

'I didn't care *where* they took you. I'd have sold you to the SS during the war… In danger, this is what happens: panic doesn't think. I saw you raving, throwing and breaking things, trying to strangle the doctor, I was quite sure it would be my turn next. Most of all I was afraid you would tear up my opera, I feared that worse than being killed myself…'

'Now *you* are crazy. I never harmed anyone but myself. I had told you about those attacks before, Michael saw them, Richmond saw them, why didn't they panic?'

'They aren't me. I dread violence. I'm terrified of all irrationality. I'm never afraid on 'planes, I just fear people… Perhaps it's something to do with being shot at when I was six.'

'You are a very frightened person' said Michael calmly.

I broke down and sobbed.

'What happened is that my moment of greatest weakness coincided with *your* greatest weakness… We shall never get over it, you'll always resent it, you'll hate yourself and blame the guilt on me…'

'Not any more. We should have talked about it before, but you always insisted on talking as if nothing had happened. *That* I resent: how could you be such an ostrich? Why not face up together to the situation?'

But the burden had already gone. M. had used the word 'weakness,' and weakness is of course forgivable: I had been accusing myself of utter, deadly selfishness. And once he'd enabled me to forgive myself, how could I not forgive him? The two pardons were inseparable. All my venom dissolved into tears.

This morning I wrote him a short letter, telling him what he's managed to do (just when he'd given up in discouragement). But I had wept so much that I was ashamed of leaving my room; that's where a pair of dark glasses would really have helped! I did a page of orchestration first, took the letter, found M. out and pushed it under his door. Later I looked for him […], found him and spent two hours on small talk, knowing he must be drained after so harrowing a conversation. I felt light and carefree, at peace with myself and with him, and though he'd been depressed when I found him, by the end he smiled and chatted very easily.

And he still hasn't read my letter: he is out tonight.

27 February

Michael on my Milford Sound[9] experience:

'When you've had a revelation like this, you shouldn't merely rejoice in it, but act on it. You see its value and beauty, but you treat it as an end in itself: you admire the key, but don't use it to open the door...'

Who since G. L. would have told me this?

This was last night, towards the end of our second serious talk, less harrowing than the first but no less crucial. I've managed to tell him what I can't bring myself to mention even in the book: my father's name (and therefore presumably mine), the operations... About the book we're now wholly in agreement, and he'll help me with the style when I've got the story down. Meanwhile he's turning my holiday into a cure...

I told him about the trick I played on him last Saturday, so now there is no concealed antagonism. I love him as I never have before: there is both more *to* love and more to love *with*.

I've just re-written the end of the suit episode, which was very vague and out-of-focus. I think it far better now. Eve will have something new to see on my return...

3 March

Michael on the book:

'You must learn humility about your sufferings, André. Look at that cripple who sells lemonade on the beach: does he flaunt his crutches? You only have to say the word 'ghetto' to evoke horror and compassion in your listeners. But suffering is not measurable, or proportionate to its causes, and people go through hell for apparently trivial reasons – a hell no less harrowing than yours. I have a fear of water. Do you know why? Because Dad used to punish me by holding my head under water till I nearly drowned. Your circumstances were far worse than that. But one doesn't suffer according to the circumstances, only according to one's own capacity, and how do you measure that? Don't turn the ghetto into a martyr's status symbol: it's unworthy both of you and of your tragedy. We love you for yourself, not for what you went through, not for any of your attributes...'

5 March

Miami–London
It's a whole day since I left Rio, but I still feel dazed – and it's not jet-lag.

---

[9] Reference to a trip Tchaikowsky took in New Zealand with one of his lovers.

About Michael I simply can't speak 'Was für ein Lied soll Dir gesungen werden?'[10] It would have been extraordinary enough if we had merely done away with the backlog – fifteen years of misunderstanding, mistrust, anger and resentment. I have never before seen that happen: it is like Long Day's Journey into Night with a happy end.

But Michael gave me so much more than that. His newly found self-knowledge, the object of a deliberate and often painful quest, is beyond the reach of most people, and he made me free of it all. His knowledge of me also far exceeds my own, and he made me a present of it too. There was nothing in either of our lives or minds that we didn't feel free to explore and discuss together. I shall not set it down, but I certainly shan't forget it either.

Michael's original vocation was neither to act nor to write: he wanted to be a pianist. How poignant our relations must have been to him! He still feels that deprivation, but by now his other vocation has begun to emerge – that of a healer. He already resembles G. L. more than anyone else I know has ever done (G.L. also had started by wanting to be a pianist); he learns from his own pain and passes on whatever he has learnt.

No wonder he has so often been tempted to wallow in mud: it's polarity! Michael is pure through and through, incapable of grudge, malice or calculation: his anger, violent and terrifying as I remember it, was always sword, not poison. He showed me some of his private diaries, kept at the time of his deepest depression, on his journey down to South America. At times pain and anger make him almost incoherent. But venom? He's never heard of it.

The diaries include a letter to his mother, whose attitude has always been thoroughly destructive; he's never sent it, it was just to 'get her out of his system', but *even there* he's never cruel or unfair. No wonder he finds my book so unpleasant! Even I now hardly have the heart to go on with it. Only the thought of Eve makes me want to continue it; I now write it for her, not myself. Most of my scars have now healed. Or am I once again kidding myself? I can't tell till I've taken myself through the ghetto chapters, whether I'm conscious of the need or not.

9 March

Oxford
This is being written while waiting at a barber's shop.

---

[10] First line of a Paul Heyse setting in Wolf's *Italienisches Liederbuch* (1896): 'What song can I sing to you?'

I've come back to a crowd of events, which I can only try to enumerate rather than describe:

1) Richard T.[11] has sent me an application form for an Arts Grant to enable me to complete *The Merchant* with as few interruptions as possible. The grants come in two sizes: if I get £5000, I'll limit next season to only the engagements I am already committed to play (only about 10); if 3000, I'll postpone the start of the season till November and stop earlier, say in May of next year. If I get nothing, I'll be only too glad to accept any concerts than may come my way!

As I needed two references, I asked Hans and Stephen. Both complied at once, but Stephen's letter was partly burnt when a Post Office van transporting it caught fire! The cinders arrived this morning with an apology from the Oxford head postmaster. I am surprised Hans' letter didn't succumb to spontaneous combustion: he speaks of me almost as Schumann did of Chopin or Brahms. Stephen said he'll write again, this time directly to the Arts Council so as to save time.

Later – 2) Another startling letter from Halinka:

Dear André, I can't understand why writing to you should prove so indescribably difficult. Your last letters should have caused me joy, but they contained far more than you yourself suspect. They negate my *entire* attitude towards life and people. The blow has proved accurate and painful. You've discovered my lack of authenticity, the fact that my personality consists of having *no* personality, that I always ham something up through guilt and a conviction that the best purpose of life is to turn yourself into others' *raison d'être*. And now I've lied so long that I'd give a lot to know what I do feel. Perhaps it's not your first attempt at unmasking me, but it's the first time you've managed it. I've suddenly felt toward you like a superannuated actor, requested to stop reciting the part and merely say what he means, in an ordinary everyday way. And it turns out that he has no idea what to say, feels sterile and empty, ashamed of that emptiness and obsessively aggrieved at losing his job. This is how I feel. But it would be most amusing if you also felt like that; if you too found it difficult to speak to me. This I expect, for something unprecedented has occurred between us. I've got utterly lost in this. The game is over. Is this good or bad?'

Of course it's GOOD! Why, it's an absolute break-through. I never realised that Halinka's 'I'll-be-whatever-you-want-me-to-be' attitude, that used to drive me nearly homicidal, was not confined to myself; in retrospect, it explains so much, notably her two disastrous marriages. She had never

---

[11] Richard Toeman (1933–2005), a representative of Josef Weinberger, Tchaikowsky's publisher.

been able to say 'no', as she was always less aware of any feelings of her own than those of her partners. It was a relief to her to fall into step with anyone who at least thought he knew what he wanted. With me she felt confused: what exactly *did* I expect of her? Did I want her to be mother, sister, wife, mistress, doormat? And all I wanted was for her to stop asking herself those very questions. Now she has! and feels utterly lost.

I cabled her: 'The game is over but life is only just beginning have courage love André' and followed it up with a letter inviting her over for June. I know it won't be easy but at least we now know the real difficulties. I concluded with: 'the Halinka I love is the one who lives independently of anyone's expectations, including my own, and I greatly desire to see her'.

At any rate there no longer seems any danger of a complete break! She's showing tremendous honesty and courage. Shall I measure up?

15 March

3) Unable and unwilling to attend E.'s 21st birthday party, I invited him to dinner here on the actual day (the party being on the nearest Saturday), i.e. last night. It proved very pleasant and relaxed, better perhaps than any previous meeting. He asked me if I'd play him Op. 109[12] as a birthday present, and though I hadn't played [it] for two years I really couldn't bear to refuse; the result was surprisingly creditable, and at last I felt free of that confounded old anxiety to impress him; free also to see that he really *has* become fond of me, for all my hard trying! He is a delightful friend to have, and may well prove a lasting one.

4) For a long time, I've been meaning to write a solo piano piece for Stephen. He started me off by suggesting variations on, of all things, *The Pink Panther*; my counter-suggestion, variations on the opening theme of Bartók's viola concerto, struck him as too high-brow ('Oh André, but that's *art!*'). I'll still try to write those variations, which I had partly sketched in Perth, WA, in '74, meanwhile I still had to find something to suit Stephen. While learning half of the Debussy studies, I had toyed with the idea of writing a set dealing with the same technical problems, but Stephen objected again: 'too much work'. Finally we agreed on a set of dances, with S. reserving the right to specify one dance beforehand: 'a mazurka or a polonaise'. For some time I could not think of either, but on a walk in Rio's botanical garden the theme for a mazurka came to me and on my return I rang him to report the grand feat of having written the first eight bars. 'Good', he replies, 'and *now* I want a tango!'

[12] Beethoven's Piano Sonata No. 30 in E major (1820).

And that very day, while shopping in Oxford, I found myself besieged by the corniest and most vulgar ideas, all in tango rhythm. Having seven concerts in the next three weeks (K. 537[13] tomorrow, a recital in Guernsey and K. 595[14] in Luton next week, K. 453[15] three times in Denmark and a radio recital in Oslo) I had forsworn all composition, but these ideas were as insistent as tarts, with whom they seem to have so much else in common, and I spent the next two evenings jotting them down. My attitude is a mixture of priggish embarrassment and amusement, as if I walked about dressed in drag; Stephen is delighted. So far he only knows about it from my 'phone report, but I've never known him so impatient to see anything of mine. I hope he'll like it, it's certainly cheeky enough to amuse him. But I really must try to keep off it till after the 2nd of April!

5) Eve came last Sunday, was thrilled about everything concerning Michael, very pleased with the suit scene, but worried about the ending of the piano scene. I'll take it to London (she is putting me up tomorrow after hearing me play the Abdication concerto[16] in Hatfield) and consult her in detail. Perhaps I shall be able to finish *1948* on my next trip?

30 March

Copenhagen airport

This stay proved a threefold success:

Apart from an unaccountable slip at the first of the three concerts (not *exactly* a memory lapse, though it must have sounded like one: I was so relaxed and pleased with the performance that, having dropped to *pp* in order to let the flute and the first bassoon through and duly heard them, I actually stopped playing!), I did a very creditable K. 453 at each successive evening, especially at the 'big' final concert whose importance had made me sufficiently nervous to overcome the increasing smugness. By sheer coincidence, which however it would be foolish to despise, I also got positively ecstatic reviews in all the main papers! What's more, I've already been invited to play a recital and a chamber concert the same time next year, the latter an all-French programme of my own devising built round the Debussy and Fauré settings of the same Verlaine texts.

Anton Kontra, the leader of the Sjellands orchestra, also leads a string quartet and asked me if I had written anything for the medium! Having both the music (score and parts, as I was correcting it) and the recording of

---

[13] Mozart, Piano Concerto No. 26 in D major (1788).

[14] Mozart, Piano Concerto No. 27 in B flat major (1787–91).

[15] Mozart, Piano Concerto No. 17 in G major (1784).

[16] Apparently a private joke: Mozart's Piano Concerto No. 26, ᴋ626 (1788), bears the nickname 'Coronation'.

the first performance, I played it to the four players half-way through their rehearsal of the Dvořák A-flat; two followed on the score, the other two on their respective parts. Anton said he wanted to play it in the summer of next year! I wrote to my publisher and asked him to let them have the material; even if it doesn't come off, the reaction was encouraging. And after all they might carry it through: having played all the Bartók quartets they shouldn't find mine too intimidating

The third success was negative: there was certainly nothing enjoyable about it. I might call it an *inverted* success. At last I have been compelled to realise that I've outgrown my outings to the usual haunts! I felt depressed and nervous at the mere prospect, and only made myself go because it was the only such occasion for a year; I hated it at the time; I left after an hour and a quarter of boredom and disgust having not gone beyond a brief half-hearted grope (if I had done any more it would have been a degrading, mendacious self-rape). I felt tears on my cheeks as I walked back to the hotel: nausea can make one weep as well as vomit…

In all this there is no disapproval. Let all those to whom it appeals enjoy it, as I did for so many years. It just no longer suits *me*.

8 April

Paris
Today I finished *1948*.

No doubt I shall have to revise it later, along with all the rest. But the end, which for once I wrote according to my original plan (Rimbaud and all) seems to work better than most other parts. I read it to Eve on the 'phone and she found it 'beautifully written'; I was especially glad to have finished it today as it is her birthday. I showed it to Kazik,[17] whose general attitude towards the book is surprisingly positive (he objects neither to factual changes and sheer invention or to my presentation of himself), likes the last page or two best of all. He had read all the rest of it at one sitting on my first evening in Paris, showed great interest and has just asked me to send him photostats of any future fragments as they came! His one objection is that there is not enough direct presentation of myself in it: the reader gets to know me only through my reactions towards other people. True enough, but isn't it a book about conflict? He would prefer me to include more of my own consciousness, my thoughts in solitude, especially my attitude towards music. I feel that the book is not about me but about one aspect of my life: my orphanhood, and my fight against the various contenders for my

[17] Tchaikowsky's cousin Charles Fortier.

mother's place. Music is a large enough subject to demand a separate, far longer and altogether different book, nor is it one that has ever tempted me: I've never yet seen a successful description of music in words. Anyway in this story it would merely cloud the main subject.

I am so happy about this ending I daren't believe it. Can I really have managed it so that the quotations from *Adieu*[18] don't seem pretentious? Then I should really have achieved some kind of union with my demon lover – the person I should so have loved to have been if I had the guts. (Though it's lucky for me that I could never even try to emulate him! He does make one feel that happiness is just a poor man's consolation prize, but I am not big enough to wish for anything else.)

I've had very good talks with Kazik. Both of us are now learning to *listen*, and consequently to know each other; we enjoy not merely respect, our different preference, temperaments, selves, and I could even tell him of my faith without any fear of being mocked. He's never asked me for anything, although he always gave whatever he had! No wonder I keep coming back.

Altogether, a heart-warming stay.

11 April

Cumnor
Just woke up from the following dream:

I was a guest at a small monthly reunion of the C. S. Lewises', only four guests being present (including me). One of the guests was a young anthropologist, so during drinks there was much merry banter about primitive rituals etc. This part of the dream was so rapid that I can't remember what was said, but took in just the lightness of the atmosphere. At a call from our hostess, we moved into the dining parts of the big room (the drinks were taken in the library, but the two rooms had been knocked into one). As I write this, I have an intense feeling that this is an actual place I know from my waking hours, and I still hope to indentify it.

However, at reaching the round table, I saw on it an open visitor's book. Each guest's place was marked with a card, and the letter he sent to accept the invitation was also present, envelope and all, to be removed no doubt when he had signed the book.

What a lot of ritual! I thought. Then I remembered that the Lewises were fond of legends and obsolete customs.

There was a chair next to me against the wall, just to my left as I was waiting to sign the book. Suddenly on that chair appeared G. L.'s ghost.

---

[18] A poem in Rimbaud's *Une Saison en enfer.*

For a second or less I was overjoyed. Then I remembered he was dead[19] and fell down to my right, into the corner. I was just passing out when I woke up.

And now I understand the general horror of ghosts. My love for G. L., the fact that there is no person in the world I'd rather see, that he had only come to give me joy, out of his own love, perhaps even out of his need, all counted for nothing. What counted was the sheer shock of his being dead, a ghost, the feeling that he had no *right* to be there. It was horribly unfair to him.

I am no longer a Christian, but on waking up I got out of bed, knelt down and prayed for G. L.'s soul. It is not something I have ever wanted done for my own soul, but G. L. was just the kind of person who'd have welcomed it.

Perhaps it's relevant that this dream was preceded by a very affectionate one in which M. R. and I were again lovers and, among many other things, discussing dreams!

Now I also realise why most nights I take Mogadon: it inhibits dreams.

21 April

I shan't receive the Arts Council Grant.

The intensity of my discouragement shows how confident I was of getting it. Now I can't even *wish* for a long free stretch in which to finish *The Merchant*. On the contrary, I am worried by the scarcity of concerts next season: so far I've only got twelve and I'd need at least three times that to make ends meet! How shall I live?

Still, practically all the artists I most admire worked under the strain of continual financial struggle. I should worry, if at all, about less trivial matters. Indeed I resent having to worry about money at all! And yet, this is an essential part of life, like physical illness: its function is to prevent one from feeling too 'special', to preserve a necessary sense of kinship with all the people who don't write operas…

At least they've answered fast, so I have time to humble myself and collect whatever concerts come my way! *Moi qui me suis cru mage ou ange…*[20]

I hate petty worries.

5 August

I am more than half-way through the *Epilogue*, though some of the earlier fragments are still not fully harmonised. This would mean that I am dead on schedule. But there are worries.

---

[19] He was also a different colour from the rest of us, greyer, more transparent. –AT

[20] 'Me, who called myself a magus or angel', another line from Rimbaud's 'Adieu'.

5.8. – I am more than half-way through the epilogue, though some of the earlier fragments are still not fully harmonized. This would mean that I am dead on schedule. But there are worries.

The first of these is no doubt shared by any modern producer of the Merchant. How does one keep the last scene from dullness? Shakespeare's audience laughed at the Jew and identified with the lovers (or at least took an affectionate interest in them). Today, with Shylock off-stage, every viewer begins to fumble for his cloakroom ticket. Except for the Midsummer Night's Dream, this is the only comedy I know in which all the lovers are united and happy before the last act. After the tension of the trial scene, who can still care about that ring quarrel? Perhaps I should have had the guts to scrap the last scene (as Verdi scrapped the first act of Otello) and finish on Shylock's tragic final exit. Well, I still may : the opera does seem overlong. But I'll write it first, despite all my present misgivings.

The other worry is the disastrous deterioration of my piano playing. I've made a point of practising two hours a day but this system, which worked so well during my first summer at Cunmor, is inefficient unless I am truly interested in what I am doing and now I feel no interest in the

211

The first of these is no doubt shared by any modern producer of *The Merchant*. How does one keep the last scene from dullness? Shakespeare's audience laughed at the Jew and identified with the lovers (or at least took an affectionate interest in them). Today, with Shylock off-stage, every viewer begins to fumble for his cloakroom ticket. Except for the *Midsummer Night's Dream*, this is the only comedy I know in which all the lovers are united and happy before the last act. After the tension of the trial scene, who can still care about the ring quarrel? Perhaps I should have had the guts to scrap the last scene (as Verdi scrapped the first act of *Otello*) and finish on Shylock's tragic final exit. Well, I still may: the opera does seem overlong. But I'll write it first, despite all my present misgivings.

The other worry is the disastrous deterioration of my piano playing. I've made a point of practising two hours a day but this system, which worked so well during my first summer at Cumnor, is inefficient unless I am truly interested in what I am doing and now I feel no interest in the piano whatsoever. I've waggled my increasingly clumsy fingers dutifully and resentfully, with an eye on my watch so as not to prolong the ordeal by a single minute, and my thoughts on *The Merchant* or irrelevant trifles. In vain did I select the most difficult new works – op. 101,[21] Chopin's B-flat minor sonata – even they didn't jog me into more than an occasional moment of alertness.

The moment of truth came last Friday, when I was asked to replace Pascal R.[22] in Beethoven III. I played through the concerto and realised that there could be no question of playing it, or anything else, in public! Every run was uneven, my fingers seemed to have grown too thick to play between black keys; my muscles ached from effort. Deeply in debt as I am, I had told Terry I'd be available for cancellations; now I had to revoke the offer. And I trembled at the prospect of the coming season, the very first programme of which ends with the Chopin B-flat minor sonata…

The answer, I decided, was to stop practising altogether, so as to free both mornings and evenings for composition. Since I am obviously unable to divide my attention, the only chance for next season is to finish the *Epilogue* as soon possible, rest a few days, and then concentrate entirely on the playing. Perhaps I really need a pitch of desperation, obsession, compulsion, to get anything worthwhile done? And what's true of this summer will no doubt be even truer of the next, with the huge trial scene to be written!

Having made this decision, I have done nothing throughout the weekend! It's typical of me to feel tired *before* any strenuous work, and yesterday I got up at 1.40 p.m. – with what an effort! Perhaps it's nature's way to store up energy? Well it's now 11.15 on Monday morning, so let's see what the rest has done for me. On with my first morning composing session!

21 August

I didn't want to re-open this diary till I could report the completion of the *Epilogue*, and tonight I can! Or, at least, it does *seem* complete: one so often has doubts and second thoughts…

[21] Beethoven, Piano Sonata No 28 in A major (1816).
[22] Pascal Rogé, French pianist (b. 1951).

Last Saturday I reached the last page, which I am truly delighted with! Everything is there: morning light, the first bird-calls, Antonio's loneliness, the mystery of impending bridal night... A sudden hush descends on the characters as they notice the dawn: let's hope this reaction will be shared by the public.

After a day of prostration on Sunday and a somewhat tiresome but inevitable social interlude, I went back to fill in the earlier bits that had eluded me – the off-stage *Allegretto* and 'How sweet the moonlight sleeps upon this bank' both of which were far too complicated and bogged with supposedly clever counterpoints. I hope it's all right now, though I'll reserve judgment till some time has elapsed (month rather than hours).

I notice with surprise that only two weeks and two days have elapsed since the last entry, so if I start practising on Friday I shall only have missed out three weeks. *And* I have six weeks left till the first concert, so if I work as wholeheartedly on the piano as I now did on *The Merchant*, I do have a chance...

Well done, Tchaik!

28 August

Apart from having finished the *Epilogue* (and it looks promising, I've already started work on the orchestration) there are two causes for joy:

1) Michael, at last, likes the biography – *1948* did the trick. Perhaps even it will make him like other chapters in retrospect? And any rate, he has come to believe in the book. And how I needed it!

2) E. now rings, writes, confides in me and our relations couldn't be friendlier. [...]

I've re-read Camus' *La Chute* and was immensely struck by it; I was too young for it the first time. Indeed, the titles of the books I'd taken out of the city library for the long weekend speak for themselves: *La Chute, The Affair of the Poisons,*[23] *Crimes of Passion,*[24] *The Night of the Long Knives,*[25] and *The Satanic Mass!*[26] No wonder I am in such a cheerful mood.

---

[23] Frances Mossiker, *The Affair of the Poisons: Louis XIV, Madame de Montespan, and one of History's Great Unsolved Mysteries*, Alfred A. Knopf, New York/Victor Gollancz, London, 1970.

[24] Of all the books to have been published with this title, the closest in date to the time when Tchaikovsky was writing seems to be an anthology of Terry Stokes published by Alfred A. Knopf, New York, 1973.

[25] Either the book by Nikolai Tolstoy, Ballantine Books, London, 1972, or that by Max Gallo, Harper & Row, New York, 1972, but more probably the former.

[26] Perhaps Henry T. F. Rhodes, *The Satanic Mass: A Sociological and Criminological Study*, Rider, London and New York, 1954.

I've resumed practice and it's not as bad as I had thought (at least so far); best of all, I now really enjoy it. But today I've strained my left arm, so I had to desist after two hours. Will it be better by tomorrow?

Here is the list of books I mean to read: *Witchcraft Today*,[27] *The Last Ten Days of Hitler*,[28] *Medieval Heresy*[29] (I'd like to find out more about the Anabaptists) and the new English translation of *Eugene Onegin*.[30]

La Chute is full of epigrams and aphorisms in the best French tradition, one of which: 'On voit parfois plus clair dans celui qui ment que dans celui qui dit vrai'[31] could be used as the motto of my 'biog' (as Michael calls it), since I can't pitch Goethe's candid title *Dichtung und Wahrheit*.[32] But better still is Proust's 'Se souvenir c'est déjà un peu oublier'[33] and this I now think I'll use. It is beautiful in itself, explains my motivation in writing the book, illustrates its subject and, best of all, anticipates any charge of untruthfulness!

13 September

Since completing the *Epilogue*, I've been leading a pleasant, regulated, uneventful life. I haven't been anywhere further than Oxford, and contented myself with playing hosts to such friends as felt like visiting me.

My practice has stayed at three hours a day, though a fourth wouldn't come amiss! I am still way below form. But I begrudge the extra hour, which could only come at the expense of the daily page of orchestration – a far more demanding, but also more rewarding job. Soon the pressure of the season will force me to step up the practice; meanwhile I enjoy the rare sensation of balance between the two activities.

Each day I start with a different Mozart concerto, then come the *Kreisleriana* or the Chopin B-flat minor sonata (which I had never dared tackle till now); these I practise on alternate days. The recent spell of delectable weather has been driving me out in the afternoons, and evenings

---

[27] Gerald B. Gardner, *Witchcraft Today*, Rider, London and New York, 1954.

[28] Hugh Trevor-Roper, *The Last Days of Hitler*, Macmillan, London, 1947.

[29] Malcolm D. Lambert, *Medieval Heresy: Popular Movements from the Bogumil to Hus*, Holmes & Meier, Teaneck (New Jersey), 1977.

[30] Novel in verse by Aleksandr Pushkin first published in serial form between 1825 and 1832; the first complete edition appeared in 1833. Charles Johnson's new translation was published by Penguin Books, Harmondsworth, in 1977.

[31] 'We sometimes see more clearly into the liar than into the one who tells the truth.' A quote from *La Chute* by Albert Camus.

[32] *Aus meinem Leben: Dichtung und Wahrheit* ('From my Life: Poetry and Truth'; 1811–1833), Goethe's autobiography, published in 1833.

[33] 'To remember is already to forget a little'. Reference to Proust's *À la recherche du temps perdu* ('Remembrance of Things Past'), a novel in seven volumes, published in France between 1913 and 1927.

are spent over books and records: I have developed an unexpected crush on
Die Meistersinger.[34]

Financially I am in a curious position – my overdraft is higher than my
mortgage!

Mr Pooter[35] would be proud of this page.

3 October

I am making my will.

The main beneficiaries were obvious. Eve will get this house and
contents (minus £5000 which will go to Terry); Michael the proceeds of
the Life Insurance; Stephen the Steinway. Eve will also get any posthumous
royalties, with Terry and Alan G.[36] being literary executors. As a burlesque
touch, my skull is to go to the Royal Shakespeare Co, 'for use in theatrical
performances': I doubt if they'll accept it,[37] but it should counteract the
oppressive solemnity of reading the will.

A wonderful letter from Michael, who has just fallen happily in love (for
the first time since leaving England). And a weird, disquietening [*sic*] one
from J. I had heard from Sally[38] that he'd returned home from Bangkok
instead of coming on here as he had planned, and felt hurt that having
written to announce his arrival and asked for money towards his travelling
expenses, he then had not seen fit to inform me of his change of plans. He
had given me very short notice to transfer the money, the letter arrived four
days before the end of his stay in Bangkok; but I rushed to London, had it
cabled through, and cabled him information on where to collect it. Since
then, silence. No J. and no further message. If it wasn't for Sally, I'd still be
waiting for him now!

So I wrote him a dry little note, asking whether he'd duly received the
money and expressing a sardonic hope that he didn't mind my knowledge

---

[34] A music drama by Richard Wagner, premiered in 1868 in Munich.

[35] *Cf.* p. 56, above.

[36] Alan Golding, Tchaikowsky's accountant.

[37] The Royal Shakespeare Company eventually used Tchaikowsky's skull in a four-month run of *Hamlet* in Stratford-upon-Avon in 2008 but announced that its use would be discontinued when the production transferred to the West End of London because audiences had begun to over-react to its appearance (*cf.* Urmee Khan, *loc. cit.*, and p. 80, above). In the event, the skull was indeed used in the London run, and also subsequently in a BBC TV screening of the production. In 2011 the Royal Mail marked the 50th anniversary of the RSC by issuing six postage-stamps, one of which featured David Tennant as Hamlet holding Tchaikowsky's skull. Tchaikowsky is, of course, not the only composer to have featured on a British stamp but is probably the only one to have done so in this manner, let alone share the space with a prominent actor.

[38] Sally was a friend (possibly the girlfriend) of J., the man in New Zealand with whom Tchaikowsky fell in love in 1977.

of his new address. He answered immediately, but in what a way! There remains little of him but a faint Ariel spirit; he has hardly spoken a word to anyone for months; all Sally saw was his corpus (sic!); he would write more but he's only a mind left, a spirit and the pen is so heavy. Is he drifting towards schizophrenia? I can see that he's always been an ideal subject for it. This, then, was at the back of that mysterious, angelic, other-worldly charm that made me love him as nobody else! And he, who at last made me feel at home in the world, has found no place for himself in it; by the time I next see him, in February, his tenuous link with reality may have snapped, or more probably gradually fade out altogether.

The letter threw me into two different states at once: this concern and awareness of my helplessness, and the usual Racinian fury at being unwanted. For several hours I wondered what I could write to hurt him most (I've lost the power to touch him, so hurt is all I have left[39]); then, fortunately, I overcame this reaction, realised it had nothing to do with J, and contrasted his isolation and wretchedness with my prevalent enjoyment of life, the richness of it, the range of joys I derived from nature, music, books and, most relevant, friends. That was J.'s work: he had enabled me to take what the world offered. And could I do *nothing* for him?

By the evening, I managed to write him a long, affectionate, blood-transfusing letter; what effect it will have I cannot know – he is going where I cannot follow. But I love *him* as I did none of my previous lovers. And I now want to hold him for his sake, not mine: he has no other link with life, no one has ever won his trust except myself. It would be an appalling tragedy if I *could* help him and yet failed him through possessiveness.

1 November

I am 44 today.

This is being written on my way to London, where Eve insists on giving me a treat! My birthday matters far more to her than it ever could to myself. But I look forward to the outing: the film of Büchner's *Woyzeck* and a cosy tête-à-tête dinner with my lovely friend.

I've spent most of this journey trying to get my short story started. So far it's rather clumsily informative, but perhaps I should set the bare facts down before worrying about the way to convey them? Perhaps one can only know what to omit if one has put it down on paper first.

---

[39] While writing this, I realised I had unwittingly quoted Racine: Je percerai le cœur que je n'ai pu toucher. ['I pierce the heart that I cannot touch': *Andromaque*, Act IV, scene 3] –AT

The Monday recital went fairly well, but I found it somewhat patchy and lacking in impact: little drama in the first movement of the Beethoven, several lapses of control in the *Kreisleriana*. The second movement of the Beethoven went much as I like it. What surprised me was the general conspiracy in favour of my *Kreisleriana*: Misha [Donat], Peter Frankl and Stephen (who touched me by turning up in person) all praised it in extravagant terms, and only Radu demurred. Alas, I don't like it and doubt if I shall ever tackle that cycle again, or any work that I don't feel utterly dedicated to! (The only exception will be complete series like, say, the Mozart concertos, which might include an odd work or two that I should never think of learning by itself). However many times I've made a mess of the Liszt sonata, the Ravel l[eft] h[and] concerto, or the *Davidsbündler*, I shall always be tempted to have another go at it: this gives even my failures a certain character and intensity. But, for all my hard work, I'd never got beyond *dabbling* in *Kreisleriana*: I could not bring myself to love it. From now on I shall only play works whose value strikes me as beyond all question, and play them in a way in which I can wholeheartedly believe. Whatever else may fail, let it never again be conviction.

Since then no practice, but several sessions on Stephen's out of date mazurka; with luck, I may yet finish it this weekend, which will be my last chance for some time!

2 November

Last night was a mild disappointment. *Woyzeck*, though beautifully done, proved arty and self-conscious, with the murder scene in slow motion accompanied by a baroque oboe solo! The prophetic quality of the play is its very rawness, so to stylise it *today* seems downright perverse. And arty and self-conscious are also the right adjectives for 'September' restaurant, which had greatly appealed to Eve a year ago and where she'd been meaning to take me ever since. The atmosphere was twee, the waiters tried too hard, and it proved so expensive that I could not possibly let Eve take the bill! This in turn disappointed her, as she had particularly wanted to provide my entire birthday treat.

I now wish we had not gone to *Death of a Salesman*,[40] which I saw at the Lyttelton Theatre today. I had wept on re-reading it, but seeing it in performance turned me into a one-man irrigation system! Free umbrellas should be given my neighbours.

---

[40] 1949 play by Arthur Miller: an elderly travelling salesman, Willy Loman, retreats from failure into delusional rants, accusing his two sons, Biff and Happy, of themselves being failures.

And yet it was not entirely successful: neither of the sons was up to his part, Happy in particular being a camp falsetto-voiced nonentity. Biff might have done for a minor part, but only a great young actor can carry the weight of the pivotal conflict of the play! And I mean young, 25 or so, perhaps less, so as not to have to work at being young in the flashbacks. This, of course, goes for Happy too: then in the main body of the action they would merely *look* older, but only superficially, two eternal adolescents who'll never grow up. Whatever possessed the producer to make the compulsive womaniser Happy camp?

But the parents were heartbreaking. Willy was Warren Mitchell,[41] whom I'd never seen: Linda someone called Doreen Mantle,[42] of whom nobody seems to have heard. Mitchell's performance confirmed Kazik's contention that any good *comic* actor can achieve tragedy without special effort – not, presumably, heroic tragedy but sheer human pathos. Tonight Willy Loman's plight was simply unbearable; I don't know how I sat through it.

What would it have been if a young, deceptively tough, but infinitely vulnerable Biff had sat down on his suitcase in that hotel room! There is no greater tragedy than destruction through *mutual* love, and almost every family can testify to this appalling fact.

18 November

Brussels

Well, I did do a generally good Beethoven IV, at any rate on Friday night, where I had Patrick and Taeko[43] as well as the local VIPs in the audience. The Saturday afternoon repeat performance was not nearly as good, for the following reason:

In addition to going well, the first concert went 'down' very well: numerous curtain calls, rhythmic applause of the kind that one hears at political rallies, briefly an ovation. By the sixth curtain call I could no longer find the conductor,[44] whom I had last seen walking away with a bottle of mineral water, and I had to re-appear alone twice in succession. Unwilling to be singled out like a prima donna after so symphonic a concerto, afraid

---

[41] British actor (b. 1926) who achieved fame as the Cockney bigot Alf Garnett in Johnny Speight's BBC TV sitcom *Till Death Us Do Part* (1965–75) and its sequels.

[42] South African-born British actress (b. 1930), who likewise achieved fame in a BBC TV sitcom, as Jean Warboys in *One Foot in the Grave* (1990–2000).

[43] The Belgian Patrick Crommelynck (b. 1942) and Japanese Taeko Kuwata (b. 1945) formed the Duo Crommelynck in 1974, the year of their marriage. In 1994, after two decades of success, they committed suicide: it seems that Taeko, discovering that Patrick had hanged himself, decided to end her own life in the same manner.

[44] André Vandernoot, Belgian conductor (1927–91).

of being taken for one, and yet encouraged by the applause to endear myself further, I said:

'Mesdames et Messieurs, pardonnez-moi de réparaître sans la chef d'orchestre: il avait trop soif.'[45]

I can now see the tasteless Wunderkind cuteness of this remark, but at the time it struck me as natural and likeable (there is a false naturalness as well as a false modesty). Needless to say, it brought a further ovation and a few minutes later I had forgotten all about it. I spent a relaxed and happy evening, conscious of my achievement in this most elusive and exposed concerto, conscious also of the general appreciation.

The next day I was in danger of being only too relaxed; luckily, I was also aware of that trap. Everything changed within seconds of going out on stage, when the conductor greeted me with:

'Et surtot, ne fais plus d'annonces publiques à la con! Tu me fais prendre pour un ivrogne maintenant. Tu n'avais plus qu'à leur dire que je suis en train de baiser une fille dans les coulisses!'[46]

'Comment, un ivrogne?' I asked, surprised, 'Je n'ai pas spécifié la boisson...'[47]

Too angry to stop, he shouted on while I spoke:

'Ça ne s'est jamais vu au Palais des Beaux-Arts!'[48]

'Tu veux quand même que je joue?'[49] I asked with that icy ironic politeness that is my own customary expression of anger.

'Ah, mais il ne manquait plus que ça! Il ne veut peut-être plus jouer maintenant.'[50]

The secretary of the Société Philharmonique looked at me with anxious compassion. The conductor was putting himself in the wrong: a brutal, humourless, stupid boor, who waited till the last moment before the performance to attack and upset his soloist. Any further remark on my part would have jeopardised my own moral superiority.

I suppressed the desire to retort. But I could not prevent my rising anger from marshalling devastating repartees, improvising an annihilating letter, briefly foregoing all concentration on the work at hand. Once the opening bars were out of the way (and these went just as well as on the previous night) I had the whole long *tutti* to sit through, with no activity to counteract the

---

[45] 'Ladies and gentlemen, forgive my reappearance without the conductor: he was too thirsty'.

[46] 'Above all, don't make any more idiotic public announcements! You'll make people think I'm a drunkard now. You might as well have added that I was shagging a girl in the wings! '

[47] 'What do you mean, drunkard? I didn't specify the drink....'

[48] 'Such a thing has never happened in the Palais des Beaux-Arts!

[49] 'Do you still want me to play?'

[50] 'That's all we need! Maybe he doesn't want to play now.'

surge of venom flooding me from within. Though far from good, the first movement was not nearly as bad as it might have been in the circumstances: the runs were rushed but generally not fluffed, the ensemble better (having said his piece, the conductor now paid more attention); but all atmosphere and serenity had, of course, departed, and all that came through was the concern for the next run. The reception was also less enthusiastic, though a few people called 'Bravo!'

Afterwards, I shook hands with both conductor and leader as usual, forwent all attempts at explanations, left during the symphony and limited the farewell to the following note:

> Cher André
> Au revoir et merci.
> André.

He is no doubt too thick-skinned to realise the irony and contempt so perfunctory a goodbye note implies. But it really was not worth a post-mortem. Even if I had told the public that he is actually getting *drunk* backstage, no man with a sense of humour and of his own dignity could have treated it as anything but a joke. Possibly it had reached him in a maliciously distorted version, as he has many enemies in Brussels. But Patrick and Taeko think that the real reason was professional envy: he couldn't help resenting the contrast between the faint applause he'd got for the *Egmont* ouverture[51] with the exceptional ovation that greeted my performance. At any rate, he behaved like a boor, whereas I had been guilty of nothing worse than thoughtlessness.

Patrick and Taeko were adorable again, hospitable and helpful in a way at once affectionate and discreet, enthusiastic about the performance, attentive, amusing, stimulating and relaxing all at once. I've told them about the Radio 3 short story, outlining the plot and the approach. Will this prove a mistake? It often is, and I was well aware of the danger. At any rate, I shall soon find out…

17 December

Cologne–Paris
[…] Schmöhe[52] is naïve, jovial, warm-hearted and somewhat flamboyant, a Papageno[53] dressed to look like Diaghileff,[54] with a charmingly absurd

---

51 From Beethoven's 1810 incidental music for the 1787 play *Egmont* by Goethe.
52 Georg Schmöhe (b. 1939), German conductor.
53 A character from Mozart's opera *The Magic Flute*, who appears dressed in bird feathers.
54 Sergey (Serge) Diagilev (1872–1929), Russian impresario, founder of the Ballets Russes in 1909.

result. His conducting is of a piece with the rest of him. I like him very much, but we should need a frank talk before being friends: he overestimates me and I pretend to overestimate him. Or does he also pretend? An amusing possibility, but I doubt it: after all, he did ask me to play with him after our K. 453 in Caracas and he did push the engagement through. And, after all, I did play well for him (though not, as he maintained, impeccably). I think he and Gisele complete each other exceedingly well! She provides the head and he the heart.

The rest of the trip was a barely disguised fund-raising expedition. Drowning in debts (£2250 overdraft, £550 owed to Access, over £1000 to Terry and £880 to Inland Revenue) I've decided to borrow money from Stefan [Askenase] and Kazik, about £1000 each. Neither made any problems and Stefan told me he is surprised by my bothering to pay him back! 'Why, whom do you take me for?' I asked. 'For a very old friend.' I took his DM 5000, added most of my modest Bielefeld fee and had it telexed to my bank in London. Tonight or tomorrow I'll get the promised 10,000 francs from Kazik. It is a great relief to owe money to well-disposed people rather than to anonymous, inflexible institutions! But this still covers only a half of my debts.

I made a point of asking Ingrid[55] if she agreed to the loan. This was a formality, but I know how easily she can turn from love to hate, and she is incapable of anything but extremes. I must confess that I do not like her, that her continuous shrill intensity tires and irritates me (part of the fatigue may be due to my poor German, which has suffered from recent neglect) and that I am downright afraid of being next-in-line on her list if anything should happen to Stefan! (He is, after all, 83, though he does not show it.) She had used every form of emotional blackmail to marry him, and the result had made him very happy. Once widowed, will she set her sights on me? If she does, she'll stop at nothing. Even now, Stefan told me, she is subject to bouts of insanity.

This is the real cause of my fatigue: hypocrisy. I hate lying, but I fall over myself to please and flatter Ingrid, lest she should once again become a barrier between me and Stefan! The first time she tried that, they were not married and he could afford to disregard her threats; now that he's happily settled and used to the kind of desperate constant attention that would give anyone else radiation sickness, he'd sacrifice me to preserve the peace of his new home. For his sake I shall keep the act up as long as he lives, but I can't lie without despising myself, and it was a great relief to me when I left.

[55] Second wife of Stefan Askenase.

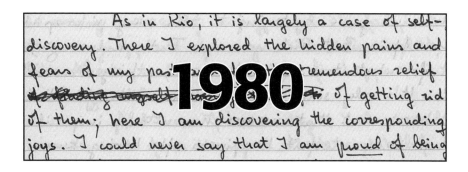

As in Rio, it is largely a case of self-discovery. There I explored the hidden pains and fears of my pas... ...tremendous relief ...of getting rid of them; here I am discovering the corresponding joys. I could never say that I am proud of being

12 January

Jerusalem

This is my happiest sojourn anywhere since Rio.

As in Rio, it is largely a case of self-discovery. There I explored the hidden pains and fears of my past and felt the tremendous relief of getting rid of them; here I am discovering the corresponding joys. I could never say that I am *proud* of being a Jew, for what have I done to become one? But for the first time in my life I actively *enjoy* being a Jew. the word has lost its ghetto connotations.

Always and everywhere, I have felt myself to be different. I felt equally out of it among Jews and among Gentiles, among homosexuals and family men, in all communities and with most individuals. Three years ago John made me break through that isolation, and since then I have found it much easier to achieve contact with people to assume welcome rather than rejection, often to extend it. J. told me of Maharishi's phrase about 'the forgiveness of differences' and I happily imagined humanity as a vast orchestra, to which my timbre could contribute the more for being distinctive.

But here I've found myself in a land where everyone is different. Short of the Yom Kippur war, could anything surprise the Israelis? They've seen every physiognomy, heard every accent within every language, witnessed and often created every creed and philosophy, known every crime, every passion, every form of financial fraud. My past, so heavy to me, is a routine affair in Israel; it meets with sympathetic understanding, not oppressive pity. They know how it feels: we are brothers. Questions which would be wildly indiscreet elsewhere – such as that of my real name and how I came to be called Tchaikowsky – do not prompt me to the usual evasion, or create more than a mild residual embarrassment.

To my surprise, I really like the Israelis. They are often assertive, argumentative and indiscreet, they have little use for tact and social graces, but they have all the corresponding virtues: warmth, spontaneity, humour,

Jerusalem, 12.1.80. — This is my happiest
sojourn anywhere since Rio.

As in Rio, it is largely a case of self-
discovery. There I explored the hidden pains and
fears of my past and felt the tremendous relief
~~of~~ of getting rid
of them; here I am discovering the corresponding
joys. I could never say that I am proud of being
a Jew, for what have I done to become one? But
for the first time in my life I actively enjoy being
a Jew: the word has lost its ghetto connotations.

Always and everywhere, I have felt
myself to be different. I felt equally out of it
among Jews and among Gentiles, among homosexuals and family men, in all communities and with
most individuals. Three years ago John made me
break through that isolation, and since then I have
found it much easier to achieve contact with people,
to assume welcome rather than rejection, often to
extend it. John told me of Maharishi's phrase about
"the togetherness of differences" and I happily
imagined humanity as a vast orchestra, to which
my timbre could contribute the more for being

26

an emotional immediacy that would create instant panic in England. They
are more openly human than most other nations: few people have an official
or social 'image' or 'persona', they are as fully themselves at work as at home,
and use the word 'Mensch' as the highest praise. Status is a rare and comic
preoccupation, and most Israelis totally ignore it: they'll deal in just the
same way with an Arab camel-driver and with the emperor of Japan.

And now I realise why I have always hated the isolating VIP treatment most people considered my due. This is the society I was looking for! I can now only laugh at my earlier plans to emigrate to, of all places, Australia, or even New Zealand: the latter, is, of course, heaven on earth, but I belong here, not in heaven. Everything shows me that this is my natural environment, and I've come to realise how many of the things I like in myself are due to my Jewish ancestry: the respect for learning, the fascination with books, the tendency to live almost entirely 'in the head'; the impatience with small talk and social rituals; and, of course, the emotional intensity.

Twice in my youth I have made the same huge mistake: in judging women by my grandmother and in judging Jews by the hateful, claustrophobic, paranoiac Diaspora communities. If those are Jews, then Israel is the best place to get away from them – the 'final solution'.

Of course Israel is full of self-created and self-contained ghettos. It tolerates everybody, including the intolerant. But it's amusing to notice the mixture of boredom and humour with which the Israelis treat those visiting professional Jews, whose sole conversation is the Jewish problem and who is or is not a Jew! They have no further need to prove their national identity: they did that by emigrating or being born here; now they can turn their attention to the universal daily task of being human.

One thing Israel does have in common with many Jewish communities is that it is an intellectual and artistic power-house. There can hardly be a town of comparable size and population in which so much gets thought, done and made as in Jerusalem – or, for that matter, one of comparable age which has been treated with such respect and discernment by modern architects. Also, the contrasting civilisations that succeeded one another in cities like Rome or Constantinople survive and flourish simultaneously in the crowded Old City of Jerusalem. Some of them are hopelessly debased and commercialised, as can be seen at the Disneyland fair called the Church of the Holy Sepulchre; but such places as the Muslim Dome of the Rock, and most Jewish temples, have preserved all their uncompromising awesome dignity.

I wish I could convey the complex heterogenous flavour of that crowded city. Here are a few examples:

1) Stage manager, telling the conductor (Uri Segal) that it's time to go on stage and start the concert:
   'Nu, Urele?'
2) An Arab at Damascus gate to Eve: 'I'll gladly give 500 camels for you'.
3) An Armenian postcard vendor near Jaffa gate:

'You André Tchaikowsky, right? I take no money from you, take the cards free! But next time play Bach on the cembalo...'

This is being written at Mishkenot Sha'ananim, an artists' and creative thinkers' residence. No one else can get in and a special committee meets four times a year to decide who is eligible; but once they've invited you, you're guest of the city, and are given a huge, quiet, beautifully furnished and designed apartment, serviced daily except on Saturdays, for anything up to three months. (Once you've completed your appointed job, you are charged just enough to meet their costs). This, like the guest house of the Israeli Philharmonic which I don't yet know, testifies to that reverence for creative thought which I am glad to recognise in myself, and the atmosphere is the most congenial I have ever met. The employees are students, and it's a matter of course to have a strenuous intellectual discussion or a well-fought game of chess any evening with any of them; there is no barrier between them and the guests. Last night I had a talk with one of the night porters, a philosophy student called Doron; it turned out that he had earlier studied comparative literature, and I suggested that we each write down our ten favourite writers and compare the lists; seven out of ten were identical.

My first thought on entering the place was: 'What pretext can I find to get back here?' and on the very next day, my first day in Israel, the wish was granted. Lili Kraus, who was due to give a series of master-classes here, fell ill and I was asked to replace her. The series was due to take place while I was playing my three concerts here, but it was postponed by a week to give me a better chance. In fact I did not play the concerts as well as I had hoped, as the very anxiety to do my very best proved predictably counter-productive; the first performance was particularly patchy. But the orchestra, which is youthful, merry and full of enthusiasm, took me to their hearts and so for some unfathomable reason did the audience; it's true that I had aimed at absolute perfection, so no doubt even a failure was worthwhile enough. Since then I have given one class and am down to do four more in the next four days; judging by my first two students, the standard is as impressive as I should have expected. One student, an arrogant religious zealot complete with skull-cap, provoked me into giving him a deliberately harsh treatment; but he turned my hostility into respect (though not into affection) by responding to criticism in a positive and professional way, so that half-way through my attack turned into encouragement!

Like any other country, Israel has its share of bores. But these are less insistent than I had expected. Most Israelis are, if anything, overactive; they are too busy living their own lives to find time for spoiling mine. And in a country where concert pianists outnumbered truck-drivers, who would bother to fuss around me? I have yet to meet a full-time local parasite.

20 January

Tel Aviv–London

Israel has cured me.

I had never realised to what extent my crippling insecurities were not social or even sexual, but racial. In the last two weeks they had simply left me – I did not notice them. At some point I realised that I've been saying just what I meant to people, doing largely what I wanted, without asking myself what they expected of me and whether I was acceptable to them. If I wasn't, it was their problem: I had just as much right to be there as they did.

This is something I had felt in no other country. To G. L., Eve, Michael and J. I could relate without reservations (though not always without anxiety), take risks, speak my mind, be myself. Many other people accepted me just as I was, including faults I concealed from myself but which were clear to them. But I could not be persuaded of this: I had to make myself acceptable, to pay my entrance fee to every social group. At each new meeting I silently asked: 'What is it that you want from me? Am I to be the charmer, the witty eccentric, the genius, the failure? Do you get more fun out of admiring or of pitying me? I can work to measure. I can be the helpless baby for you to mother, the idol you pray to, the riddle only you can solve. All I need are your exact requirements.'

My own wishes I discarded as irrelevant, and for a time I would manage to repress my true feelings – in the strict Freudian sense of being utterly unconscious of them. But never for long. And then, to make up for past hypocrisy, I should rebel and turn brutal and cruel, break off relations, reject and humiliate the person who, whether taken in by my previous act or seeing through it, had truly loved me.

Not that in Israel I necessarily assumed unconditional acceptance! It was better than that: I no longer even needed it, and just as concerts go better when one is not desperate to succeed, I found myself free and happy to meet everybody, answered every 'phone message, found or made time for anyone I liked, gave each new acquaintance a chance to make friends with me. It made for the busiest time I've ever had, but to my surprise I managed to cope with it all – sometimes better, sometimes worse, but I ignored virtually nobody. And this made me realise how much energy had gone into my previous lying and play-acting, the unconvincing over-politeness, and above all the constant anxiety.

Shall I be able to keep what I've found? All my habits are of course against me, and most old relationships have assumed fairly rigid patterns. But I know that there is a land where my rights and equality are not merely written on paper, and that within me there is an embassy of that land. I can carry my freedom and self-respect wherever I go.

But I'll have to be on my guard – no longer against other people but against myself. Israel showed me the limits of my self-knowledge: it is far more deficient than I had suspected. It has also made me aware of my hidden potential: once free of fear, there is no knowing what I may do or become. The first surprise was my decision to try and meet my father! If I had been told of it beforehand, I should have cancelled my entire visit.

We all cling to what we know, even if we hate it. For five years I had grumbled about life in London without moving out. For most of my life I had fought what I was in favour of what I had wanted to be. Perhaps my insane egocentrism is only a reaction against my constant efforts to meet the supposed expectations of other people, and will give way once this habit is broken?

31 January

Aarhus–Copenhagen

Most of my week in Denmark having proved pleasant but relatively uneventful, I shall devote this entry to jot down the impression of my last few days in Israel.

I had told Halinka M[1] about my book soon after arriving in Jerusalem, and her reaction exceeded all my expectations: she has always regarded it as our *duty* to write an account of what had happened to our generation, and often reproached herself for not finding the time or the courage to do it herself. She thinks our joint exploration of our common past may help herself as much as me, and is ready to confront for my sake any terrors that are bound to come up.

Nor, to my surprise, does she object to my writing the book as a novel! (I still think she will later, when she realises the extent of my liberties with reality). […] The effect of that stay was not, however, to stimulate my work on the book. With so much evidence still to come, and now at last so readily available, it seems silly to go on writing sections I shall only have to scrap and rewrite when I have got the undistorted facts. What I shall do instead is to *make time* for the research on the book, spend a few weeks in Israel collecting information, and only then write it. I have already applied for permission to stay for three-four weeks at Mishkenot Sha'ananim, if possible next November; by then, with exceptional luck, the totally missing trial scene of *The Merchant* may have been completed. In my application,

---

[1] Halina (Halinka) Malewiak, Tchaikowsky's cousin.

I suggested combining the orchestration of that scene with work on the book, so I shall not be staying there under false pretences! Hans[2] has written another incandescent letter to back me up (this time he may have better luck) and the committee meeting is due *today*, so I shall have an answer within a week or so; if they accept me, I shall inform Halinka. I couldn't imagine better conditions for strenuous mental work than the calm seclusion of Mishkenot, without any professional or social obligations that I could never avoid on tour.

No, the real effect of my stay in Israel is so startling that, if I had been told of it beforehand, I should no doubt have cancelled the entire trip. I have decided to seek out my father! I'll try to meet him unannounced, so as not to give him time to prepare a refusal to see me or a triumphantly accusatory speech: his face will tell me what I really need to know. This may mean that I may never be able to use the *1948* chapter, and I'll be sorry to waste that but what is the book but a most inadequate compensation for *having no parents*? If he should say one word that touches my heart, I'll no doubt scrap the entire Paris section. And he might: I am no longer as prejudiced against him as I was. I still think him a pompous, stupid, coarse bully, conceited through being the only educated member of a barely literate family, unaware of anybody but himself. But that is Truth: one does not choose one's parents. And he had suffered two mortifying rejections for marrying morally 'above his station': both Mother and myself walked out on him.

And now he's 70; soon he may die. Who knows if he's still alive now? I do want to see what he's like and how he feels about me while I have the choice.

Copenhagen–London, p.m.

I had spent so much energy in Israel that I expected a huge reaction: days in bed, possibly with a headache; no question of work; disastrous concerts. Well, so far none of this has happened. Rick came to stay the day after my return and I was as happy as ever to have him around; I practised a lot and with interest; I played, on the whole, surprisingly well, though the finale of the B-minor sonata[3] is still very far from being 'fit for public consumption'. The rondo of the E-minor concerto[4] was also somewhat patchy last night, but the first movement was better that it has ever been; and whatever their faults, nothing at either of the Danish concerts suggested fatigue. Israel may have taken all I had, but it gave even more than it took.

---

[2] Hans Keller and his wife, Milein Cosman, spent two periods at Mishkenot Sha'ananim, in 1977 and 1979. The result was Keller's *Jerusalem Diary: Music, Society and Politics, 1977 and 1979*, illustrated with Cosman's drawings and published by Plumbago Books, London, 2001.
[3] Chopin, Piano Sonata No. 3, Op. 58 (1844).
[4] Chopin, Piano Concerto No 1, Op. 11 (1830).

18 February

Auckland
Yesterday was my first day in New Zealand, my first summer day in mid-winter, and just about my first free day this year.

The summer part proved most untypical. The unseasonably mild winder in England is being paralleled by freak weather here, gales, rain and sub-antarctic temperatures. Not unexpectedly, I spent most of that first day asleep. My banal tourist dream of spending it at the beach, dozing in the sun, was reduced to a brief walk along it, during one temporary respite from the rain. The local regatta was abandoned mid-way, but I saw some of it before they gave up.

[…] I have deliberately left *The Merchant* behind, so as not even to be tempted into orchestration! Three years ago, my pianist duties were confined to alternating two relatively easy concertos, K. 595 and Beethoven I. This time, the three Viennese programmes demand all the concentration and practice I've got, and I leave for Hong Kong next day but one after the last concert. Not till late spring shall I be able to resume work on the *Epilogue* again.

The book, on the other hand, is with me. On the way over, I've copied out, shortened and partly corrected the early part of 1945; I hope to be able to dabble in it sporadically now and then (mainly, no doubt, on planes). With luck, the corrections may lead to some ideas for its continuation – at the moment, my mind is quite barren.

In Christchurch, I shall be staying with Ian Dando, Christchurch's and New Zealand's first music critic and, of recent, a personal friend.

19 February

Auckland–Christchurch
For many years, Ian treated me to rave reviews. The sub-editor of the *Christchurch Star* being addicted to alliteration, Ian produced the title: 'Glowing Genius Glorifies Gargantuan Goldberg'. I replied by telegram 'Dashing Dando Dispatches Dizzying Dithyrambs' and he surprised me several years later by pulling that carefully folded cable out of his wallet. Now and then we'd meet and discuss music and look at each other's scores – the opening of Act I of *The Merchant*, Ian's very competent Second string quartet. We never discussed any personal topics. […]

When he heard of my projected trip to New Zealand, he invited me to stay with him. I replied cautiously, warning him of my pathological untidiness and adding that during my last stay I had fallen very happily in love and should hate to rule out any chance of a Da Capo: if that should happen, I'd have more freedom in an hotel. Ian assured me that the young lady was just as welcome as I was myself. I took the plunge and made matters clear.

Back came six pages of hero-worship, praising my honesty and courage as if I had confessed to at least necrophilia! He all but apologised for being exclusively straight himself. As for the untidiness, he's used to having his sons stay with him: 'surely you can't make more of a mess than three little boys?' So we've agreed to my staying with him, unless either of us should find urgent and delightful reasons for wanting to be on his own. […]

2 March

Dunedin

And now a word about my professional activities.

The Hamilton recital went quite well on the whole, despite the horrid piano; I had aimed it at S.,[5] who, as it transpired later, hadn't turned up! Afterwards I was driven to Auckland, where they had arranged a lecture for me at the university. I felt perfectly at ease about it until I heard, within minutes of starting, that they had advertised it as a 'lecture-recital'; after all, I can always talk, but a recital demands some preparation and a stricter mental attitude.

However, it went strikingly well. A lecturer, unlike a pianist, has to *face* his audience; I saw them smile affection[ately] at me, laugh at my jokes, admire the beauty of the illustrations. And I found myself loving them, wanting to do my best by them when the time came, to leave them with a lasting experience of shared beauty. And this has one practical consequence.

My last concert in Auckland is on the 14th; my single recital in Christchurch two days before. I had asked J. – there is no keeping that lad out of any single entry! – to spend the night of the 12th with me, all of it, and he's agreed. But now I realise this would mean a tired, perfunctory performance in Auckland, and the Diabelli[6] demand all the presence of mind I've got; moreover I could no longer treat the concert as an *event*, but only as an anticlimax. So I shall try to persuade J. to come with me to Auckland and share with me my final free day, by which time my duties will have been completed and my reward earned. But can he? Will he? He hates to refuse me, and this in turn makes me afraid to ask, lest he agree out of sheer tenderness of heart, without real willingness or enjoyment.

And yet how little time we have for each other! When shall we listen to music together, or play chamber music (J. is surprisingly able on the

---

[5] A New Zealand-based acquaintance.
[6] Beethoven's *33 Variations on a Waltz by Anton Diabelli*, Op. 120 (1819–23).

violin), or read poetry together? (I'd love to introduce him to W. H. Auden.) Now that the thorns have gone, is the rose to blush unseen and waste her fragrance on the desert air![7] Shut up, Tchaik, you're about to mix up Gray and Blake.

The Dunedin recital went acceptably well, no better than that, some excellent playing alternating with feverish rushes in *Les Adieux*[8] and small lapses of concentration in the outer movements of D. 960.[9] Indeed, I spent much of its first movement analysing the panic spots of *Les Adieux*! But the *Andante* of the Schubert was the best I have ever played it. I suppose what I really missed is a sensitive friend to play to. With, say, Eve in the audience the recital might have been terrific.

No, the real achievement of my stay here was far more unexpected: I have finished copying and revising the opening pages of 1945! That was one thing I could not hope for amid so many concerts, but the result seems reasonably satisfactory. Now I've caught up with myself and can break fresh ground!

13 March

Auckland

'Do you love me?' I asked again.

No answer.

'You *know* you do,' I insisted gently.

'Yes', he whispered. And all life stood still.

It was the quiet inward climax of an almost unbearably crowded ten days, and it resolved all accumulated tensions. It brought me just that peace that had always lain beyond my reach. This is why I had come, though of course I could have no such hopes! This was why I had played, and worked, and loved, and lived. I only recognised my goal when I had attained it: that quiet centre of the world, the only place where our two hearts could meet.

I am now far too peaceful and contented to want any post-mortem of the intervening harsh vicissitudes. I'll do that on Sunday, on the long flight to Hong Kong. There'll be no chance till then: tomorrow I am repeating the Diabelli – D. 960 programme that had brought me such a unique reward last night in Christchurch, and on Saturday – dare I believe it – J. is coming here to see me off.

---

[7] 'Full many a flower is born to blush unseen,/ And waste its sweetness on the desert air': a line from the poem *Elegy Written in a Country Church-Yard* by Thomas Gray (1716–71).

[8] Beethoven, Piano Sonata No. 26 in E flat major, Op. 81a (1809–10).

[9] Schubert, Piano Sonata in B flat major (1828).

Lord, help me to deserve my present joy. Teach me to love as well as I am loved. Open up my heart.

24 March

[…] And now a few words about my visit to the astrologer in Auckland, the day before I left.

His name is David Ingram and he's a friend of Elaine's.[10] Like her, I liked him at sight, before knowing who he was. He radiates warmth, goodwill and generosity.

The last named quality showed in his announcing beforehand that the chart was a present from him and Elaine, just as I wondered how much such things cost. A handsome gift: it must have taken him hours of work to produce the three documents he showed me, only the first of which I could have identified as a horoscope (the other two being something like an isotope graph and a table of figures). And he spent 2½ hours explaining his finding to me, forsaking lunch and missing the opening of a Menotti matinee he was taking his two children to see.

He recorded his interpretation and advice on a cassette which he then gave me. I have not yet heard it, so I only remember the criticisms and warning: these always stay on in the mind.

I cannot judge his ability as an astrologer, but he is certainly a shrewd psychologist. I shall return to his comments when I've heard the cassette, as I am bound to have missed or misunderstood most of them; all I'll record now is the resultant advice.

30 March

'NEVER EXPECT', he wrote in capitals over the chart. My weakest spot lay in relationships, where my habit of analysing people and situations, coupled with my overactive imagination, constantly pre-empted and prevented any real contact. I was too enslaved by my own ideas and expectations of them that I could never see what they did have to offer. From now on I was never again to wait for a letter or a telephone call, never try to manipulate anybody's feelings, never depend on anyone but myself, and then everybody would come to me freely and lovingly, and give me all they had to offer, which was more than I ever imagined.

Nor did I have any choice in the matter, he added; if I persisted in letting imagination intrude on my private life, my torment would become intolerable. Neptune will keep luring me with false promises, and his present

---

[10] A friend of Tchaikowsky's in New Zealand.

conjunction with Venus will undermine my most precious relationships. The next three years won't be easy, he warned: I'll have to keep revising my old attitudes.

As an example of the practical application of his words, I remember this little exchange:

I: 'You mean I should just put my own cards on the table saying 'This is how I feel. How do *you* feel?''

DAVID: 'No! Never ask them how they feel. It's their business. If they want to tell you, they will.'

For all the wisdom of his advice, I should have rejected it as hopelessly beyond my powers had not my recent […] [experience] convinced me of the absolute necessity to learn how to relate to *people*, and not just their reflections in my mind. I had already turned my back on past attitudes: David showed me what I should now aim at.

But old habits die hard. Even while writing this I hope impatiently that J. will be able to free himself and visit me in June; he did say he would try, but I don't know what his chances are – he had tried to come over a year ago and was overruled. Is this hope one of Neptune's tricks?

For once, though, I know that I too have something to offer. J.'s ear for music and sensitivity of response are phenomenal, and yet being in New Zealand he's been deprived of any music lover's daily bread: he knows no Beethoven quartets, no Mozart operas, no Schubert song-cycles as far as I know. If he comes, I shall *give* him music, guide him through it, hear ten different records in one night or the same one ten times, as he prefers… This is why we are trying for June – it's the one month in which he can have *all* my time, energy and enthusiasm, with no competing duties and no pressure.

14 April

It's a fortnight since I've seen my father.

I have delayed describing that meeting till I had time and concentration to do justice to so rare an event. But that time came, and I still had no desire to start on this entry. At first I just felt too tired to embark on what obviously had to be a long and detailed description. But gradually, a deeper reason for my reluctance emerged: disappointment.

Rare the event undoubtedly was: we had not met since 1948! But it was less of an event than I had expected, nothing like the breakthrough I'd experienced in Israel, where I first conceived the idea of visiting Father. It taught me nothing new, and I had only gone there in order to learn – to find out who I am and where I come from.

It took me some time to realise I was disappointed, because my first reaction had been one of dazed relief. It had all gone so well, after all! And there had been every reason to fear.

It was fear that had made me decide to give him no advance notice of my visit. I thought that his initial reaction might be in my favour, or at least would reveal his true attitude toward me, whereas any delay would be fatal. I wanted to give him no time to brood over his real and imaginary wrongs, to prepare an accusatory speech, perhaps even to refuse to see me (I had twice refused to see him). But while all the friends I had consulted applauded my resolution to see Father, they unanimously disapproved of my intention to take him by surprise. Some feared that the shock might induce a heart-attack or an apoplectic stroke; others accused me of seeking a cheap histrionic effect. Everyone condemned the idea as flippant, callous and in wretched taste.

None of this made any difference. I was determined to find a short cut to Father's heart, by-passing all the accumulated bitterness and hurt pride; and I was confident that the actual meeting would upset him far less than a mere prospect of it. Also, I preferred the slight risk of being thrown out to the very real probability of a refusal to see me, or an attempt on his part to dictate the terms of the meeting.

Finding him proved already a problem. I had delegated that to Jadzia,[11] who had proved so valuable in providing information for the early chapters of my book; devoted, tactful, discreet, she was obviously the ideal ally here. But Father was not to be found in the Paris 'phone book; for all we knew, he might have gone back to Austria or Germany; nobody Jadzia consulted knew anything of his recent whereabouts.

Jadzia's letter reporting her failure was contradicted by a post-scriptum which gave his address and 'phone number. She also informed me that Father now had Parkinson's disease, that he was currently in hospital so that she's only been able to speak to his second wife, and that I had a half-sister.

Reading this reversed my previous attitude. I could no longer bear any prehistoric grudges against a man who shook with palsy and couldn't walk without fear of falling on his face: he had become vulnerable, perishable, human. I was also extremely curious to meet my half-sister. How old would she be? I imagined her in turns as a child and as a teenager.

Jadzia had told my stepmother that she was speaking on behalf of a Polish friend of my mother's who was visiting Paris. 'Yes, I know about his Polish first wife,' answered my stepmother, 'he even has a son by her who refuses

---

[11] A colleague of Tchaikowsky's cousin Charles Fortier.

to acknowledge him'. At any rate, there was no doubt that Jadzia had found the right person. I was only surprised to hear of this long-term grievance so freely expressed to a stranger.

Two weeks ago I arrived in Paris and Jadzia rang them again under the same pretence. Yes, Father was now home; yes, he could see his first wife's friend (*une* amie) at 2 o'clock. I bought a bunch of roses and went.

They live just outside Paris, which explained Father's disappearance from the 'phone book. The place was easy to find, I had over an hour to kill, so I had lunch in a nearby bistro. I was nervous, ridiculously anxious to make a good impression, anxious also to avoid all solemnity.

I rang their bell punctually and found myself confronting a comfortable-looking, portly lady of about sixty. For a moment I could not think of anything to say, so I tendered her the flowers in idiotic silence.

'Mais, monsieur…' she faltered with the beginning of unease in her voice. She had been told to expect a lady, not an unknown man. Did burglars really offer roses to their victims?

Finding no ready explanation for my presence, I mentioned my name. 'Je m'appelle André Tchaikowsky. Savez-vous qui je suis?'[12]

'Bien sûr,' said the lady calmly. 'Vous avez mis du temps…'[13]

Meanwhile Father had appeared at the end of the corridor; his rigid Parkinson gait made me think of Eric von Stroheim.[14]

'Monsieur,' he started in turn, but he was interrupted by his wife:

'Comment "monsieur"! Mais c'est ton fils!'[15] she cried joyously as if it was an obvious and regular visit.

'Eh oui,' I said, advancing towards him with a smile, 'je suis ton fils.'[16]

'Viens,' he said without the slightest hesitation, 'je vais tout t'expliquer'.[17] Taking him unawares obviously did not spare me that oppressive 'speech'. I had underestimated my father: he would always have a speech at his command.

But it was not the prosecution speech I had expected. Far from accusing me, he concentrated on defending himself, and thinking over his loss of me in the long intervening years he had come to realise the precise object of my resentment, though it had not been voiced in 1948. He knew that the trouble had started before I was born or conceived; he now realised that

---

[12] 'My name is André Tchaikowsky. Do you know who I am?'
[13] 'Of course. You took your time.'
[14] Erich von Stroheim (1885–1957) was an Austrian-born film star of the silent era.
[15] 'What do you mean, "monsieur"! It is your son!'
[16] 'Yes, I am your son.'
[17] 'Come, I will explain everything to you.'

Tchaikowsky's father, Karl Krauthammer, at the time of their meeting in 1980.
He was to outlive his son by a year.

I also knew it. One example of our estrangement was his having to ask in what language I now preferred to speak.

I followed him into the drawing-room, took the indicated seat and listened. His wife was tactfully going to leave us alone, but he said he had no secrets from her, and I was also glad of her calm benevolent presence.

He talked on. I was aware of the many facts he suppressed or distorted. But what did it matter compared with the uncontrollable trembling of his left hand and right foot? Who could hold a distant past against a man reduced to such a state? I no longer cared for the truth of 1934 or '48. But I let him have his say, for his own sake.

'Well,' he asked at last, 'and what has made you decide to see your father after 32 years?'

Again I realised that I had nothing to say: my reasons for the meeting sounded unconvincingly nebulous. It was, of course, easy to invent more plausible reasons, e.g. remorse, but I am glad that I did not choose that easy escape. I tried to tell him about my experience in Israel, my decision to find my own roots; it sounded flat, bookish and impersonal.

'Et je suis venu sans te prévenir,' I concluded, 'par peur que tu refuserais de me recevoir. Tu serais dans ton droit, j'ai tous les torts.'[18]

He reminded me of my refusal to see him after a concert in 1958 or thereabouts.

'Oui, je l'ai fait: j'étais très monté contre toi. Dès ma naissance, je n'ai jamais entendu que du mal de toi, et à notre rencontre tu as voulu me faire abandoner la musique...'[19]

This was the only fact I could uphold against him, as it was the only one I knew at first hand. All the rest could be blamed on Grams, who was dead and could not be harmed.

Again he explained his earlier position, with all the classical arguments. A bad doctor or lawyer may make less money than a first-class one, but at any rate he makes a living; a bad musician, or simply an unsuccessful one, has nothing to eat. The argument is irrefutable, for only people with a vocation of their own will ever understand what vocation means.

'This gave Grams more ammunition,' I said, by-passing an impossible explanation. 'She could now say that only with her I'd become a pianist. It gave her a fresh hold over me, on top of all she had already: I now owed her simply everything.'

'My mistake was in providing for you alone, instead of offering to support her as well,' said Father. 'I had too strong a grudge against her to volunteer that.'

This was ridiculous: Grams would never have accepted a centime from a man she loathed and despised, and they would have torn me apart between them. But I did not contradict Father: there was no point.

'Wait,' he said. 'I want to show you something.' He got up with some effort and took a book from a cabinet. It was a German musical lexicon. Father invited me to look myself up. I read:

– TCHAIKOWSKY, André... Verlor seine Eltern im Krieg –[20]

I don't know if I blushed, but I felt ashamed. I could just imagine what had happened, a friend telling Father that his son was in that lexicon, Father rushing through Paris to the German bookshop, buying the lexicon, eagerly seeking out my entry and reading that he'd been pronounced dead.

I apologised. I knelt in front of his armchair and kissed his hand. I asked his forgiveness. Had anybody told me I should do any of these things, I'd

---

[18] 'I came without warning you for fear that you would refuse to see me. You would have every right, and I am in the wrong.'

[19] 'Yes, I did, I was very much against you. Since my birth, I have never heard anything good about you, and when we met you wanted me to abandon music.'

[20] 'Lost his parents in the war'.

At the home of his father in Paris in 1980

have cancelled the project of our meeting. But this was, firstly, because I had always assumed that he'd *demand* an apology: he did no such thing. Only his face showed his pain and bitterness. I now saw the preceding decades as a story of his long, awkward, unrequited, humiliated love. And secondly, I realised something I had overlooked. Under all the personal emotions, there existed a basic, archetypal level, a level at which Father was Father and Son was Son, whatever the individual circumstances, attitudes and feelings. And on that level, it really wasn't too much for a father to expect to be able to have his son's address, to hear from him, to see him occasionally. I now realised that Father had been robbed – who cares by whose fault? – of his natural right. All right then, he was a stupid bastard: who's ever said that stupid bastards do not love their sons? They merely do not know how to deal with them, alienate them and suffer without ever understanding why. I was guilty however either of us felt.

This was the one true lesson of the meeting, and perhaps it was worth it for that alone, worth it for me as well as for him. Thinking back on it makes me realise the possible reason for my strange resistance to *Oedipus, King Lear,*

Phèdre: in every case, I could not afford to accept the dramatist's premise, which is the existence of obligation which depend not on a person's feelings but on his very identity. Oedipus couldn't plead ignorance – he *had* sinned in ignorance but he knew it to be irrelevant. I'd long been aware of a barrier in my appreciation of *Lear* and *Phèdre*, but put it down to Grams' incessant and interminable catalogues of her misfortunes and my ingratitudes. I was wrong: the barrier lay in me. I could not acknowledge Goneril and Regan guilty without admitting myself to be so, and their subsequent crimes struck me as gross unfairness on the writer's part. (They still do, but I now know myself to be at fault.) I am only waking up to the horrid possibility that guilt may not just be a feeling, but a fact.

I tried to leave after that and I wish they had let me, as my only other discovery was far less exalting. I recognised in myself instantly that bored polite resignation with which everyone has learnt to listen for hours to a ranting parent. Put in the baldest terms, the discovery ran: A PARENT IS SOMEONE TO WHOM ONE LIES. Assuming music to be the one bond between us (whereas in fact it was the chief barrier), Father now treated me to a good hour's lecture on music. His specialty lies in value judgment, but he is too circumspect a person ever to back anyone but a winner: he reserves his admiration for stars and best-sellers. Thus he saw fit to inform me that Pollini had talent, that Horowitz had been a great pianist, that Menuhin was no longer worth hearing, at least to someone who'd had the privilege of witnessing his wunderkind triumphs; he gave a plug to Beethoven's most popular sonatas, the ones with a nickname; he recommended Mozart and gave Schubert a qualified pass. Anything from Debussy onwards was, of course, dismissed, but so were Beethoven's last sonatas: Father merely said he didn't understand that music, but his tone of voice made it plain that it was always the composer's fault.

'And do you also play jazz?' he asked.

'No.'

'Good, because jazz is just shit for me.'

Listening to all that I realised how convenient for me his invalid condition was. For one thing he now took fourteen tranquillisers a day, which reduced his once tonitruante voice to a mezzo-forte; I found myself thinking that he should have taken them all his life, for his kin's and friend's sake. For another, there was no longer any danger of his turning up at my home or one of my concerts and embarrass me with his pompous vulgarity. If we could choose our fathers, most of us would never be born; are parents ever as ashamed of us as we are of them? At least if they are they can say so.

Before they at last let me go they invited me to dinner the following evening to meet my half-sister Catherine. She is now 26 and has been

Reconciled: Tchaikowsky with his father and half-sister, Katherine Krauthammer, in 1980

married for two years. Both parents agreed that Catherine's character is very difficult, but that their son-in-law Michel is very nice. [...]

I left with renewed apologies (nobody asked me for them, which is why I wanted to make them) and went back to Kazik's relieved, touched and nearly in tears.

Father's illness has deprived him of reading, since he cannot hold a book steady and is too proud to use a pulpit (or a stick in walking). 'C'est une sale maladie,' he said. 'Si je n'avais ni femme ni fille, je saurais quoi faire!'[21] This makes him dependent on such music as he does enjoy, so the obvious present was records. In the hour he spent on the subject I had learnt his favourite works and performers, so the choice was easy. I also took two bottles of champagne, which nobody finally drank, as Génia, my charming

---

[21] 'This is a filthy illness! If I didn't have a wife or daughter, I would know what to do!'

step-mother, showed her Russian provenance by an overwhelming display of hospitality. The fatted calf is not a Christian monopoly.

Again I arrived punctually and was told Catherine and Michel would be late. This gave Father time for a very revealing piece of information.

'You asked after your uncle and aunt,' he began. 'Well, we're no longer on speaking terms.'

Two thoughts coincided in my brain: 'Father is running true to form' and 'Good, at least I'll be spared the tedious round of family visits.'

The first thought proved unfair. Both Father's siblings broke relations with him because he had allowed his daughter to marry a Gentile! 'J'aurais moi-même préféré un Juif,' he added gently. 'Mais pourquoi?' 'Je ne sais pas, c'est quand meme plus proche.' [22]

It was nice to be able to side with Father for once on some point. His atavistic hankering for a Jewish son-in-law gave more value to his acceptance of the one he had. Génia indignantly confirmed the story of the family quarrel and I trusted her enough to accept the facts.

Catherine and Michel proved nice, if banal, and I saw no evidence whatever of her difficult character. I felt more contact with Génia and Michel than with my two blood-relations (this no doubt is the usual way). The dinner was a relaxed and merry affair, and it was only the sudden almost pathological exhaustion afterwards that made me realise the effort involved: I thought I had been natural when I had merely *acted* natural, and there is no more strenuous act.

One other curious fact emerged during dinner. According to Father, I was born not in 1935 but '36! This, if true, would knock out David Ingram's detailed horoscope, which struck me as so uncannily accurate a fortnight before! I wrote to him and told him of this most unexpected possibility. But Kazik thinks Father has got it wrong, and as he had been chaperoning my mother through much of the courtship, I cannot altogether dismiss his view. Another possible witness is Halinka M. in Israel. But there can be no concrete evidence: my birth certificate must have been burnt in 1944, along with all of Warsaw. I do have a vague memory of Grams changing my birth date late in the war…

Catherine and Michel saw me off at the station of their little suburb. On the way she said:

'Father and I didn't always get on, and I often considered setting off to find *you* – I knew you'd understand me.'

[22] 'I would have preferred a Jew, myself.' 'Why?' 'I don't know; it's closer, anyway.'

'Did Father talk a lot about me, then?' I asked, surprised at the place I had occupied in the thoughts of a girl whose very existence was unknown to me.

'No, he never did. Never! But maman did.'

'But she had never met me!'

'All the same, we talked of you quite often.'

I had left them all my address and telephone number (the latter was vital, as Father can't write and may become critically ill any moment) and invited Catherine and Michel to look me up at Cumnor. I knew they'd be impressed with the house, garden, piano etc., and report it all to Father who values nothing more than money and success. Let him be glad at the thought that his son has 'made it': that will make him feel a bit of a success as well, and he has few other comforts. […]

Another 'correct' thing I might do is visit Father in a German clinic which specialises in Parkinson's disease. He is on the waiting-list and will go there when they can find a bed. He won't take Génia, as he can't afford to keep her for a month in an hotel, and she would get very bored outside the short visiting hours. Now, this mention of 'short visiting hours' was exactly what decided me: I should only get bored during them. Let Father exhibit me as his genius son to nurses and fellow invalids! I'll swallow the embarrassment for an hour a day. But the rest of the time will be mine, to fill up with orchestration, work on the book, reading or the study of German… And of course I should not stay a month, but a few days.

As for visiting them at home, I took care to tell them I could not come to Paris till next year. Father seemed disappointed, but did not protest. Perhaps he is relieved? There seems little point in taking fourteen tranquillisers while being subjected to such emotions as these.

As for me, I still don't' know how I feel about it. I am at once relieved, disappointed and confused. No doubt the subject will crop up again in this diary…

21 April

I shall copy out here the letter I've just written to Father:

'Mon cher Papa,

Merci beacoup de ton coup de fil. Je comprends ton réaction – tu ne peux tout de même pas m'accueillir après trente-deux ans comme si rien ne s'était passé. J'étais même stupéfait que vous m'ayez tous reçu les bras ouverts, sans réservations ni reproches!

Tu me demandes pourquoi j'ai voulu te revoir. Je regrette de te dire que ce n'était ni par amour filial, ni par un sens de devoir, ni par remords. Toute ma vie je m'étais senti déraciné, et en Israël j'ai enfin commence à sentir mes racines, à voir que j'appartenais quelque part. Ma première racine, c'était toi: j'ai donc décidé d'essayer de te retrouver pour me trouver et me connaître moi-même. Jamais je n'ai pensé que tu me demanderais de revenir; au contraire, je m'attendais à être mis à la porte!

Quand j'avais pris cette décision, je ne savais même pas si tu vivais, où tu habitais, j'ignorais tout de l'existence de Génia et de Catherine, sans parler de ta maladie. Et je croyais fermement que tu me haïssais, de façon que j'ai eu besoin de tout mon courage pour aller te voir.

Tu me demandes aussi la raison de toute cette longue rancune: pourquoi ai-je cru que tu me haïssais, pourquoi ai-je refusé de te voir? Eh bien, voilà: ma grand'mère t'avait accusé de très graves torts envers maman, y compris celui d'avoir refusé de la faire sortir de Pologne an début de la guerre et d'être ainsi responsable de sa mort. N'oublie pas que je n'avais que douze ans quand elle me l'avait dit, et que je n'avais jamais entendu cette histoire d'un autre point de vue; que j'adorais éperdument maman et que je ne me suis jamais remis de sa perte (alors que je n'aimais pas du tout ma grand'mère, bien que j'aie longtemps essayé). Et souviens-toi qu'ayant passé deux ans de mon enfance au ghetto de Varsovie et deux ans caché dans une armoire où je ne pouvais ni bouger ni parler, j'avais tout un système de neurasthénies qui m'empêchait de voir clair.

C'est pour cela que tu as très bien fait de commencer par m'expliquer l'histoire de ton premier mariage: personne d'autre n'aurait pu me mettre au courant des faits dont j'ignorais la plus grande partie. L'obstacle entre nous était formé dès avant ma naissance. Et que de circonstances pour l'aggraver!

Maintenant, c'est à toi de décider si tu veux rester en contact avec moi. Quoi que tu fasses, je respecterai ta volonté. Eu attendant, mille amitiés à toi, Génia, Catherine et Michel,

Ton fils prodigue,

André.

PS. Pourquoi me dis-tu que tu veux m'envoyer un cadeau pour 'ne pas rester en dette' envers moi? Tu ne me dois rien! C'est moi qui suis et resterai toujours en dette.[23]

---

[23] 'Many thanks for your call. I understand your reaction; after all, you can't welcome me after thirty-two years as if nothing had happened. I was even dumbstruck that you all received me with open arms, with neither reservations nor reproaches.

You ask why I wanted to see you again. I'm sorry to tell you that it was neither because of filial love, nor a sense of duty, nor remorse. All my life I had felt uprooted, and in Israel I have at last begun to feel my roots, to see that I belonged somewhere. My first root was you; I therefore decided to try to find you again to find myself and get to know myself. I never thought you would ask me to come back; on the contrary, I expected to be shown the door!

Poor Dad! He's reached the *brooding* stage. Now I know where I've got it from…

28 April

I have at last met Christopher Hampton.

The Observer is running a rather modest theatre festival in Oxford, and one of the events was a 'playwrights' forum', with C. H., Tom Stoppard and Stephen Poliakoff.[24] It took place this afternoon at the Playhouse and quickly proved very uneventful indeed. The questions fired at them by members of the largely student audience were, inevitably, vague and naïve, and the writers never seemed sure which of the three was being addressed. I minded none of that: I had only come in the hope of meeting Hampton.

None of the organisers seemed sure where to find him, but I set off toward the stage entrance, saw him coming down the street with Stoppard, accosted him and introduced myself. He was extremely pleasant and co-operative, apologised for not finding his translation of *Une Saison en Enfer* ('I'm pretty sure it's in my mother's garage') and asked me to ring him by the end of May, by which time he'll have come back from America and I shall have completed the season.

He asked me how far I had got with *Total Eclipse* and I explained to him that I was still in the middle of my previous opera. I did not add that it now looks very doubtful indeed whether I shall ever be able to take up the other

---

When I took this decision, I didn't even know if you were alive, or where you were living, I didn't know anything about Génia or Catherine, without mentioning your illness. And I firmly believed that you hated me, so much so that I needed all my courage to go and see you.

You ask me the reason for this long bitterness: why did I believe that you hated me, why did I refuse to see you? Well, here it is: my grandmother had accused you of behaving very wrongly towards mother, including refusing to make her leave Poland at the beginning of the war and thus for being responsible for her death. Don't forget that I was only twelve years old when she told me that, and I had never heard this story from another point of view; that I adored mum madly and I never got over her death (whereas I didn't love my grandmother at all, although I tried for a long time). And remember that, having passed two years in the Warsaw ghetto and two years hidden in a cupboard where I could neither move nor talk, I had an entire system of neurasthenias which prevented me from seeing straight.

That's why you did very much the right thing by beginning by explaining to me the story of your first marriage: no one else could have made me aware of facts of most of which I was unaware. The barrier between us had been formed even before I was born. And look at the circumstances that made it worse!

Now it's for you to decide if you want to stay in touch with me. Whatever you do, I shall respect your will. In the meantime I send you, Génia, Catherine and Michel much friendship.

Your prodigal son.

André

PS: Why do you say you want to send me a present so as not 'to stay in debt' with me? You owe me nothing! It is I who am and will always be in debt.'

[24] Tom Stoppard, British playwright, b. 1937; Stephen Poliakoff, British playwright, script writer and director, b. 1952.

project! The ENO have refused *The Merchant*[25] and I am so far in debt that I had to yield to Terry's arguments and agree to go back to the piano in October. This means writing the trial scene in three months instead of six, and I'll have to be extremely lucky (as well as diligent!) to complete my last act in that time. If I do, it will be the most I have ever achieved.

But even assuming that to have been done, there are still hundreds of hours to be spent on the orchestration, the piano reduction, correcting of the parts etc., all of this without any definite prospect of performance. To pay off my debts, I've already agreed to play right through next year, shelving all composition. (This makes me realise I've actually lied to C.H. when I said that I couldn't start work on his play till next summer!) And having done all that, shall I want to assume the long-term burden of another opera, still with no hope of performance? Not a chance! I want to *hear* what I've composed: it is the only way of learning.

Also, my obsession with Rimbaud and C.H.'s play has abated somewhat: I am now drawn to a broader and less bitter conception of life. And my very admiration for the play inhibits me: it is so nearly perfect on its own terms that I could hardly avoid spoiling it! I first used the idea as a bait to catch Hampton's attention: that, of course, failed, but it is typical and amusing that now that he at last has responded to the extent of suggesting a meeting, the project that had once come to mean so much to me should have reverted to its original trivial function.

Still, perhaps Hampton's personal influence shall make me take up the whole project again, despite all practical considerations? It certainly wouldn't happen for several years, as I want to follow the ten-year stint on *The Merchant* by a few shorter works (the piano suite for Stephen, the viola concerto for Uri[26]). I doubt if I'll be ready to undertake another opera till I've seen and heard my first. But if I do decide to write another, then *Total Eclipse* offers the best safeguard against the danger of repeating myself.

Meanwhile, in our few minutes of talk, I was aware of an instant rapport. He saw at once what I meant when I mentioned my musical need for lyric expansion, and that this would have to come from an inclusion of Rimbaud's own text, since in his play, very rightly, neither Verlaine nor Rimbaud speak the way they write. 'Yes,' he said, 'and I was criticised for that.' While

---

[25] On its first submission, that is, thus occasioning Hans Keller's letter supporting the opera to Lord Harewood, which led to its audition in December 1981: *cf.* pp. 328–34.

[26] Tchaikowsky had undertaken in 1981 to write *Six Dances for Piano* for pianist Stephen Kovacevich, but finished only the Mazurka and Tango. They have been recorded by Colin Stone for Merlin Records (B00004Y28P). No sketches of the Viola Concerto have been found.

speaking, I completely forgot my doubts about the project, and he seemed impressed with the professionality of my approach.

At any rate, his manner was most cordial. I am to ring him and he'll come to a meal!

6 May

A difficult period.

Financially, I have never yet been so far out of depth. Even before the start of my free period I am several thousand pounds in debt! What will it be by December?

I discussed the situation with my bank manager, who offered me unlimited credit facilities, and Terry, who warned me against contracting more debts than I can pay off and talked me into shortening my writing period by half, just in case he can find me a few concerts from October onwards! This faces me with my most stringent challenge so far: can I complete *The Merchant* in three months instead of six? I am absolutely determined to forgo my writing spell altogether next year, so as to collect the summer pianistic engagements and climb out of debt that much quicker. If I do, there'll be plenty of secondary writing to keep me in touch with composition next year: orchestration, piano reduction, proof-reading etc. But if I don't, the prospect is too awful to contemplate: two seasons of zombie performances, my mind obsessively chasing the elusive pages of the incomplete score, my whole being torn into two conflicting halves. I remember that state from the time I'd had to abandon the piano concerto unfinished, and spent a whole season playing disastrously. I then thought I was finished forever.

The best chance for *The Merchant* would, of course, be to start it at the end of this month, immediately after the last piano engagements. But – and this brings me to my most agonising difficulty – my elusive love J. *may* arrive on the 3rd of June, for a month's holiday which sounded so idyllic till Terry insisted on my being available to play by October. [...]

1 June

Terry rang three nights ago and asked me if I'd take over a tour of South Africa, starting on the 9th of June. He expected me to refuse, but I was only too glad of that providential bout of occupational therapy and professional discipline, of a change from emotional devastation to finite and definite practical problems! By the next morning the tour was confirmed.

It consists of eight concerts, seven with orchestra and one recital. The last date is on the 3rd of July in Durban and I'll be back on the morning of the 5th. This, of course, pushes back still further my work on *The Merchant,* but

Terry agreed to letting me off for most of October in exchange for playing this tour (the first definite booking of the season is on the 28th Oct.), so I can still have up to three months.

The combined fees will go more than halfway towards cancelling my elephantine overdraft.

30 June

Johannesburg–Durban
The ten days I spent in Pretoria were comfortable and pleasant.

Of the concerts, the Liszt in Bloemfontein had gone quite well, the Prokofieff in Pretoria on the following day adequately but no more; real excitement arose with the repeat of the Prokofieff two days later in Jo'burg. A severe 'flu epidemic was ravaging the orchestra, and the conductor, Leo Quayle,[27] was barely fit enough to get through the first concert, and utterly unable to conduct the second. His assistant, a young Englishman called John Mitchell was barely recovered from the 'flu when he was given the score of Prokofieff III at 11 p.m. on the eve of the concert; he had never conducted the work and hardly knew it. The rest of the programme consisted of Tchaikovsky V and the *Ruslan and Ludmila* overture.[28] I don't know how familiar he was with those works; he certainly seemed to know thoroughly the Tchaikovsky, but I'm not sure whether he'd had much practical experience of it, as opposed to mere homework.

A last-minute rehearsal had been called to acquaint John with the Prokofieff. The public actually waited outside while we went through it, and the concert started half an hour late! Nothing else was rehearsed: John merely announced to the orchestra the way he would beat a couple of details in Tchaik V.

The orchestra responded with all the zeal and alertness the occasion demanded. The leader, ill herself, got out of bed on hearing about the emergency; this, of course, assured some continuity of experience between the two concerts. Everyone watched the beat as never before – including myself, who am normally quite oblivious of my partners' efforts.

Indeed, the orchestra's general willingness and team spirit are utterly admirable, especially compared to the abler but jaded orchestras of England. It's perhaps the only full symphony orchestra I know that has the personal cohesion and intimacy of a chamber group (except perhaps for the NZ Symphony). Nor is there a barrier between the players and

---

[27] South African conductor (1918–2005).
[28] Overture to Glinka's opera by the same name (1842).

the administration: the administrator himself is one of the 'cellists, fully committed to music and sharing all his fellow players' problems. He was a reputedly capable soloist till he was stricken by multiple sclerosis; this, however, has so far taken a mild enough form to enable him to keep up practical music-making within the orchestra. A graver tragedy is that his only son is going blind! And yet old Aubrey goes on working at both jobs, a pathetic, endearing, stoic and for some reason slightly absurd figure. Right now he is in bed with that same 'flu.

The manager of the orchestra is a terrific chap called Vic, who manages to take over everybody's job without ever appearing tired or hurried. He plays and teaches percussion, tackles all the transport and stage-building problems, distributes parts and still manages to fit in a love-affair with a girl flute-player (I think). Without that, he'd be just too good.

Another remarkable man is a Dutchman called Fred, who started life as a hairdresser and hated it, switched over to engineering and is now devoted to converting SA audiences to drama and music (a daunting task). He works from 5 a.m. till 1 a.m., arranging sets, lights, etc., undeterred by the fact that this is his one yearly holiday! Fred's other claim to distinction is his being in love with his own wife, after at least twenty years of marriage.

Both the leader and the first 'cello are female, Jewish, and exceedingly competent. The leader, Annie, is from Amsterdam, and shares my adoration of Zinman! The woodwinds are virtually all young, keen and generally handsome, and impart great freshness to the orchestra.

The conductor, who has now recovered, is middle-aged and experienced, pleasant to work with and avuncular in manner. He likes being called 'Prof'. By last night, after I had appeared for the Ravel L. H. with my right arm in a sling (with Vic's compliments) and had the orchestra in hysterics, followed by a supper at which the Swiss first clarinettist demonstrated how to cook rösti, I genuinely regretted having to leave.

In Bloemfontein I scored my one political success to-date. Aubrey had told Terry that I should have mixed audiences everywhere, but this now varies not just between cities but from hall to hall, and on arriving at Bloemfontein I was informed that the university, where I was to play, was still closed to blacks. I used the press and radio interviews to say what I thought of this, and met with surprising support. The interviewer, far from editing my comments out as I had feared, switched them round to the very beginning of the interview, and sent a copy to Johannesburg for use in the national news programme (I don't know if they did use it); the papers were glad of a foreign guest endorsing their views; and the rich lady who sponsors this series of concerts promised me not to renew her support unless they were thrown open to mixed audiences! (Unlike her US counterparts she is young, pretty and 'with it'.)

But dare I admit it? I hardly care if there are any Africans in the audience or not. Surely they are being debarred from far more basic privileges! And about that I can do nothing. Nor do they come even in places where they are allowed, any more than I should consider going to an evening of African music! Why, even white South Africans are utter philistines: the very name of Mozart puts them to flight, that of Debussy is no doubt unknown (I didn't mention Bartók in fear of arrest). The orchestra helped me enjoy the symphonic concerts, but my single recital in Johannesburg proved a funereal affair – the 7½ people present reached an almost cataleptic state, and it was all I could do to keep awake myself.

What I really miss in South Africa is any general interest in culture. There is not one string quartet in the country! It makes one wish even for that nauseating snobbery that makes American millionaires sponsor chamber music. Sooner or later the musicians themselves give up trying against the prevailing apathy. The existence of censorship is less of an evil than the fact that no doubt nothing of moment would happen if it was removed.

No, my true sympathies lie with the striking BBC musicians, who get no strike pay and are almost certain to be starved into submission and further starvation.[29] If I prove myself of any use, let it be to them! So far I've done nothing.

John O'Brien[30] came over from Gaborone and we had a pleasant, relaxing, not very eventful weekend. He helped me make the necessary cuts in the trial scene, with some optional bits being left in square brackets – it will depend on the musical development whether they're left in or out. It hardly took an hour to work this out, but three months won't be too much for setting it to music!

By now, of course, I am on the long return flight. Apart from its usefulness in reducing the overdraft and its value as occupational therapy, this really was a very enjoyable tour! Durban itself is a vulgar sprawling holiday resort, clearly modelled on similar waterfront places in England, but what I saw

---

[29] Early in 1980 the BBC proposed tackling its mounting deficits with a cost-cutting plan that involved the disbanding of no fewer than five of the eleven orchestras it then maintained. The Musicians' Union responded with a strike: its members would not play for any BBC engagement, which meant that the beginning of the 86th season of Henry Wood Promenade Concerts, scheduled for 18 July, could not go ahead. Instead, the players of the BBC Symphony Orchestra presented an alternative 'First Night' in the Wembley Conference Centre. The dispute was finally resolved on 24 July and voted on by the members of the Musicians' Union by early August and so, on 7 August, the Proms were able to resume, almost three weeks late.

[30] Librettist of *The Merchant of Venice*.

of its surroundings is magnificent, and the climate at this time of year is a joy in itself. I quickly gave up the idea of using my two free days there to go on with the orchestration, and surrendered to a delicious sleeping-sickness (due, I'm told to the sudden drop of altitude, as well as to fatigue). I even wished I had arranged to stay a day or two longer, enjoying banal pleasures – the sun, local seafood and wines, beach-gazing and buying myself floral Indian shirts. Next time – for I am quite determined to return if I can! – I'll make more time for Durban and stay at a delicious hotel called the Oyster Box, twenty minutes north of the centre. *And* I may go on to Rio to see Michael…

But it is also fun to be going home, no doubt to a pile of letters (I wonder if that two-faced little sneak B. will have the nerve to write, and if so what he'll find to say) and, I hope, a new start including some revision of my habits. Firstly, the watch will go into a drawer, to be consulted only on special occasions, such as timing meditation, catching a bus or a radio programme – time is a notorious factor of anxiety. This in turn should make it very much easier to deal with insomnia – I'll go to sleep whenever my body demands it, without reference to mechanical *or* chemical devices. Then, I shall follow Chris' excellent advice to start improvising again for a while every day; that might free the flow of new ideas. Finally, I'll try to stop biting my nails by using that foul-tasting stuff I had already tried in Rio.

Best of all, now is the time to get cracking on the trial scene! July may prove somewhat difficult as I am being besieged by well-meaning people. Ian Dando is coming to stay for ten days and wants me to introduce him to Hans, Terry and Basia;[31] Staszek, the first man in my life, is in London for a month (I don't look forward to *that* meeting at all); John Schofield has invited himself for a weekend, and my aunt Celina wants to see me. Well, I'll do what I can to fit some work in. But from August onwards, I shall be lost to all except *The Merchant*! The target date is the 30th of September – how near it can I get? In a way, it's good to have all the interruption combined (in my list, I've just overlooked Uri and his family). Let them all entertain one another – Ian, for instance, already knows and likes Uri. The odd man out is Staszek, whose English is no doubt derived entirely from books and who is reported to have become extremely misanthropic – I am one of the six people he claims to like, so *noblesse oblige*! He is a sterile human dead-end.

There is still so much I don't know about the trial scene, but I hope it will become clear step by step as I work at it. Certainly I am more confident

---

[31] Halina Janowska's daughter Basia Lautman, Polish-born British artist based in London.

and determined than I used to be! The thing to remember is not to let the critical instinct inhibit invention, but just go on as well as one can at the time, without stopping to wonder if it's 'good enough'. Yet another habit to revise! [...]

12 August

August, unlike July, had been almost entirely free of interruptions, and my almost desperate determination has enabled me to reach and complete Shylock's outburst yesterday – just in time, as I am showing it to Hans tonight! Never since adolescence have I written so quickly and spontaneously. Last summer my work on the *Epilogue* was even easier and more pleasant, but there I had the help of many earlier ideas from discarded pieces: the octet, the violin concerto and the piano invention that I'd replaced by the present No. 5.[32] This time I had to start, as with the trio two years ago, with hardly an idea in my head. Well, they all started coming just when they were needed! First came Antonio's lament, then the duke's Chaconne, then Shylock's outburst – all of it 'in order of appearance' as if my very subconscious had been disciplined. A third of the trial scene is now ready, and I shall do my best to maintain the pace: the sooner I complete it the more thoroughly I'll be able to prepare the coming season. The latest deadline is the end of September, but it would be a great help to be ready with *The Merchant* earlier – say by mid-September?

Let's hope my relative freedom from my usual inhibiting critical sense has not impaired the quality. I am very curious of Hans' reaction.

I shall also consult him on a possible and, I now think, desirable cut in the libretto, from Shylock's 'The pound of flesh that I demand of him/is dearly bought, is mine and I will have it' to the announcement of Portia's entrance. This means sacrificing Shylock's rejection of Bassanio's offer and, more regrettably, his threats to the duke ('If you deny me' etc.) as well as the heckling chorus of Gratiano and Co., but it seems worthwhile for the sake of the dramatic irony which would juxtapose Shylock's 'I will' with the unexpected arrival of the one opponent who can defeat him. Also, it's difficult to make Shylock thunder any more than he already has (in the play he starts the trial scene much more soberly, having already raged at Antonio in Act III) without a sense of repetitive anti-climax. Boito and Verdi sacrificed the entire first act of a much greater play,[33] and no one minds!

---

[32] *Cf.* p. 370, below.
[33] *Falstaff* (1893), Verdi's last opera, based on Shakespeare's comedy *The Merry Wives of Windsor* (1602).

13 August

Hans was particularly impressed by Shylock's outburst, agreed with the cut, queried a detail of the duke's arietta which I corrected on the spot and suggested a total re-write of Salerio's entrance, which I had never felt satisfied with. The cut means that the work is even further along than I'd thought, so I may well take a few days off and allow ideas to come to the surface spontaneously (if they don't, I shall eventually prod them on). Eve is coming for the weekend, so I'd only have two working days before the next break; I think I'll forgo them. […]

23 August

I've just completed Portia's speech on mercy. Nothing in the third act so far has given me so much trouble: virtually all of it had to be written more than once, and the first version of the opening was very discouraging. I found it difficult to avoid my usual 'sexy' harmonies, continual false relations and clever counterpoints. But the result has proven a real breakthrough.

It's all there: clear, simple, pure, grateful to sing and transparently accompanied. I woke up before dawn today, started working just after six and finished it by about eight o'clock. I felt as excited by what I'd done as Hugo Wolf in his manic phases (this is ominous). Unable to keep it to myself I called Chris as soon as was civilised – and it was really hard to wait till then! – and asked him over to see the aria. He came, sang it in a voice that gave us both fits, and pronounced it to be beautiful. It's the first time he has liked anything of mine, but this time I was sure he would.

I played him the middle part of Shylock's aria, which now strikes me as better than I thought at the time of writing (I then preferred the *Allegro* bits but Hans said the *Lento* was marvellous) and the duke's chaconne, which I no longer like as much as I did: the harmonies now strike me as too complicated, too tense and ultimately monotonous. But it's hard to believe that I've started the act a month ago with hardly an idea in my head!

PS. – From Hugh Trevor-Roper's *The Last Days of Hitler*:[34]
'In interrogation pressure must be uninterrupted, but persuasion needs pauses.'
I must try to remember the last three words.

[34] *Cf.* p. 261, above.

17 September

I have finished Act III.

All that remains to do is the interlude linking it with the *Epilogue*. That had better be good, as with the curtain down and some three hours of solid listening already behind them, the audience are all too likely to get fidgety! My model is the final interlude in *Wozzeck*, or that in Act IV of *Pelléas*: an intense, passionate, climactic lament, clinching the entire piece, so that the quiet last scene be felt as a resolution and not an anticlimax. Whatever else, it must not be *clever*.

The one bit I am not sure about is Antonio's second aria, which gave me great trouble and shows it! After two verses I came to feel that if he sang any more he'd outstay his welcome, but he still had something to say, so I made it overlap with Bassanio's rejoinder. This in turn made it difficult to hear the vital words about his wife, so that I was now driven to change the text from 'sacrifice them all' to 'sacrifice my wife' (by that time Antonio *had* mercifully stopped singing) so that Portia's retort should at least become intelligible. But the whole short duet of the two men is laboured for every note, not only in the vocal part but in the accompanying 'cello *obligato*. Perhaps Hans will suggest an improvement…

What I do like is the scene of Shylock's defeat, which contains touches any producer of the play might envy. His final plea to be allowed to leave is made to the same Jewish beggar's whine he'd parodied to Antonio in Act I, except that now it's no longer a parody: he's been reduced to just that condition. His exit is accompanied by a sudden *ff* cry of 'Jew!' by the hitherto unsuspected off-stage chorus. I expect great things from that sudden *ff*. But the most daring touch, the one that shocked even me, is that of making Portia taunt Shylock with 'Why doth the Jew pause?' and the final 'Art thou contented, Jew? What dost thou say?' to the very theme she had just used for her speech on mercy! This doubles the irony, for while she's being ironic at Shylock's expense, the music does the same at hers: she most certainly doesn't practice what she preaches, and this drives the point home most uncomfortably. I was almost aghast at myself when I thought of it.

Perhaps I should have dared to bring the curtain down immediately after Shylock's exit, but for one thing it seemed an easy way out of a problem that no producer can shirk – anti-climax; and for another such little plot as there is in the epilogue hinges entirely on the tedious ring business! I did make it as short as I could. The sheer length of the whole opera gives me great misgivings. I hope never to write anything quite so long again…

I am showing it to Hans on the 22nd, so I have barely five days in which to write the interlude. Of course I never promised to complete the work by that or any other date, but it would be lovely to have it all ready for him! Last week I wrote over four pages of the libretto in just four days – an all-time record! But I *still* daren't count my chickens.

23 September

I have finished *The Merchant of Venice*.

I was not sure whether I had or not until Hans confirmed it last night. The interlude proved particularly difficult and the very look of the sketch shows it – a tangle of crossings, erasures and alternative versions. It will also prove difficult to score, as it's the kind of close polyphony that can easily turn into confusion; but it *can* be done. Hans and I had a close look at the most problematic passage, which I had marked with a query in the margin, and he's managed to allay my misgivings.

He is also unexpectedly satisfied with Bassanio's answer to Antonio's farewell aria. Is it because my misgivings, which I'd expressed beforehand, made him expect something worse? He agreed that it will require particularly careful preparation, but was relieved to see fewer notes in the orchestra than I'd given him reason to fear. Altogether, he has never yet suggested so few and such minor corrections, which I made there and then in a few minutes, and his own serious concern was over the ENO's rejection of the score! He will now write to Lord Harewood[35] about this. [...]

30 September

Last night, a celebration: Eve took me to the Prospect production of *The Merchant* with my idol Timothy West as Shylock.

When we first saw the advance publicity leaflet, I immediately decided to go in the hope that it would give me ideas for the trial scene. It seemed very frustrating that the run should not start until late September towards the end of my composing period! What I did not envisage was the possibility of my completing Act III before the Prospect's opening night.

So it became a treat and a reward. Of course I couldn't help comparing many details of the production with the way *I'd* set them; but this only enhanced my enjoyment. It was a beautiful production, incomparably the best I have seen! Except perhaps as King Lear, Timothy West has been

[35] George Lascelles, Seventh Earl of Harewood (1923–2011), a first cousin of Queen Elizabeth II, was variously involved with opera throughout his life, *inter alia* as editor of *Opera* magazine (1950–53), director of the Royal Opera House, Covent Garden (1951–53 and 1969–72), Managing Director of English National Opera (1972–85) and chairman of its board (1986–95). He was also director of the Edinburgh Festival (1961–65).

great in every part I've seen him do; but nothing has been as striking as his Shylock. Stooped, squinting, furtive and suspicious, with every nerve constantly on the alert, he radiates an almost animal sense of fear and danger. His unparalleled magnetism, and his own consciousness of it, enables him to understate all the most obviously powerful lines, so that they speak for themselves: he reaches the interval (unusually early in this production, after II, 7) without once having raised his voice. His voice and accent are strikingly like Radu's, and he even contrives to look like him! Eve pointed this out. His whole attitude is that of a cornered rat, sniffing, snarling, yet always ready to take cover, the exact opposite of that usual rhetoric that passes for tragedy in Shakespeare.

And Portia was a dream. Feminine, witty, a-flutter with Bassanio, purposeful in court, she showed a range I have never yet seen in the part. Her particular achievement was not to forfeit any sympathy in her triumph over Shylock; throughout the scene she had proceeded from initial brisk optimism to contempt and loathing (this was particularly noticeable when Shylock refused to have a surgeon present). After that, she was obviously acting in righteous indignation, so that even *I* couldn't blame her! Indeed, I now realise that I have loaded the dice in Shylock's favour at that point. And the business of the rings in the last act was deliciously funny (though both Bassanio and Gratiano were hopeless) and there was no suspicion of an anticlimax: perhaps I needn't have worried. Her name is Maureen O'Brien.[36] If she could sing, she'd be the most perfect Fiordiligi ever.

Nerissa, who has hardly twenty lines in her whole piece, looked and acted so charming that there was no overlooking her. She's a South African called Lois Butlin. My other favourite was a teenage, eager and endearingly absurd Lorenzo: Christopher Fulford.

After the show, we went round to see Timothy West, who received us most affably. I told him about the opera and he said: 'Great! This we must celebrate. Come to the pub next door and let me buy you a drink'.

We did that and talked for some ten minutes. He is very keen on music, particularly opera, and asked me lots of questions, which I answered somewhat awkwardly (I was thrilled, but shy). He ended up asking me to let him know if anything hopeful should happen about it.

1 October

By the strangest coincidence (Jung would call it synchronicity) Christopher Hampton called me on the 21st of September, the very day I finished *The*

---

[36] British actress (b. 1943) and also the author of a number of detective novels.

Merchant, to say that he has completed his translation of 3 fragments from *Une Saison en Enfer* and 5 of *Les Illuminations*! Last night I found them here on my return from London, with this note:

Dear André,
(if we may drop the formality) – I must stop playing about with these and let you have them. Let me know what you think and then let's meet. I hope the high of completing your opera still persists.
All best wishes,
Christopher.

I had told him on the 21st about his uncanny timing, and he told me that each time *he* completed a piece, he felt elated for two days and terribly depressed afterwards! Hence the last sentence of his note. This time I felt no elation after finishing the job, perhaps because it took me so long to believe it really was finished! Part of it was, no doubt, the sheer novelty of the situation, but the essential reason seems to me that for once I had to aim not at a closing double bar or curtain, but an interlude dovetailing into the previously written epilogue: the curtain was in fact going *up* as I stopped writing. This of course made it unsettlingly inconclusive! Correspondingly, I have felt no dejection since – fatigue, yes, but also a growing, calm, untypically *steady* satisfaction. It's utterly unlike my state after leaving Auckland – *that* kind of elation is, no doubt, only available outside reality. But I'll never regret that holiday in a fool's paradise. The joy was real, even if the situation wasn't.

I read Christopher's fragments through last night, was thrilled by some of his trouvailles (including the very title, *Ravings* for *Délires*) but was disappointed by several instances of his present tendency to tone down Rimbaud's abruptness and brutality. He was closer to him in the days of *Total Eclipse*! Today I've had it photostated, so that I can scribble on the margin without giving offence. How impertinent would it be if I told him what I've just said here? Am I competent? Neither English nor French is my first language; nor am I a writer. *I* think, of course, I know a lot: but this is just the conviction that leads so many fools to bore me with pretentious rubbish about music.

Just at present I am more thrilled with his friendliness than with the translation. How eager have I been to have it, how impatient, how piqued! As David [Ingram] so valuably says, 'it doesn't matter if you only have in six months what you'd like to have immediately'.

19 October

Red pen out for a red-letter week!

To begin with, Hampton. All that time when nothing seemed to happen wasn't wasted: when we did meet, he immediately treated me as an old friend. It's amazing how much he managed to tell me about himself in the 4½ hours we spent together: his literary projects, his own and his wife's background, his recent bereavement (two close friends died in the last few months, both of heart attacks!). It says something for the ease and naturalness of our relations that I did not say anything *for effect* – nor was I even tempted to display anything except my familiarity with his own works and my great admiration for them. Neither of us ever tried to steer the conversation: we spoke of plays, music and our respective lives, following our thoughts wherever they would take us.

Thus I found myself telling him about my long estrangement from my father and our surprisingly uneventful meeting earlier this year. There was a perfect freedom from compulsion and embarrassment alike: I could have told him about J. with equal ease if it had arisen. Anyway, it was soon obvious that he sensed and observed more about me than my mere words conveyed. One moment early on in the meeting revealed it most tactfully and touchingly:

Christopher: 'A South African friend of mine got married in the States and I happened to be able to attend the wedding. As he's not allowed to go back home, all his relatives flew over and saw him for the first time in years… It was very moving. I realised what it must mean to be an exile…'

I: 'I've often wondered what it's like to be anything else.'

C.: 'Of course. Having left Poland at twelve…'

I: 'I was an exile in Poland too.'

C. 'Yes, of course.'

I: 'Why of course?'

At that Christopher looked confused and lost for words, so I came to his rescue.

I: 'You mean because of my being Jewish?'

He nodded and smiled. I really loved him at that point, loved the combination of sympathy and discretion that made him wonder for a moment if he'd gone too far.

After that, nothing would have been 'too far'. I can still feel the calm glow of that meeting. […]

The next day I went to Blackwell's and sent him a box of the Mozart string quintets. For once even Eve has agreed that the gift was perfectly warranted! My heart was so full, I hardly stopped to think whether it was socially 'the right thing' or not.

10 November

Amsterdam airport

The Beethoven[37] displayed my usual sharp fluctuation: the first concert was very good, the second *appalling*, the third positively excellent – way beyond my usual level (if indeed there is such a thing). The orchestra showed a similar unpredictability, but they were off form on the first night and at their best on the second. Part of the trouble with the second performance is that the success of the first had once again lulled me into a false sense of security; I unconsciously took it for granted that at last I had 'licked' the piece, shed my nearly lifelong neurotic phobia of it, and now merely had to go on as I had started. A fool's paradise only exists for the sake of eviction; the mood gets shattered by the first ridiculous trifle.

This particular trifle was so absurd that I am ashamed to confess it even here! Uri had told me that it was very bad to keep my watch on while performing, and I am nervous about leaving valuables in my dressing-room, so I decided to put it in my pocket. Now, the button of my back trouser pocket is missing, and no other pocket seemed deep enough to be safe, so I put the watch on my wallet, which immediately developed a monstrous bulge, and stuffed the whole in my breast pocket. Looking like an Amazon, I walked on stage, played the opening calmly and well, and felt the pressure of the wallet at the very opening chord. Suddenly, while Uri conducted a most beautiful first *tutti*, I was seized by an almost physical panic. What will happen during the runs! It will be fine at the top of the keyboard, since the bulge is in my right breast pocket, but any *downward* run is bound to be impeded by my lateral pregnancy. All my life I've been terrified of the first downward run, the one I missed in Walthamstow, and this additional obstacle doomed it in advance. I could hardly produce anything so prosaic as a *wallet* during the opening *tutti* of a sublime concerto! But the worst was that it was all my own fault, that I hadn't thought of trying it out beforehand (even though we'd had a short rehearsal), that I had stupidly sacrificed the performance to a watch that had cost £10! (Not that I'd have been justified to jeopardise the performance for a diamond watch). Any external circumstance could actually have challenged me to a better performance, but for guilt I know no remedy. Of course I missed the first run, and nearly all the subsequent ones! Of course I rushed hysterically, especially in the rondo, miscounted the bass toward the end and got briefly out of phase with the orchestra; I must have sounded as if I had piles (superstition nearly prevented me from writing down that sentence). To my surprise, I got an

---

[37] Piano Concerto No. 4.

ovation, and both Uri and the orchestra seemed less disappointed than I'd have expected. And to my great relief, of all the people I know only the fool Rickenbacher[38] heard that particular concert, while my new German agent came to the last one, which really made me sound like a first-class pianist.

He is delightful, younger than me, new to the profession, knowledgeable in music and, above all, an enthusiast. He'd heard me in Berlin when I was young and he a schoolboy and liked me ever since. Yesterday's Beethoven confirmed his belief in me and we immediately took to each other personally (I particularly appreciated his wisdom in not introducing himself till after the performance, as the anxiety to impress him could only have spoilt it). By the time he saw me off at Oberhausen station, we were on hugging terms, let alone 'Du' and first names! His name is Heiko Hermes, and I find both his names delightful. He's also very interested in my compositions, asked for scores and cassettes of my string quartets and offered to intercede with German opera houses on *The Merchant*'s behalf. He truly believes in all the people he represents and I truly believe in him: I even think that he will prove a friend first and an agent second. He already feels like an old friend. No, a new friend, for there is also the joy of discovery! And both Terry and I feel he might be gay – that would give us yet another link! It's so rare and so welcome to meet a homosexual (if indeed he is that) who is not embarrassingly camp, but natural, warm and spontaneous… […]

15 November

Bergen–London
This was a very pleasant little tour.

I don't think I've ever played in such small places, but they showed up to far better advantage than I could have expected. All the audiences were attentive and appreciative, and to my surprise Bartók's *Out of Doors*[39] went down as well as anything, despite the fact that the individual pieces were left unnamed and even unmentioned in the perfunctory printed programme, so the audience had to take it in purely as music! In Flekkefjord I got a standing ovation, and in Olen one-tenth of the population attended the concert (i.e. a hundred people, but in London that would have been a million); Odda turned out to have a magnificent Steinway, bought recently at great cost from the Oslo Philharmonic; of the four little towns, only Nærbø had

---

[38] Karl Anton Rickenbacher, Swiss conductor (b. 1940); he succeeded Christopher Seaman as chief conductor of the BBC Scottish Symphony Orchestra (1978–80).
[39] Set of five piano pieces (1926).

nothing but good-will to offer.[40] And despite the crowded itinerary, the tour proved far less 'stressing' than both the organisers and myself expected.

The highlight of the trip was the spectacular road from Olen to Odda, which reminded me very strongly of the fabulous trip to Milford with J. The breathtaking scenery put me into an affectionate frame of mind, and I sent him a postcard that expressed that in a quiet way. (Thank God I never sent that insanely vicious letter! It would have shamed me each time I thought of it, perhaps to the end of my days). It was the first time I saw partly or wholly frozen waterfalls, the birth of stalactites caught in the act! And my pleasure was further enhanced by an element of slight fear: the road was virtually a tightrope at times, only a flimsy low barrier, a foot high if that separated it from the deep-lying fjord, and there was ice on it as well (I didn't learn till later of the existence of their special ice-resistant wheels, though I suspected they must have something of that kind). It all led to a very decent recital in Odda!

And I did start on *Le Fils du Soleil*,[41] with more speed, ease and zest than I should have thought possible! I had one session on it yesterday afternoon before the last recital and it didn't interfere with my concentration; another early this morning, as I'd woken up at three and could not go to sleep again. It is a great incentive to want to have something to show Patrick next month: his English is hardly up to the original, and he is full of his usual irresistible enthusiasm for the project. As long as I wanted him to admire my translation, I kept putting it off; but now I want him to know and admire the play, and there is no other way of showing it to him, so all my inhibitions disappeared. It is the same with playing, of course: I always feel freer and play better to an audience that does not know the piece, but is sensitive enough to appreciate it on discovery. For then I concentrate on the piece and forget my own obtrusive self. Could I learn to do this more often?

1 December

Jerusalem

This is the nearest I've come to having a holiday this year.

I owe this freedom partly to the disorganisation of the Jerusalem Music Centre. For a start, they seem to have two directors, who predictably disagree with each other. One, a newcomer who had just taken over the job when I was here last January is brilliant, knows his worth and can't resist showing

---

[40] The four towns are all in the southern part of Norway.
[41] A reference to Tchaikowsky's translation of Christopher Hampton's *Total Eclipse* ('fils du soleil' was one of Rimbaud's epithets for himself: *cf.* Robert Greer Cohn, *The Poetry of Rimbaud*, University of South Carolina Press, Columbia, 1999, p. 12).

that he knows it. This of itself would be enough to breed resentment, and his enemies find a weapon in his not being a professional musician: he knows all he needs to know about music, but he hasn't got a piece of paper saying that he knows it. He is, in fact, one of those natural polymaths, a Renaissance man, but certainly not Machiavelli; in fact, he could do with a few lessons in diplomacy. When Isaac Stern, the *éminence grise* behind the Centre, asked bluntly: 'Eleasar, what exactly are your qualifications as a musician?' Eleasar replied: 'Isaac, I don't deny that you play the Bach E-major concerto *much* better than me'. This, of course, implies that Eleasar would be better than Stern in the Bach A-minor concerto, not to mention the rest of the violin repertoire or, indeed, all music.

Stern's power politics are too subtle to allow a direct reaction. But he has a marionette on the premises, a competent violinist and teacher called Mendi Rodan; and Mendi duly started vetoing all Eleasar's suggestions. One of these concerned my master-classes here: needless to say I couldn't understand E.'s reluctance to go ahead with that project, after he'd asked me to do them and I'd agreed. The first alternative he suggested, some two months before my arrival, was a composer's workshop; I replied truthfully that I understood no contemporary music except my own and was thus in no position to teach it. Then he asked me if I'd visit a few conservatoires in selected cities, and I agreed.

Alas, I didn't know that in Israel a conservatoire is not the advanced but the medium stage of education! I'd have had to teach kids between nine and fourteen years of age. Besides, while on my first day here they still didn't know what I was supposed to do (sic!) [*sic!*], by the next morning they produced a back-breaking schedule of daily trips, 4 hours teaching sessions etc. and at no point had any remuneration for my work been mentioned.

I thought I was stuck with it, and decided to go through with the programme; but under protest. However, I had barely uttered two words of the latter, when Eleasar cried:

'But you're not committed! Don't do any of it if you'd rather be free. We've always known that your reason for coming here was your own work…'

At that time I knew little of the situation, and didn't want to disappoint Eleasar, whom I greatly like and respect. Only a few hours later did I begin to realise that I was helping him by refusing the work. He must have said all along that I shouldn't have wanted to do it, and my reaction vindicated him. This was made clearer by Mendi's huffiness. A few days later I asked Eleasar if my guess was right and he confirmed it.

So my life here runs much as originally planned: practice in the morning (only since yesterday), a couple of hours on the Schubert and Chopin sonatas. Then a spell in the sun, working on *Le Fils du Soleil* (I finished Scene

2 today). Then a walk, TM and a nap, and finally a page of orchestration. It's certainly a *working* holiday!

And I'm seeing no people at all.

3 December

I've just woken up from a dream in which, at some elder female relative's instigation I had been handling buried radioactive material. As a result, the skin on my hands was already peeling and I was showing them to the woman concerned (whom I cannot identify), reproaching her, scared of further changes.

For once I think I can explain the dream. The buried dangerous stuff is my Ghetto past; for the past two weeks I have been delving in it, with increasing horror and revulsion; I've made myself read the Ringelblum Ghetto archives, which appalled me, and Wojdowski's novel on the subject,[42] which I cannot bring myself to continue. I now realise how little I knew, how sheltered I had really been, and how egocentric.

For some time now I've felt disinclined to continue the work on my book. The bitterness that impelled me to write it had worked itself out: the therapy had been so successful as to make itself obsolete. Each time I murdered an old foe in the book (Grams, Father, Dorka[43]) I'd find myself free of them and either forgive them or stop thinking of them. Still, it seemed a pity to abandon so much good writing, and I thought it possible to continue the book freely, not out of compulsion. But that bitterness was my fuel: once gone, it took the motivation to continue with it. No doubt it was the worst possible reason for writing a book, but such as it was it had been mine and I no longer had it.

So I had doubts about the project before even coming down here. Then on the flight down I started reading the Wojdowski and realised how incompetent, superficial and uninformed I was. This was *the* novel of the Warsaw ghetto: there would be no need for another. Before landing I knew my piece was a non-starter. One proof of Wojdowski's work being the real thing is that I can't bear to read it!

But the most instructive discovery is that of my own self-centredness. I've always known it of course, but never till now had I realised how much it made me miss in terms of perception, compassion, sheer humanity; never till now have I been so ashamed of it. Why, it's positively indecent to devote

---

[42] *Chleb rzucony umarłum* ('Bread for the Departed'), a 1971 novel by Bogdan Wojdowski (1930–94), himself a survivor of the Warsaw Ghetto.

[43] Dorota Swieca, sister of Tchaikowsky's grandmother.

a whole book to petty personal vendettas while ignoring the appalling catastrophe that went on all around me! It's like quarrelling at a funeral. One could write a good book about a neurotic grandmother and a nasty aunt, but NOT in the context of the Warsaw ghetto. Some of the people who contributed to the Ringelblum archives were just as interesting as me, and led equally complex personal lives; but they chose to describe the *common* fate, and a footnote in small print invariably informs one that they came to share it. However special they were (and some of the writing and perception is astonishing) they all became part of that same heap. And in the middle of that universal waste I stand complaining *of a nasty aunt!!*

This must be what Michael had meant when he told me to learn humility about my sufferings.

14 December

Tel Aviv–London

I'm not flying home, just to London for a couple of days to rehearse the Dvořák quintet[44] with the Amadeus.[45] The performance is on Wednesday in Brussels, but they insisted on rehearsing in London to cut down hotel bills. It's a bit awkward for me, but I can see the sense in it.

What fills me with misgivings is the actual concert. In my 25 days in Israel, I did next to no practice; and yet it could hardly have been less like a holiday (even though I made a point of sitting in the sun for a couple of hours till the weather changed, usually translating Hampton). I am so tired I may be incapable of true concentration, quite apart from being out of fingers. I am too tired even to *care* how I play. But though I do repent the weakness and laziness that made me miss such opportunities for practice as I had, I can't regret the main reason for my fatigue: the revelation of life and death in the Warsaw ghetto and the camps (mainly Treblinka). It was something I needed to know, to take in, to feel some of its weight: *some*, indeed very little, but enough to depress me, and for once I accept the depression.

I won't write down here the details that particularly crushed my spirits. They haunt me and will go on doing so, no doubt; I don't need a special reminder. Anyway, I've still got the Archives, on a long-term loan from Halinka M.,[46] so there is no need for putting it down here. Nor do I want to record any other aspects of this visit: they don't matter compared to this.

---

[44] Piano Quintet No. 2 in A major, Op. 81 (1887).
[45] String quartet founded in 1947, consisting of Norbert Brainin and Siegmund Nissel (violins), Peter Schidlof (viola) and Martin Lovett (cello), all but the last refugees from Nazism.
[46] *Cf.* note 2, p. 22, above.

Oh yes, my family did make a good job, not only of saving but of sheltering me. I thought I knew it all, but what I saw or knew was a drop in the ocean! My mother went to die deliberately in order to increase my chance of survival; other mothers ignored the cries of their forcibly separated children, just as deliberately, in the hope of avoiding their fate. If any of them did survive, how can they live with themselves?

This is the worst part: not what was done to us, but what we did. All the most unbearable details document not just our death, but our own dehumanisation. Long before they destroyed the body, there was nothing but the body left.

To avoid discouragement, I shall treat this free period as if the freedom had been my own choice. It is, of course, ironic ~~that~~ when ...ancial difficulties have forced me to re... period for the first time in ten years, I should yet have it after all because no one wants me! Never mind, though: the mai...

1981

14 January

Cumnor

From David Ingram's letter to me, written last September:

'...the next two years will see the real burying of the past, the real acceptance of the death of your mother, as a liberation of yourself, not as an emotional shackle.

The simple fact is that if you don't break up the deeply ingrained habits for yourself then you will attract circumstances that will break the habits for you, and in a far more painfully destructive way – and like clearing out an attic – you have to take everything out into the light – to decide what needs discarding.'

Events have an uncanny way of proving him right. I haven't yet reached the stage of burying, breaking or discarding anything, but a lot within me *has* come to light as a result of that recent Israeli trip. Only now am I experiencing some small fraction of the true response to those events, including some shadowy sense of kinship with the dead – all of them, not only my mother. They seem that much less dead to me, and I less alive. And now that I see myself as one of them, my fate strikes me as incredibly lucky, almost indecently so, as if I had stolen my survival. I had considered myself spectacularly unlucky to be there at all! But luck, as I've come to realise, is determined by statistics: where six million are tortured to death, the handful that survive could almost be ashamed of their good luck. (The Swiss are supposed to feel somewhat guilty at having made neutrality pay – hence Andorra[1] and The Fire-raisers.[2]) And though on the surface I live on much

---

[1] Play (1961) by the Swiss dramatist Max Frisch (1911–91) which takes place in a fictional town called Andorra: the Teacher claims to have rescued from the neighbouring anti-Semitic 'Blacks' a young Jewish boy, Andri, who turns out to be his illegitimate son and thus not Jewish; when in any event he is met with anti-Semitism, he goes to his death identifying with the Jews.

[2] Another play by Frisch, *Biedermann und die Brandstifter* (1958), where, in a metaphor for the complacency with which the rise of Nazism was tolerated, Biedermann takes in two pyromaniac

as usual, something seems to be missing – perhaps simply an active interest in what I am doing. I do practise four hours a day, I am aware of playing Beethoven IV³ at the Festival Hall on Sunday, I enjoy cooking and eating good meals, I do notice a handsome face in the street now the students are back; and yet that photograph of those naked Lithuanian women, standing on the edge of a mass grave they had no doubt just dug out themselves and awaiting the shot, that picture that didn't seem to affect me at all when I saw it at Yad Vashem a month ago – that and what it stands for interposes some alienating wall, alienating from all that happens to me today and all that surrounds me. It is not exactly painful, rather numbing; it deadens initiative, puts all seemingly important events in perspective, and leaves me sober, calm, tired and listless.

How did *they* feel? Were they still capable of feeling anything at all? And those parents, deported first, who before execution were forced (forced *how*?) to write descriptions of their supposed comfort and affluence to lure to their death the children they wanted to warn – how did they feel? What does it take to do something like that? I do hope I never find out.

19 January

Nothing to brag about.

The Beethoven IV at the RFH yesterday was nervous, patchy, frequently smudged and generally hanging by one thread; I had to fight for every run, and the headache that had woken me up at six yesterday morning showed its nervous origin by a fresh pang at the base of the neck just after every precariously navigated passage…

But it did pass: most, perhaps all of my friends in the audience seemed satisfied, even Terry, whose profession has made him normally so hard to please. Perhaps it did go better than I think, though not nearly so well as I know I *can* sometimes play it. Perhaps the intensive practice of recent years makes me take more for granted than I did.

But I'm too tired to take any great interest in life or in work. That's bound to show at least as much as practice! And practice didn't show all that much…

The main thing is to go on, of course.

terrorists who store petrol in his attic and eventually burn his house down.
³ Piano Concerto No. 4.

29 January

London
The last two recitals showed that the current recital programme is coming
on, and in particular that there should be no need to replace the Schubert
G-major sonata.[4]

But I am still somewhat depressed. At the back of it all lies, of course,
Yad Vashem, along with the Ghetto Archive,[5] and it will no doubt take
considerable time for me to digest that experience. (Some people never
have, of course, but then they received it full in the face to begin with.)

Last night I discussed it with Hans, who suggested that instead of giving
up a book, I start it again, without any artistic pretentions, merely by jotting
down loose memory at a rate of half an hour a day. He said I'll be surprised
by the flood of memories this will release. No doubt he is right, but I don't
feel ready for it yet. Surely I'll sense an urge to take up that work if ever I
am ready for it. At the moment I don't feel I have anything to say that would
be of value or interest, either to those who have experienced it or to those
who haven't.

Hans argues that the situation in question having been among the most
complex in the whole history of mankind, any light that can be shed on it
can be of value. But my torch pointed inwards, not outwards – what is the
value of that?

The present stage is one of sheer fatigue, and that hardly favours
originating a new project. The incentive has gone, and since I believe in
letting things happen rather than making them happen, I shall certainly not
try to manufacture a phantom incentive: it would only pre-empt and falsify
anything that *may* yet one day generate within me. I might have become
more of a musician more quickly if Grams had not worked quite so fast to
turn me into one – and that's a less mysterious field.

No, Hans' advice is excellent in the sense that this is the best way to tackle
the work *when the time comes;* but he could quite understand that I did not
feel ready for it. Only I can sense that readiness. Perhaps it never will come.
Perhaps I only want to get away from it, to face my past merely in order to
be able to shed it. Or perhaps all I can do is to multiply rationalisations for
nothing more 'special' than FUNK.

I've lent Hans the archives so he can read the German bits.

---

[4] Piano Sonata No. 18 in G major, D894, Op. 78 (1826).
[5] *Cf.* note 14, pp. 26–27, above.

The other reason for my depression is incomparably more trivial: I'm sinking into an ever deeper financial morass. Lord Harewood[6] wrote to ask whether I had a vocal score of *The Merchant* and suggested that I take part in a playthrough with another pianist, one of us playing the vocal part, the other the orchestra! Now of course there is *no* vocal score, which would take years to prepare and cost about £3000! Hans put me onto Susan Bradshaw,[7] who does such things and would be very happy to take on *The Merchant*, but the union rate is £10 per page, and neither I nor Richard T[oeman]. have been able to find anyone ready to grant or even lend me the money for the work involved. It's a vicious circle, for the various societies that *could* help will only consider works that have been accepted for public performance, with a firm date, while the ENO won't even consider *The Merchant* without a playthrough – i.e. a vocal score. Richard is willing to advance me £500 against future royalties: that would not cover the cost of Act I. I rang my bank manager and renewed the mortgage on the house, which was due to run out within three months.

Even this doesn't greatly help: the amount of the mortgage is £5000, and my present overdraft is, I'm afraid, nearly £7000! The bank manager transferred £5000 from the overdraft into the loan account but put a £2000 limit on my overdrafting facilities. This leaves me only Richard's £500 to play with. Still, we can't let such a chance go by, so Richard urged me to get Susan started; as luck would have it, her 'phone is out of order today. But what am I letting myself in for?

11 February

Caracas

Now that the increasing pressure of petty aggravations preceding my departure is over and that I've experienced my first relatively carefree day for some time, the deep horror that inhabits me has begun to come to the surface. It just showed in the following dream:

A conversation over a meal with Mel[8] and Grazyna has led us to discuss contraception and Mel's catalogue of increasingly unsavoury practices has led to this remark:

---

[6] *Cf.* note 35, p. 301, above.

[7] British pianist (1931–2005) especially associated with new music, not least that of Pierre Boulez, with whom she had studied. In 1961 she and Keller perpetrated the notorious 'Piotr Zak' hoax, whereby they recorded themselves making a series of random noises in a studio and broadcast the result under the name of a supposed contemporary Polish composer. Tchaikowsky commissioned Bradshaw to make a piano reduction of *The Merchant of Venice*.

[8] Canadian-born Mel Cooper, founder of *Opera Now* magazine. His father was the previous owner of Tchaikowsky's house in Cumnor.

'Of course, if all else fails, you can always burn the foetuses!' or something to this effect.

I was greatly perturbed and found myself warning him that at the next such allusion to his no doubt very dashing past I should break off relations! This, predictably, put some strain on the company and Mel's difficulty in knowing what to say next made him say –

WHAT?

I don't know what he said, or what he was about to say. Cutting through this was a middle-aged German voice (perhaps that of the amiable old German whose daughter lets me practise on her piano, and who can be seen both around the house and on a photograph standing on the same piano):

'Du, da war *noch* etwas!'[9]

And suddenly, in that split-second before the shock woke me up, I was about to see, I actually caught the first glimpse of what the German had seen, of the reason for my upset with Mel: the ovens, the lot.

I am afraid.

My first reaction to the dream was to jump out of my bed, drop on my knees and pray God to preserve my soul – the despair I had just sensed would be enough to destroy it. My conscience wouldn't let me add a prayer for my bodily safety. As I did so, I took in my surroundings and realised where I was.

Of course I have an excellent excuse to fuck it, to skip the experience. I am playing the K. 488[10] here on Sunday, with the first rehearsal tomorrow, so now is just the time to take Valium and Mogadon. And I decided to take it, after jotting down this most confusing dream – fear distorted my actual perceptions in it, so I'm not merely being inarticulate: it's a distortion of vision, not of description. For tonight no doubt, the chemical safety curtain will no doubt come down.

But I am frightened of the five-day holiday in Miami on the way back. What will befall me there at night, alone with my subconscious in an hotel room? I badly need a holiday. But is this what I need it for? To bring THAT to light?

Still, I hope I can somehow cope. If not, it will remain unidentified and poison me from inside. I can't afford to carry such stuff with me indefinitely!

BOŻE, BĄDŹ WOLA TWOJA.[11]

I'm afraid.

---

[9] 'Roughly, 'What, again?'
[10] Mozart, Piano Concerto No. 23 in A major (1786).
[11] 'Lord, Thy will be done.'

Practising before a concert in Oslo, 1981

16 February

The K. 488 went very well yesterday! I love the work and it shows. Somehow the sustained peacefulness of the first movement lends its calm to my own attitude (the equally peaceful *Allegro moderato* of Beethoven IV does, of course, nothing of the sort) so that I can attend to each detail without haste or panic. I see it as a Madonna, with the *Andante* as a Pietà – not that I believe in inventing programmes for pure music!

A few minutes after the last entry I met my host in the kitchen, told him I'd just had a nightmare and had a short but satisfyingly open talk with him. He is, as it happens, a German count, 54 today (so he was barely twenty in 1945) and a wonderfully kind and sensitive man. He helped me a lot by asking directly if I had been in a concentration camp and we discussed my recent discoveries in a way that brought me true comfort. It is wonderful to find a German of that generation quite unhindered by the usual collective guilt complex!

26 February

Miami–London

A blissfully uneventful stay in Miami: the practice came to 1½ hours in all, the orchestration to two pages! Moreover I was too tired to feel either lonely or bored, and actually welcomed the utter banality of the place. In those five days, I did exactly one hour and a half of practice, and two pages of orchestration, and I resented every minute even of that usually so congenial task. What I enjoyed was the sun on my face, the warmed swimming-pool of the hotel, the taste of fresh crab and some of the gay films at the pornographic cinema I discovered by accident and re-visited on my last evening there: all restfully trivial pleasures! My only regret was not to be able to stay more than five days.

28 February

Since starting this entry, I've completed the journey to Grizedale in the English Lake District, where I am playing a totally unprepared recital tomorrow, skipped practice and slept for eighteen hours! Now I feel very well indeed. But how shall I sound? It may prove one long embarrassment!

Even so, I confess I no longer care. I've done too much. Whatever happens tomorrow, I forgive myself in advance.

2 March

Lancaster–Oxford

Well, it went quite well! Nobody would have known that I had done nothing to prepare the recital. The Mozart C-minor sonata, in particular, went worlds better than in Abingdon and in Caracas; there it had been so patchy that I had thought it wise to shelve if after this performance, but yesterday it was controlled and effortless. Short as it was, the holiday in Miami has already helped, and so did the long sleep after arrival. Moral: it's always better to rest than to work when one is tired – provided, of course, that one has worked at some point beforehand!

Another surprise is that while at the time I felt totally devoid of emotion, merely paying cool, professional attention to each detail as it came, taking fast impulsive passages at a cautious tempo and actually smiling at the occasional wrong note, the tape made by the promoter gives exactly the opposite impression: the playing sounds impulsive, lyrical, at times exaggerated, and very much faster than I was aware of playing! Perhaps I should try to cultivate a deliberately cool attitude? But can one *choose* one's attitude? Uri is right about the advantages of a casual approach…

And now for home!

14 March

Copenhagen

A day of convalescence.

I've decided to spend two days in Copenhagen to recover from the strenuous and in some ways frustrating week in Denmark before starting on my round of visits (Stefan,[12] Heiko,[13] Papa and my family in Paris). The frustration didn't come from the concerts, which by and large went well (especially the group of French songs with Edith Mathis,[14] towards whom I've developed an almost Cherubino-like attitude, so that my sensuous delight in their exquisite harmonies melts into my admiration of her voice, artistry, looks and androgynous charm). Occasionally I made a mess of things, especially in the underpractised Debussy prelude, the last but one of the *Valses nobles et sentimentales*[15] and the finale of the Fauré C-minor quartet,[16] but that was only the odd patch of nervousness, and the songs bore a charmèd [*sic*] life. And my dissatisfaction with these mishaps showed my increasing demands on myself.

No, the frustration came from my humiliatingly precarious financial position, the scarcity of work, the, for me, almost impossible need to sound people out about possible engagements. I learnt in Israel that I was not nearly so special as I'd thought, and this commonplace, trivial worry rubs the lesson in. It helps nothing to think of Mozart's penury or Dostoyevsky's debts: their glory lay in themselves and didn't need the help of circumstances. I have no genius, only talent, and therefore need the support of success. And I am weak, vain, spoilt and far too proud for the role that is now being forced on me.

10 August

Kitzbühel[17]

I shan't write much tonight: I can't be bothered. I have eaten too much, drunk too much, talked too much; I feel full, heavy, stupid and bovine. More and more I'm becoming aware of my true vocation of laziness – or rather of that constant undertow that makes nonsense of any true vocation I might have.

For instance, I didn't play remotely well in Bardonecchia.[18] I blush to admit the more personal cause of that: my stupid habit of biting my nails made me bite off a piece of skin on the right forth finger, which proved painful whenever I had to play between black keys! The other reason was the hopeless piano, and I blamed it all on that. What should worry me more

---

[12] Stefan Askenase.
[13] Heiko Hermes, Tchaikowsky's agent in Germany; *cf.* p. 306, above.
[14] Swiss soprano (b. 1938).
[15] Composed by Maurice Ravel in 1911.
[16] Gabriel Fauré's Piano Quartet No. 1 in C minor, Op. 15 (1883).
[17] Small mediaeval town in the Austrian Tyrol.
[18] Town in north-west Italy, by the French border (it is the westernmost *commune* in Italy).

is that I enjoyed my stay there so much in spite of that! I liked the people and could see they liked me (though not enough to invite me again); I finished *Madame Bovary*,[19] the cumulative effect of which is still with me several days later, and followed it up with the German translation of *A Doll's House*[20] in Kitzbühel; I relished the scenery and the meals. I am an utter hedonist and a dilettante, and can't even summon up the energy to be really annoyed with myself: I have grown complacent.

How shall I play here? The first rehearsal today has gone well enough for that kind of semi-professional occasion. But what about Dartington? Shall I panic in time to rise to the occasion through last-minute strenuous practice? Or will the unwarranted smugness persist, as so often, till the sudden collapse of all self-confidence during the performance?

Let's face it: I resent having to practise, I only work with a will at composition, or when learning something new, like the 24 preludes[21] recently. Perhaps the answer is to set myself fresh challenges by crowding my repertoire with difficult new works? I'm sure I should have played better in Bardonecchia if I had practised a different programme in between... Autumn must be devoted to learning some new Beethoven sonatas, perhaps even op. 101![22]

Back to *Madame Bovary*: let's re-read the trial!

18 August

Dartington Hall

Well, I played awfully well again at Dartington! The only serious casualty was the very last Chopin prelude, in which a manic tempo produced panic and countless wrong notes. I had trained myself to take the tempo from the chromatic scale in thirds at the climax, but since then I've practised the thirds and learnt to play the run very fast indeed, so I now have to find some other passage to determine the tempo – no doubt the group of seven when it comes in octaves. What was funny was that I got all the runs and missed virtually everything in between the runs! It was a regrettably ill-fitting conclusion to an otherwise consistently impressive recital. Even the B-flat minor prelude suffered only minor flaws, and the E flat major was too fast and lacked poetry (as well as several notes). But it's been a long time since I've been both so relaxed and so concentrated for nearly two hours – and that in a place which I expected to scare me out of my wits!

[19] Novel by Gustave Flaubert (1856).
[20] Henrik Ibsen's prose-play in three acts (1879).
[21] Those by Chopin, Op. 28 (1835–39).
[22] Piano Sonata No. 28 in A major, Op. 101 (1816).

9.4.81.

30 THE PARK
CUMNOR
OXFORD
OX2 9QS

Dear Lord Harewood,

Thank you so much for your kind letter of the 25th of March, which I am sorry not to have answered sooner! The reason for the delay was the need to look in on Susan Bradshaw to see how the score is shaping up, and the concert engagements that prevented me from paying that visit until yesterday.

I am delighted to say that she is doing a wonderful job at a positively phenomenal speed! At her present rate of progress, the first two acts will easily be ready by

October, and I shall let you know as soon as I receive them; we can then find a date for the playthrough that would suit everyone concerned.

It's very kind of you to warn me of the dangers of premature optimism, and I do realize that your interest in the piece does not mean that you will like it and accept it. If you do, of course, I shall be thrilled into temporary insanity! But if you don't, I'll comfort myself by putting it down to the economic crisis (an ever handy face-saving device) and simply start work on another piece.

With all best wishes,
Yours sincerely,
André Tchaikowsky.

Tchaikowsky reports to Lord Harewood on the progress of The Merchant of Venice

Not that Dartington is what it was in the Glock[23] reign. I couldn't know it when playing the recital, but the place has a dying air: it's limp and anaemic, and the audiences have lost no less in vitality than in number (though my own recital was sold out, and chairs had to be put on stage; I also got an ovation at the end). What's happened is that Maxwell-Davies's[24] policy falls between two stools: it's neither conservative enough to please the 'old dears' whose compulsive faithfulness once made the place so claustrophobic, nor radical enough to attract the young 'with-it' crowd that used to follow Max like the Pied Piper. The atmosphere is stale, limp and tepid; the lectures and classes are ill-attended and followed with scant interest. The general level of the performing students is low – at least in my class, and I am told the violin class is not better. And I am told that students who were offered bursaries to come here free of charge have turned them down! This is a shocking humiliation for a place that used to have such unique prestige. There have been too many years of mindless, repetitive inertia, too little initiative: what was spirit had turned into habit.

Shall I tell Max any of this? I hardly know him: he might take it amiss. And yet what do I risk? I don't care if I'm never asked back: the only reason

---

[23] Sir William Glock, CBE (1908–2000), British music-critic and administrator, founder of the Dartington International Summer Music School in 1953 and Controller, Music, at the BBC from 1959 to 1972.

[24] Peter Maxwell Davies, British composer (b. 1934), knighted in 1987.

for my playing in the summer is lack of funds, and they pay very little. (John Amis[25] rang shortly before the course started to ask me to reduce my fee by 20%, a request I naturally granted; so, I'm told, did everybody else.) And Elaine[26] made a strong impression on me with her demand that I act on my thoughts *regardless of consequences*! Besides, I have a feeling that Max likes me and will take it well…

Now I'm off to Hans' daily lecture. I went to one yesterday: even he sounded tired, and the whole thing had an air of carefully preserved ritual. I'd prefer to see him as artistic adviser: he at least has guts!

Later: I did speak to Max and found him welcoming, determined and optimistic. He's demoted John Amis whose adherence to William's ancient régime was blocking all new ideas, got financial backing which will end his dependence on the old dears, and intends to start his new reign next year! I might even attend his composition class

1 September

Unless some cancellations come my way, I've just played my last concert for over two months.

To avoid discouragement, I shall treat this free period as if the freedom had been my own choice. It is, of course, ironic, that when financial difficulties have forced me to forego my free period for the first time in ten years, I should yet have it after all because no one wants me! Never mind, though: the main thing is to use it. I have already started on the tarantella towards Stephen's suite, and scored the first two pages of the trial scene, and I am conscious of having, if anything, too little free time. God knows, there is enough to do even without concerts! Stephen wants three more dances, which then have to be arranged for piano duet before the end of the year (I haven't even arranged the Tango), as Patrick and Taeko[27] are to record the suite in January; Susan's version of Act III needs to be corrected, and both acts learnt in time for the ENO playthrough next month; moreover, I've recently realised that Act II needs to be *revised*, cut and partly re-written! Then there is the orchestration of the huge trial scene, the translation of the revised *Total Eclipse* (though that's of course a hobby) and, with or without concerts, I can hardly forgo practice for more than ten days!

In fact, I am worried about my piano playing. I thought I had played K. 491 very well on Sunday; but I could tell that none of my friends thought

---

[25] English writer, broadcaster and administrator (1922–2013)
[26] Tchaikowsky's New Zealand friend.
[27] *Cf.* note 42, p. 265, above.

so, and Stephen, at my request, delivered a rather devastating post-mortem. Only in mid-July Terry had accused me of eccentric exaggeration in Beethoven III; mindful of that, I concentrated on restraint, and this time I seem to have underplayed: Stephen said it didn't sound like a performance. The most alarming thing is that I should have liked my own playing, both now and in July! Obviously I can't tell how I play…

Could I use this respite to re-learn spontaneity? For it has to be learnt: most of us are too thoroughly conditioned to sleep when we're sleepy and eat when we're hungry: instead, we go by the watch. Right now, I am about to make dinner because my watch tells me it is dinner-time – my stomach has not made a sound. Suppose I left my watch unwound in a drawer except when I do need it? I've meant to do just that so many times! Tonight, or tomorrow, I shall give it a try, and shed the neurotic slavery that, in common with all our crazy civilisation, watches and clocks have imposed on me. For a start, I'll take my watch off *now*, and go to bed at my body's behest! […]

25 October

Lord Harewood's secretary rang on Thursday to say that he has managed to muster 'everybody' (whatever that means) for the 21st of December, so that it's now the date of my playthrough! It suits me ideally, as the last concert of the present batch in on the 6th of December so I'll still have a fortnight in which to concentrate exclusively on the opera, and can give the next six weeks over to my piano work almost as exclusively. (Almost, not quite: the last third of Act II still needs correcting and partly re-writing, and the ENO pianist who is to partner me in the playthrough will no doubt soon start clamouring for the score, so I'll have to find an occasional hour for that work in between the concert.)

The first engagement is a BBC studio recording in Birmingham with the first half of my Chopin programme in Brussels, plus the C-minor nocturne which I shall play in Rotterdam; both these concerts are in the first week of November. Though the BBC date is for the day after tomorrow, it only came through a few days ago: the producer wanted me to record it on the 1st of December and I twisted his arm to let me do it now as a try-out before playing it in public, so he found me a studio at short notice!

I shan't write any more, as I've written a huge pile of letters yesterday and can still feel the beginnings of a writer's cramp… I've also shelved the orchestration work, completed just over a third of the trial scene. How did all the Big Folk manage to write, not only so well, but so MUCH?

1.9. – Unless some cancellations come my way, I've just played my last concert for over two months.

To avoid discouragement, I shall treat this free period as if the freedom had been my own choice. It is, of course, ironic, that when financial difficulties have forced me to forego my free period for the first time in ten years, I should yet have it after all because no one wants me! Never mind, though: the main thing is to use it. I have already started on the tarantella towards Stephen's suite, and scored the first two pages of the trial scene, and I am conscious of having, if anything, too little free time. God knows, there is enough to do even without concerts! Stephen wants three more dances, which then have to be arranged for piano duet before the end of the year (I haven't even arranged the Tango), as Patrick and Taeko are to record the suite in January; Susan's version of Act II needs to be corrected, and both acts learnt in time for the ENO playthrough next month; moreover, I've recently realized that Act II needs to be revised, cut and partly re-written! Then there is the orchestration of the huge trial-scene, the translation of the revised "Total Eclipse" (though that's,

21.

28 October

The Chopin recoding (*Polonaise-Fantaisie*, six mazurkas, the C-minor nocturne and the 4th ballade) went quite creditably in Birmingham yesterday: an auspicious start to the season! But the 24 preludes, which

I have just played to Colin[28] and which I am due to play in a week in Rotterdam, are in a total mess. It is surely no coincidence that Colin has just retired upstairs with a headache…

A touching surprise today was a birthday present from Papa, a huge book on Schubert. My attitude towards him has largely changed: he makes no demands or reproaches, accepts the fact that I see him about once a year, and shows his own affection in the only way I have left him – that is, by remembering my birthday. Not long ago, I had a dream in which we were wandering around Montmartre, hand in hand, talking affectionately about past misunderstandings…

20 November

Cumnor

It is now three days since playing my own concerto in Hagen; the delay in entering it here is not due to any disappointment with the event, but simply with a trivial but tiring tummy – but that has been plaguing me since the night after the performance. (It was quite providential the attack had not started sooner!) The pain and diarrhoea have now stopped, but I am still in a fairly depleted state, with a sub-normal temperature and less than sub-normal level of energy. Even this entry is somewhat of an effort.

But the Hagen performance was certainly worth recording (I mean in this diary, not on records!). The piano part had been cleaner in Ireland, but the ensemble was incomparably better: my friend Yoram David[29] both loves and thoroughly understands the piece, and his enthusiasm compelled the frankly mediocre local orchestra to a clearly unwonted degree of attention. At first he was, as he put it, too overawed to extend his remarkable alertness and control to my own part, but at the final rehearsal I made several quite crude mistakes, and this luckily convinced him that having composed the piece confers no infallibility in performing it, and he agreed to show me the more dangerous entrances just as he did to everybody else. And his technique is impeccable: the only way to miss his beat would be by looking elsewhere, and the few times we were not together were due precisely to my looking at my hands in a difficult passage, rather than at him. Even so, he could no more teach inferior musicians to play in tune than a maverick soloist to stick to the beat, and the intonation was at times very questionable! But what he did obtain was a positive attitude to the work on the part of virtually the whole orchestra (one or two chromic grumblers apart); they

---

[28] Colin Stone, British pianist (b. 1961), currently a professor of piano at the Royal Academy of Music.
[29] Israeli conductor (b. 1948), currently living in Italy.

clearly did their best, and one violinist shouted 'great piece!' at me during curtain calls. I had had no such response in Ireland.

Nor was the public in Dublin and Cork nearly as enthusiastic as that of Hagen. I'd been warned to expect a dull, philistine, middle-class audience, just what I'd have expected anyway in a small German town. But I got an ovation! Now I am not interested in public success as such – a few musicians' approval means more to me than a crowd's applause – but it *is* encouraging to see that my piece, complex as it is, does not depend on intellectual comprehension for its effect, but can secure an ignorant audience's response through sheer emotional impact! The 30-odd people who came to the informal discussion of the piece afterwards posed very sensible questions, and most of them could obviously read music, since the score was being passed from hand to hand. But they could not have ensured the general reaction; that came from the music alone; and I am greatly encouraged to see that my concerto does not need to be preceded by a lecture with blackboard and side-slides, but speaks for itself, at the most naïve unconscious level, as all music should. [...]

Having written all this, I feel better.

20 November[30]

London–Copenhagen
After 5 days of nothing but soup and dry biscuits, the wretched tummy-bug is still with me! The symptom (i.e. diarrhoea) returned with positively explosive force last night, just when I had every reason to think that my restraint had earned its due reward. Isn't the thing supposed to last only three days? And haven't I been GOOD? My first reaction was a cross feeling that the other side is *not playing the game,* and that for all the difference it makes, I might as well indulge in gravad lax and my other Scandinavian favourites.

Certainly I am extremely tempted to eat whatever they'll serve on this flight, not through hunger but to see what happens. Was there ever a more childish temptation? But then my whole attitude to the illness is childish: I still feel that the débâcle last night ought not to have happened and that *somebody* has let me down – be it God, the bug or my G.P.

A more serious worry is the state of my preparation for the recital on Wednesday night. Last Wednesday was, of course, spent travelling, and Thursday was going to be a day off anyway, but I was in no condition to work on Friday either, so I valiantly but perhaps rashly tried to compensate

---

[30] Same date as previous entry; apparently a slip on Tchaikowsky's part.

over the following two days, doing 4½ hours on each. (Today is Monday.) It is the programme I played in the summer, but the Schubert sonata has gone rusty and the Bach was rhythmically unsteady till last night: the rondo of the Schubert is still a special danger point. And then there are the Chopin preludes, which may suit me 'ideally', but which technically are only just within my grasp! Perhaps it was that latest spasm of effort, coupled with that of writing the protest letter to the authorities responsible for the Cumnor building project,[31] that brought on the famous relapse.

But now I have only tomorrow to put the programme back on its feet, and the combination of restaurant food and practice in a piano shop with no toilet is not likely to improve my condition! Meanwhile the SAS meal has arrived: shall I eat it? YES!

11 December

Oxford station

Havoc!

Each time England gets a blizzard, it reacts as it might to nuclear war. Now they have satellites to show them the approaching weather, but obviously no equipment for dealing with it when it comes, so the foresight is of little help.

I am supposed to play a recital tonight near Manchester, and am not too sure of getting there in time. At first the venture seemed downright impossible, and my initial reaction was one of unmixed relief: true, I can ill afford to forgo the £500 which is only a part of my current debt to Terry (this is why I accepted the engagement at such an awkward date), but if it was a case of force majeure and no one could blame me for staying at home, what a blessing! I might even get that day off I've been pining for: yesterday I spent three hours on Susan's unplayable version of *The Merchant*, and got through only half of Act I, and this morning I woke up with a headache, not all of which has cleared up. If anything, it seems to be coming back! Too much is happening all at once – the yearly nightmare of Christmas, the ENO audition which I'll never be able to prepare adequately, social distractions, Florian's visit next Thursday for three days, dinner at Stephen's the day after tomorrow – and not a chance to stay put and quiet, to clear my crowded head after the arduous work on the QEH programme; no chink of respite.

Most of all I am worried, of course, about the ENO playthrough: I've booked a rehearsal with Tom Wade for Wednesday, and I'm not even sure

---

[31] A reference to a draft plan submitted to the local council to build 510 houses in Cumnor, 15 of which were to be built directly behind Tchaikowsky's back garden. He wrote a letter which was read out at the first meeting of the residents, which he could not attend. He also signed a petition against the proposal.

I'll have a chance to complete *sightreading* the piece before then! But what I resent most is the trivial hypocrisy of Christmas cards and presents, forced on me by other people (e.g. the bore D. who sent me a present well in advance, as if to remind me to add him to my list!), and aggravated by the obligatory pretence to *enjoy* the whole detestable fuss. (There are perhaps five or ten people in the world to whom I'd send Christmas cards of my own accord.) Needless to say, my real friends are carefully kept off the ever growing list: I've hardly ever sent a card or a present at Christmas without resentment, so I should only insult them by treating them as I do my G.P. and bank manager (both of whom are quite nice, by the way). It's snowballed from year to year, but this time the coincidence with the ENO audition is downright disastrous! I wish I had the guts to ignore everyone's presumed expectations and see who still likes me after I've failed them. But my own guilt might prove more strenuous than the farce I'm playing now, and I might end as the only person who has not forgiven the omission. […]

28 December

It is now a week since the ENO audition, and I still haven't quite recovered from it! This entry will no doubt have to be written in instalments: it's likely to be as long as my opera, and I can't afford to exhaust myself further.

The fortnight preceding the event was exceedingly strenuous. Susan has tried to put *everything* in, from the piccolo flute to the double basses, and the result makes the piano score of *Wozzeck* look like 'Chopsticks'! She realises it's unplayable, but argues that any professional corepetiteur [*sic*] is adept at leaving things out, and that singers prefer to have as much information as possible, so as to know what to listen for. This has been confirmed by, among others, Richard Rodney Bennett,[32] who does a piano score first and plays from it himself: but my training as a professional pianist bred into me the need to play all the notes at all times and I can't fail at this without feeling guilty and frustrated. Perhaps if it was someone else's piece I could manage better; at any rate I'd certainly feel less flustered. I was more nervous about *playing* the two acts than about any other aspect of the audition.

Such was my state when I arrived at the ENO to rehearse with the pianist in charge of the vocal parts. His name is Tom Wade; he's shy, middle-aged, kind and extremely accomplished in his way: he astonished me by singing most of it, words and all, tapping his chair to simulate percussive effects

[32] The British-born composer Richard Rodney Bennett (1936–2012), based in New York from 1979. His best-known film scores are those for *Far from the Madding Crowd* (1967), *Nicolas and Alexandra* (1971) and *Murder on the Orient Express* (1974). He was equally esteemed as a composer of concert music and as a jazz pianist.

and whistling at the end of Act I. His main fault proved to be a tendency to rush everything, which made my hopelessly overwritten orchestral part even more unplayable.

The night before that rehearsal I suddenly noticed that a page in Act II was missing! In a panic I rang Susan at 11PM, but she couldn't find it, and John Schofield at Weinberger's couldn't either, so I went to London early next morning and transcribed the page myself from the full score. It was ready just in time for the rehearsal, and Tom played from it at sight.

Having had no time for breakfast or lunch, I suggested a cup of tea at the ENO canteen before starting work. Tom happily agreed, and we were joined by the chorus-master Hazel Vivienne, an adorable woman who did all she could to re-assure me.[33] I didn't have to play it all through, she said; I could talk about it and play a scene at a time; they were quite used to composers not quite able to play their own work, and the whole thing was quite informal; 'take it as it comes'! This was a huge relief: I can always *talk*. Having spent the previous three days fighting my way through the piece and getting constantly bogged down in details (each act took three hours or more, and I had never managed to play either act right through) I decided there and then to treat myself to a free day when I got back.

But the rehearsal was not a success! Tom kept rushing ahead without listening to me, and his way of trying to keep it together was by using his head or a momentarily free hand to give a beat I was nearly always too busy to watch! It was as time-consuming to rehearse that opera as to practise it, and though Tom made me a present of an extra half-hour, by six o'clock we had barely got through the two acts. [...]

And all that time I was taking tablets. The more tired, anxious and irritable I felt, the less I was inclined to take a rest: instead, I swallowed more and more Foselite – a combination of phosphorous and vitamin C. I took three pills, then four, then eight or ten; also, of course, plenty of strong coffee. I was quite willing to fall ill the next day after the audition, to make myself ill, as long as I managed reasonably on the 21st.

An additional strain was, of course, the annual upheaval of Christmas. I can't be bothered to list the trivialities that further bit into my time, energy and attention! Suffice it to say that I've decided to give up Christmas, or at least to limit it to the minimum from next year on. By the end I found it hard to sign a Christmas card without wishing the addressee a sudden death.

---

[33] When Vivienne was appointed chorus-master of the English National Opera in 1976, she was the first woman to occupy the post – although she later had a sex-change and took the name Victor Morris.

Then there was the weather. Another blizzard was announced for the weekend before the audition! It was just as well that I went down to London on the eve and spent the night at Terry's: on the day, Paddington was closed, so once again the whole thing would have had to be put off.

I had arranged to meet Tom at twelve and go through a few danger spots. The audition was at 2.30 and we worked on till within an hour of that; John Schofield had arrived about one with scores for everyone and accompanied me to the canteen for a quick lunch. Painstaking Tom stayed to have another look at the score.

The panel consisted of seven people: Lord Harewood, Mark Elder,[34] Edmund Tracey,[35] the new assistant conductor Peter Robinson,[36] the new director of production David Pountney,[37] Hazel and an assistant of Lord Harewood's called Jeremy something who remained silent throughout. Of the seven, two people were late: Mark Elder and David Pountney. John whispered that as Peter was present, Mark would probably not come. That didn't indicate a particularly keen interest on the company's part.

'Well, why don't you just play us Act I?' asked Lord Harewood. We went ahead, with John turning my pages while Tom managed by himself. The panel sat along a row of tables put end-to-end in a straight line, Peter with the only full score, the rest with vocal scores. Now and then I could hear them whisper.

Tom and I came badly apart several times, but we kept catching up with each other as best we could and managed to keep going until the finale. That, however, I had never had any intention to play – not at least since speaking to Hazel. I stopped and said:

'I am afraid this finale is just not playable on the piano. The fugal subject is a *glissando*, which of course I can't reproduce, and there's so much going on that any attempt to play it would only be misleading and confusing.'

'Why don't you just do what you can?' suggested a blond being of angelic beauty whom I was seeing for the first time. 'And we'll all do what we can: we'll sing and whistle and help you out.'

This was Mark Elder. I don't know when he had come in. Then I became aware of a dark young man of almost equal beauty, who turned out to be David Pountney.

---

[34] British conductor (b. 1947), knighted in 2008.

[35] British dramaturg (1927–2007).

[36] British conductor, Assistant Music Director at ENO in 1981–89, now Artistic Director of British Youth Opera, and a Professor at the Guildhall School of Music and Drama.

[37] British opera-director (b. 1947), the Intendant of the Bregenz Festival from 2003 until 2013, now Artistic Director of Welsh National Opera.

Well, there was no question of refusing either of those two anything! I was already half in love with Hazel and at that point I fell for the whole panel. We loners are prone to such crushes: no individual love can ever satisfy the lifelong pent-up need to be 'part of the family'. I had experienced it several times before.

If at that point a cable had arrived from the Met, offering a fortune for the rights to the first performance, I should have said: 'Sorry, I must wait to hear from the ENO first'. There was nothing professional left in my attitude. I was merely a wooing lover with a bunch of red roses in my hand, and it was not my piece but myself that they would now accept or reject.

We panted and floundered our way through the finale, and I expected and needed a break.

'Well done!' said Lord Harewood instead. 'How about Act II?'

"Can I please have a glass of water?' I gasped.

There already was one by my side, unobtrusively provided by Tom in the 30 seconds since he had stopped playing. We launched into Act II and played it right through, ploughing doggedly through pages of indescribable mess, especially in the long finale.

The first voice to be heard after the last chord was Edmund Tracey's:

'Exactly 45 minutes.'

They had asked me how long each act was and I replied that I didn't know, as this was the first time I should play a whole act without stopping!

MARK: 'But it wouldn't go *quite* so fast, would it?'

I: 'No, we panicked.'

This was only one of innumerable, exceedingly detailed and practical questions they asked. This was the most encouraging aspect of the audition: they were behaving as if the work had already been accepted and they were planning the production! A few examples?

M: 'Will the Duke be a bass or a baritone?'

I: 'A baritone.'

M: 'That's good, as basses are thin on the ground.'

Or:

M: 'Are you having both the piano and the harpsichord in the pit? You realise that this means fewer strings as there'll be less space?'

I: 'I could do with an upright.'

They also asked me if I'd be prepared to rewrite anything that didn't suit a particular singer, and of course I said yes (it wasn't beneath Mozart's dignity). They even asked me if I had any particular singers in view and

I said: 'Well, on a Walter Mitty basis, if I had magic powers I'd have Tom Allen[38] as Shylock (signs of dismay, as he's not in their company) or a baritone who has sung Wozzeck (this wasn't much better, as they haven't done *Wozzeck* in recent memory, if at all), and Elizabeth Connell[39] as Portia (she *is* with them and I really think she'd be ideal).

Lord Harewood: 'What's the exact composition of the stage consort?'

I told him, forgetting the tabor.

To my surprise, no one commented on the difficulty of the piece, which I'd expected to be the chief objection. Perhaps they're used to worse, after all the avant-garde stuff they've done! Later I asked Hazel if she thought it difficult and she said: 'In parts'.

They encouraged me to talk about the dramatic aspect of the work, the psychology of the characters, the motivation, and I found myself chatting my head off! I felt perfectly at ease by now, and I was aware of intense attention on everyone's part. Mark charmed me further by saying: 'I don't know the play very well, can you tell us the story?' and Lord Harewood asked how closely John O'Brien had followed the original text. 'Oh, almost word for word', vouched Edmund Tracey (it doesn't, of course).

Hazel made me correct one mistake in prosody and Mark persuaded me to add an accent for similar reasons. We talked for quite a long time, but no one seemed ready to break up. Then Lord Harewood asked:

'Have you got any more with you?'

I had the *Epilogue* in full score, the first third of Act III in full score, and the whole remainder of the opera in sketches. But all I could play were slow bits. I showed them Portia's speech on mercy, the beginning of 'How sweet the moonlight' (to my shame, I couldn't play it right through), the beginning of the stage consort's D-major *Larghetto* and, of course, the very last page, which I preceded by a brief description of the final scene.

The audition was now at an end. But it did not end in the way I had anticipated. Lord Harewood merely said: 'Well, this was very interesting, thank you very much' and within a minute or two the room was empty, except for Tom, John and me.

I was stunned. Of course I knew no answer could be expected till they reached a decision among themselves, but there was no reference of any kind to its having been an audition organised for a specific purpose: no 'we'll be in touch', 'we'll let you know' or even 'Don't expect a reply for the next X months'. They behaved for all the world as if all those VIPs had

---

[38] Thomas Allen, English baritone (b. 1944), knighted in 1999.
[39] South African-born mezzo soprano, later soprano (1946–2012).

given me so much of their precious time and intense affection for mere idle curiosity's sake.

I knew this could not be the case. All the same, I was shattered. Why, I'd been naïve enough to expect us all to have a cup of tea or a drink together! And just because I was too shocked to think, I did exactly the right thing: I fell back on clichés. The few words I spoke were a meaningless chain of Merry Christmas, Thankyouverymuch and Nicetohavemetyou. A born-and-bred Englishman could not have done better.

I asked Tom and John for a cup of tea at the canteen and there once more we were joined by Hazel. She said: 'I'd get cracking on the rest if I were you, and let Lord Harewood know when the whole thing is ready. We'd have another playthrough, and it might be as well to repeat the first two acts as well: people forget…'

This was a clear indication that Hazel, at any rate, was on my side. But I wanted to know my chances, so I said 'Well, I don't want to nag at Lord Harewood'. If I had hoped to hear: 'Oh, but he's most interested' (and I must have) I was disappointed. Hazel merely said: 'Oh, but it wouldn't be nagging just to let him know you've finished it!'.

I left with John, accompanied him to his office, went on to Terry's, meditated and fell asleep. By the time I woke up and reached his office Christmas party, there were only a few stragglers left. I was asked how the audition went: I replied truthfully that I did not know. I was still dazed.

I had expected the reaction to take the usual form of a headache, but what I got instead were stomach cramps. At times I couldn't move, and yet I had to get back home, deliver the last Christmas presents, do some shopping – all the boring stuff, but I almost welcomed boredom after so much excitement. The cramps abated after a few days, but today (29.12 by now) is the first day I've been up to sustained work.

And all the well-meaning people who kept interrupting my work beforehand to wish me good luck now rang again to ask how it went. At first I refused to talk about it as yet; then I related the event to a few friends, emphasising the emotional air-pocket I had fallen through (rather like being prickteased). Most of them said it sounded very auspicious indeed! Kazik said that 'we'll be in touch', the words I was so disappointed not to have heard, are just what one says when one *doesn't* want to get in touch. Grazyna said I was a fool to expect a drink with them afterwards: how could that happen without their being drawn into the very discussion they weren't ready for? But the most positive reaction was Hans', who had originated the whole thing by writing to Lord Harewood in the first place, and who now offered to write again and ask how the audition went! He and Chris think it ill-mannered of the panel not to have said anything more at the end; most people think there was nothing that *could* have been said. Next time I'll try to be more rational about such auditions!

And I must also learn to defend my solitude firmly and without guilt. I am getting somewhat better at it but oh, how slowly! Perhaps next Christmas I'll be able to get away and escape most of the compulsory sociability.

The people I'd like to see and get to know better are Mark Elder, David Pountney and Hazel Vivienne, and not only because of *The Merchant*! If they do accept it, it promises to be the most enjoyable collaboration yet: the 'vibes' are terrific.

1982

2 January

Frankfurt airport

[…] My GP diagnosed colitis and gave me some antispasmodic pills. Asked how long it would take me to recover, he replied: 'How long is a piece of string?' I hope the pain will come to an end before the pills do…

22 January

Mainz

Now I know a great deal more about that colitis! On the 7th of January, the day after the course ended, I went to Bonn to visit Stefan and his loathsome wife. She can no longer even try to control her pathological possessiveness and jealousy of anyone Stefan loves: he told me how she'd isolated him from his sister with a wild attack, how she constantly reproaches him for enjoying other people's company more than her own (small wonder!). It was a poisonous evening.

When, towards the end of my trip back to Mainz, I got an unusually severe attack of colitis, I naturally blamed it on Ingrid. Didn't my GP's booklet say that an emotional crisis is almost certain to bring on a flare-up? Also, the severe cold could, I thought have something to do with it: the cramps started just as I left the compartment for a noticeably colder corridor. I barely made it to the taxi, barely managed to regain my room at the hotel. I immediately took two of my GP's tablets and lay down, fully dressed. I didn't worry: the two tablets were bound to do the trick. I lay there and waited for the savage cramps to abate.

They did not abate. About an hour later I called the porter and asked him to find me a doctor. All I wanted was an injection, not a diagnosis: I knew what I had. I used to get injections for my tension headaches which were just as excruciating, and yet lifted within a few hours.

The doctor came about half an hour after I called. I had unthinkingly locked the door, and now had to drag myself to it, groaning and grunting, to let him in. I told him about my colitis and asked him if I'd be able to fly on to Paris as planned the next day. He thought I could: those acute attacks didn't usually last. The injection soon began to work. It was perhaps half past two when the doctor left.

Some time after that, perhaps a couple of hours later, I tried to undress without getting out of bed. This immediately brought on a different pain, fiercer than the cramps: a stabbing from the left into my lower belly, made worse by the slightest movement. It was really difficult to dial '8' for the porter this time. While waiting for the doctor, I heard myself groan and shout, but my part of the hotel seemed deserted – there was no reaction.

'This is something new', said the doctor. ' I can't tell what, though: could be a kidney stone or a spinal nerve inflammation. I'll give you an injection, but this may need further looking into.'

I liked this kindly and patient doctor, whom I had already twice dragged out of bed.

'Would you take me on as your patient?'

'I can't, I specialise in gastric diseases. But I can recommend you to a hospital where you'll be well treated.'

Hospital: things were already snow-balling. I asked to ring my agent Heiko Hermes, who lives in Wiesbaden. It was, by then, 6.45. The doctor had to dial the number.

Heiko and his lover Wollo arrived about ten and at once set about arranging my transportation into hospital. This involved a lot of red tape: the previous doctor was already at work, and a new one had to be found to authorise the request for admission and an ambulance. He specified that I was to be taken on a stretcher (I still couldn't sit up), gave me yet another injection and left. I called Vivi,[1] who expected me in Paris, and told her the news; she took it admirably. Heiko and Wolfgang packed my stuff, paid my bill, took care of every detail. They have been utterly wonderful throughout my illness; Heiko must have neglected his work to look after me.

It was about one o'clock by the time I got to the hospital. Once there, however, things speeded up enormously. I was at once subjected to a long series of tests, conducted with a truly German thoroughness. Then I was wheeled across to the X-ray room.

It was during the X-rays that I became aware something was badly amiss. The X-ray operator and the nurse whispered together in unmistakable dismay. 'We'd better show this to the doctor at once', I heard. 'Let's do another picture, just to be sure', and they did.

---

[1] The wife of Tchaikowsky's cousin Charles Fortier.

A beautiful young lady came into the X-ray room and asked me about my illness. I rattled off all I knew about my colitis, my English doctor's reassurance etc., but I was increasingly aware of an almost painful compassion in her eyes. What *was* going on?

Having wheeled me back to the room where the tests had been taken, the nurse said: 'You may have to wait a while, I don't know if the surgical department is ready'. I felt weak: for all my hypochondria I had not anticipated this. 'You don't mean I am going to have an operation?' 'Yes, I think so.' 'Is it cancer?' I faltered. 'No', she said, 'that it is not'. (Her English was fairly Teutonic). 'It's a perforated intestine'. Then she added: 'I was not supposed to tell you. Say nothing.' I agreed.

Within minutes, the surgeon arrived. He beamed at me and flashed a row of gold teeth. 'You have a perforation!' he announced joyfully. 'Your life is in danger. It *must* be operated!' He made it sound like a treat. I've never seen a better bedside manner; his high spirits were so infectious that I found myself smiling back at him.

'Can you promise to spare me as much pain as possible?'

'You can't expect too much there', he answered frankly. This later proved to be a huge understatement.

'How long will it be till I recover?'

'Two weeks.' Another understatement: it was two weeks since then yesterday, and my release still hasn't been mentioned. Besides, a second operation will be necessary.

'Can I make a telephone call?' I asked.

'Yes, we'll wheel you to a 'phone on the way to the operating theatre. Will you sign this form?'

I signed. I wanted to ring Vivi as well as Heiko, but while speaking to the latter I heard that the theatre was ready, so I gave him her number instead. He sounded so distressed that it made me pretend to be brave. 'Think of it as a concert', I said.

Another nurse spoke to me with great compassion: I saw tears in her eyes and was touched. Meanwhile, I was being transferred to a stretcher by two cheerful young lads (ambulance and stretcher service in Germany is entrusted to conscientious objectors in lieu of military service). They wasted not a minute: the whole sequence of events unrolled at a surrealistic speed.

While being carried along corridors, I broke my private ban of petitionary prayers. It was no longer just 'Thy will be done.' 'Please, God', I prayed, 'remember I'd always prefer death to pain.'

And perhaps I should not have come to if they had not made me. At some point I became confusedly aware of harsh lights, my face being slapped and my name being shouted by German voices. I tried to ignore all this and sink back; they persisted. It was a most reluctant and unpleasant awakening.

What followed was the longest and worst night in my life. It was only next day that I learned it had been one night: it seemed infinite, and I estimated it at about a week. Never before had I known such horrendous pain. It came in sudden spontaneous spasms, and my shrieks startled everybody in the intensive care unit, including myself. I had never known myself capable of uttering such sounds. The head nurse fell on her knees by my bed, pleading:

'Um Gottes Willen, schreien Sie doch nicht so schrecklich! Die andere Pazienten werden vor Schreck aus dem Bett hinfallen...'.[2]

The night superintendent tried sterner tactics. He stood hard by the bed and shouted angrily:

'Herr Tchaikowsky, es gibt einen Pazient in jedem Box, die haben auch Schmerzen! Sie müssen mit diesem Lärm sofort aufhören.'[3]

But I couldn't stop, nor could I even wish to. The spasms were so sudden that there was no time even to bite my teeth: the pain and the shriek were simultaneous. I screamed as one bleeds.

Unable to stop me, the man began to hate me. I've seldom seen so much cold hatred in a human face. It showed in his voice too, when he refused me a pain-killing injection. The way he said 'Nein' was a perfect illustration of the word Schadenfreude.

The other night attendant was kind and patient, mopped my forehead and moistened my mouth (I was not yet allowed to drink). But the general attitude was brisk, professional and matter-of-fact, without any attempt at compassion. This was not just a hospital, but an intensive care unit: they hardly ever saw a patient who was not at death's door. They reacted to my agonised complaints with injunctions to bite my teeth or remarks like 'Na ja, Schmerzen dürfen Sie schon haben.'[4]

Throughout that night I had visions of long grey corridors with a tiny red opening visible just at the end of them; each spasm of pain would whisk me down the whole length of the passage into the red area. Then the corridor would re-appear as before. The sequence repeated itself hundreds of times.

It was truly a season in hell.

---

[2] 'For God's sake, don't scream so terribly! The other patients will fall out of bed with fright.'
[3] 'Herr Tchaikowsky, there's a patient in every cubicle, they have pains, too. You must stop this noise immediately.'
[4] 'Well, pain's something you should be expecting.'

'Wie geht es Ihnen?'[5] asked the surgeon. There were several other doctors present. I didn't know where I was: had they transported me somewhere? They hadn't, but my sense of place and time were still confused.

'Die schlimmste Nacht meines Lebens', I answered, 'War es wirklich nur eine Nacht? Oder mehrere Nächte?'[6]

They assured me it was only one night. Then the surgeon's beaming golden smile came back.

'Sie hatten eine Tumor!' he exclaimed triumphantly. 'A tumour!' he shouted in English, lest I had misunderstood my good luck.

'Malignant?' I asked.

'We don't yet know, it's being analysed. Die ist aber weg! Ganz weg! Sie haben grosse Chance, normalerweise alt zu werden....'[7]

Having never assumed anything else, I could not share his jubilation at the prospect. When he had said my life was in danger, it simply had not sunk in. Now he seemed to me to be saying the same thing in a different phrasing, and this time I took it in to the hilt.

'Die Tumor war noch so, dass man sie völlig beseitigen konnte. Ich habe alle Lümpfknoten – Lymph-knots! – weggenommen, und alles untersucht: cs war nirgends mehr Tumor zu sehen. Sie werden natürlich alle sechs Monaten untersucht werden müssen.'[8]

I could see a new life beginning, a life of fear and hospitals. Didn't cancer usually come back? Since then I've heard that cancers of the bowel have a better prognosis than most.

The revelations were not over yet.

'Sie haben einem künstlichen Anus!'[9] yelled the surgeon. He could be informing me of an inheritance.

'Wo?' I asked, aghast.

'Hier!' he shouted, striking athletically his solar plexus.

Now I felt truly sick. This was the ultimate degradation: a grotesque, nauseating, ridiculous and shameful disfigurement. I had always been squeamish, and the prospect of having shit come out of my chest crushed and humiliated me more than any aspect of my disease. For days I was to be haunted by Baudelaire's lines:

[5] 'How are you?'
[6] 'The worst night of my life. Was it really only one night? Or several nights?'
[7] 'But it's gone! Completely gone! You have a good chance of growing old normally....'
[8] 'The nature of the tumor was still such that it could be completely removed. I have taken away all lymph-nodes and examined everything: there was no more tumour to be seen anwhere. Of course, you will have to be examined every six months....'
[9] 'You have an artificial anus!'

Oh Seigneur, donnez-moi la force et le courage
De contempler mon corps et mon cœur sans dégoût![10]

'War es also keine Perforation?'[11] I asked.

'Die Tumor war perforiert!' And an elderly, senior doctor, who later
proved to be the chief of the department, explained complacently in English:

'This complication – this perforation – enabled us to help you better.'
He was to say this sentence at least twice more on successive visits. He was
obviously impressed with this stroke of luck: the tumour had not shown on
X-ray plates, but the perforation had. Later I heard I had also had peritonitis.

The surgeon must have noticed my reaction to the news about the
artificial anus, for he said:

'Nur für Monaten! Dann werden Sie wieder operiert, noch zwei Wochen
im Krankenhaus und fertig.'[12]

So: three months as a freak of nature, then yet another operation, with
no doubt the same amount of pain. I felt punch-drunk. I'd never heard of
artificial anuses; apparently they're quite common, but of course no one
admits to having such a thing….

'Jetzt müssen Sie aber mitmachen! Schön husten, immer wieder stark
husten! Sonst bekommen Sie eine Pneumonie….'[13]

What, pneumonia too? I could react no more. I was like Macbeth
confronted with the eight successive Banquo apparitions. Coughing,
besides, would be entirely intolerable: the wound was just below the navel. I
was instructed to hold it down with both hands to lessen the pain.

It did not prove very effective. The pain, severe at all times, became
intolerable at every cough and every movement. And I was continually
being made to move: the modern medical practice is to keep patients mobile
in order to avoid thrombosis, and already on that first day I was forced,
despite screams of pain and protest, to get up and walk to the window, each
step bringing on a fresh cramp. They kept lowering my bed to measure
something or other, which for some reason proved agonising as well, and
they were very parsimonious with pain-killers and sleeping injections. One
hardly ever sleeps in an intensive care unit, and not only because of the
pain: there is no day and no night, the noise is always equally intense, and
no nurse ever seems to think of lowering her voice or closing a door softly.

[10] 'Oh, Lord, give me the courage, and the strength,/To contemplate my heart, and my body without
disgust!' The last lines of Baudelaire's poem *Un voyage à Cythère*.
[11] 'Was it not a perforation, then?'
[12] 'Only for months. Then you'll be operated on again, two more weeks in hospital and you're done.'
[13] 'But now you have to get on with it. Cough properly, keep coughing forcefully. Otherwise you'll get
pneumonia….'

The 'phone rings all the time, and various gadgets add strident noises of their own. I really couldn't feel guilty at the sounds I was making myself, loud and harsh as they were.

There was luckily no mirror in my 'box', but I was aware of looking like a science-fiction creature. A tube reaching down to my stomach came out of my nose, another out of my penis (this caused urethritis), yet another out of my now disused rectum. There were several drips from the wound dragging on the floor on either side of me. I was being fed intravenously through an opening in my neck, which also served for drawing blood and other such pleasures (I privately called it 'the Dracula treatment'). When they would get me up, I was made to drag the carrier with the infusion bottles along with me, while two sisters arranged the drips on either side.

The first three days I was too annihilated by shock, pain, and the sudden death-blow to all my hopes and projects even to want recovery. Pain is a full-time job: I was no longer anything but my belly. I experienced the full truth of Auden's terrible lines in *Surgical Ward*: 'They are and suffer: this is all they do' and 'For who when healthy can become a foot?' When Heiko and Wolfgang visited me on that first day, I could only burst into tears. They left in dismay, without speaking.

Indeed, there was something almost Aristotelian in my sudden fall. Two days before, I was an apparently healthy, active, self-confident man, full of ambitious projects and optimistic prospects. 1982, after several years of financial worries, promised enough lucrative engagements to get me out of debt altogether; my compositions were at last beginning to arouse interest. And where was I now? The £3000 I had hoped to earn in Norway, a sum heavily borrowed against and paid in advance, were already lost; the second operation, for the removal of the ghastly artificial anus, could only take place in three months, which would put paid to the even more lucrative spring tour with the Utrecht orchestra; and meanwhile bills would keep coming in, bank orders would go through, till only the immediate sale of the house could cover the debts; and after that I'd have nothing even to borrow against, and nowhere to live. (Assuming, of course, that I *should* live). And how much would the present treatment cost? In England it would have been free, but I had no choice in the matter, and here I was taken on as a private patient. The hospital stay alone was nearly £100 per day – and what about the operation and the various doctor's fees? It looked as if I could hardly *afford* to recover, whatever my chances were.

And, following the Aristotelian rules of tragedy, I noticed that I had the required tragic fault: that of hubris. For far too long I'd been intent on living my life entirely on my own terms! I'd come to regard happiness, that mirage beyond most people's reach, as sine qua non, almost as a natural right. I had made a fetish of comfort. I barricaded myself with objects destined to ensure it, an Ansafone to avoid interruption, an electric blanket to make my bed more voluptuous in a way that would make no demands on myself, innumerable pills to assuage or prevent the least vestige of pain and discomfort. (It was ironic having all those pills with me here, where I suffered unprecedented agonies, and being unable to take them; the head-nurse was utterly dumbfounded when she found my collection, and became even stricter as a result.) And of all my many fears, that of physical pain was by far the most intense and deep-rooted. It was that, no doubt, that foiled my attempt to re-live my early years in imagination. Harsh, as the present lesson was, it was deserved and accurate: it covered exactly my areas of greatest weakness.

I already realised that I should have to live differently, indeed *be* different, if I recovered. Hemingway's striking sentence: 'The world breaks everyone, and afterwards some get stronger in the broken places'[14] seemed to apply to my case exactly. Perhaps I'd now find the guts to brave poverty, give up the piano and devote myself entirely to composition? I had a very strong suspicion that my organism had produced the disease to force on me that very decision, to turn me back into the person I was born to be, doing the thing I was born to do. My career as a pianist, pleasant as it often was, was like having married for money; the wife was nice as well as rich and deserved to be loved for herself, but I did not love her, and in choosing her I had turned my back on my very identity. I still remember my grandmother's words: 'If you are a composer, you'll be famous after you're dead! What good will that do you?' I knew myself too little to realise that my first wish, or rather need, was not to be famous: it was merely to be myself. It takes the whole of one's life to acquire self-knowledge, and it often needs a collapse like my present one to bring it about.

If I am right in assuming that I grew this cancer as it were deliberately to shed a life that did not answer my deepest needs, then I can hardly afford to ignore such a warning. If I did, I'd no doubt develop another tumour, or some other equally drastic disease, and that time I might be less lucky.

On the other hand, how should I live if I gave up the piano? I have yet to meet a composer who makes a livelihood out of his gift, unless he write film-music like Bennett.[15] If my reasoning was right, I had the choice between returning to the stage and succumbing to cancer or some other disease within a few years, or giving it up for a longer and happier life or composition and semi-starvation. I'd either make money I'd have no time to

---

[14] Slightly misquoted, from *A Farewell to Arms* (1929).
[15] *Cf.* note 32, p. 328, above.

need or need it chronically without being able to make it. The decision was made difficult by the impossibility to ascertain my prospects. If I knew I was doomed, I shouldn't hesitate to devote the little time I had to composition. The surgeon thought, however, I had good chances of a normal old age. There could be no certainty: there never had been. Why, I might leave the hospital in perfect health and be run over on my first day out!

Amid all these reflections, I remembered G. L.[16] saying: 'Each time life frustrated my plans, I reaped unexpected benefits' and wondered how it would apply to my case. I never doubted his words and his wisdom and can now confirm his experience at first hand.

The first timid appearance of joy came about 24 hours after the operation, when I was allowed a sip of cold peppermint tea. Nothing I'd ever drunk had tasted so delicious and every successive sip was a fresh rapture (they were well spaced). It was my first foretaste of that renewal of sensibility that was to make me so sharply aware of every taste, sight and feel: everything was being rediscovered. Like a child, I became fascinated by the whiteness of snow, the shapes of bare trees outside my window, the freshness of air when the window was open, the taste of each successive food I was allowed. The process only became noticeable within the last week, but it started with that sip of tea.

It culminated in my first bath. No Roman emperor had ever known such luxury! And yesterday (it's now the 28th) I set the seal on my recovery by tossing myself off. This, too, proved more enjoyable than it had been for years. I had won a new appreciation of everything I'd always taken for granted.

Most of all, I have become more aware of my friends. The news of my illness provoked them to an overwhelming display of love and concern, and my recovery owes a lot to their moral support. Heiko and Wolfgang came to see me every single day; Heiko also rang Terry and my cousins in Paris and has acted as a liaison officer between me and Rabbit's-friends-and-relations ever since. His 'phone can hardly ever have stopped in the first few days: as the news spread, more and more people wanted first-hand reports on my progress. Cables poured in from Stephen, Kaarina, Kyung Wha, Derek P., Jean Redcliffe-Maud; flowers from Heiko, Kyung Wha and a German friend of Richard Toeman's;[17] and within two days of the operation I was told not to worry about money or anything practical, as Terry and

---

[16] George Lyward – *cf.* p. 102, above.
[17] Stephen Kovacevich, Kaarina Meyer (from Harrison Parrott), Kyung-wha Chung, Lady Redcliffe-Maud (*cf.* p. 143, above) and Richard Toeman from Weinberger, Tchaikowsky's publisher (*cf.* p. 252, above).

Uri would take care of all the current expenses, and Derek said he could wait a year if need be before any money came into my moribund account. To prevent boredom, Heiko lent me a miniature radio set and a cassette recorder, along with several books; more books arrived from Terry, Eve, Kazik, Jadria, John Schofield, Alan Golding, Yoram and Hiro; Heiko and Yoram spent hours recording cassettes for me. Truly, I'd need a relapse to read and hear everything I've been given!

And I haven't yet mentioned the visits! Eve, who of all my friends can least afford such a trip, was the first to arrive (she'd have come over at once, but Heiko told her I was not well enough). She stayed five days and her presence was a blessing. We touched on our recent difficulties and got their aftertaste out of our system.

Terry arrived the next day, laden with books and – yes! gay magazines! I didn't actually want the latter, but I couldn't help being touched and amused by his going to such extravagant lengths to cheer me up. He worked out the financial aspect of my stay here and is covering almost the whole cost (along with Uri). The first day, his vitality betrayed me into talking and laughing more than was good for me: the pains came back and Terry got really worried. By the next day, I was better and we had a very welcome quiet talk about the possibility of my giving up the piano in favour of composition.

That was on Friday, one week after the operation. Patrick and Taeko tried to come on the Saturday on their way to Russia, but the project misfired. I was relieved: I wasn't yet up to so much company, and both Eve and I badly wanted to be alone together; I asked Heiko and Wolfgang not to come the next day, and enjoyed Eve's quiet undemanding presence.

Uri arrived on Sunday and did me a world of good with his sunny, relaxed personality. Stephen flew in on Monday, between Paris and London; by that time I was up on my feet, which reassured him, and we spoke as much about his own recent problems as about mine. […] He also offered to lend me money; I declined, at least for the time being, but asked him to try and get some organisation to commission my suite of dances for him and help me that way. I intend to make the same request to Kyung Wha.

There followed a lull between this spate of visits and the next. My father rang, mainly to complain about his own health! This was his best opportunity to show his affection; I cannot say he made the most of it. The week confirmed my conviction that it's the mind, not the blood, that forms one's true kin: my real family had gathered round me.

It included, of course, people who *are* related to me by blood: Vivi arrived from Paris with precisely the things I requested, specifically chosen books, a chess-set and towels, plus a box of sweets. Unfortunately I couldn't long enjoy her calm beneficial company, as Radu arrived on the same day!

Expecting, no doubt, a skeleton, he was overjoyed to find me up and about and, moreover, in very high spirits (it's been a great surprise to me as well to find myself so *happy* here, once the gruesome first few days were over); so he stayed for eight hours, played several games of chess and lost them all (has the operation improved my chess? he invariably beat me before), and ended up asking my opinion about his own recurrent depression, for which there are at present no objective reasons, and which may be due to some obscure chemical disorder as well as his overprotected upbringing. I was touched and flattered by his confidence, but pretty tired by the time he left. […]

The doctors and nurses have also shown me increasing affection. The head-sister said: 'Sie haben so eine Ausstrahlung'.[18] But it is from Dr. Grund, who's been looking after me since my release from the intensive care unit, that I've received the most generous gesture. A keen music-lover, he lent me his cassette recorder and several cassettes (some transcribed from the radio, some from records), and I showed my gratitude by halving my nightly dose of Mogadon (till he did that, I was deaf to all his arguments). He talks of music whenever he can spare the time and I've come to like him so much that I intend to stay in touch with him after my release! Already I've invited him to my concert in Frankfurt on the 17th of May: it now looks as if I might be able to make it!

31 January

The artificial anus is to be removed tomorrow.

This is wonderful news! For one thing, it shows the positively Olympic speed of my recovery (the normal delay is three months); for another, it will enable me to come out of here as an anatomically normal human being, not as a shameful freak, handicapped by a humiliating secret, shunning society, condemned to mess about with revolting, stinking plastic bags. I was dreading that period between the two operations, and was determined to spend it 'in hiding'; thank God I've been spared it.

It also means that I have good chances of salvaging the spring tour with the Utrecht orchestra! Considering my recuperative powers (the X-rays showed that my colon was completely healed 2½ weeks after the operation) two months should be quite enough time for my convalescence. I should be out of here by mid-February, and the first concert is on the 17th of April: it *should* work! Will it?

---

[18] 'You have such charisma.'

10 February

I'll be released on Monday the 15th.

I shall not dwell on the second operation, the discomforts of the first few days and the recovery; I've already covered that ground. Yesterday, for the first time in just over a month, I was allowed out and spent a few minutes in the nearby supermarket, buying wine for Heiko (it was his birthday). Today is a real spring day, and I've already been allowed to go for a walk in the park after the doctor's second visit!

The score and sketches of Act III are already in Paris; Pascal Rogé was to take them across on Monday, and he may even drop them at my cousins'. How I look forward to staying with them! It will be marvellous to be looked after, to save such energies as I may have for practice and orchestration, to face no bills I cannot pay (my home must be flooded with them), to have a total respite from all the trivial pressures of life, like the child I've never stopped being. The upright piano I used in my Paris days is now standing in the very room I am to occupy; how it still plays I don't know but then I don't know my own present ability either, and it should certainly prove adequate for the inevitable technical drudgery of the first few weeks. When last did I have a chance to spend up to two months in PARIS?!

25 March

St Malo
I do not want to write about it, so I'll just jot it down quickly: the ENO have refused *The Merchant*.

I've had the news more than two weeks ago, but I couldn't bring myself to record it then. The letter from Lord Harewood was curt and officialese, quite unlike his charmingly personal notes before the audition. Far from trying to soften the blow, it even included an additional sting: it said that having had such good advance news of *The Merchant* they had felt duty bound to hear the piece, but that having done so they saw no reason to alter the ENO's commitments to several other new works already planned. The last sentence dotted the i's brutally: 'so I'm afraid that my letter must rule *The Merchant of Venice* out for the ENO' as if I was the type to climb in through the window after being pushed out of the door.

Once again I'd been too optimistic. Why, they didn't even wait to hear the crucial trial scene and the *Epilogue*! I had always thought that would absolutely clinch the deal, and regretted their decision not to wait till the work was complete. And I still cannot quite help thinking that things would have gone differently if they had got the climax and the shape of the entire work.

My first reaction was to feel devastated: it was like another operation. My second was to go right back to the score and increase the daily rate of orchestration! This was both occupational therapy and a vote of confidence in the work, but I overdid it, wrote three big pages in one day and made myself ill. So my third reaction was, of course, a headache.

I've now got nearly two-thirds of the trial scene (Shylock is just about to draw out his knife) but I shall have to put it aside in favour of practice: the tour is only three weeks away. I shan't be able to re-open the score till June. And yet how impatient I am to finish it! Now that the prospect of seeing it soon has disappeared, the whole thing has become a huge drag: it stands between me and new, practical, accessible projects. It's a year and a half since I last experienced the joy of completing a new work (*The Merchant*, in fact): I need it again, and Kyung Wha is awaiting her pieces with all her usual impatience. It will all have to get done in the summer... [...]

19 April

Utrecht

Yesterday I played my first concert in 1982.

That it went pretty well is scarcely more surprising than the fact that it took place at all: the last few weeks of my Paris stay were increasingly uncomfortable, with constant indigestion and itinerant abdominal pains, and my cousin's family doctor suggested an immediate check-up! Now I obviously preferred this to be done in the clinic where I was operated, so I rang my friendliest doctor there (the one who lent me the cassette recorder) and arranged for the check-up to take place in April, instead of May as originally booked. But I had to wait out the Easter holiday, so I could only start the tests last Tuesday, and was released on Thursday, the day before the first rehearsal in Utrecht! This meant four days without practice immediately before the first concert, as Easter Monday was devoted first to getting to Mainz and then to shitting (the preparation for the tests is a massive dose of laxatives, as most tests consist of sticking various instruments up one's arse; I even had a microperiscope in it, and came to realise where the word 'arsenal' must have come from). The time was not altogether wasted for work, as I've managed to add three pages to the full-score of the trial-scene, which is now just past the two-thirds mark; but there could of course be no piano practice till I reached Utrecht on Thursday afternoon, and I am still pleasantly surprised at having managed to put in a session that evening, after all the discomforts and fatigue of the tests.

The latter were made more painful by the fact that I have recently developed piles! I thought in Paris it was just a spot, but the chief surgeon

10.2. – I'll be released on Monday the 15th.

I shall not dwell on the second operation, the discomforts of the first few days and the recovery; I've already covered that ground. Yesterday, for the first time in just over a month, I was allowed out and spent a few minutes in the nearby supermarket, buying wine for Heiko (it was his birthday). Today is a real spring day, and I've already been allowed to go for a walk in the park, after the doctor's second visit!

The score and sketches of Act III are already in Paris: Pascal Rogé was to take them across on Monday, and he may even drop them at my cousins'. How I look forward to staying with them! It will be marvellous to be looked after, to save such energies as I may have for practice and orchestration, to face no bills I cannot pay (my home must be flooded with them), to have a total respite from all the trivial pressures of life, like the child I've never stopped being. The upright piano I used in my Paris days is now standing in the very room I am to occupy; how it still plays I don't know, but then I don't know my own present ability either, and it should certainly prove adequate for the inevitable technical drudgery of the first few weeks. When last did I have a chance to spend up to two months in PARIS ?!

99

in Mainz, the very man who had so brilliantly operated on me in January, scared half the life out of me by saying: 'Sie haben dort eine Thrombose!' Thrombosis, like cancer, is a tremendously fear-laden word, and I had no idea that it could be applied to hemoroids [*sic*] (or, no doubt, varicose veins). Scalpel-happy as ever, the surgeon then offered to operate on them

('In einer knappen Woche sind Sie ja wieder heraus'[19]), but I preferred to save the tour by resorting to less drastic means. These seem to be working well, and already I am much improved.

The result of the tests was all one could wish. Sometimes, indeed, microscopic bits of the tumour escape the scalpel and start proliferating again! But so far no sign of them has been revealed (the final diagnosis will take another six days, till the analysis has been completed). My numerous tummy-aches are simply due to my having been operated in a state of peritonitis, which causes the once-infected tissues to become inflamed once again in the very process of healing. But it's a bore, and I've arranged to see a doctor here tomorrow in the hope of being able to counteract this and my numerous muscular pains. The latter, said the chief surgeon, were also a normal aftermath of having lain still for so long in hospital; but the explanation doesn't lessen the pain in my right hip, which regularly wakes me up in the small hours.

But enough grumbling! The main thing is that I seem to be cancer-free, that I've been medically authorised to go on with the tour, that the first concert, while by no means perfect, would have been creditable enough even before the recent vicissitudes. There were many wrong notes in the first movement and a predictable tendency to rush in the rondo; but in between the mishaps and the nerves, the music-making went on unimpaired, and the *Larghetto* was perhaps the best I have yet played it. I'm to play it eleven times more on this tour (only three German towns have chosen Mozart), so no doubt there'll be time to master the nerves and the notes, before fatigue spoils the work again.

The conductor, Lamberto Gardelli, is a most accomplished old professional and a good musician, but his avuncularly patronising and didactic attitude to me, his childish egomania and constant prattle about himself do not entice me to seek his company. I let him talk without the least indication of my attitude: with fifteen concerts still to come, it would be madness to create an antagonism that would undermine the performances. But I've already told the manager who'll travel with us that I prefer to go by bus with the orchestra rather than with him and Gardelli in his car; there is a plausible reason for that, as we both want to sit in front (I get car-sick in the back). But quite apart from that, I couldn't have taken so many hours of anybody's self-advertisement! 'In Italy they called me the new Toscanini, in Vienna the second Furtwängler. But this is stupid! I'm the first Gardelli!'

---

[19] 'You'll be out again in under a week.'

I never try to compete with that kind of talk, so the maestro graciously praised me for my modesty. Little does he know.

24 April

Utrecht

I am again in hospital, recovering from an evening of great pain and fear! The pain started just after a light lunch (a croque-monsieur, which is all my hotel provides by way of lunch) and persisted through repeated and, indeed, exaggerated doses of Buscopan combinate and Glifanan,[20] which only ended by bringing on nausea. At five o'clock I dragged myself to see a young doctor recommended by the hotel; he couldn't help and tried to waive the fee, but I insisted. At ten, in ever greater pain and by now thoroughly alarmed, I got the receptionist to call a doctor to my bedside; he spoke to me first on the 'phone, then offered to come.

He proved both competent and sympathetic, but his tentative diagnosis exceeded my worst fears: he suspected something called ileus, or intestinal adhesion, a condition that can only be cured by surgery! In January I had agreed to an operation without virtually batting an eyelid: since then I have learnt what it's like. The ruinous loss of the tour (though how could I play or travel in such acute pain?) was almost nothing compared to the sheer stark terror of a third operation in 3½ months. I told the doctor I had to try and keep playing if at all possible, that I'd be ruined if I didn't, that my failure to play the second concert in Utrecht would constitute a breach of contract, etc. He undertook to explain all this to the surgeon at the hospital, and rang him there and then; as far as my guess would allow, he did explain my personal and professional predicament. He ensured my immediate admittance and examination, and told me to go straight there by taxi.

The taxi took me to the wrong hospital, so it was nearly twelve when I arrived at last at the right place! The surgeon explained again that in the case of ileus he'd have no choice but to operate, and ordered X-rays and a blood test. The former proved unclear, the latter would take some hours to develop: the surgeon suggested I stay the night under observation. He promised to let me attend the morning's rehearsal if at all possible, and I promised to return from it to the hospital.

With two Mogadons and a pethidine[21] injection, I still stayed awake, I think, the entire night. But this morning in the nick of time, the surgeon

---

[20] Buscopan is the trade-name of a drug, Butylscopolamine, used to treat abdominal pain; it can be combined with paracetamol. Glifanan is the trade-name of the pain-killer Glafenine.
[21] Pethidine is another analgesic; once common, it is now prescribed only rarely.

Some of the last photographs: Tchaikowsky rehearsing in Utrecht in April 1982

came to say I had nothing worse than acute constipation (meanwhile already relieved by a clyster) and could do the rehearsal and the concert! He recommended, however, that I came back to the hospital in between the two, and it can't be denied that I feel safer here than in an hotel, so here I am again in relative comfort. The pain has all but gone, and the doctor in attendance today confirmed emphatically that there could be no question of ileus! Asked about the cause of so much pain, he charmingly suggested metastasis... Just as well I've had this check-up.

And despite all these vicissitudes, everyone seemed to like my 595[22] very much indeed at this morning's rehearsal! God grant me the right frame of mind tomorrow... I do so want to play well, whatever the available 'excuses'.

25 April

Well, I did get away with it, though I was very nervous in the first movement! I had to fight for every note, and there *were* a few minor slips (and innumerable near-slips which luckily only I knew about). But it seems to have gone down very well, better than the Chopin, where I was in no position even to aim at perfection, and therefore had to be content with a

---

[22] Mozart's Piano Concerto No. 27.

far less accomplished performance. To me the Mozart today sounded timid and small-scale, but several people assured me that it 'carried' well. Next time perhaps I'll be able to enjoy it myself.

The pains in my belly have gone down to an occasional sharp twinge, and the doctor assured me I was now out of trouble; if all goes well, I shall be off to Bonn tomorrow evening, and play there the next day (the Chopin I again, with Stefan in the audience!). Another improvement is in my attitude towards Lamberto, who really is kind, good-natured and a very good musician: even his egotism is innocent compared, say, with Rubinstein, who manipulates others into praising him, till one has no thought of one's own left! I am now truly ashamed of my bitchy earlier comments about L.

29 April

Salzburg

The concert in Bonn went very well, an intensely concentrated and committed performance. Chopin I being what it is (and I what I am) it was by no means impeccable, but it was just the kind of playing where wrong notes don't matter. Stefan called it 'phenomenal' but criticised the exaggerated *rubato* and an imperfectly pedalled opening of the *Larghetto*. After the concert, I had the pleasure of repaying the first instalment of my debt to him.

In fact, even if I don't fall ill and do manage to play all the concerts of this crowded tour, it will only just cover the most pressing debts! Yesterday Heiko showed me two more bills from the Mainz clinic, totalling another DM 9000; he told them I should pay this and other bills still to come immediately on completing the tour. He estimates the total hospital costs at DM 25,000; more than half of this has been paid by Terry and Uri, but I'll still be left with at least 10,000 to pay. And there's my debt to Kazik and the rest of my debt to Stefan, not to speak of Heiko's and Terry's commissions! No, there will be nothing left to come home with, and nothing to live on till next season, unless I do get refunded for some of my medical costs...

André Tchaikowsky died at 6.45 in the morning of Saturday, 26 June 1982; he was 46 years old.

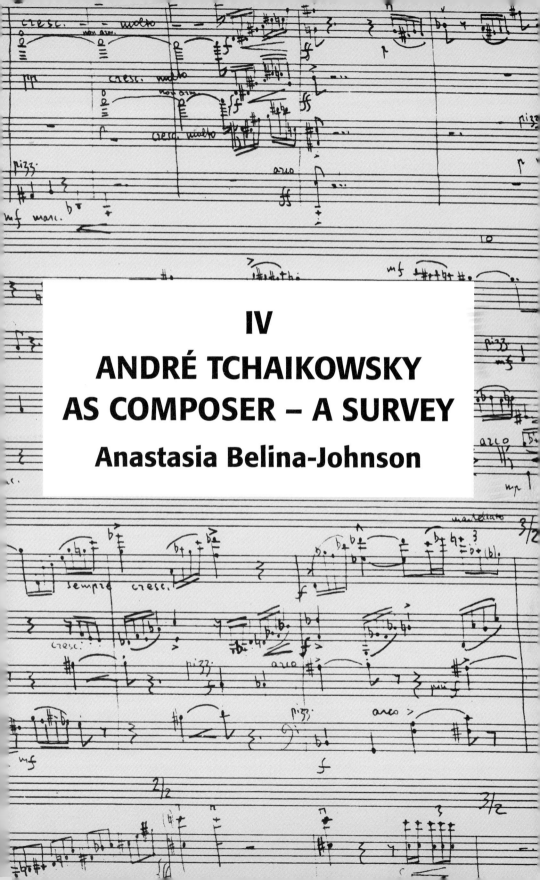

IV
ANDRÉ TCHAIKOWSKY
AS COMPOSER – A SURVEY
Anastasia Belina-Johnson

Although composition was André Tchaikowsky's true calling, he did not promote himself as a composer. The conductor Christopher Seaman remembers:

> He hated the word 'career'. He actually hated the word. On one occasion when I was with him, he was reading something and the printing was very bad. He misread the word career. He misread it as being the word 'cancer'. He read it again and saw that it was 'career'. Then he said: 'How interesting it is that I've misread that word like that'. He was completely unaffected by media hype. If someone introduced him to the most famous conductor in the world, it's really quite possible that André really wouldn't have heard of this guy. If he'd heard this guy conduct something and didn't like his work, he wouldn't be interested in meeting him.[1]

Composing fulfilled Tchaikowsky, and it was the one area of his profession where he never procrastinated: on the contrary, he had to force himself not to compose when on tour or when preparing for concerts because composition entirely took hold of him.

Because he could not dedicate himself to composition on a full-time basis, his legacy is small – but that does not mean it is unimportant. Apart from two piano concertos, two string quartets and a number of compositions for voice, piano and other instruments, his opera *The Merchant of Venice* is a profound and moving work that deserves a place of honour in the operatic repertory of the twentieth century.

Some of Tchaikowsky's works have a somewhat 'just finished', improvised quality – like, for example, those of an earlier virtuoso pianist, the Russian Anton Rubinstein, who wrote copious amounts of music that he seldom revised. Tchaikowsky, by contrast, wrote a very small number of works but he, too, did not always have the time or the opportunity to revise them. In Martin Anderson's words:

> Some composers are consolidators – like, say, Brahms, Bruckner or Nielsen – who step determinedly from one work to the next, refining and improving their expressive armoury as they evolve. And others – Schubert is the obvious example – are improvisers: Schubert would drop a piece in mid-composition once he had learned what he wanted from it. Even though AT's

---

[1] Christopher Seaman, interviewed by David Ferré, 8 April 1987, Oxford.

output is obviously much smaller than Schubert's and his pieces took much longer to emerge, he seems to have had the same desperate rush to move on. That, I think, is what gives his music its freshness – the *Inventions*, for example, even the Op. 4 Piano Concerto, often sound as if they are being made up there and then. Of course, we'll never know what might have happened if health and wealth had allowed him a productive middle age, but I suspect that the nervous energy that powered him through the life he did have would have continued to drive him to explore, to write and move on.[2]

As a pianist Tchaikowsky had Arthur Rubinstein as his champion at the early stage of his performing career; as a composer he had the support of Hans Keller in developing and promoting his works. Keller was one of the first people to hear excerpts from *The Merchant of Venice,* helped organise a play-through of the opera in December 1981 at English National Opera, and wrote a glowing letter of recommendation for the work.[3]

On 24 August 1971 Tchaikowsky was scheduled to play the 'Goldberg' Variations at a Promenade concert in the Royal Albert Hall. Gerald Larner, music-critic of *The Guardian*, asked him for an interview. Tchaikowsky thought Larner one of the better critics and granted the interview, which shows him as composer and performer.

Tchaikowsky Mark Two

I came across André Tchaikowsky in the street, humming to himself, his head bobbing in time not with his feet but with the imagined music, his fingers drumming on the imagined keyboard. So I asked him what he was playing. 'Oh, I'm writing a piano concerto. One movement is not finished yet'. When it is ready he will play it, of course, but he would rather not give the first performance: 'I would get so nervous'.

He gets very nervous, anyway, about playing in public. 'Sometimes I wish I could drop dead before a concert.' But he would never give it up. If composition is, as he said, 'what makes me tick', playing the piano is what makes him tock. Even if he could earn a living as a full-time composer, he would still play the piano: 'I couldn't live without it'. Not that he does make money out of writing music. 'I have not made a penny out of it, and I don't think I ever will.'

'Who plays it?' I asked. 'Practically nobody', he said. But Gervase de Peyer has played his Clarinet Sonata (published by Weinberger), the Lindsay Quartet will perform his String Quartet, and Margaret Cable has sung his

[2] E-mail to Anastasia Belina-Johnson, 17 September 2013.
[3] *Cf.* pp. 387–88, below.

cycle of Seven Shakespeare Sonnets. He has also written a violin concerto[4] and Novello is about to publish some piano pieces called *The Inventions*.

Most young soloists could not find time for composition even if they had the inclination. 'Writing is a pretty obsessive occupation. I don't do it when I am on tour. It is too demanding.' So, in order to tick, he takes a few months off every year, usually June and July. A couple of years ago it was three winter months in the mid-season, which is professionally unheard of. In order to make sure that he is tocking properly, he also takes time off to visit 'an old lady in the Lake District' who apparently has a 'fantastic ear'. She listens to his playing and, without concerning herself with interpretation, picks holes in his technique. 'She treats me as if I were six. She's very bad for my self-confidence.'[5]

Obviously, André Tchaikowsky is no ordinary career pianist. His reputation of being 'difficult' still lingers on. This has only partly to do with his musical principles – that he won't play works he is not 'crazy about', like the Grieg, Tchaikovsky and Rachmaninov concertos, which are 'corny'. He has doubts even about the 'Emperor' and Bartok's Third, though Bartok has been one of the major influences on his own music. Bartok's Second is 'just too difficult. My arms would drop off'. But he plays the Schumann and Beethoven's Third and Fourth, which are his favourites outside of Mozart. 'Mozart comes first every time. Most people would agree that humanity and perfection are mutually exclusive, but the exception is Mozart.'

Nor is his reputation for being difficult due to the occasional awkward encounter with conductors. 'I don't get on with grand old people', he admits, and prefers to work with young ones. 'Old conductors are much bossier and less flexible', particularly some senior German ones who apparently like to maintain a military discipline and expect him to salute and 'Jawohl' rather than discuss the interpretation. His fingers drummed on the keyboard again, and the baldish head bobbed in time.

Eventually, before he came to settle in this country, 'everyone was sick to the teeth with me. They thought I played the piano rather well but they found me insufferable'. But he finds that it is only a 'false situation' which brings out the worst in him. Even in England, which he regards as a 'supremely civilised

---

[4] The *Concerto Classico* of 1962–64 *cf.* pp. 377–78 below.

[5] The reference is to Stephanie Hess,

whom André loved very much [...] she knew a great deal about music and musicians. [...] Stephanie lived in a small village near Bassenthwaite called Sunderland and André used to go and stay there a lot. She was also close to Peter Schidlof and left him her house when she died. [...] Stephanie was indeed very forthright about piano technique and used to complain about most pianists (not André) that they did not have proper left-hand voicing, which for her was the key. [...] She lived alone with her adored dog, an indeterminate breed called Kerry of whom André used to mutter that you needed a gas mask whenever Kerry was in the room. Stephanie of course ignored this.

E-mails from Anthony Phillips to Martin Anderson, 17 and 18 September 2013

Tchaikowsky with Stephanie Hess, the 'old lady in the Lake District', photographed on the steps of Judy Arnold's home in Highgate, North London, c. 1968

country – the first in which a central-European refugee like me could feel really safe', he had a difficult time at first. He had so little work between 1960 and 1962 (having got on the wrong side of his manager) that he had to borrow money from his teacher, Stefan Askenase.

Now, however, he seems quite happy. Certainly, I found him very polite and unusually modest, with a cheerful sense of humour. The more he feels at home, the better the sense of humour works. New Zealand, for example, he regards as 'Arcadia, so innocent, so unspoilt, no snobs, no rat race'. And it was in New Zealand, on a recent tour with Christopher Seaman, that, for an encore, Tchaikowsky conducted the orchestra and Seaman played the piano. The orchestra was as surprised as the audience: 'For heaven's sake', André told the orchestra, 'don't pay any attention to me.'

Another place where he is happy, and popular as a teacher, is the summer school at Dartington. 'Where else can you play to an audience two-thirds of which you are sexually attracted to?' I said I didn't know. He said that once when he could not be at Dartington he sent a postcard saying simply, 'I love you. Will you marry me?' They pinned it to the notice board. He was there again this summer.[6]

But do these statements reflect what Tchaikowsky really felt? Or was he saying what he thought people wanted to hear? Only a few months before his death, he articulated his true calling unambiguously: composition was what he wanted to do.[7] It is obvious that had he lived, composition would have become his main occupation.

---

[6] *The Guardian*, 24 August 1971.
[7] Diary entry dated 22 January 1982; *cf.* p. 342, above.

CHRONOLOGICAL LIST OF COMPOSITIONS

I. EARLY WORKS

All the works in this list are for solo piano unless otherwise indicated.

1948

Nocturne

1949

Ten Dances
Ten Etudes

1950

Sonatina in G Major
Suite for Piano (1. Preludium, 2. Variations, 3. Waltz, 4. Lullaby)
Piano Sonata in F minor
Piano Sonata in A major
Variations on a Theme of Handel[8]
Variations on a Theme of Cohen[9]
Variations on an Original Theme
Concerto for Piano and Orchestra
Concerto for Violin and Orchestra
Sonata for Violin and Piano
Concerto for Flute and Orchestra

1953

Prelude and Fugue

1954

Two Preludes

1954–55

Sonata for Viola and Piano (I: *Largo non troppo*; II: Theme and Variations; III: *Allegro Agitato*)

1955

Two Études
Song for soprano and piano

---

[8] Which Handel theme he used is unknown.
[9] Jean-Léon Cohen (b. 1934) studied at the Paris Conservatoire with Vlado Perlemuter (in 1954 he became the first Perlemuter student to win a *premier prix*) and with Maurice Hewitt. From 1959 to 1988 he taught a piano class in the Conservatoire in Rennes. Because all earlier works by Tchaikowsky have been either destroyed or lost, it was not possible to establish what was the theme used for this work.

All these compositions, between the *Nocturne* of 1948, the earliest work that Tchaikowsky mentioned in an application to the Youth Circle of the Polish Composers' Union on 13 June 1950,[10] and 1955 are presumed lost: his aunt Mala, who lived in Paris, kept all his manuscripts, reviews and any related documents, but when Tchaikowsky found out about it, he asked her to destroy everything and she appears to have complied fully with his request.[11] Seemingly the only work to survive from this period is a Sonata for Viola and Piano, dating from 1954–55: the manuscript was found by the pianist Maciej Grzybowski and violist Krzysztof Chorzelski in 2012, in a box Tchaikowsky had left with Halina Janowska when he left Poland for the last time in 1956.

II. Mature Compositions

1956–57

Piano Concerto ('No. 1'[12])

1958

Sonata for Piano

1959

Sonata for Clarinet and Piano, Op. 1

1960

Two Songs after Poems by William Blake

1961

Octet

1961–62

10 *Inventions* for Piano, Op. 2

1962–64

Concerto Classico for violin and orchestra

1964–65

Arioso e Fuga per Clarinetto Solo

1966

Incidental music for *Hamlet*

---

[10] *Cf.* p. 40, above.
[11] Halina Malewiak, interviewed by David Ferré, 29 November 1985, Israel.
[12] Tchaikowsky did not give a number or opus to this concerto, and it is not certain if it is the same concerto he started to compose in 1950.

1967

Seven Sonnets of Shakespeare

1969

Ariel (three songs from Shakespeare's *The Tempest*)

1969–70

String Quartet No. 1, Op. 3 (in A major[13] and four movements)

1966–71

Piano Concerto, Op. 4 ('No. 2')

1973–75

String Quartet No. 2, Op. 5 (in C major and three movements)

1978

Trio Notturno for piano trio, Op. 6

1981

Six Dances for Piano
(unfinished, *Tango* and *Mazurka* completed)
Five Miniatures for violin and piano
(unfinished, three miniatures completed in sketch form)

1968–82

The Merchant of Venice: opera in three acts, Op. 7

Works for Piano and Orchestra
Piano Concerto (No. 1; 1956–57)

Tchaikowsky composed this piano concerto while living, studying and touring in Brussels, Warsaw, Sofia, Paris and Fontainebleau, before coming to live in England. When in Paris, he visited Arthur Rubinstein every day, showing him the Concerto as it developed, and was advised: 'Open up! Let your soul sing! You're very talented, child, a golden talent. You should write as to make everybody in the audience cry'.[14] But Tchaikowsky did not want to 'end up with the fifth concerto by Rachmaninov',[15] and instead asked the opinion of the conductor André Vandernoot, who told him:

> Oh, such a beautiful theme! Isn't it a waste to use it for the piano? Turn it into a symphony. What do you need this typewriter for? It was fashionable during

---

[13] Tchaikowsky, unusually for him, indicated the keys of both his string quartets.
[14] Letter to Halina Janowska, dated 18 June 1957.
[15] *Ibid.*

its era. In ten years' time, almost nobody will be playing it. Listen, mate, the orchestra plays much better when no twiddle, twiddle interrupts her.[16]

Tchaikowsky wrote to Halina Janowska:

> Under Rubinstein's influence I wrote a theme which all my friends consider to be terribly sweet and weepy. Under Vandernoot's influence, I added accompaniment on the post twelve-tone series with 'concrete' whispers on percussion, pianissimo kettledrums, glides and trills in the quartertones. God only knows how it's going to turn out, but I'm looking forward to the first performance, and I feel we are all going to have a lot of fun. I can just imagine the look on the faces of the orchestra during the first rehearsals. [...] It will be nothing less than a zoological symphony: Drums growling, clarinets meowing, brass roaring and flutes barking. But the real menagerie will be the audience.[17]

Tchaikowsky dedicated the concerto to the American pianist John Browning in the hope that he would perform it, but Browning was not interested in the work. The premiere took place on 18 March 1958, in Brussels, with the composer playing the solo part, and André Vandernoot conducting the National Orchestra of Belgium – its only public performance. The complete score is held in the Josef Weinberger André Tchaikowsky archive, and a copy can be found in the library at the Royal Conservatoire of Antwerp: Tchaikowsky gave it to Marcel Cuvelier, the president of the jury of the 1956 Queen Elisabeth Piano Competition, where Tchaikowsky received third prize.

The first movement has two main contrasting elements. The first is wistful, longing, with a number of demanding, inquisitive instrumental exclamations, and the second is observational and lyrical. Activity increases towards the end of the movement, which ends with a fast, toccata-like piano part, with a full support of dramatic, intense orchestral sound, and frenzied rhythms in the percussion section.

The second movement opens with a slow, dark and quiet introduction lasting about three minutes. The strings and woodwind stealthily creep out of their lower registers, bringing out a lyrical and dramatic melody. The wandering nature of the piano part imbues this movement with a searching, longing quality, and the overall spirit of the movement is dark, with ominous, dramatic, pessimistic colouring.

---

[16] *Ibid.*
[17] *Ibid.*

The finale is energetic, erratic and unsettled, where bursts of activity are interspersed with intensely romantic episodes that feature not only the piano but also solos of different orchestral instruments. The piano-writing in this concerto is effective and virtuosic, and shows the pianist's technical prowess, but only to the extent demanded by the music, never for its own sake.

Piano Concerto, Op. 4 (1966–71)

The second piano concerto was composed in London, and premiered on 28 October 1975, at the Royal Festival Hall, with Rudu Lupu as soloist and The Royal Philharmonic Orchestra conducted by Uri Segal. It was published in 1975 by Josef Weinberger.

Tchaikowsky began the composition sporadically in 1966; only in 1970 did he start working on it systematically, completing it in December 1971. Radu Lupu agreed to perform the work before it was finished, recalling meeting Tchaikowsky in the offices of their agent Harrison Parrott in London, where Tchaikowsky appeared carrying the manuscript under his arm. He recounted their conversation:

> Lupu: What are these papers?
> Tchaikowsky: My piano concerto.
> Lupu: Oh, I will play it.
> Tchaikowsky: You do not know it.
> Lupu: Tell me then.
> Tchaikowsky: It has a slow introduction...
> Lupu: I adore slow introductions.[18]

With Hans Keller's help the premiere took place four years after its completion. It was difficult and took Lupu nearly six months to learn, requiring an enormous amount of hard work. Perhaps that is why Tchaikowsky, who originally dedicated the concerto to the memory of George A. Lywaid, changed the dedication to Radu Lupu in the published version. Writing in *The Times*, Joan Chissell commented:

> The work is in three continuous, interlinked movements lasting for about 27 minutes. No one but a virtuoso of the first order could tackle the solo part. Yet not a note is there for mere display. Piano and orchestra are as closely integrated in a disciplined, purposeful argument as in the concertos of Brahms. Although, in his introductory note, the composer let us into formal secrets (a passacaglia to begin with, followed by a scherzo-like *Capriccio* and a *Finale*

---

[18] Radu Lupu, interviewed by David Ferré, 6 September 1986, London.

combining fugue and sonata), there was little about underlying 'programme' [*sic*]. Yet the work is dramatic and intense enough, in an often strangely ominous, disquieting way, to suggest very strong extra-musical motivation. There are moments of melancholy just as deep and tortured as in Berg opus 1.[19] Not for nothing is the glinting central *Capriccio* headed *vivace con malizia*: it is a 'danse macabre' ending in catastrophic climax. Even the *Finale*, at first suggesting emotional order won by mental discipline, eventually explodes in vehemence before the sad, retrospective cadenza (picking up threads from the opening *Passacaglia*) and the hammered homecoming.

If nearer in spirit to composers of the Berg-Bartok era than the avant-garde, Tchaikowsky still speaks urgently enough in this work to make his idiom sound personal. Much of it is also strikingly conceived as sound, with telling contrasts of splintered glass and glassy calm in the keyboard part. The *Capriccio* is a spine-chilling tour de force for the orchestra too.[20]

Max Loppert, writing in *The Financial Times*, was only slightly less impressed:

> It was, from the outset, rather impressive to encounter music of this kind concerned with 'strict construction' (the composer's phrase), made with clean-cut neo-classical materials purposeful and determined […]. At best, in the central *Capriccio* movement, something of an individual personality, quicksilver, angular and hard-edged, can be detected through the Stravinskyian cut-and-thrust, the late-Prokofiev flourishes and moto perpetuo passagework. Elsewhere, in the *Introduction* and *Passacaglia*, but more so in the *Finale*, brandishing its fugue, sonata and toccata, a slight greyness threatens to seep out from the basic material, a want of burning organic energy to be revealed behind the formal gestures.[21]

In *The Guardian* Edward Greenfield noted the unusual forbearance of the opening:

> 'I made a determined effort not to write a prima donna's favourite', Mr. Tchaikovsky explained in his programme note, and, for the first five minutes, that seemed the understatement of the year. Like the B flat minor concerto [by Piotr Tchaikovsky], the new Tchaikovsky first starts with an introduction, but in the composer's own words, 'it is slow and austere', and the piano for three whole minutes never gets a look-in, while the thematic material for the whole work is grittily outlined. After that, flamboyance still rejected utterly,

---

[19] Alban Berg's Piano Sonata, most probably composed in 1907–8, and published in 1910. It is Berg's only piano composition with an opus number.
[20] *The Times*, 29 October 1975.
[21] *The Financial Times*, 29 October 1975.

the pianist enters with a long and ruminative solo, which sets the pattern of wrong-note romanticism in gently flowing lines.[22]

The concerto was later performed by the National Orchestra of Ireland, conducted by Albert Rosen, with Tchaikowsky at the piano, in Dublin on 1 October, and Cork on 2 October, 1978. On 17 November 1981 Tchaikowsky gave his own final performance of the work in Hagen, Germany, when the conductor was Yoram David. A review in the *Westfälische Rundschau* reported:

> André Tchaikowsky (age 46), especially appreciated as a Mozart virtuoso all over the world, played the piano part at the Hagen City Hall concert himself. Is the concerto calculated such that the piano part is dominant? André Tchaikowsky: 'This is what I've tried to avoid. The instruments are introduced in groups and separately. The work is so polyphonic as to make great demands on every member of the orchestra'. [ ] Yoram David, the conductor of this event, says: 'This concerto for piano and orchestra is a phenomenally good work, tremendously crafted and is without a superfluous note'.[23]

After Tchaikowsky's death, the concerto was performed in Copenhagen on 12 September 1986, with Norma Fisher as soloist and the Tivoli Summer Orchestra conducted by Uri Segal. It was also performed in Poland by the Polish pianist Maciej Grzybowski on 8 February 2008 in Kalisz and 15 February 2008 in Bialystok, and on 17 August 2008 as part of the festival 'Chopin and his Europe' in Warsaw. Grzybowski performed it again on 22 July 2013 in Bregenz, with the Vienna Symphony Orchestra conducted by Paul Daniel.[24] It was published by Josef Weinberger in 1975, both in full score and a two-piano reduction made by the composer.

The Op. 4 Concerto is a powerful, complex and extraordinarily difficult work. It places huge demands on the soloist, who has not only to deal with technical difficulties, but also with sophisticated rhythmical, harmonic and musical details. A review in *Kultur* on the day after the Bregenz performance noted the complexity of the music:[25]

---

[22] *The Guardian*, 29 October 1975.

[23] Anon., 'Deutsch Uraufführung – Tschaikowsky', *Westfälische Rundschau*, No. 270, 18 November 1981.

[24] It is this performance that, along with solo-piano works by Tchaikowsky, appears on Toccata Classics TOCC 0204 (2013).

[25] *Kultur*, review by Silvia Thurner, 23 July 2013 (http://kulturzeitschrift.at/kritiken/musik-konzert/ gipfelstuerme-klangkaskaden-und-ruhepole-2013-das-erste-orchesterkonzert-bei-den-bregenzer-festspielen-beinhaltete-gegensaetze).

Close relationships between the instruments of the orchestra and the piano created forms of dialogue that were always changing [...]. Particular sound effects emerged in the intensive exchange of the piano with the timpani, drums and marimba.

[...] Although the work had some striking moments, it was above all the coherent order of the musical development and the rich interrelationship of events within the smallest confines that left a deep impression. Surprising twists and sensual pools of sound ensured balance between tension and relaxation in the dense musical texture.

Works for Solo Piano
Sonata for Piano (1958)

Tchaikowsky began composing the only mature sonata he wrote for his own instrument while on holiday in Madrid with his cousin Charles Fortier. When he finished one movement, he played it to Arthur Rubinstein on the hotel piano over the phone. Rubinstein was on tour in Australia, and the cost of the call was enormous.[26]

On 19 April 1959 Tchaikowsky included the work in a solo recital in Orchestra Hall in Chicago but attributed it to an unknown composer, Uyu Dal. Writing in *The Chicago Daily Tribune* Seymore Raven saw through the subterfuge:

A modern work on the program was a just completed Sonata (world premiere) by Uyu Dal. The feeling persisted that Dal is Mr. Tchaikowsky's pseudonym. A companion feeling was that in composing this music, Dal was very much inspired by Prokofiev but much more gentle in temperament despite the very brilliant pianistic idiom that darted in and out of the terse, quicksilver scoring.[27]

Tchaikowsky never played the Sonata again. The manuscript, dated 'May/June 1958, Madrid-London', is held in the Josef Weinberger Archives.

Inventions for Piano, Op. 2

The set of ten inventions was composed in London between 1961 and 1963. Each piece was dedicated to one of Tchaikowsky's friends, and the first performance was given to the ten dedicatees in a private performance at the home of Charles and Lydia Napper on 22 January 1963.[28] Encouraged by the private success, Tchaikowsky performed the *Inventions* on 7 June 1968 on BBC Radio 3 (repeated on 22 July 1971). The pianist John Ogdon,

---

[26] Charles Fortier, interviewed by David Ferré, 28 December 1985, Paris.
[27] *The Chicago Daily Tribune*, 20 April 1959.
[28] Letter to Beatrice Harthan dated 19 December 1962.

The first page of the 1958 Piano Sonata

a supporter of Tchaikowsky, heard both the 1968 and 1971 BBC broadcasts. At the time, he was associated with the music publisher Novello and was selecting contemporary piano compositions for publication. He contacted Tchaikowsky, and by 1975 the *Inventions* had been published by Novello. In the decade and more between composition and publication, Tchaikowsky made some changes in the dedications (the revised dedication is given in brackets) and substituted a new piece for the original *Invention* No. 5:

1. *Allegretto tranquillo*; to Peter Feuchtwanger
2. *Adagio serio*; to Fou Ts'ong and Zamira Fou (Fou Ts'ong)
3. *Leggiero e vivace*; to Ilona Kabos
4. *Velocissimo*; to Robert Cornford
5a. *Semplice*; to Charles and Lydia Napper (deleted in published version)
5b. *Placido*; to Patrick Crommelynck (not in original manuscript)
6. *Con umore*; to Stefan and Anny Askenase (Stefan Askenase[29])
7. *Allegretto scherzando*; to Tamás Vásáry
8. *Vivacissimo*; to Sheldon and Alicia Rich
9. *Brusco*; 'To Wendy – or Beatrice? – Harthan'[30]
10. *Lento transparente*; to Michael Riddall

The first recording of the *Inventions* was made by the British pianist Colin Stone (who had briefly been coached by Tchaikowsky) for Merlin Records (MRFD 20033) in 2001. The *Inventions* were also performed in Bregenz on 20 July 2013 by Maciej Grzybowksi and reviewed in *Kultur*:

The Inventions op. 2 (1961–62) are short and concise pieces. The dedicatees are various personalities from the composer's circle and not least because of that each invention had an independent musical character. André Tchaikowsky built his works on distinctive motifs that were contrapuntally linked with one another. [ ] Interval relationships and the resulting tensions played a special role. Motivic lines sounded stringent and clearly interwoven

---

[29] Anny Ashkenase had died in the meantime.
[30] Beatrice Harthan was born in 1902 in England. She was trained as a musician and played the organ at her parish church. In 1925, she married a minister/missionary and moved to China. Her husband, observing her hard work with children, called her 'quite a Wendy-girl'. The nickname stuck and she is known as both Wendy and Beatrice. Beatrice was introduced to Tchaikowsky by Peter Feuchtwanger. If Stefan Askenase was Tchaikowsky's father-figure, then Beatrice was his mother-figure. She had a drill-sergeant personality but was supportive to struggling musicians. Tchaikowsky secretly harboured ambivalent feelings about her and the *Invention* is marked *Brusco* and *Grottesco*. Their relationship ended when one day he announced, 'I don't want to see you any more, Wendy'. When Harthan asked why, Tchaikowsky said: 'Because that is what I want, and if you go to my concerts, you must not go "round to see me afterwards"'.
E-mail from David Ferré to Anastasia Belina-Johnson, 17 September 2013

The dedicatees of the Inventions, left to right from the top: Peter Feuchtwanger, Fou Ts'ong, Ilona Kabos, Robert Cornford, Charles and Lydia Napper, Patrick Crommelynck, Stefan Askenase, Tamás Vásáry, Sheldon and Alicia Rich, Beatrice ('Wendy') Harthan and Michael Riddall

and also gathered in sonic concentrations. Some of them were treated as ostinato figures or linked together in a sweeping stream.[31]

Mazurka and Tango from *Six Dances for Piano* (1981)

The dances were commissioned by Stephen Kovacevich and are dedicated to him. Only the Mazurka and Tango were finished; Tchaikowsky arranged the Mazurka for piano duet and presented it to the Duo Crommelynck while he was at the Crommelynck home in Paris recovering from his cancer operation in January 1982. The original scores are held by Stephen Kovacevich and Josef Weinberger Ltd.

Works for Clarinet
Sonata for Clarinet and Piano (1959)

Tchaikowsky wrote the Sonata for Clarinet and Piano, Op. 1, for Michael Riddall and dedicated it to him. The premiere was given by Gervase de Peyer, clarinet, and André Tchaikowsky, piano, on 4 July 1966, for a BBC broadcast. The score was published in 1969 by Josef Weinberger, with the following programme note:

> A quiet, meditative opening explores the upper and lower reaches of both instruments' range: this is the first subject. The second subject is a brisk and rhythmical theme announced first by the clarinet, then taken up by the piano. A subsidiary theme follows a short cadenza and proceeds to develop the phraseology of the second theme, with anacrusic semi-quavers and wide intervallic movement. With the return of the broad and expansive first subject the development section commences; however, the accompaniment now highlights the melody by shifting from lively static octave embellishment to flurries of movement. The clarinet eventually joins the piano in a frenetic exchange over pedal points on A flat, and C sharp (the enharmonic tonic, though the work is not in any particular key). The recapitulation is fairly free in construction and includes a short solo section for the piano which ruminates on the first subject. The sonata closes with the clarinet becoming less apparent amidst the piano's singing melodies and ringing chords.

Performances of the Sonata for Clarinet and Piano include another BBC broadcast, with Janet Hilton, clarinet, and Peter Frankl, piano, on 17 June 1973 and a third BBC performance, again with Janet Hilton, this time with the composer, on a date that has eluded precision. The first live public performance took place on 27 October 1985, at the Wigmore Hall

---

[31] *Kultur,* review by Silvia Thurner, 27 July 2013 (http://kulturzeitschrift.at/kritiken/musik-konzert/eine-eindrueckliche-musikalische-begegnung-2013-inventionen-und-sonette-von-andre-tchaikowsky).

The Mazurka from the unfinished Six Dances for Piano

Gervase de Peyer with André Tchaikowsky, c. 1967

in London as part of the Josef Weinberger Centenary Concert Series, with Julian Jacobson, piano, and Anthony Lamb, clarinet. Gervase de Peyer performed it on 14 January 1987, at Merkin Hall in New York City with Carol Archer, piano, and in London on 12 February 1987, with Gwenneth Pryor, piano.

Arioso e Fuga per Clarinetto Solo (1964–65)
When Tchaikowsky met the clarinettist Gervase de Peyer, then first chair in the London Symphony Orchestra (a position he held from 1956 until 1973) and a founder-member (in 1950) of the Melos Ensemble, he promised to write him a solo work for clarinet. The result was the *Arioso e Fuga per Clarinetto Solo*, dedicated to de Peyer. It received its world premiere in Bregenz on 22 July 2013 by Heinz-Peter Linshalm. The original manuscript is kept in the Josef Weinberger archives.

Works for Voice
Two Songs after Poems by William Blake (1960)
This work was composed between March and May 1960 in London and Paris and is scored for soprano, oboe, flute, violin, cello and harpsichord. Tchaikowsky selected 'The Lamb' (from William Blake's *Songs of Innocence*) and 'The Tyger' (from his *Songs of Experience*). It was his first composition for voice, preceding his song-cycles *Seven Sonnets of Shakespeare* (1967)

and *Ariel* (1969). The work has never been performed and the original manuscript is held in the Josef Weinberger archives.

Seven Sonnets of Shakespeare (1967)

Tchaikowsky met the contralto Margaret Cable at the Dartington Summer School in 1965 and, impressed by her abilities, wrote for her the *Seven Sonnets of Shakespeare*.

Fascinated by Shakespeare and able to recite much of his work extensively from memory, Tchaikowsky chose the following sonnets:

No. 104, 'To me fair friend you never can be old'
No. 75, 'So are you to my thoughts as food to life'
No. 49, 'Against that time (if ever that time come)'
No. 61, 'Is it thy will, thy image should keep open'
No. 89, 'Say that thou didst forsake me for some fault'
No. 90, 'Then hate me when thou wilt, if ever, now'
No. 146, 'Poor soul the centre of my sinful earth'

Cable, to whom the work is dedicated, premiered it on 18 June 1968 in a BBC broadcast from the Royal Festival Hall, London, accompanied by the composer. The first public performance took place four days later, in the Purcell Room next door. Tchaikowsky wrote about the concert in a letter to Halina Janowska:

> A week ago there was the first performance of my song cycle, *Seven Sonnets of Shakespeare*. There were quite a few musicians there: Andrzej Panufnik and his wife [Camilla Jessel], Daniel Barenboim and his wife [Jacqueline du Pre], Gervase de Peyer, and Fou Ts'ong's wife. Fou Ts'ong was playing somewhere that evening. It turned out the cycle is first class, undoubtedly better than anything I've written so far. As a result, Andrzej Panufnik's wife gave birth to a child two weeks prematurely, but the baby seems to be normal.[32] The cycle went like a bomb. The audience was delighted, the reviews were terrible, so everything was as it should be, and I'm happy with one and the other.[33]

The cycle was never published, although it received both the broadcast and public premieres as well as another performance in Amsterdam in the same year; it was revived in Warsaw in 2007 and in Kraków in 2010. On 20 July 2013 in Bregenz the cycle was performed by Urszula Kryger and Maciej Grzybowski.

---

[32] The baby became distinctive later in life, as the composer Roxanna Panufnik.
[33] Letter dated 29 June 1968.

The sonnets chosen by Tchaikowsky are dark and speak of unhappy or doomed love; an atmosphere of heavy foreboding permeates the entire work. The music is inventive, descriptive and starkly emotional; with it the composer paints a world devoid of hope and full of sorrow and unfulfilled dreams. In the fifth sonnet the pianist has to play the piano strings either pushing the hammers directly or by plucking them, and at times some piano keys have to be pressed silently. The resulting silence between sounds is striking. A visual equivalent might be Edvard Munch's *The Scream* (1893), in which the scream, although silent, is also deafening in its emotional intensity.

Ariel (1969)

Ariel is a set of three songs from Shakespeare's *The Tempest*, scored for mezzo soprano, flute, oboe, clarinet in A, horn in F, bassoon, piano/celesta and harp. The premiere took place on 7 October 1977, in St John's, Smith Square, London, performed by Margaret Cable and the Melos Ensemble, with the composer playing the celesta.

In 1974 Tchaikowsky had met Chad Varah,[34] rector of St Stephen Walbrook in London, and founder of the Samaritans, who, believing that all of his compositions should be heard in concert, arranged for a performance of *Ariel*. Varah described the circumstances of the concert:

> André told me that the only work of pure genius amongst his compositions to date was *Ariel*. He said it will never be performed because it is for nine instruments, including a mezzo soprano, and who can afford to gather nine soloists for a piece that lasts five minutes? I told André that I was determined he should have a performance. I said that he should not go to his grave without hearing his work of genius. What I did was arrange a concert at St John's, Smith Square, in aid of the restoration of the church, St Stephen Walbrook, and worked out a programme that would use the players in other compositions.
>
> […] We assembled the requisite players and André played the piano himself and also played the celesta. He said jokingly afterwards it had been rather expensive to hire the celesta, which was largely a visual aid because the sound from it was so slight. You could see him playing, but you could hardly hear him. […] This was the only time I was ever annoyed by André. We had arranged for a professional recording van to be parked outside St John's, Smith Square, and made a recording of the whole concert, but particularly to make a separate little tape of *Ariel*. Margaret Cable missed a bar in the performance. It didn't ruin the whole thing, but it left a little bit out, and André was so

---

[34] *Cf.* p. 102, above.

disappointed with the tape, because it wasn't 100 percent perfect that he had it destroyed. I took the view that, since I had paid for this concert, for his pleasure, even if he didn't like the tape, he ought to have given it to me, or at least mentioned it to me before having it destroyed.[35]

The tape Tchaikowsky destroyed cost £83 to produce. The concert was reviewed by Max Harrison in *The Times*:

The sensitive melodic lines, expressively sung by Margaret Cable, indicate a style that is astringently romantic rather than in any way modern. The most interesting sections of the instrumental part were the interludes, which are quite densely contrapuntal. However, Mr Tchaikowsky's ensemble scoring was effective throughout, each detail pulling its weight. *Ariel* was, in fact, an agreeable piece, well crafted, although not at all memorable.[36]

Ariel was performed in Denmark in 1985. The music has never been published and, after these two performances, has never been heard again publicly. The work is dedicated to Robert Erwin, a New Zealand friend. The manuscript is held in the Josef Weinberger archives.

Works for Violin
Concerto Classico for Violin and Orchestra (1962–64)
The composition of the *Concerto Classico* started immediately after Tchaikowsky met Sylvia Rosenberg in Stockholm in March 1962. By the time of its completion in July 1964, Tchaikowsky and Rosenberg were close friends and had even formed a piano-violin duo, giving concerts and broadcasting on the BBC. Tchaikowsky completed the scoring of the concerto, wrote a piano reduction, and dedicated the work to Rosenberg, but the friendship became strained, and the concerto was put aside. Many years later, there was a complete reconciliation and their thoughts turned back to the concerto, but Tchaikowsky died before any kind of performance could be scheduled. The manuscript, now in the Josef Weinberger archives, was found after Tchaikowsky's death among other papers at the bottom of a laundry box at the home of Eve Harrison.

Five Miniatures for Violin and Piano (1981)
Tchaikowsky had agreed to form a piano-and-violin duo with Kyung-wha Chung for an Italian tour in April–June 1983, and was preparing a set of *Five Miniatures* for performance in Trieste, Perugia, Florence, Genoa and Turin. Unusually, Tchaikowsky proposed to perform his own music.

---

[35] Chad Varah, interviewed by David Ferré, 11 August 1987, London. *Cf.* also p. 196, above
[36] 8 October 1977.

The first page of the solo part of the Concerto Classico

The composition was to be dedicated to Kyung-Wha Chung but was left unfinished at Tchaikowsky's death in June 1982. Chung considered playing the reduced suite for her concert tour, but there was insufficient material, and the suite remains unperformed. Three of the five miniatures are nonetheless complete in sketch form and are in the Josef Weinberger archives.

String Quartets
String Quartet No.1 in A major, Op. 3 (1969–70)
The First String Quartet consists of four movements: *Pastorale*, *Notturno*, *Scherzo* and *Variazione*. It was a present to Stefan Askenase on his 75th

birthday, in the celebrations of which Tchaikowsky took part. The premiere took place at Bad Godesberg, Germany, on 10 July 1971, with the Lindsay Quartet. The Lindsays played it again, on 18 November 1971, for the BBC in London, and then a live performance was given on 15 March 1972, in London. The quartet was published by Josef Weinberger in 1974.

String Quartet No.2 in C major (1973–75)

Like the First String Quartet, the Second was dedicated to Stefan Askenase and presented at his 80th birthday. Tchaikowsky wrote his own programme notes:

> In July 1971, the Lindsay Quartet gave the first performance of my first quartet and immediately suggested I write another. I was flattered by the request and eager to show my gratitude. But I could think of nothing more to say in the medium and was afraid of repeating myself, so I merely promised to think about it. Some months later, I heard the Lindsay Quartet play the Shostakovich sixth quartet. The slow movement of that work is a simple and beautiful passacaglia, a form I should never have dared to attempt in a string quartet for fear of boring the cellist. Bernard Gregor-Smith suggested a passacaglia with a varied bass, and this immediately helped to focus my ideas. Even then, the cellist was still restricted to going 'round in circles', so I decided to compensate in the outer movements by giving him conspicuous and flamboyant solos. The next logical step was to extend the concertante treatment to the other players. This at once allayed my fears of producing an identical twin of my first quartet, in which my chief aim had been a close-knit truly chamber texture, and I now relished all the display I had denied myself before: high positions, single and double harmonics, quick alternations or arcato and pizzicato, and so on. It was quite a surprise that, with all of this, the new quartet is easier than the first. Dynamically, the work is shaped like a 'V'. The first movement is a rapid, tense sonata, which calms down towards the end to set the mood for the sombre passacaglia. The last movement is a continuous accelerando. As its speed increases, so does the resemblance to the first movement from which it is derived.

The Lindsays premiered the String Quartet No. 2 at St John's, Smith Square, on 23 January 1978, in a performance broadcast by the BBC, but after only a few performances the group had to put the work aside in favour of other repertoire. Josef Weinberger published the Second Quartet in 1980. The dedication in the published version was changed to the Lindsay String Quartet.

The work was also performed in Bregenz on 21 July 2013 by the Meccorre String Quartet from Poland: Wojciech Koprowski and Magdalena Makowska, violins; Michał Bryła, viola; Karol Marianowski, cello. The

The opening pages of Tchaikowsky's two string quartets
(No. 1 marked up for the typesetter)

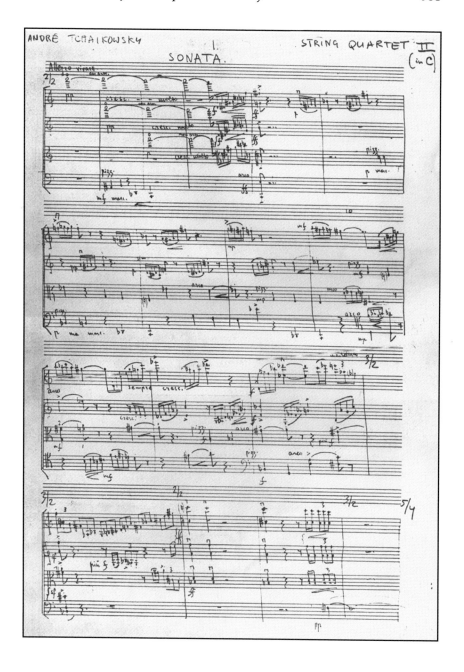

reviews noted the intricacy , serious nature and contrapuntal writing of the work, and its affinity with Shostakovich's Sixth String Quartet.[37]

Other Chamber Works
Octet (1961)
Dedicated to Anny Askenase, the Octet is scored for clarinet, horn, bassoon, two violins, viola, cello and double-bass. Tchaikowsky did nothing to promote a performance of his work and it remains unperformed. The original score is held in the Weinberger Tchaikowsky archives in London.

Trio Notturno, Op. 6 (1978)
Peter Frankl, pianist in the Frankl-Pauk-Kirshbaum Trio, wanted something for his ensemble and in 1976 asked Tchaikowsky for a composition. Tchaikowsky recorded the request in his diary on 1 August 1978.[38] The composer wrote his own programme notes:

> Some years ago Hans Keller gave a lecture at Dartington about the basic incompatibility of piano and strings. Classical harmony, he explained, used to bridge the gap. With the decline of tonality it became all but impossible to blend the disparate sounds. 'All right, Hans,' I said, 'if ever I write anything for piano and strings it shall be dedicated to you.'
>
> And so it is. When Peter Frankl asked me to write for his trio, I naturally remembered Hans Keller's warning – or challenge – and my promise. I decided to tackle the problem head on by emphasising the disparity of the instruments. This in turn led me to conceive the whole work as a study in contrast, and I did all I could to increase the polarity of the two movements.
>
> Thus the *Allegro* is a movement of extreme rhythmic irregularity, full of short abrupt phrases and swift changes of register, with a preference for the dark low notes of the piano, while the *Andante* is a calm lyrical movement without a single change of metre, full of flowing melodic lines and clear, crystalline harmonies. And, lest the contrast thus attained prove too 'pat', I wrote an agitated central section, culminating in the climax of the entire work and followed by a sudden silence, a shortened recapitulation and a long, static, reminiscent coda. It is as if Florestan had briefly invaded Eusebius' territory,[39] before being finally subdued.

[37] Silvia Thurner, 'Eine eindrückliche musikalische Begegnung – Inventionen und Sonette von André Tchaikowsky, *Kultur*, 27 July 2013 (http://kulturzeitschrift.at/kritiken/musik-konzert/eine-eindrueckliche-musikalische-begegnung-2013-inventionen-und-sonette-von-andre-tchaikowsky); Fritz Jurmann. 'Ein 'Treffen' der Musikrevolutionäre', *Voralberger Nachrichten*, 23 July 2013 (http://www.vorarlbergernachrichten.at/kultur/2013/07/22/ein-treffen-der-musikrevolutionare.vn).
[38] *Cf.* p. 223, above.
[39] A reference to Robert Schumann's two opposing artistic personalities.

The *Trio Notturno* was first performed at Tchaikowsky's funeral on 2 July 1982, and officially premiered on 4 July 1982 at the Cheltenham Festival. William Mann wrote in *The Times*:

> Having pledged himself to balance anew the unwieldy, sometimes inequitable, partnership of violin and cello with modern grand piano, [Tchaikowsky] proposed a linear basic texture, its outlines ornate, almost baroque, rich in harmonic density, passionately argumentative in expression. The two abruptly contrasted movements challenge instrumental virtuosity at every turn; they might have sounded simply hard going, but were revealed, with formidable cogency, as invigorating to play, and listen to, especially in the rapid middle section of the second movement, an alarmingly brilliant feat of imagination. [...] Textural considerations are paramount in the *Trio Notturno*. It was inspired by an allegation (from the ever-provocative Hans Keller, to whom the work is dedicated) that piano and strings are basically incompatible. André Tchaikowsky approached the problem in much the same way as Bartók did in the two mature violin sonatas, emphasising the differences rather than attempting to effect a compromise.
>
> The *Trio Notturno* is thus not the most comfortable work written for violin, cello and piano. It is, however, despite its echoes of Bartók, one of the most original and personal of its kind. The silence observed by the audience at the end – although the composer himself might have preferred applause to reward an admirably dedicated first performance – was an appropriate reaction to a work of such integrity.[40]

The Frankl-Pauk-Kirshbaum Trio performed the work worldwide. Other trios have performed the *Trio Notturno* in concert, including the violinist Daniel Phillips, cellist Carter Brey and pianist Edward Auer at the Sante Fe Chamber Music Festival on 9 August 1983, and the Capricorn Ensemble on 10 November 1985 in the Wigmore Hall. The Frankl-Pauk-Kirshbaum performance in the Library of Congress in Washington, DC, on 13 December 1985 was broadcast on National Public Radio.

As part of the Tchaikowsky programme in Bregenz in 2013, the *Trio Notturno* was performed by the Altenberg Trio: Christoph Hinterhuber, piano; Amiram Ganz, violin; and Christoph Stradner, cello, on 30 July in the Kunsthaus, Bregenz.[41]

The *Trio Notturno* was published by Josef Weinberger in 1982.

---

[40] 5 July 1982.

[41] A review by Silvia Thurner was published on 31 July 2013, and can be viewed at http://kulturzeitschrift.at/kritiken/musik-konzert/gute-musiker-maessige-werke-2013-das-altenberg-trio-wien-spielte-das-einzige-kammerkonzert-im-rahmen-der-201ekunst-aus-der-zeit201c-bei-den-bregenzer-festspielen.

Incidental Music
Hamlet (1966)

Tchaikowsky's close friend Michael Menaugh was an actor who, scheduled to appear in an Oxford production of *Hamlet* in 1966, asked Tchaikowsky if he would compose music for it. He remembers:

> He agreed and he was fascinated by Hamlet. It was one of those plays that he knew particularly well, and it obsessed him just as it obsessed me. We had a big correspondence about the play. He came three days before the performance and supervised the recording of the music. He was a great help to me during a very tense time because it's no easy matter to both direct and play Hamlet at the same time.[42]

The originals of the music for *Hamlet* are in possession of Michael Menaugh, who kindly provided the description of four parts:

> Part 1 – Fanfare and Entrance of the Players (Act II; Scene II)
> Part 2 – Entrance of the Players (Act II, Scene II) (continued)
> Part 3 – Fortinbras' Army (at the bottom there is a note: 'Col Legno: Sticks only, beaten against each other' ...where col legno is an instruction to strike the string with the stick of the bow, rather than by drawing the hair of the bow across the strings. This results in a quiet but eerie percussive sound.
> Part 4 – Fortinbras' Army (continued).

Opera
The Merchant of Venice (1968–82), Op. 7

Opera in three acts and an epilogue after William Shakespeare
Libretto by John O'Brien

Roles:
Jessica – high soprano
Portia – mezzo-dramatic soprano
Nerissa – mezzo-soprano
Antonio – countertenor
Bassanio – tenor
Lorenzo – lyric tenor
Shylock – baritone
Salerio – baritone
Solanio – bass
Gratiano – bass

---

[42] Michael Menaugh, interviewed by David Ferré, 1 December 1987, Brazil.

Duke of Venice – bass
A boy – soprano
Aragon and Prince of Morocco, suitors to Portia (unsung roles)
SATB Chorus: People of Venice and Boys' Chorus
Augmented full orchestra
Stage Band:
descant recorder
treble recorder
lute
oboe d'amore in A
oboe da caccia in F
two bassoons
harpsichord
tabor

Except for the last 24 bars of orchestration (completed after the composer's death by Alan Bousted[43]), the work that took Tchaikowsky almost a quarter of a century was finished at his death. It was completed and published, in both full score and piano reduction, using the memorial fund established by his friends and literary executors.

John O'Brien and Tchaikowsky met in London, at Finchden Manor, where O'Brien directed theatrical productions. In spring 1968, they decided to work on an opera together, at first planning to use the dialogue in Act V of Shakespeare's *The Merchant of Venice*. O'Brien remembers:

> Quite soon after that, he said, 'Why don't we try an entire opera, the entire *The Merchant of Venice*? I think it must have occurred to him that it would, as an opera, give him an opportunity to look at a whole lot of fairly crucial things in his life. At first it seemed odd, that he, a Jew, would want to take Shylock on, particularly at a time when there was a feeling that Shakespeare was anti-Semitic, which is a nonsensical thing anyway. There was the portrayal of some anti-Jewish feeling, yes, but that's not the same as anti-Semitism. This was really the starting point of the opera.[44]

---

[43] British composer, orchestrator and conductor (1931–2001), best known as a much-sought-after music copyist working for most of the larger London publishers (he was very accurate) and the copyist of choice for several composers (Peter Maxwell Davies, amongst others). He completed Arthur Benjamin's last opera *Tartuffe*, conducting its premiere in 1964 in Sadler's Wells. For Josef Weinberger, Bousted worked as copyist for many orchestral works and prepared full scores for operettas by Lehár and Kálmán, and reconstructed the original nonet version of Brahms' *Serenade* in D.

[44] John O'Brien, interviewed by David Ferré, 2 January 1987, New York.

John O'Brien, librettist of The Merchant of Venice, *in 1964*

O'Brien began writing the libretto, and Tchaikowsky left for an extended tour of Australia. They exchanged letters when in different countries, and met to discuss the work when Tchaikowsky was back in England. By 1970 the libretto had begun to take shape, and in the summer of that year, while Tchaikowsky and O'Brien were on a working holiday in Corsica, they made so much progress that libretto was finished in three weeks. In August 1972 Tchaikowsky showed the opera to Hans Keller, who expressed his astonishment at its quality.

By the summer of 1978 about two-thirds of the opera was composed. Finally, on 1 October 1980, Tchaikowsky wrote to Michael Menaugh:

Dear Michael,
Rejoice with me – I have finished *The Merchant of Venice*! It took Hans to convince me that I really had. I kept fussing and fiddling with it, changing tiny details that I would then change back to their previous version, merely because I couldn't adjust to the new situation. Hans then offered to write to Lord Harewood, who is chairman of the ENO [English National Opera], on my behalf. I doubt whether his recommendation can override the English economic crisis, but it is good to see him so impressed.

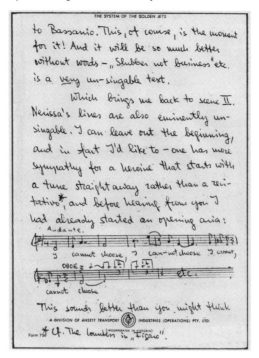

*Tchaikowsky writes to John O'Brien from Australia in 1968
to discuss* The Merchant of Venice

A play-through was scheduled at the English National Opera, with Hans
Keller's help, for 21 December 1981. In attendance were the director of
the ENO, Lord Harewood, orchestra director Mark Elder, director David
Pountney, chorus-master Hazel Vivienne, a staff pianist and Tchaikowsky.[45]

Hans Keller wrote another letter of recommendation in July 1984:

> I am intimately acquainted with André Tchaikowsky's opera, *The Merchant of
> Venice*, and have no hesitation in describing it as an outstanding work, both
> musically and theatrically. For those of us who knew André Tchaikowsky's
> previous compositions, the considerable musical substance and weight of the
> work did not come as a surprise; but that a composer, however inventive,
> should write his first opera as if he had developed his sense for the theatre
> over many years is surely a surprising fact which one could almost honour
> with the adjective 'sensational'.
>
> There are many successful operas which aren't half as stage-worthy as is
> Tchaikowsky's opera; what is even more striking is that every crucial dramatic

---

[45] *Cf.* pp. 328–34, above.

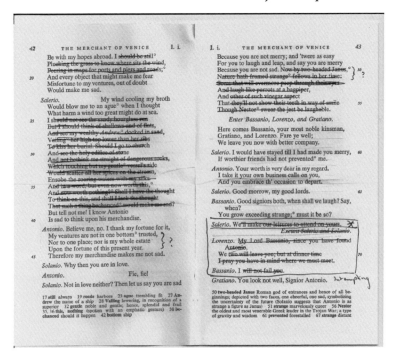

An example of John O'Brien's cuts to Shakespeare's text

corner is supported by music which would retain its fascination if one had no idea of the dramatic situation to which it applied. Needless to add, I would be able and prepared to substantiate this considered opinion in detail, on the basis of the score. Meanwhile, let it be said that, although the composer's style is very eclectic, there isn't a phrase, not a harmony, in the entire score which doesn't disclose his clearly and well defined creative personality.[46]

Susan Bradshaw wrote to Eve Harrison on 30 July 1984:

Dear Eve,
Having just finished making the vocal score of André Tchaikowsky's opera, *The Merchant of Venice*, I thought I must write and tell you what an outstanding work I feel it to be, particularly in the way it manages to communicate all the passionate involvement that went into its composition. There is a wealth of striking detail here, both musical and dramatic (in the glittering orchestration as well as on stage) and the vocal lines, though not always easy, are intensely singable throughout. I am confident that the work will one day be given the full stage production it undoubtedly deserves as a significant contribution

---

[46] A copy of this (undated) letter is kept by Eve Harrison in her André Tchaikowsky archive.

to the modern operatic repertoire (and one with a good chance of appealing to the opera-going public); meanwhile, wouldn't it be wonderful if we could manage to arrange a concert performance, to whet the appetite, so to speak.

The composer's dying wish was for the opera to be performed.

Synopsis by Keith Warner:

Act 1

Venice. A city full of ambiguities but also a mercantile trading centre of worldwide notoriety. The Merchant, Antonio, is depressed. Two tabloid journalists, Salerio and Solanio, are always hanging around picking up or creating gossip. Gratiano is there, too, looking for any opportunity to advance. We discover that Antonio's great friend (and much desired) Bassanio wants him to stand surety for a loan: Bassanio needs money to pursue his courtship with an heiress, Portia. Unfortunately, all of Antonio's capital is bound up in a series of shipping interests – all currently at sea. He must seek a loan to help his friend. Shylock, a Jew, is much maligned by the majority Christians but nonetheless he agrees to loan Antonio the three thousand ducats needed. They make a half-joking agreement that if the surety fails, Antonio will forfeit a pound of his own flesh as recompense.

On the day of a wild street carnival, Jessica, Shylock's teenage daughter, is kept locked up at home; her mother, Leah, has died. Jessica hates her father's overbearing control of her life. While Shylock is away, arranging the loan for Antonio, her secret pursuer, Lorenzo, enters ever-ready to carry her and her father's riches off. She agrees to convert to Christianity and marry him. She passes him a love letter as his friends help him arrange and then enact her elopement that very night, and most importantly they revel in the robbing of Shylock's riches. Ever more distraught, Antonio and Gratiano meet and discuss Bassanio's imminent departure to win Portia. Antonio and Bassanio bid each other farewell. Shylock returns to discover his daughter gone and his house robbed – the crowd only mock him. He swears revenge.

Act 2

Belmont. A lakeside country house. Portia complains about her life to her companion, Nerissa. Portia, according to her father's will, can only marry a suitor choosing her portrait from one of three caskets: gold, silver and lead. The princes of Aragon and Morocco fail the test, while her servants and guests look on amused.

Gratiano arrives to introduce Bassanio, but Nerissa is immediately eyeing him as potential partner for herself. Bassanio enters, very eager to get on with the competition and choose the right casket. Portia counsels prudence, while Nerissa sets up the trial. He chooses the lead casket – and wins his bride. They celebrate their betrothal as Nerissa and Gratiano also announce their marital intentions.

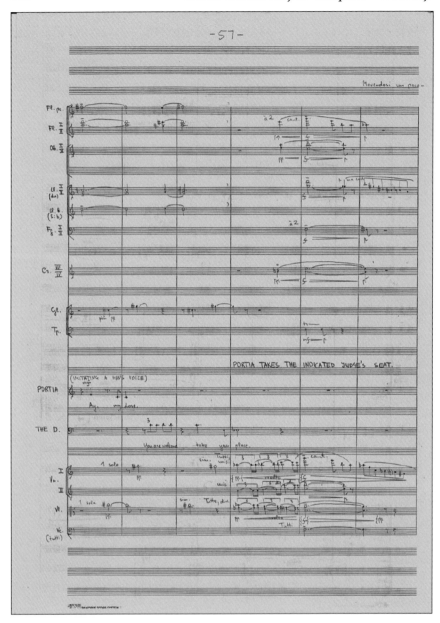

Two pages from the full score of The Merchant of Venice

A letter arrives from Antonio with Jessica and Lorenzo and Solanio. It reveals Antonio is ruined and his fortune lost. Shylock is insisting on the forfeiture of his bond being paid: one pound of flesh. Portia counsels her new husband's return to Venice. Meanwhile, she says, she and Nerissa will await their men's return in a nearby cloister.

Act 3
Venice. Outside the courthouse, Solanio and Solerio bait Shylock teasing him about his dead wife's ring, which they say Jessica stole and sold wantonly to further her new 'Christian' lifestyle. Shylock is driven mad by sorrow and anger. Even when Antonio enters and tries to calm him, he promises no mercy.

The courtroom. The duke of Venice counsels prudence on all sides, but Shylock simply and unwaveringly demands his pound of flesh. Portia and Nerissa arrive disguised as a young lawyer and his clerk. They are not recognised. Despite recommending mercy from Shylock he will not relent and Antonio is prepared for the knife. At the last moment, Portia brings up a point of law. Although his bond allows him the flesh, it does not allow for any drop of blood to be spilled. On top, for threatening a Christian life by his claim, Shylock must beg for mercy or be executed himself, lose all his property and convert to Christianity. His life shattered, he stumbles from the courtroom, attacked by the crowd, as the others rejoice. Portia and Nerissa, still disguised as the lawyers, ask for the two rings they originally gave as wedding tokens to Bassanio and Gratiano, as payment for their successful legal advice. Out of gratitude, the men feel obliged to comply.

Epilogue
Belmont. The atmosphere is dreamy and melancholic – Jessica and Lorenzo sing of an idealised love. Portia and Nerissa, now changed back to their own clothes again, demand their rings back from their husbands, who can only bluff their excuses. Finally all is resolved with the revelation of the truth. The men are forgiven. Antonio joins the lovers, saved, rich again, but still sadly depressed.[47]

The opera is a real testament to Tchaikowsky's talent and predilection for stage and drama. It is unusual, for a composer about to enter into his prime, to create a first work in the genre so well crafted and dramatically impressive. It is obvious that Tchaikowsky found his own voice almost, it seems, effortlessly. His music cannot be easily explained in terms of influences, or associations with other composers: he had his own individual interpretations, and he presented his ideas in music with mastery. Complex

[47] Keith Warner, synopsis for the programme at the Bregenz Festspiele, 2013.

textures in the orchestra form a kind of spider's web reflecting the complexity of human emotions.

There is no musical copying in *The Merchant of Venice*. Even if one hears a bar or two that are reminiscent of a composer such as Berg or Bartók, it remains but a flash that never develops in that style. The conductor of the Bregenz premiere, Eric Nielsen, believes that Tchaikowsky knew and must have studied early music, particularly Bach's *Musical Offering,* because the echoes of Bach and Beethoven are heard in his use of short motifs that generate layers of musical material.[48] The orchestral writing is polyphonic and contrapuntal, with very difficult instrumental parts, such as highly chromatic timpani and virtuosic woodwind.

Tchaikowsky was also clearly well acquainted with French grand opera, as can be seen in his adroitly humorous characterisation of the Princes of Aragon and Morocco, the two roles that require no singing. Flashes of French influence extend to the way Tchaikowsky tries to avoid dissonances and to the spacing of intervals so as to create an impressionistic sound. Indeed, the music often sounds consonant because of the space created by wide intervals, even if the notes involved, put closer together, would have sounded dissonant.

The notation is precise, and everything is articulated clearly in the score (down to whistles, laughs, knocks and key-turns), which makes it both easier and harder for the singers and orchestral players. It is obvious from the composer's very clear directions that he is asking the performers to do what he writes, and does not easily encourage 'interpretation'.

The Merchant of Venice is not 'about' being Jewish, nor is it about anti-Semitism. It is about alienation from society, from self. Shylock and Antonio are alienated for different reasons, but the result is the same – loneliness, sadness, not being understood. The opera ends with a seemingly happy resolution, with all lovers united, and with Antonio's flesh intact, but the intense melancholy in the ending reminds the audience about one man who was humiliated in his last hours in society and another who will always be alone even among friends. David Pountney wrote about the opera:

> In the very limited world of English language opera, the impact of *The Merchant of Venice* is considerable. After all, the competition is thin. The greatest English language opera composer of that era, Britten, ducked the issue of a serious Shakespeare, and his *Midsummer Night's Dream* is a skilful, charming but slight affair. There was, as I recall, a rather unfortunate shot at Hamlet by Humphrey Searle with, to the audible relief of the Covent

---

[48] Conversation with Anastasia Belina-Johnson, 16 July 2013, Bregenz.

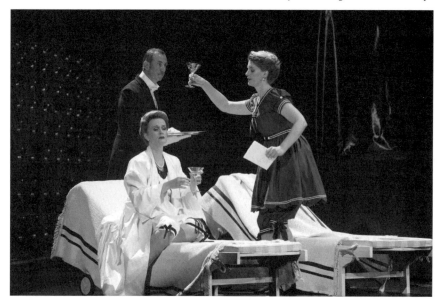

Scenes from the Bregenz premiere of The Merchant of Venice:
*Act II, Belmont Scene : Portia (Anna-Magdalena Hoffman) complains
that she cannot choose a suitor*

*Act II, Court Scene: uproar ensues as Shylock (Adrian Eröd) rejects the payment
of forfeit from Bassanio (Charles Workman)*

Act II, Casket Scene: the Princes of Aragon and Morocco (Juliusz Kubiak and Elliot Lebogang Mohlamme) try to choose the casket containing Portia's portrait.

Act III, Epilogue. Antonio (Christopher Ainslie) attempts to deal with the traumatic experience of the Court Scene

Garden audience, the Players scene done as a Tchaikovsky parody – not *this* Tchaikovsky obviously. Walton's *Troilus and Cressida* is worthy but not more, and Samuel Barber's *Antony and Cleopatra* is a failure *d'estime,* and Reimann offered a very strident and, to my ears, extremely crude version of *Lear*, composed in German of course. So Tchaikowsky's subtle, intelligent and well-paced version of one of Shakespeare's most serious and at the same time problematic plays is a hugely significant contribution to the repertoire.

The Merchant of Venice itself is another obvious example of time, fashion and history transforming the meaning of a work of art. Shakespeare may well have originally imagined Shylock as a comic character who when he discovers that his daughter has eloped, cannot quite decide which he mourns most: 'My daughter, my ducats, my daughter, my ducats.' But such is Shakespeare's genius and instinctive sensibility that he cannot help creating an ambiguous space in which sympathy for Shylock can grow. As in the case of Malvolio, we come to be shocked, horrified even, by the spectacle of a man we have begun by despising and ridiculing destroying himself before our eyes – the smile slowly freezing on our faces. No doubt Tchaikowsky perceived the musical possibilities of this transformation, and his music grasps the opportunity to re-define Shylock in the course of the piece as a tragic figure.

Tchaikowsky may be expected to identify with Shylock, although he always resisted overt identification with Jewish causes or identity, but perhaps identified even more closely with another character, Antonio, who speaks the opening lines of the play:

In sooth, I know not why I am so sad:
It wearies me; you say it wearies you;
But how I caught it, found it, or came by it,
What stuff 'tis made of, whereof it is born,
I am to learn;
And such a want-wit sadness makes of me
That I have much ado to know myself.

This touching definition of depression – even if time had not yet invented that term as a medical condition – is a remarkable opening to a comedy, and together with the implication that Antonio's fatal loan to Bassanio is made as much under the influence of homo-erotic attraction as pure friendship, suggests that there may be an element of self-portraiture here. Of course the fact that Antonio makes the loan to his friend precisely so that the latter can go off and woo a woman gives added piquancy to its consequences. I have the feeling that Tchaikowsky would have deeply understood that. And there is one final melancholy point to observe about the piece. It oscillates between a male world of money, men and malice and a female world of music, love and laughter. When all are enfolded in love and laughter at the end of the play, two men are left out in the cold to contemplate the silence: Shylock and Antonio.

I suspect that was as important to Tchaikowsky in his choice of material as the redemption of the Jew.[49]

In *The Merchant of Venice* every character was equally important to Tchaikowsky, where even the shortest roles are given multi-faceted musical treatment. Tchaikowsky's identification with Antonio is perhaps the reason he makes his character more clearly homosexual than does Shakespeare. It is evident through the very first opening lines that allude to Antonio's melancholy, and through the choice of counter tenor, a possible allusion to homosexuality. Falling intervals in Antonio's vocal part reflect his depression, and the melodic writing is that of word-painting. Whenever Antonio sings of hope, the vocal line goes upwards, but inevitably it ends in disappointment and downward slopes. 'I am so sad' is a defining line of this character. In the 1970s, when Tchaikowsky was working on *The Merchant,* writing for counter tenor was still in development, and not many composers used this voice in their compositions. Tchaikowsky's writing for counter tenor is somewhat lower than usual, by at least three to five pitches. As a result the lower register of the voice is occasionally lost in rich orchestral textures – a point Tchaikowsky would have undoubtedly addressed had he been able to hear the opera performed.

Shylock is perhaps the major role in the opera. Musically, there are some stock Jewish intervals that are reminiscent of synagogue-type of singing, such as a touching 'I pray you let me go from here' in the court scene in Act II. There is also a *bel canto* element, and word-painting, as with Antonio. When Shylock mocks Antonio in Act I, imitating his high voice, the effect is striking, and would not have been easily achieved had the roles been written for similar voices. Shylock's identifying instrument is trombone, which plays only when Shylock is on stage, or a reference to him has been made.

In the vocal part of Shylock's daughter Jessica, Jewishness, although not as obvious as that of her father, is still a part of her musical characterisation. The opening of Jessica's part is very melodious, and it is especially beautiful when she sings of her love for Lorenzo.

Tchaikowsky's Portia is a dramatic soprano, who must have tremendous volume and agility and at the same time be able to be lyrical. Both power and stamina are required of her in the court scene that demands dramatic intensity, but also humour when she asks Bassanio to give her his wedding ring.

---

[49] Quoted in Anastasia Belina-Johnson (ed.), *André Tchaikowsky: Die tägliche Mühe ein Mensch zu sein,* Wolke Verlag, Hofheim am Taunus, 2013, pp. 12–14.

The two non-singing characters are the Princes of Morocco and Aragon, Portia's suitors. Tchaikowsky's music is so sensitive to stage action that the two are inseparable. The scene with the caskets in Act II is witty, sarcastic and hugely entertaining. There is a parody of Tchaikovsky's Symphony No. 4, heard in the bassoon, when the supremely vain Prince of Aragon admires his reflection in a mirror. For those who knew André Tchaikowsky's intense dislike of his Russian namesake's music because of what he thought was exaggerated romanticism and overstated emotion, this allusion does not come as a surprise. Wagner's 'curse motif' from *The Ring* also makes an appearance in Act II, when Portia gives Bassanio the ring. Tchaikowsky uses it as texture, rather than a motif, thus disassociating the motif from Wagner's.

The Merchant of Venice finishes with an Epilogue which presents a complete change of mood and location. The lovers are reunited, the loss of rings is explained to Portia and Nerissa, the true identity of the young lawyer and clerk are revealed to Bassanio and Gratiano, and everyone retires to enjoy marital bliss – apart, that is, from Antonio and Shylock. The bliss of happy couples is a sharp contrast to the two lonely figures who will continue along their paths alone.

Early Reviews

The reviews published after the world premiere on 18 July 2013 in the Bregenz Festspiele show that the opera impressed many commentators. For example, *The Financial Times* published Shirley Apthorp's account, which states that

> Tchaikowsky's music [...] defies attribution to any one definite style of 20th-century composition. The score is intricate and dark, with moments of both brutality and lyricism, not to mention flashes of acerbic wit. Shakespeare's theme of the tension between mercy and justice fascinated the composer. It is hard to imagine who else could have set this opera with such lack of pathos and so refined a sense of ambivalence.[50]

The review in *The New York Times* tried to 'identify' the music of the opera in familiar terms:

> Its music, complex and impressively crafted, is basically atonal, yet it can accommodate late-Romantic expressiveness in a way that recalls Alban Berg.

---

[50] Shirley Apthorp, '*The Merchant of Venice*, Bregenz Festival, Austria – review', *The Financial Times*, 22 July 2013 (www.ft.com/cms/s/2/d1ac5a6a-f2b3-11e2-a203-00144feabdc0.html#axzz2bE7T13Dc; accessed on 18 August 2013).

It also has recourse to other idioms when they can serve the drama. For instance, just before the introduction of Shylock – a character Tchaikowsky must have identified with – brooding woodwinds articulate a lugubrious, vaguely Oriental theme surely meant to signify his Jewishness. Further listening would reveal other details of characterization in the densely packed but rather introverted score.

Still, the opera shows a lack of theatrical savoir faire attributable, no doubt, to Tchaikowsky's inexperience. After cogently setting up the central plot in which Antonio, serving as surety for Shylock's loan to Bassanio, promises his pound of flesh, the drama meanders as the setting shifts from Venice to Belmont, and other characters – Shylock's daughter Jessica, Bassanio's beloved Portia, the latter's suitors and others – are introduced.

Yet the scene also brings engaging musical details, like fanfares drawn from Beethoven and (the other) Tchaikovsky, Renaissance dance rhythms and even Wagner's Ring leitmotiv, heard when Portia gives Bassanio a ring. Things get back on track at once following the revelation of Antonio's catastrophic shipping losses. The courtroom scene is gripping, and the epilogue supplies a pleasant, if unduly long, afterglow.

Also problematic is John O'Brien's libretto, which preserves much of Shakespeare's original language. Its fidelity may be a boon to those who know the play inside out, but otherwise the text – which was sung in English with German titles – was difficult to follow. What can audiences make of lines like Shylock's 'take no doit of usance for my moneys' when sung at them? [51]

In *The Sunday Telegraph* John Allinson wrote:

Darkly lyrical and hard to pin down stylistically, the music is marvellously responsive to John O'Brien's libretto and Shakespeare's moods.

Keith Warner's elegant, flowing production evokes the time of the *Dreyfus Affair*, yet cleverly alludes to the skull episode (in the Prince of Morocco's dance), while sensitively suggesting a resemblance between Shylock and the composer himself. [52]

In her blog 'Co W Duszy Gra' Dorota Szwarcman wrote:

[…] *The Merchant of Venice* is a wonderful piece of music, worthy of exposure on the best stages in the world.

---

[51] George Loomis, '*Merchant of Venice* and *The Magic Flute* at Bregenz Festival', *The New York Times*, 30 July 2013 (www.nytimes.com/2013/07/31/arts/31iht-loomis31.html?_r=0; accessed on 18 August 2013).

[52] John Allison, '*Die Zauberflöte/The Merchant of Venice*, review', *The Sunday Telegraph*, 28 July 2013 (www.telegraph.co.uk/culture/music/classicalmusic/10205054/Die-ZauberfloteThe-Merchant-of-Venice-review.html; accessed on 18 August 2013).

[…] In 1981 the opera's style – with audible echoes of Berg, Britten, and even Hindemith – may have seemed too traditional for the modern stage. Today, however, it is judged simply by its quality. And its quality is outstanding.

While much of Czajkowski's chamber music is inherently bleak, with a quality of something reduced to ashes, in *The Merchant of Venice*, we hear a great deal more variation in atmosphere. Acts I and III are of course quite gloomy, but the second act – in which Portia chooses a husband – is satirical. It features no shortage of musical citations; referencing Beethoven's Leonora Overture No. 3 and… Symphony No. 4 by Andrzej's namesake, Pyotr Tchaikovski, whose music he sincerely hated and never played. The epilogue that follows Act III – though a little wordy – features exceptionally beautiful, lyrical, and dreamlike music.[53]

Other reviews included those published in *Die Welt*[54] and *Opera News Magazine*,[55] and are all available online.

Tchaikowsky's *The Merchant of Venice* makes a substantial contribution to the interpretation of Shakespeare in the world of opera since the nineteenth century. In this monumental work, the composer deals with the issues of personal and cultural identity, depression, love, homosexuality, friendship and loyalty. The opera is remarkable for its psychological depth, humour, lyricism and its masterly orchestration. Given that it was Tchaikowsky's first attempt at the genre, one might speculate that had he lived, he would have made an impressive mark on the world of twentieth-century, even 21st-century, opera. But even the small number of compositions he left are important because they show the development of an extraordinary artist, who combined in his work the entire western musical legacy and reinterpreted it with his own unique voice.

[53] Dorota Szwarcman, 'The Two Sides of Andrzej Czajkowski', translated by Alena Aniskiewicz, Co W Duszy Gra, 21 July 2013 (http://andretchaikowsky.com/composer/polityka_01_en.pdf; accessed on 18 August 2013).
[54] Stephan Hoffmann, 'Der Komponist ist seit 30 Jahren tot: *Der Kaufmann von Venedig*, die einzige Oper des Polen André Tchaikowsky, feiert posthum Uraufführung in Bregenz', *Die Welt*, 20 July 2013 (www.welt.de/kultur/buehne-konzert/article118222875/Orchesterschreie-aus-ohnmaechtiger-Wut.html; accessed on 18 August 2013).
[55] A. Goldman, 'Tragic Dimension', *Opera News Magazine*, May 2013, Vol. 77, No. 11 (www.operanews.com/Opera_News_Magazine/2013/5/Features/Tragic_Dimension.html; accessed on 18 August 2013).

Appendix One
Recordings of Tchaikowsky's Compositions

Piano Concerto (1956–57)
André Tchaikowsky, piano; National Orchestra of Belgium cond. André Vandernoot, Brussels, 18 March 1958; private recording, only known example held by Michał Wesołowski

Piano Concerto, Op. 4 (1966–71)
1. Radu Lupu, piano; Royal Philharmonic Orchestra cond. Uri Segal, London, 28 October 1975; Polskie Radio Archive, Warsaw
2. André Tchaikowsky, piano; National Orchestra of Ireland cond. Albert Rosen, Dublin, 1 October 1978; private recording
3. Norma Fisher, piano; Tivoli Summer Orchestra cond. Uri Segal, Copenhagen, 12 September 1986; private recording
4. Maciej Grzybowski, piano; Sinfonia Varsovia cond. Jacek Kaspszyk, Warsaw, 17 August 2008; source Polskie Radio
5. Maciej Grzybowski, piano; Vienna Symphony Orchestra cond. Paul Daniel, Bregenz Festspiele/ORF, 20 July 2013, Toccata Classics TOCC 0204 (2013)

***Seven Sonnets of Shakespeare* (1967)**
1. Margaret Cable, mezzo soprano; André Tchaikowsky, piano; BBC radio broadcast, 18 June 1968; also released as a private LP by Sound News Productions
2. Urszula Kryger, mezzo soprano; Maciej Grzybowski, piano; Polish Music Festival, Kraków, 8 November 2007
3. Urszula Kryger, mezzo soprano; Maciej Grzybowski, piano; Bregenz Festspiele/ORF, 20 July 2013

String Quartet No. 1 in A major, Op. 3 (1969–70)
1. Lindsay Quartet, BBC broadcast, 18 November 1971
2. Meccorre String Quartet, Toccata Classics TOCC 0205, 2014

String Quartet No. 2 in C major, Op. 5 (1973–75)
1. Lindsay Quartet, BBC broadcast, 23 January 1978; also released on ASV Records CD DCA 825
2. Meccorre String Quartet, Bregenz Festspiele/ORF, 21 July 2013, Toccata Classics TOCC 0205, 2014

Trio Notturno (1978)

1. Peter Frankl, piano; György Pauk, violin; Ralph Kirshbaum, cello; BBC broadcast, 1 November 1985; Library of Congress Music Division concert, 13 December 1985 (sound recording RWB 2063-2064)
2. Julian Jacobson, piano; Elisabeth Perry, violin; Timothy Mason, cello; Wigmore Hall, London, 11 November 1985; source Josef Weinberger
3. Nico de Villiers, piano; Sebastian Müller, violin; Alfia Nakipbekova, cello; Toccata Classics TOCC 0205, 2014

Sonata for Clarinet and Piano, Op. 1 (1959)

1. Janet Hilton, clarinet; Peter Frankl, piano; BBC broadcast, 17 June 1973.
2. Janet Hilton, clarinet; André Tchaikowsky, piano; BBC broadcast, c. 1976
3. Gervase de Peyer, clarinet; Carol Archer, piano; live concert, Merkin Hall, New York, 12 February 1987; private recording

Sonata for Piano (1958)

Nico de Villiers; Toccata Classics TOCC 0204, 2013

10 Inventions for Piano (1961–63)

1. André Tchaikowsky; BBC radio broadcast, 7 June 1968; also released as a private LP by Sound News Productions
2. Norma Fisher; BBC radio broadcast, c. 1985
3. Colin Stone; Merlin Records CD MRFD 20033, 2001
4. Gabriela Glapska; Akademia Muzyczna (Bydgoszcz), 29 September 2011
5. Daniel Browell; British Music Society Piano Awards, 2004
6. Maciej Grzybowski; Bregenz Festspiele/ORF, 20 July 2013
7. Jakob Fichert; Toccata Classics TOCC 0204, 2013

Mazurka and Tango for Piano[1]

Colin Stone; Merlin Records CD MRFD 20033, 2001

The Merchant of Venice

Adrian Eröd (baritone: Shylock), Christopher Ainslie (countertenor: Antonio), Charles Workman (tenor: Bassanio), Kathryn Lewek (soprano: Jessica), Magdalena Anna Hofmann (mezzo soprano: Portia), Richard Angas (bass: Duke of Venice), Adrian Clarke (bass-baritone: Salerio), Norman Patzke (bass-baritone: Solanio), David Stout (bass-baritone: Gratiano), Jason Bridges (tenor: Lorenzo), Verena Gunz (mezzo soprano: Nerissa), Hanna Herfurtner (soprano: a boy), Vienna Symphony Orchestra cond. Erik Nielsen. Bregenz Festspiele/ORF, 18 July 2013, Arthaus-Musik DVD

Many of these recordings can be accessed at http://andretchaikowsky.com/composer/index.htm.

---

[1] The only two of an intended *Six Dances* to be composed; *cf.* p. 372, above.

Appendix Two
Tchaikowsky's Recorded Performances: A Chronology

1. Radio Recital
Programme:
  Chopin, *Étude* in A minor, Op. 25, No. 4
  ———— Mazurka in C minor, Op. 56, No. 3
  ————, Mazurka in B major, Op. 56, No. 1
  ————, *Impromptu* in G flat major, Op. 51
  ————, *Étude* in F major, Op. 10, No. 8
  ————, *Étude* in D flat major, Op. 25, No. 8
  ————, *Étude* in A flat major, Op. 10, No. 10
  Schubert-Godowsky, *The Trout*
  Rameau-Godowsky, Minuet in A minor
  ————, *Elegy* in E minor/major
  Prokofiev, Sonata No. 3 in A minor, Op. 28
  Falla, *Cuatro piezas españolas*: Nos. 2, 'Cubana', and 3, 'Andaluza'
Date: c. 1954
Source: studio recording, Polskie Radio

2. Radio Recital
Programme:
  Szymanowski, Mazurka in C major, Op. 50, No. 5
  ————, Mazurka in E flat major, Op. 50, No. 14
  ————, Mazurka in D major, Op. 50, No. 15
  ————, Mazurka in A major, Op. 62, No. 1
Source: studio recording, Polskie Radio
Date: c. 1955

3. Concerto Recording
Programme: Prokofiev, Piano Concerto No. 3 in C major, Op. 26, with Orchestre
  National de Belgique cond. Franz André
Date: 31 May 1956
Source: Royal Conservatoire of Antwerp, Belgium
Note: from the 1956 Queen Elisabeth Piano Competition

4. Piano Recital
Programme:
  Bach-Liszt, *Fantasia* and Fugue in G minor, bmv542
  Beethoven, Sonata in E major, Op. 109
  Szymanowski, *Masques*, Op. 34
  Debussy, *Études* Nos. 10 and 7

PROKOFIEV, Piano Sonata No. 7 in B flat, Op. 83
Date: 14 June 1956
Source: Polskie Radio archives

5.   Piano Recital
Programme:
  RAVEL, *Gaspard de la Nuit*
  PROKOFIEV, *Visions Fugitives*, Op. 22
Date: 4 June 1957 (recorded); October 1957 (released)
Source: RCA Victor LSC-2145 (stereo); RCA Victor LM-2145 (mono); RCA Victor
  RB-16046 (UK)
Note: recording location Salle Wagram, Paris

6.   Concerto Recording
Programme: MOZART, Piano Concerto No. 25 in C major, K503; Chicago Symphony
  Orchestra cond. Fritz Reiner; cadenza by André Tchaikowsky
Date: 15 February 1958 (recorded); March 1959 (released on RCA Victor)
Source: RCA Victor LSC-2287 (stereo), RCA Victor LM-2287 (mono), RCA Victor
  VICS-1167 (UK), Idlewild Records JDLR 116; RCA Victor/BMG BVCC-38397,
  Forgotten Records FR-680
Note: recorded in Orchestra Hall, Chicago

7.   Concerto Recording
Programme: BACH, Concerto for Clavier No. 5 in F minor, BWV1056; Chicago
Symphony Orchestra cond. Fritz Reiner
Date: 15 February 1958 (recorded); June 1980 (released RCA Victor); 22 November
  2006 (released RCA Victor/BMG)
Source: RCA Victor DPM1-0444 (stereo), RCA Victor/BMG BVCC-38397
Note: recorded in Orchestra Hall, Chicago

8.   Concerto Recording
Programme: ANDRÉ TCHAIKOWSKY, Piano Concerto 'No. 1'; Orchestre National de
  Belgique cond. André Vandernoot
Date: 16 March 1958
Source: private recording held by pianist Michał Wesołowski

9.   Piano Recital
Programme:
  MOZART, *Fantasia* in C minor, K475
  ———, Sonata No. 14 in C minor, K457
  ———, Sonata No. 10 in C major, K330
Date: 26–28 January 1959 (recorded); August 1959 (released)
Source: RCA Victor LSC-2354 (stereo), RCA Victor LM-2354 (mono), reissue
  Forgotten Records FR-680
Note: recorded at RCA Studios, New York

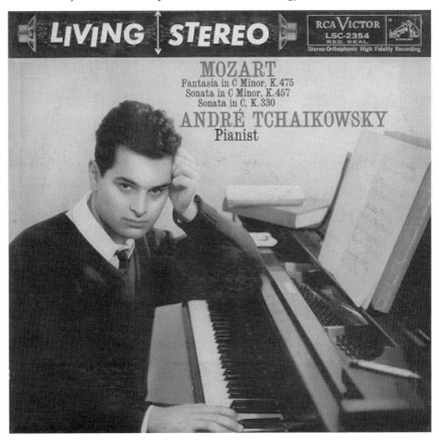

10. Piano Recital
Programme:
    CHOPIN, Preludes, Op. 28
    ————, No. 18 in F minor
    ————, No. 2 in A minor
    ————, No. 14 in D flat major
    ————, No. 4 in E minor
    ————, No. 5 in D major
    ————, No. 8 in F sharp minor
    ————, No. 19 in E flat major
    ————, No. 20 in C minor
    ————, No. 23 in F major
    ————, No. 24 in D minor
    ————, *Barcarolle* in F sharp major, Op. 60
    ————, *Étude* in A flat major, Op. 10, No. 10
    ————, *Étude* in C major, Op. 10, No. 7
    ————, Mazurka in A minor, Op. 59, No. 1
    ————, Mazurka in A flat major, Op. 59, No. 2

————, Mazurka in B major, Op. 56, No. 1

————, *Ballade* No. 3 in A flat major, Op. 47

Date: 10–12 March 1959 (recorded); October 1959 (released)

Source: RCA Victor LSC-2360 (stereo), RCA Victor LM-2360 (mono)

Note: recorded in RCA Studios, New York

11. Piano Recital

Programme: BACH, 'Goldberg' Variations, BWV988

Date: 12–15 May and 30 November 1964 (recorded); 15 June 1965 (released on Columbia)

Source: Columbia Records SAXF-1036 (stereo), Columbia Records FCX-1036 (mono), Dante Records, HPC 022 (stereo CD) (Volume 1)

Note: recorded Salle Wagram, Paris

12. Symphony Concert Television Broadcast

Programme: PROKOFIEV, Piano Concerto No. 3 in C major, Op. 26, with Swedish Radio and Television Orchestra cond. Sixten Ehrling

Date: 15 April 1962

Source: National Library, Stockholm

13. Radio Broadcast

Programme: HAYDN, Piano Sonata No. 14 in E flat major, Hob. XVI:49

Date: 19 June 1962

Source: BBC

14. Radio Broadcast

Programme: MOZART, Piano Sonata in C minor, K457, Saarbrücken, Broadcasting House Halberg (Funkhaus am Halberg)

Date: 14 February 1963

Source: private recording

15. Symphony Concert

Programme: MOZART, Piano Concerto No. 27 in B flat major, K595, with Symphony Orchestra of Norddeutscher Rundfunk cond. Karl Böhm

Date: 4 March 1964

Source: private recording

16. Radio Broadcast/Symphony Concert

Programme: RACHMANINOV, *Rhapsody on a Theme of Paganini*, Op. 43, Saarbrücken Radio Symphony Orchestra cond. Rudolf Michl

Date: 25 April 1964

Source: private recording

Note: broadcast by Broadcasting House, Halberg (Funkhaus am Halberg), Saarbrücken

17. Piano Recital

Programme:

    SCHUBERT, *12 Ländler*, Op. 171

———— *Valses*, Op. 18, No. 1, 2, 6, 8–10
————, *Danse allemande*, Op. 33, No. 7
————, *Ländler* No. 12 in E flat minor, D366
————, *Deux danses allemandes*, D769
————, *Valses nobles*, Op. 77, Nos. 9 and 10
————, *Valses*, Op. 9, Nos. 19, 21, 22, 26, 29, 30, 32 and 34–36
————, *Letzte Walzer*, Op. 127, Nos. 15 and 18
————, *Valses sentimentales*, Op. 50, No. 1, 3, 7, 12, 13, 15, 19 and 27
Date: 14–16 April and 1 June 1965 (recorded); October 1965 (released on Columbia)
Source: Columbia Records (EMI) SAXF-1057 (Stereo), Columbia Records (EMI) FCX-1057 (Mono), Dante Records, HPC049 (Vol. 4), Electrola (EMI) SME 80988 (Stereo)
Note: recorded Salle Wagram, Paris

18. Piano Recital
Programme:
CHOPIN, *Nocturnes*, Op. 62: Nos. 1 in B major and 2 in E major
Date: 17 May 1965
Source: recorded in Studio 3, Sender Freies Berlin (SFB), held as private recording

19. Radio Broadcast
Programme: ANDRÉ TCHAIKOWSKY, Sonata for Piano and Clarinet, Op. 1, with Janet Hilton (clarinet)
Date: 4 July 1966
Source: BBC

20. Piano Recital
Programme:
HAYDN, Sonata No. 49 in E flat major, Hob. XVI:49
———— *Andante et variations* in F minor, Hob. XVII:6
————, Sonata No. 23 in F major, Hob. XVI:23
Date: 4–7 January 1966 (recorded); August 1966 (released on Columbia)
Source: Columbia Records (EMI) CCA-1097, Dante Records, HPC029 (Vol. 2)

21. Piano Recital
Programme:
MOZART, Sonata in F major, K533: *Allegro* and *Andante*
————, Rondo in F major, K494
————, Sonata in G minor, K312: *Allegro*
————, Rondo in A minor, K511
————, March in C major, K408
————, *Menuet* in D major, K355
————, *Gigue* in G major, K574
————, *Adagio* in B minor, K540
Date: 6–8 September 1966 and 17 January 1967 (recorded); June 1967 (released)
Source: Columbia Records (EMI) CCA-1106 (stereo), Dante Records, HPC035 (Vol. 3)
Note: Recorded in Salle Wagram, Paris, as *Prélude au XIXème siècle*

22. Radio Broadcast
Programme: MOZART, Piano Sonata No. 13 in B flat major, K333
Date: 10 February 1967
Source: BBC

23. Radio Broadcast
Programme: BRAHMS, *Variations on an Original Theme*, Op. 21, No. 1
Date: 19 March 1967
Source: BBC

24. Piano Recital
Programme:
    CHOPIN, Mazurkas, Op. 50, Nos. 1–3
    ———, Mazurkas, Op. 56, Nos. 1–3
    ———, Mazurkas, Op. 59, Nos. 1–3
    ———, Mazurkas, Op. 63, Nos. 1–3
    ———, Mazurka, Op. 67, No. 2 in G minor
    ———, Mazurka, Op. 68, No. 4 in F minor
    ———, Mazurka in A minor
Date: 18 and 19 January and 22 May 1967 (recorded); June 1997 (released)
Source: Dante Records, HPC060 (Vol. 5)
Note: recorded for Columbia/EMI but never released by them

25. Symphony Concert/Radio Broadcast
Programme: RACHMANINOV, *Rhapsody on a Theme of Paganini*, Op. 43, with Symphonie-Orchester des Bayerischen Rundfunks cond. Colin Davis
Date: 31 January 1968
Source: private recording
Note: concert in Herkulessaal, Munich

26. Radio Broadcast
Programme: ANDRÉ TCHAIKOWSKY, *Inventions*, Op. 2
Date: 7 June 1968
Source: BBC

27. Radio Broadcast
Programme: ANDRÉ TCHAIKOWSKY, *Seven Sonnets of Shakespeare*, with Margaret Cable (mezzo soprano)
Date: 18 June 1968
Source: BBC

28. Piano Recital/Radio Broadcast
Programme: RAVEL, *Valses nobles et sentimentales*
Date: 29 April 1969
Source: private recording
Note: recorded in Studio 3, Hessischer Rundfunk, Frankfurt

29. Symphony Concert
Programme: MOZART, Piano Concerto No. 21 in C, K467, with Symphonie-
Orchester des Bayerischen Rundfunks cond. Leopold Hager
Date: 30 April 1970
Source: private recording
Note: concert in the Herkulessaal, Munich

30. Symphony Concert
Programme: BEETHOVEN, Piano Concerto No. 4 in G major, Op. 58, with
Saarbrücken Radio Symphony Orchestra cond. Rudolf Michl
Date: 9 May 1970
Source: private recording
Note: concert in Kongresshalle, Saarbrücken

31. Radio Broadcast
Programme: BRAHMS, Piano Quartet No. 1 in G minor, Op. 25, with Amadeus
Quartet
Date: 7 April 1971
Source: BBC

32. Radio Broadcast
Programme:
    BARTÓK, *Out of Doors* Suite, SZ81
    BEETHOVEN, Sonata No. 15 in D major, Op. 28 ('Pastoral')
    SCHUMANN, *Fantasie* in C major, Op. 17
Date: 23 April 1972
Source: BBC
Note: broadcast from the Queen Elizabeth Hall, London

33. Private Concert
Programme: FAURÉ, Piano Quartet No. 1 in C minor, Op. 15, with Michael
Belmgrain (violin), Lars Grund (viola), Ino Jansen (cello), André Tchaikowsky
(piano)
Date: June 1972 (recorded); July 1996 (released)
Source: Dante Records HPC049 (Vol. 4)

34. Symphony Concert
Programme: BACH, Piano Concerto No. 1 in D minor, BWV1052, with Serenata of
London, leader Emanuel Hurwitz
Date: 24 July 1973
Source: private recording
Note: concert held at Royal Albert Hall, London (Prom 5, 1973)

35. Piano Recital
Programme:
    BEETHOVEN, Piano Sonata No. 27 in E minor, Op. 90
    SCHUMANN, *Fantasiestücke*, Op. 12: No. 1. 'Des Abends', and No. 5, 'In der Nacht'
    DEBUSSY, *Images*, Book I: No. 2, 'Hommage à Rameau'

Stravinsky, *Three Movements from Petrushka*
Chopin, Mazurka No. 40 in F minor, Op. 63, No. 2 in F minor
Date: 25 November 1973
Source: BBC
Note: concert held at Queen Elizabeth Hall, London

36. Radio Broadcast
Programme: Mozart, Piano Concerto No. 24 in C minor, k491, with Bournemouth
    Sinfonietta cond. Theodor Guschlbauer
Date: 15 February 1974
Source: BBC

37. Piano Recital
Programme:
    Schubert, Piano Sonata in D major, d850
    Bach, Prelude and Fugue in F sharp minor, *The Well-Tempered Clavier*, Book
        II, No. 14, bwv 883
    ————, Prelude and Fugue in D minor, *The Well-Tempered Clavier*, Book I,
        No. 6, bwv851
    ————, Prelude and Fugue in F sharp major, *The Well-Tempered Clavier*, Book
        I, No. 13, bwv858
Date: 4 November 1974
Source. BBC
Note: concert given in the BBC 'Lunchtime Concert' series held at St John's, Smith
    Square, London

38. Radio Broadcast
Programme:
    Haydn, Piano Sonata No. 61 in D major, Hob XVI:51
    Beethoven Piano Sonata No. 31 in A flat major, Op. 110
Date: 12 October 1976
Source: BBC

39. Piano Recital
Programme:
    Debussy, *Études*: No. 7. 'Pour les degrés chromatiques'
    ————, No. 6, 'Pour les huit doigts'
    ————, *Préludes*: Book II, No. 1, 'Brouillards'
    ————, Book II, No. 5, 'Bruyères'
    ————, Book I, No. 6, 'Des pas sur la neige'
    Chopin, *Fantasy* in F minor, Op. 49
    ————, *Polonaise-fantaisie* in A flat major, Op. 61
    ————, *Barcarolle* in F sharp Major, Op. 60
Date: 6 December 1976
Source: private recording
Note: concert held at Lancaster University

40. Radio Broadcast
Programme:
  Rachmaninov, *Rhapsody on a Theme of Paganini*, Op. 43, with City of
    Birmingham Symphony Orchestra cond. Uri Segal
  Ravel, *Concerto for the Left Hand*
Date: 30 December 1976
Source: BBC

41. Symphony Concert
Programme: Mozart, Piano Concerto No. 27 in B flat major, k595, with
  Saarbrücken Radio Symphony Orchestra cond. Lothar Zagrosek
Date: 15 April 1977
Source: private recording
Note: concert held in Kongresshalle, Saarbrücken

42. Symphony Concert
Programme: Mozart, Piano Concerto No. 27 in B flat major, k595, Saarbrücken
  Radio Symphony Orchestra cond. Lothar Zagrosek (repeat performance)
Date: 17 April 1977
Source: private recording
Note: concert held in Kongresshalle, Saarbrücken

43. Radio Broadcast
Programme: Mozart, Piano Concerto No. 13 in C major, k415, BBC Scottish
  Symphony Orchestra cond. Christopher Seaman
Date: 1 August 1977
Source: BBC

44. Piano Recital
Programme:
  Bach, *Italian Concerto* in F major, bwv971
  Schubert, Piano Sonata in B flat minor, d960
Date: 20 March 1978
Source: BBC
Note: concert given in the BBC 'Lunchtime Concert' series held at St John's, Smith
  Square, London

45. Symphony Concert
Programme: André Tchaikowsky, Piano Concerto, Op. 4, with National
  Orchestra of Ireland cond. Albert Rosen
Date: 1 October 1978
Source: private recording

46. Piano Recital
Programme:
  Bach, *Partita* No. 6 in E minor, bwv830
  Bartók, Three Studies, sz72
  Beethoven, Piano Sonata No. 14 in C sharp minor, Op. 27, No. 2, 'Moonlight'

SCHUMANN, *Davidsbündlertänze*, Op. 6
RACHMANINOV, *Étude-tableau* in E flat minor, Op. 39, No. 5
Date: 15 December 1978
Source: private recording
Note: part of concert series at BBC Pebble Mill, Birmingham

47. Radio Broadcast
Programme:
BEETHOVEN, Piano Sonata No. 27 in E minor, Op. 90
SCHUMANN, *Kreisleriana*, Op. 16
CHOPIN, *Nocturne* in E flat major, Op. 55, No. 2
Date: 29 October 1979
Source: BBC
Note: concert given in the BBC 'Lunchtime Concert' series held at St John's, Smith
    Square, London

48. Piano Recital
Programme:
HAYDN, Sonata No. 49 in E flat major, Hob. XVI:49
SCHUBERT, Piano Sonata in A minor, D784
CHOPIN, *Barcarolle* in F sharp major, Op. 60
————, Piano Sonata No. 3 in B minor, Op. 58
Date: 25 April 1980
Source: private recording
Note: part of concert series at BBC Pebble Mill, Birmingham

49. Radio Broadcast
Programme:
BACH, Toccata in C minor, BWV911
SCHUBERT, Sonata in G major, D894
CHOPIN, 24 Preludes, Op. 28
————, *Nocturne* No. 13 in C minor, Op. 48, No. 1
Date: 6 December 1981
Source: BBC
Note: concert held in Royal Festival Hall (Tchaikowsky's last piano recital)

50. Symphony Concert
Programme: CHOPIN, Piano Concerto No. 1 in E minor, Op. 11, with Utrechts
    Symfonisch Orkest cond. Lamberto Gardelli
Date: 10 May 1982
Source: private recording
Note: concert held in Tonhalle, Düsseldorf (Tchaikowsky's last concert)

Index
of André Tchaikowsky's Music

An entry in italics indicates an illustration.

General
Index

An entry in italics indicates an illustration.

Content of the CD
ANDRÉ TCHAIKOWSKY IN RECITAL

André Tchaikowsky spent a period in the first half of 1975 as artist-in-residence at the University of Western Australia in Perth. He stayed in a co-educational student residence, Currie Hall, and was soon both liked and respected by the students.[1] On a number of occasions he gave private concerts in Currie Hall on an old upright piano housed in a common room. This is an amateur recording of one such concert, which took place on 2 June 1975.

In it Tchaikowsky performed music by Bach, Beethoven, Schumann, Debussy and Chopin, improvising his programme as the recital unfolded. He interacted with his audience, involving them in the decision-making. His sense of humour and wit, as well as the admiring reaction of his enthusiastic audience, are all captured in this recording, notwithstanding its technical shortcomings. The CD also allows the reader to hear Tchaikowsky's idiosyncratic speaking voice – high-toned, with a strong Polish accent (but his grammar almost never betrayed his non-English origins), nasal, nervous, melodious – and so gives an idea of the sounds behind the words which constitute the bulk of this book.

Immediately after Debussy's 'La soirée dans Grenade' he launched into the finale of Chopin's Sonata No 3 in B minor, but after less than three minutes the tape cuts out. The effect of such an abrupt end is shocking but serves as a metaphor for the tragically abrupt end of Tchaikowsky's own life.

1	**Spoken introduction**	1:34
	Bach Prelude and Fugue in F sharp minor, *The Well-Tempered Clavier*,	
	Book II, bwv882	6:58
2	Prelude	3:01
3	Fugue	3:57
4	**Spoken commentary**	1:04
5	**Schumann** *Fantasie* in C major, Op. 17: I *Durchaus*	
	fantastisch und leidenschaftlich vorzutragen	12:17
6	**Spoken commentary**	0:28
7	**Schumann** *Fantasie* in C major, Op. 17: II *Mäßig. Durchaus*	
	energisch	7:30
8	**Schumann** *Fantasie* in C major, Op. 17: III *Langsam getragen.*	
	Durchweg leise zu halten	9:20
9	**Spoken commentary**	1:37

---

[1] *Cf.* pp. 115 and 158, above.